BESIEGED

BESIEGED
School Boards and the
Future of Education Politics

William G. Howell
Editor

BROOKINGS INSTITUTION PRESS
Washington, D.C.

379.153
B554

ABOUT BROOKINGS

The Brookings Institution is a private nonprofit organization devoted to research, education, and publication on important issues of domestic and foreign policy. Its principal purpose is to bring knowledge to bear on current and emerging policy problems. The Institution maintains a position of neutrality on issues of public policy. Interpretations or conclusions in Brookings publications should be understood to be solely those of the authors.

Copyright © 2005
THE BROOKINGS INSTITUTION
1775 Massachusetts Avenue, N.W., Washington, D.C. 20036
www.brookings.edu

Library of Congress Cataloging-in-Publication data

Besieged : school boards and the future of education politics / William G. Howell, editor.
    p. cm.
    Summary: "Examines school board politics in U.S. cities at the end of the twentieth century, focusing on site-based management reforms, mayoral takeover, parental choice and competition, and standards and accountability initiatives, as well as the role of teacher unions, and assesses the promise of various governance reforms"—Provided by publisher.
    Includes bibliographical references and index.
    ISBN-13: 978-0-8157-3684-4 (cloth : alk. paper)
    ISBN-10: 0-8157-3684-3
    ISBN-13: 978-0-8157-3683-7 (pbk. : alk. paper)
    ISBN-10: 0-8157-3683-5
    1. School boards—United States. 2. School management and organization—United States. 3. Politics and education—United States. I. Howell, William G. II. Title.
    LB2831.B49 2005
    379.1'531—dc22   2004027179

9 8 7 6 5 4 3 2 1

The paper used in this publication meets minimum requirements of the American National Standard for Information Sciences—Permanence of Paper for Printed Library Materials: ANSI Z39.48-1992.

Typeset in Adobe Garamond

Composition by Cynthia Stock
Silver Spring, Maryland

Printed by R. R. Donnelley
Harrisonburg, Virginia

Contents

Acknowledgments

The chapters herein were originally presented in October 2003 at a conference entitled "School Board Politics," which was jointly sponsored by the Program on Education Policy and Governance and the Center for American Political Studies at Harvard University. I gratefully acknowledge the financial support of the Smith Richardson Foundation, the Olin Foundation, and the Center for American Political Studies for making this conference possible. Much of the early planning for the conference occurred over long lunches with Chris Berry and Paul Peterson, but were it not for the superb logistical and administrative support provided by Antonio Wendland and Mark Linnen, the conference would never have gotten off the ground. Besides those acknowledged individually in the chapters, I would like to thank the following people for their contributions to the conference and this volume: Alan Altshuler, Jeffrey Berry, Barry Bluestone, Mark Brilliant, Anne Bryant, Barry Burden, Phoebe Cottingham, Chester Finn, Charles Glenn, Eileen Hughes, Sunshine Hillygus, Lisa Graham Keegan, Christopher Kelaher, Shep Melnick, Richard Murnane, Doug Reed, Wilbur Rich, Christine Rossell, Theda Skocpol, Adam Urbanski, and Sidney Verba. In addition, Christopher Berry and I acknowledge the financial support of our work in chapter 7 provided by IES grant R305A040043, National Research and Development Center on School Choice, Competition, and Student Achievement, and we thank Francis Shen for his excellent research assistance.

Finally, I dedicate this volume to my mother-in-law, Linda Harrison, who after thirty years of working as a public school teacher is running for the school board in Woodward, Oklahoma—her campaign continues as this book goes to press.

1

Introduction

WILLIAM G. HOWELL

Today, as at no other time in American history, the federal and state governments enshroud public schools. From above, presidents, judges, legislators, governors, and bureaucrats mandate all sorts of education reforms, covering everything from curricula to school lunch programs. With their consent and under their direction, mayors have begun to enter the fray, casting an even longer partisan shadow over public schools. Today, professional politicians regularly drown out the voices and displace the visions of the individuals who have governed public schools for centuries: locally elected (and occasionally appointed) school board members.

It wasn't always so. In the beginning, schools in the United States were locally controlled. First in New England and then in the South and the West, town selectmen directed the financing, building, and governing of public schools. Then, as populations increased and diversified, special boards (sometimes called committees or commissions) assumed responsibility for overseeing and supporting schools. In many regions, these boards gained functional autonomy and a measure of independent legal authority. Given their focus on a single objective—providing educational services to the community—school boards became the engine that drove the most rapid expansion in educational opportunity the world had ever seen.

Through much of the nineteenth century, school boards were the central governing institution of U.S. schools. Although ultimately subject to state law,

1

most school boards nonetheless assumed primary control over hiring and firing, curricula, the length of the school day and year, and the observation of holidays. These quasi-municipal corporations took primary fiscal responsibility for schools, writing budgets, levying taxes, and ensuring that schools spent their allotted funds appropriately. Their members debated a host of issues that now seem somewhat antiquated, such as religious education in common schools, parental fees, and corporal punishment. And when they were not acting as executives or legislators, board members often played the role of judge, hearing and ruling on public objections to their policies.

Their control, of course, was imperfect. As public education took hold in the United States, school boards had to contend with schools whose teachers retained considerable autonomy to do as they pleased. Though superintendents managed to impose a modicum of order on and control over a decentralized system of schooling, school board members rarely could be sure that teachers would faithfully implement their policies. Data on student performance and the quality of classroom teaching were sparse; board evaluations of schools rarely took a school's employees to task; and the particular mix of school board responsibilities and powers varied widely from district to district. As the education historian David Tyack notes, "public education . . . seemed to reformers more a miscellaneous collection of village schools than a coherent system. Responsibility was diffuse, teachers had considerable autonomy in their decentralized domains, and the flow of information was erratic and insufficiently focused for purposes of policy."[1] Given that state of affairs, board members could hardly impose their will whenever and however they chose. Changing school policy often required considerable care, powers of persuasion, and attention to the various needs and interests of parents and teachers.

Still, as governing institutions, school boards were basically the only game in town. The federal government did grant public lands to states for the purpose of promoting public education, but it had little say over what actually happened within the newly constructed school houses. The Office of Education, established in 1870, collected descriptive statistics on public schools but otherwise rarely interfered. While most states had statutory and constitutional requirements for the provision of public education, local school boards retained broad discretion in administering education services. State superintendents and departments of education, such as they were, exercised only modest oversight.

Accordingly, localism thrived during the nation's early years. The purposes of schooling, public funding of schools, and even the languages of instruction—all were locally determined. Striking regional differences defined the era—in the number and quality of schools, the length of the school year, and the representation of religious and cultural norms. What held true for Boston

1. Tyack (1974, p. 33).

did not necessarily apply to Newton, just ten miles west, and the instruction in New York schools differed markedly from that in Illinois and South Carolina. Working through lay school boards, communities built public schools in their own image and for their own objectives; the federal and state governments had little say in the matter.

Federalism Asserted

Localism would not last. Beginning in the middle of the nineteenth century and picking up steam at the turn of the twentieth, new efforts to "professionalize, homogenize, and organize common schooling threatened highly prized local control."[2] Rising immigration and heightened demand for skilled labor to meet the needs of an industrializing economy became a driving force for change. Businessmen, professors, and politicians lobbied for the transformation of an agrarian, decentralized pattern of schooling into a bona fide public school system that promoted the values of centralization, efficiency, modernization, and hierarchical control. Over time, as states began to insist on the imposition of fixed standards based on scientifically proven practices, control over curricula and course offerings shifted from lay school boards and local educators to trained specialists.

Changes in schools reflected and in many instances were induced by larger developments in the nation's political structure and economy—specifically by Progressive Era efforts to remove politics from local and state governance of schools. The order of the day put rational control and expertise in the service of objectivity and efficiency; the result was the birth of the civil service, the exaltation of meritocracy and modernity, and the rise of Taylorism, the scientific management of industries and businesses. In an effort to maximize their bottom line, factories standardized almost all aspects of their operations, down to the very hand movements of assembly line workers. Concomitantly, government reformers targeted provincialism, corruption, and patronage—and by extension, the values of local control, diversity, and tolerance. Public schools and the structures that governed them could hardly avoid the political and economic reforms sweeping the nation.

Loosely knit schools, held together by school boards alone, soon gave way to a more unified, centralized system of public education. State superintendents mounted consolidation campaigns to reduce the number of school districts, each with its own local board of education. As a result, school districts declined in number, while their populations (measured at both the district and school level) increased in size. Indeed, one of the most striking developments in public education during the twentieth century was the staggering consolidation of school

2. Kaestle (1983, p. 158).

districts and their governing boards. In 1936, the first year for which reliable counts are available, the nation had 118,892 school districts with an average of 218 students each; by 1997, just 15,178 districts attended to an average of 3,005 students each. As the number of school boards rapidly declined, so did the number of members serving on them. At-large elections replaced ward-based elections, and membership on most urban school boards fell precipitously. In 1893, the twenty-eight cities with populations of more than 100,000 residents maintained school boards that had an average of 21.5 members. Two decades later, that average dropped to roughly seven, and it has not recovered since.[3]

During the second half of the twentieth century, challenges to the autonomy and prerogatives of local school boards only intensified. With the Soviet Union's launching of Sputnik in 1957, public education in the United States quickly came to be considered a matter of national security, and the federal government burst on the scene. Initially, its role was quite circumscribed: it provided funding for school construction and established grants for post-secondary scholarships. Over time, however, the federal government created funds for, and regulations governing, the provision of education services for the handicapped and the poor; wrote strict antidiscrimination statutes; required public schools to provide equal opportunities for male and female students to participate in sports; and, more recently, entered the business of demanding strict accountability systems in public schools nationwide.

School boards increasingly turned to the federal and state governments for funding, and in doing so, they relinquished considerable autonomy. In 1920, public elementary and secondary schools relied on local governments for 83 percent of their funds, on state governments for 17 percent, and on the federal government for less than 1 percent. By 2000, local revenues constituted just 43 percent of total expenditures, while the federal and state governments kicked in for 50 and 7 percent, respectively.[4] Federal agencies and state legislatures imposed an increasing number of regulations on schools, affecting what was taught, how contracts were written, and who was hired and when they could be fired. In addition, state boards of education began to do more than just provide support services for local boards; increasingly, they asserted significant control over administrative and curricular matters.

The courts, especially since the Supreme Court ruled on *Brown* v. *Board of Education* in 1954, have had a profound impact on public education. Leading the fight to desegregate public schools in the 1950s and 1960s, courts have mandated all sorts of education policies. They have set rules, for example, on which student organizations can assemble in public schools, what kinds of religious references valedictorians can make at graduation ceremonies, and what allowances

---

3. Twentieth Century Fund (1992, p. 44).

4. National Center for Education Statistics, *Digest of Education Statistics 2002*, table 156 (www.nces.ed.gov/programs/digest/d02/dt156.asp [December 1, 2004]).

and accommodations must be made for students with disabilities. State courts have had a definite impact on school finance, setting fixed standards on the level and type of funding inequalities permissible between and within school districts. And by court order, many urban districts have had to reform their school enrollment policies to advance the twin goals of racial and economic integration.

Various interest groups, teacher unions foremost among them, now influence public education. Through collective bargaining, the National Education Association and the American Federation of Teachers, along with their state and local affiliates, have gained a foothold in public education, which has given them considerable say in the kinds of curricular and administrative reforms that school board members will even consider. Unions have transformed school hiring and firing practices, arbitration procedures, tracking systems, teacher assignments, class sizes, and pay scales. Any reform-minded school board members must deal with unions; indeed, success may ultimately depend on their ability to garner union support.

Whereas school board members governed virtually all aspects of public education during the nineteenth century, today members must compete with political actors scattered throughout the federal, state, and local governments as well as organized interests in the private sphere. Almost everything that school boards do is now subject to regulations handed down from city councils, state legislatures and boards of education, the federal government, and federal courts. In 1980, J. Myron Atkin lamented:

> Increasingly local school administrators and teachers are losing control over the curriculum as a result of government action. Minimum competency laws determine which fields are to be tested, and the curriculum is expected to reflect that political decision. Teachers and school administrators are told the techniques to be used . . . in developing instructional programs for handicapped children. Vocational education and drug-abuse protection education are similarly mandated. In this process, the local administrator becomes less of an educational leader and more of a monitor of legislative intent.[5]

Since then, from Atkin's perspective, matters have only worsened. Teachers may stand alone in their classrooms and principals alone in their schools, but the voices of judges, legislators, mayors, interest groups, and even U.S. presidents bombinate ever more loudly.

During the last two decades, four trends in public education reform have beset school boards. The first took hold in the 1980s under the banner of site-based management. Touting the professionalism of teachers and disparaging bureaucratic waste, organizations such as the Carnegie Foundation called for the

5. Atkin (1980, p. 93).

wholesale restructuring of public education. Rather than strictly abiding by school board rules and regulations, principals, parents, and teachers would assert new control over and inject much-needed vitality into the education of children. While continuing to function under the direction of school boards, site-based councils (consisting of some mix of principals, professional aides, teachers, and parents) would set standards, develop the curriculum, and design programs around students' needs and interests.

While site-based management reforms failed to reorganize the basic structure of public education, they did usher in a new wave of education reforms in the 1990s that threatened the very existence of school boards. In cities such as Baltimore, Boston, Chicago, Detroit, and New York, mayors and states began to eliminate or seriously constrain the powers of independently elected school board members and to assume primary responsibility for the functioning of the public schools within their jurisdictions. To be sure, only a handful of mayors thus far have assumed control of school board operations, either directly or through a board that they appointed, and all of these takeovers have occurred in large urban districts, with the exception of Harrisburg, Pennsylvania. Still, even a few cases are enough to send a clear and potent message: school boards that do not fulfill the expectations of other political players may be stripped of the few independent powers they still retain.

Whereas takeovers shift political power away from school boards to other political actors, choice-based reforms threaten to limit government power more generally. By introducing choice and competition into an expanding education marketplace, vouchers, intra- and interdistrict public school choice, and magnet and charter schools all empower parents. In doing so, these policies transform a top-down accountability system wherein school teachers and principals answer to school boards and board-appointed superintendents into a bottom-up system wherein schools attempt to attract and retain students whose parents enjoy a wide range of educational options. In a universal voucher system, school board activities likely would be reduced to overseeing the health and safety of students (much as the Food and Drug Administration does that of consumers) and the policies and practices of school administrators (much as the Federal Communications Commission regulates the media and telecommunications industries). No longer would school boards micromanage the internal affairs of individual schools, deciding who is hired and fired, which textbooks are purchased, what curriculum is adopted, and which buildings are repaired. Instead, school boards would referee a game in which they no longer were players.

The final policy trend threatening the autonomy of local school boards is the recent push for standards and accountability, epitomized by the 2002 No Child Left Behind Act (NCLB), a federal statute that requires schools to administer standardized tests every year to students in grades 3 through 8. Schools that fail to demonstrate adequate yearly progress toward proficiency (as defined by the states) are subject to sanctions ranging from the potential loss of students to the eventual reconstitution of their operations. NCLB's sheer scope and detail—it runs more than 1,000 pages!—make it the most important federal education law since the original authorization of the 1965 Elementary and Secondary Education Act. From the perspective of school board members, however, NCLB represents yet another intrusion on local control. While states choose the tests given and set proficiency standards, local school boards must reorganize district operations so that schools advance fixed objectives identified by state and federal bureaucrats. And just as school boards did not pick these objectives, many do not want them. As Douglas Reed has argued,

> NCLB effects a structural mismatch between authority and accountability, such that the entities who have significant property taxation authority (school boards with electoral consent) are not the entities who establish the terms of accountability or its consequences. The resulting unanticipated consequence of NCLB, then, would [be] a local-level erosion of support for the generation of public educational resources, as taxpayers and voters realize that resources extracted by local school boards cannot be directed toward locally defined problems.[6]

To a greater and greater extent, the purposes of education are defined from on high, while school boards and the public schools under their care scramble to demonstrate compliance from below.

Holding On

Given federal demands for accountability and state takeovers from above and parental choice from below, school boards would appear to have few defenders and their demise to be just a matter of time. But while the decline of school boards has been unmistakable, their future remains less certain, and the pace of change is likely to remain gradual. To start, strong biases in favor of the status quo are built into the U.S. system of separate and federated powers. Minority coalitions have ample opportunities to block the enactment of novel public policies and to stall, if not derail, their implementation. Change, when it occurs, typically proceeds incrementally, as political actors tinker at the margins while leaving the whole intact. And because most political actors (especially those who are elected) are only weakly motivated to refashion governance structures, institutional change proceeds at an even slower pace. Rather than in weeks or months, a political institution's evolution typically is measured in decades.

Once a political entity has been granted certain powers, it is extremely difficult to reclaim them. This is due in part to the fact that, as noted, policy change

6. Reed (2003, p. 3).

is always tricky. But it is also a consequence of the organizing strategies of the political actors to whom power has been delegated. School board members can be expected to harness and protect whatever powers they are granted. And so they have, in the form of the National School Boards Association (NSBA). In addition to providing support services to newly elected board members, NSBA advocates on behalf of board powers and privileges. As part of its legislative strategy, NSBA opposes all voucher and tax-subsidized tuition schemes, federal unfunded mandates, and state takeover of school board functions. Concomitantly, it actively lobbies for increasing public education funding (both targeted aid and block grants) and relaxing federal and state restrictions on the use of funds.[7]

A few state courts, meanwhile, have taken some modest steps to protect school boards. Consider, for instance, a recent Colorado district court ruling to overturn the state's voucher initiative. Rather than basing his decision on concerns about the separation of church and state—the primary focus of court challenges to vouchers in Wisconsin, Ohio, and Florida—Judge Joseph Meyer of the Denver District Court declared Colorado's Opportunity Contract Pilot Program unconstitutional because it illegally denied local school boards control over education. Meyer ruled that because the law granted the state final authority to determine which students and nonpublic schools could participate in the program and because school boards had few means by which to oversee private schools, the voucher initiative represented a clear—and unconstitutional—affront to school boards: "I see no way to interpret the voucher program statute in a way that does not run afoul of the principle of local control."[8]

The greatest wellspring of support for school boards, however, does not lie among judges or organized interests. Rather, it resides within the broader public, which regularly confesses an abiding belief in the importance of local school governance. While few citizens may participate in school board elections and fewer still may attend school board meetings, the idea of local democratic control over public education resonates widely. Take, for instance, a recent Phi Delta Kappa/Gallup poll of public attitudes toward public schools. When asked "Who should have the greatest influence in deciding what is taught in the public schools?" 61 percent of respondents selected the local school board, while 22 percent chose the state government and just 15 percent chose the federal government.[9] According to a 2002 poll commissioned by *Education Week*, the public not only trusts school boards, it also believes that school boards are the

7. NSBA's legislative priorities can be reviewed online at www.nsba.org.

8. *Colorado Congress of Parents, Teachers, and Students* v. *Owens*, case number 03CV3734. P. 14, December 2003. The Colorado Supreme Court later upheld the trial court ruling: *Owens* v. *Colorado Congress of Parents, Teachers, and Students*, case number 035A364, June 28, 2004.

9. Lowell Rose and Alec Gallup, *The 35th Annual Phi Delta Kappa/Gallup Poll of the Public's Attitudes toward the Public Schools* (www.pdkintl.org/kappan/k0309pol.pdf [December 1, 2004]).

single most important institution in determining the quality of public schools—more important than parents, governors, state assemblies, or the U.S. president. According to the report, "Americans retain a strong vision of public schools as community resources and they want politicians to remain focused on the goal of strengthening that resource rather than replacing it with untested options that lack strong credibility and accountability to the citizens they serve."[10]

School boards continue to fight for their institutional survival and for the system of local educational governance on which public schools were built. To date, faced with political forces and educational reformers bent on either their radical restructuring or outright elimination, they have given considerable ground. However, the decline of school boards has been slow and sporadic, stretched out over a century, proceeding rapidly in some years and regions while occasionally retreating in others. Advocates of local democratic control have reasons for optimism, as the structure of governance favors the status quo and public opinion sides with elected school boards. As education reformers debate the merits of localism, parental control, and local accountability to the federal government, the struggle continues.

Debating a Future for School Boards

Longer-term trends toward centralization and professionalization, along with a spate of recent governance reforms, have conspired against school boards. At the dawn of the twenty-first century, school boards were fewer in number and weaker in stature than they were at the start of the twentieth. But the future of school boards is not preordained. Should state legislatures and governors so desire, they can consolidate past trends and further strip school boards of their few remaining powers. But just as the federal and state governments can take away, so too can they revitalize and restore. By granting local school boards the flexibility and resources required to address their communities' particular needs and by lifting many of the rules and restrictions that accompany funding, the federal and state governments can reverse course and recapture aspects of yesterday's localism.

But should they? What about school boards is worth defending? What about local control is worth preserving? These questions run deep, and they raise normative issues that deserve far more care and attention than I can provide here. Philosophers and education reformers have long debated the merits of localism and democratic education, and consensus remains elusive. Among policymakers, however, there is at present a lively public debate on the future of school boards and the appropriate design of the structures that govern public schools.

10. Linda Jacobson, "Public Sees Schools as a Priority" (www.edweek.com/ew/ewstory.cfm?slug=32pen.h21&keywords=education%20electorate [October 6, 2004]).

To be sure, participants in this discussion have articulated a wide variety of claims, based on a diverse assortment of first principles. Stripped of its embellishments and subtleties, however, the debate essentially pits two camps against one another. On one side are education reformers who applaud the historical decline of school boards; indeed, many eagerly anticipate their eventual demise. On the other are individuals who argue on behalf of rejuvenating the powers of school boards and returning to the days of strictly local control of education.

Consider first some of the claims of school board critics. These reformers point out that the practice of school board politics falls far short of the ideal of local participation in the democratic process. Rather than presenting a forum in which parents, teachers, and administrators can come together and jointly deliberate the civic and professional education of children, they say, school boards instead provide an institutional mechanism for vested stakeholders to extract revenues from, and impose their will on, the public school system. Notes Chester Finn:

> There may still be some tranquil towns and leafy suburbs where the platonic ideal of the elected local school board flourishes: with the community's foremost citizens running in nonpartisan elections, then selflessly devoting themselves to the best interests of all the community's children. But in the parts of U.S. education that cause the greatest concern, namely cities large and small, today's typical elected local school board resembles a dysfunctional family, comprised of three unlovable sorts: aspiring politicians for whom this is a stepping stone to higher office, former school-system employees with a score to settle, and single-minded advocates of diverse dubious causes who yearn to use the public schools to impose their particular hang-ups on all the kids in town. No wonder reform-minded cities are trying every alternative they can think of: mayoral control, state takeovers, appointed boards, etc. The inventors of school boards thought their reform would keep education out of politics. In fact, it's immersed public schools in politics.[11]

Rather than fighting on behalf of the average student or parent, school board members are beholden to the handful of voters who show up on election day, most of whom are employees of the public school system or individuals who stand to profit from it. In still darker corners of the education system, school boards are dens of cronyism and corruption wherein members reward friends and political supporters with hefty contracts and cushy administrative jobs. Little about this arrangement serves the needs of children, these reformers argue, and less is worth defending.

11. Chester Finn, "Who Needs School Boards?" *Education Gadfly* 3, no.37 (2003) (www.edexcellence.net/institute/gadfly/issue.cfm?id=120#1505 [December 1, 2004]).

A common refrain among critics is that school board members merely legitimate deeply entrenched public school practices. Rather than advocating innovative reforms or articulating new visions of schooling that address students' changing needs, board members concentrate on reassuring the public that everything is as it should be. Among board members, dissent is squelched and radical voices are marginalized. Successes are advertised widely, while failures and their root causes are routinely ignored. "In my experience," notes Lisa Graham Keegan, former Arizona state superintendent of public instruction, "those who join district boards, even those who start out reform-minded, eerily become co-opted and wind up defending the system tooth and nail. It's just like watching *Invasion of the Body Snatchers*."[12] The status quo, these reformers note, is given no fairer hearing than it is at a local school board meeting.

Others do not find school boards themselves objectionable, though they decry the inequalities that arise from the system of governance in which school boards are embedded. Social scientists have long observed that districts that rely on local property taxes for funding and assign students to schools on the basis of residence propagate all sorts of class and racial inequalities. As the political theorist Stephen Macedo observes, "Local control, when combined with local funding and district-based assignment of pupils to schools, has created a geography marked by stark inequalities centered on class and race: a new form of separate and unequal."[13] Rich districts stay rich, and poor districts stay poor. School boards, meanwhile, reinforce these tendencies by erecting high barriers to entry and by hording their funding. Well-to-do suburban districts may accept a few token central city students into their schools, and they may occasionally reach out to adjacent districts that are struggling. But that is all. The school board member who does any more to threaten the sanctity of the educational system constructed by suburban parents on behalf of their children cannot expect to remain in office very long.

Whatever larger social ailments they reinforce, school boards may have become antiquated as governing institutions. They may have worked well in small rural communities where all students attended the same school and where parents and teachers knew each other well. But as districts have grown and schools have proliferated, school boards have proven incapable of keeping pace. As Chester Finn and Denis Doyle wrote in 1985,

> Until now most states delegated control to local school boards, retaining only loose control in the state capital. That arrangement suited a stable agrarian society with a tolerance for local eccentricities, uneven outcomes, and school resources that varied with village property values and tax

---

12. Lisa Graham Keegan, "What Is Public Education?" *City Journal* 10, no. 4 (2000) (www.city-journal.org/html/10_4_what_is_public_edu.html [December 1, 2004]).

13. Macedo (2003, p. 743).

rights. Now governors and legislatures are vigorously asserting themselves. One consequence is that local school boards and superintendents are becoming obsolete: the "organizational dinosaurs of American education in the late 80s," a friendly observer calls them.[14]

Education trends over the past twenty years would appear to corroborate Finn and Doyle's argument. In an expanding education system that values choice, opportunity, and competition, school boards represent little more than a holdover from a rural past. Progress, it would seem, requires their dismantling.

Nonetheless, school boards are not without their defenders. For if not boards, then which governing institution should assume primary responsibility for overseeing a community's public schools? The state legislature? A federal agency? The office of the mayor? The courts? None of these alternatives is clearly superior to a local school board that works full-time to meet the educational needs of children living within its jurisdiction. Mayors and members of the state assembly must deal with a wide variety of social issues, from road repair to disaster relief to crime control, a fact that forces them to limit the time and resources they devote to education. As the NSBA intones, "A system run by politicians is, by necessity, mired in and must compete with all of the other municipal services and priorities that demand a busy public official's attention. Not so with the school board, whose sole responsibility is education."[15] The only mission of a school board is to govern public schools, giving them the full measure of attention that they deserve.

Because school boards focus exclusively on education, they also provide a forum for citizens to address vitally important but distressingly uncertain issues. The education of children involves much more than formulating and administering fixed lesson plans. It involves, for example, determining the merits of creationism and theories of evolution, interpreting the Civil War and the civil rights movement, understanding the value of tolerance and respect, and assessing the legacy of William Shakespeare and that of Marcus Garvey. There is no ideal sex education course, no fixed allotment of resources for chess clubs and football teams, no obvious way to discipline students. Hence communities historically have been left to figure out how to address these issues for themselves, in ways that best suit the needs of their children and the moral principles and conceptions of self to which they most aspire. If school boards are abolished, or even if past trends are allowed to continue unchecked, the only political institution that enables a community to impart its history, values, and identity to its children will be lost.

14. Chester Finn and Denis Doyle, "As States Take Charge of Schools: A New Plan" (Education Winter Survey) *New York Times*, January 6, 1985, p. 69.

15. National School Boards Association, "Do School Boards Matter?" (www.nsba.org/site/doc.asp?TRACKID=&VID=2&CID=199&DID=10888 [October 6, 2004]).

Some say that school boards have become all the more relevant precisely because the federal and state governments have assumed responsibility for much of the formation of education policy and the funding of schools. Two reasons stand out. Sarah Glover identifies the first: "For much of the last twenty years, the state has been the outside source of pressure on school districts to improve. But these are 'big box' improvements that can only go so far. By definition they cannot address needs that are idiosyncratic to a local geography or local economy."[16] Boards do the work of translating state and federal laws into local policy, they ensure that policies developed elsewhere suit their community's particular needs, and they provide the necessary institutional links between parents and teachers and state and federal legislators. The second reason relates to the first: local school boards defend districts against bad policy. Too often, the federal and state governments write education law that does more to hinder than help local educators address the needs of their students. As Thomas Shannon notes, "State legislatures have in fact adopted many oppressive statutes over the years that ruin the type of local school environment needed for innovation. As barnacles slow down ships, these laws that limit school-board discretionary authority over personnel, curriculum, and other crucial operating areas—and that substitute micromanagement by statute—hinder local initiative and stifle local imagination by undercutting boards' authority to act as local policymakers."[17] If school boards do not check these tendencies, who will?

School boards do have problems, as even their admirers readily admit. Too few citizens vote in school board elections, and board members often assume office lacking basic management skills. However, rather than turning the governance of district schools over to state or federal bureaucrats, reformers say that communities should work to enhance democratic participation on local school boards, encourage parents and teachers to run for office, draw citizens out to vote, and encourage the media to cover local education issues. On learning that the turnout in elections for state legislators is low, who would seriously argue that state legislatures should be disbanded? Why then should school boards? Improvements are needed, but the institution should not be blamed for the occasional failings of its members or the apathy of citizens who choose not to participate at all.

School Board Politics

Which arguments about school boards are most persuasive? Which alternatives to school boards, if any, should policymakers consider? These larger questions beg a host of smaller ones. Whose interests do school boards represent? Those of

16. Glover (2004, p. 13).
17. Shannon (1992, p. 30).

students? Parents? Teachers? Who votes in school board elections? When voting, do citizens consider a board member's record? How does the structure of a school board election affect its outcome? Which governing institutions retain legal authority over school boards? What evidence currently exists that mayors do any better at governing public schools than school boards do?

To begin the process of formulating answers, policymakers must distinguish their hopes and aspirations for school boards from the practical realities that boards confront. The ideals of democratic education and local control assuredly captivate the public's imagination, but a meaningful defense of school boards cannot rest on idealized conceptions about what school boards do and whose interests they serve. It must instead scrutinize school boards as they are, bumping up against the federal and state governments; negotiating with teachers, parents, and business contractors; deciding whether charter schools can open within their jurisdiction; interpreting and implementing court mandates; and coping with new accountability systems. By doing so, policymakers may meaningfully ascertain the value of school boards, and of recommendations that their powers be further restricted.

Only by examining school boards in the push and scuffle of everyday politics can policymakers identify which structural reforms deserve serious consideration. For contemporary school boards *are* political institutions—the Progressive Era notion that the administration of public education should be removed from the practice of politics long ago proved utopian. Within school boards, interests clash, power is exerted over the vocal opposition of certain constituents, alliances are made and broken, and organized groups converge in order to advance their own independent agendas. It is in this context that a board's contributions to school governance and student learning must be evaluated.

Unfortunately, scholarly studies on school boards and school board politics are startlingly sparse. In comparison with the well-developed literatures on many other aspects of public education and local politics, empirical research on school boards remains in its infancy.[18] Few studies in the social sciences concen-

18. Book-length treatments of the subject are particularly rare (Lutz and Iannaccone 1978; Bacharach 1981; Cibulka, Reed, and Wong 1992; First and Walberg 1992; Hannaway and Carnoy 1993; Education Commission of the States 1995). The Institute for Educational Leadership has published several monographs on school boards that describe valuable survey findings (Institute for Educational Leadership 1986, 1992). See also Twentieth Century Fund (1992). Other recent works on school boards have focused on issues of administration and leadership (Flinchbaugh 1993; Sarason 1997). Finally, while school boards often are the subject of a chapter or two in educational administration textbooks, the coverage tends to be descriptive and perfunctory (Blumberg 1989; Guthrie 1991; Lunenburg and Ornstein 1991; Cusick 1992). For a notable exception, see Sergiovanni and others (1992). Articles in professional journals, although more voluminous, hardly begin to fill the gap. Political scientists, surprisingly, have given school boards scant consideration. In the past four decades, fewer than twenty-five articles that directly relate to school boards have been published in major political science journals. The major issues addressed in this literature include racial politics and representation on school boards (Meier and England 1984), school

trate explicitly on the local political institutions that govern public schools. Indeed, key aspects of local school governance—elections, mobilization of interest groups, interagency relations, and notions of power—have essentially been ignored. It is hardly an exaggeration to note that more is known about the operation of medieval merchant guilds than about the institutions that govern contemporary school districts.

A Road Map

This volume presents new evidence on school board politics and their contributions to student learning. Each chapter presents empirical findings that will inform the ongoing debate about school governance structures and about local education more generally. The book covers four broad areas. First, it analyzes historical and contemporary efforts on the part of school boards to defend their powers against state and federal encroachment; second, it scrutinizes school board elections; third, it identifies the citizens and interest groups that organize to influence school boards; and fourth, it reflects on the merits of local control.

Richard Briffault sets the stage in chapter 2 by surveying the constitutional and legal authority of state governments and local school boards for public education. He identifies numerous instances in which courts have recognized the values of localism and accorded school boards and school districts de facto legal autonomy. The history of public education and the tradition of local control, he observes, have informed judges' rulings in a wide variety of cases on topics ranging from school vouchers to board elections to school finance reform. The state, however, retains primary legal control over public education and therefore has ultimate authority regarding the design of school districts and the assignment of responsibilities for local education. School boards remain "legally subordinate arms of their states," with little or no constitutional basis for asserting independent claims. While a school board in practice may enjoy the discretion to write policy that does not perfectly reflect the will or intention of the state government, as a legal matter, the state can revoke such powers at any time. States can

---

desegregation (Gatlin, Giles, and Cataldo 1978; Rossell and Crain 1982), social networks and social capital (Schneider 1997; Schneider and others 1997), and bureaucratic politics (Meier, Stewart, and England 1991; Meier, Polinard, and Wrinkel 2000). The economics literature most closely linked to school boards deals principally with issues of competition among districts (Hoxby 2000) and economies of scale related to district size (Andrews, Duncombe, and Yinger 2002). Meanwhile, sociologists and education scholars working on school boards have focused mostly on the relationship between elected boards and professional administrators, teachers, and superintendents (Greene 1992; Carver 2000; Earley 2000); site-based decisionmaking (Wyman 2000); school board training and the characteristics of "effective" boards (Streshly and Frase 1993; Campbell and Greene 1994); and board members' perception of their role in education (Newman and Brown 1993; McAdams and Cressman 1997).

launch any number of initiatives to abolish or greatly restrict the legal authority of school boards. Indeed, the future of school boards and of local control may lie with governors and state legislators.

Plenary state powers revealed themselves most fully during the rapid, indeed unprecedented, consolidation of school districts during the middle of the twentieth century—a development that local officials had no legal recourse to halt. Between 1930 and 1970, states eliminated more than 100,000 districts and their governing boards, revolutionizing school governance and setting in motion wholesale changes in public education. The most immediate result of these consolidations was that the size of school districts increased fourteenfold and that of schools increased fivefold. It is difficult to underestimate the sheer magnitude of these changes, much less their importance for framing contemporary policy debates. Advocates of small schools, for instance, are pushing for marginal changes in school size that hover around a mean established during the 1950s and 1960s by legislators intent on restricting local control over public education.

In chapter 3, Christopher Berry examines the impact of district consolidation on students' long-term monetary earnings. His findings are striking. While increasing district size had only a negligible impact on earnings, the observed effects for school size were substantial. By Berry's calculations, increasing a school's size by 100 students led, on average, to a 4 percent decline in students' earnings. The historic consolidation of school districts—and with it the elimination of school boards—yielded at least some unintended and adverse effects for children. In addition to validating past work on school size, Berry's work suggests a possible conflict for contemporary school board members. While smaller schools may benefit students, they do not necessarily serve incumbent board members struggling to maintain control over the schools within their jurisdiction. Difficulties in administration and oversight necessarily mount as schools proliferate, and schools can decrease in size only to the extent that they increase in number. School board members therefore must choose between attending to students' interests (by pressing for smaller schools) and protecting their own (by opposing them).

While the consolidation of school districts has tapered off, threats to school boards have not. Most prominently, in a growing number of large urban districts, mayors have assumed primary responsibility for the governance of public schools. In an effort to stem the tide of middle- and upper-class families moving from urban to suburban districts and to better integrate the provision of education with other government services, mayors in nearly a dozen major cities have secured control of a majority of slots on their school boards. In all, upward of 2 million students now are educated in school districts run by a mayor. In chapter 4, Kenneth Wong and Francis Shen examine the impact of mayoral takeover on districts' fiscal management, prudently noting that more experience and more time are needed before firm conclusions can be drawn about the efficacy of takeover. By their account, however, the early evidence appears rather unimpressive. Mayoral takeovers have not had any impact on staff allocations or on the percentage of funding that districts receive from the federal or state governments. There is some evidence that mayors reallocated finances from central administration toward school sites, though they also tended to cut per-pupil spending on instruction. Though mayoral takeover continues to captivate the imagination of school reformers, in practice, its short-term effects on district spending appear rather tepid.

The next two chapters focus on the willingness and capacity of school boards to faithfully implement court desegregation orders and state charter laws. In chapter 5, Luis Fraga, Nick Rodriguez, and Bari Erlichson carefully examine the San Francisco school board's handling of a desegregation consent decree during the 1980s and 1990s. Plainly, the authors note, the electoral interests of some school board members were not served by vigorously enforcing such a decree, and those members carefully calibrated progress toward the stated desegregation objectives by using their power to hire and fire the superintendent. The authors demonstrate that without the consensus of local school board members, commitments to racial progress made by judges, legislators, and even governors amounted to little. Because most of a policy's effect lies in its eventual implementation, much about an education initiative's success or failure lies with school boards.

In chapter 6, which examines school boards' treatment of charter schools, Paul Teske, Mark Schneider, and Erin Cassese take a slightly different tack. Just as school boards may circumvent desegregation decrees, so too may they ward off competition. One might therefore expect school boards, as chartering agencies, to deny the vast majority of charter school applications and accept only those that do not threaten the financial or political well-being of the public school system. Surveying national databases on charter applications and approvals, however, Teske and his colleagues suggest that school board members are not especially sophisticated political creatures. Charter laws met resistance at the local level not because school boards strategically worked to undermine them, but because board members were ill equipped and poorly trained to evaluate charter applications. School boards tended to grant as many charters, with as many waivers, to as many students as did state boards of education and universities. The authors do find some evidence that school boards granted fewer charters to "niche" schools serving at-risk students. But whereas Fraga and colleagues observed school boards deliberately shirking court mandates, Teske, Schneider, and Cassese saw school boards merely muddling along.

While mayors and courts may wield influence from above, and competition from an incipient charter school movement may present new challenges from below, it is to the electorate that individual school board members are ultimately accountable. This volume next turns to school board elections, examining who shows up on Election Day, how they vote, which groups gain representation, and what implications all of this has for student learning. To start things off,

Christopher Berry and I point out in chapter 7 that accountability in public education runs considerably deeper than it does in the federal government's latest efforts at reform, the No Child Left Behind Act. Unlike employees of government agencies that oversee the provision of welfare or health services, which are insulated from electoral pressures and hence require a top-down accountability system, most school board members must defend their performance before an electorate. Consequently, mechanisms that reward excellence and punish failure are already in place: when schools falter, voters can boot school board members out of office; when schools succeed, voters can reward them with reelection.

We examine whether voters do in fact hold board members responsible for recent trends in student learning. Scrutinizing the 2000 and 2002 school board elections in South Carolina, we find mixed evidence that voters do. In 2000, test score gains positively contributed to the probability that incumbent board members would seek reelection, decreased the chances that they would face a competitor, and increased their share of the final vote. In the 2002 mid-term elections, however, we found no relationship between incumbents' electoral prospects and student performance. We speculate that holding school board elections at the same time as presidential elections—and thereby drawing a significantly higher turnout—strengthens the chances that incumbents will be held accountable for student outcomes.

Chapters 8 and 9 examine factors affecting the racial and ethnic characteristics of school board members as well as the effects of board composition on education outcomes. In chapter 8, drawing on survey data and electoral returns in almost 200 school districts in Atlanta, Boston, Detroit, and Los Angeles, Melissa Marschall finds that African Americans won more seats in ward-based elections (where minorities, as voting blocs, constitute a majority of the voters) than in at-large elections (where their influence is more diluted), while differences for Hispanics appeared trivial. Marschall also finds that African Americans' evaluations of their local school were especially sensitive to the racial composition of the school boards, while again, those of Hispanics were not. In chapter 9, examining the experiences of Hispanics in Texas, Kenneth Meier and Eric Juenke reach slightly different conclusions. The authors trace the possibilities for and consequences of Hispanic representation straight through the electoral process, from the original votes cast to the number of Hispanic teachers and administrators hired to the performance of Hispanic students on standardized tests. Where they were a minority of the population, Hispanics gained more seats in ward elections than in at-large elections; gains in Hispanic representation on school boards, in turn, led to gains in representation among teachers and administrators; and where Hispanic teachers worked, Hispanic students scored higher on tests and attended advanced classes more often. Simple changes to the structure of school board elections appeared to have profound downstream consequences, suggesting that state and federal policymakers should pay as much attention to school board electoral reforms as to specific education initiatives designed to improve minority test scores.

Local education politics, of course, consists of considerably more than just average citizens casting their vote for their favored board member, whether on the basis of his or her race or demonstrated ability to improve student achievement. Interest groups, campaigns, and money all affect the composition of school boards and the objectives that they pursue, and this volume next examines their influence on school board operations. In chapter 10, drawing from a national survey of school board members, Frederick Hess and David Leal find that teacher unions, parent groups, business groups, religious organizations, and racial and ethnic organizations all influenced school board politics, through financial contributions or (more often) canvassing. But in most districts, Hess and Leal note, school board politics did not reveal the considerable drama that characterizes congressional or presidential elections. Instead, most school board elections were low-budget affairs wherein candidates relied on friends and family members for campaign contributions and, according to most board members, the elections themselves were rarely competitive.

While Hess and Leal surveyed a nationally representative sample of elected school board members, in chapter 10 Terry Moe surveys both winners and losers in California school board elections. By Moe's account, the politics in these elections were more contentious than Hess and Leal suggest and the most powerful of the mobilized interest groups was obvious: teacher unions stood out as the single most significant influence on who was elected to school boards and which policies they supported. Indeed, the combined influence of parents, religious bodies, business groups, and other community organizations paled in comparison. To be sure, union dominance was not complete, and Moe notes instances in which local education politics were more appropriately characterized by pluralism. But if you are going to wager on who is likely to win the next school board election and on what interests he or she is likely to serve, you would do well to check with the local teacher union.

If unions dominate school board politics, as Moe claims, advocates of local democratic control must address two issues. First and most obviously, school boards would disproportionately represent one segment of a community—and one whose interests do not always align with those of students. Moreover, because of collective bargaining arrangements, teachers and their union representatives would appear to have a virtual lock on the system. In principle, independently elected school board members are supposed to negotiate school policy and operations with teachers. But rather than standing on opposite sides of the table, school board members and teachers would appear to be partners in a common enterprise, each providing vital resources and support that the other requires. Much, of course, rides on the relative accuracy of Moe's depiction of school board politics vis-à-vis that of Hess and Leal. Depending on the verdict, existing governing arrangements either perpetuate the interests of a narrow band of the electorate or they provide a forum for competing groups to air their claims and contribute to education policy.

In chapter 12, David Campbell shifts attention away from organized interests and toward average citizens. He asks a simple but underexplored question: Who, exactly, attends school board meetings? Analyzing new survey data from forty communities across the nation, Campbell finds strong individual and contextual effects, most of which are straightforward enough. As one might expect, greater religious involvement, education, and income all increase an individual's propensity to attend local meetings, and the average education of a community correlates positively with attendance patterns. One finding in Campbell's analysis, however, appears counterintuitive. One might expect a positive relationship between religious heterogeneity in a community and attendance at local meetings, for when parents come from different religious traditions, they are likely to have different ideas about what should and should not be taught in public schools. To assert their independent interests and safeguard their child's educational welfare, parents from such communities ought to attend school board meetings with some regularity. Campbell, however, finds just the opposite. Parents from religiously homogenous districts attended more local meetings than parents from heterogeneous districts. Rather than diversity drawing parents into local education politics, it appeared to depress civic engagement. Social capital, Campbell observes, is abundant among like-minded residents who share common religious traditions.

This book, then, presents new empirical findings about who participates in school board politics, whose interests school boards serve, whether school boards can be trusted to faithfully implement policy directives from other branches of government, and what possibilities different governance reforms hold. When assigning meaning to these findings, readers should pay close attention to regional differences. The characteristics of Hispanics living in Texas, whom Meier and Juenke analyze, may not match those of Hispanics living in the Northeast or the West; California teacher unions, the subject of Moe's analysis, are obviously stronger than those operating in South Carolina, on which Berry and I based our research; and experiences of urban school boards, which receive a disproportionate amount of attention in all the chapters in this volume, may not carry over to suburban and rural districts. Taking note of such differences, the book closes with two reflective essays, by Joseph Viteritti (chapter 13) and Jennifer Hochschild (chapter 14), each of whom interprets the empirical findings presented in this volume and their implications for localism's past and future. Noting both salutary and pernicious features of school boards and the system of local democratic control that they stand for, Viteritti and Hochschild introduce larger frameworks for thinking about the normative debate that underlies this collection of essays—namely, whether policymakers should applaud or decry historical trends toward district consolidation and state and federal control over local education.

What can be expected from school boards? By my account, the essays in this volume present a rather sobering assessment. Consistent with their critics' claims, school board elections typically are low-turnout affairs, and vested interests (most prominently teacher unions) exert considerable influence on their outcomes. Citizens who do participate in school board meetings tend to have more education and higher income and to live in religiously homogeneous communities, raising problems for those who would defend school boards on the grounds that they provide a forum in which diverse interests can deliberate collectively. Meanwhile, using their appointment powers, school boards continue to thwart judicial efforts to desegregate public schools, much as they did in the 1950s and 1960s. And when mayors try their hand at school reform, they bump up against many of the political and institutional constraints that confront existing school boards.

There are some bright spots. When turnout is high, voters appear to hold incumbent school board members accountable for the test score performances of local schools, suggesting that elections may do more than merely anoint the preferred candidates of teacher unions and other organized interests. Relatively simple changes in the structure of school board elections may increase minority representation, a change that may in turn yield positive benefits for minority parents and children. And despite other claims to the contrary, school board members may not always ward off competitive threats—at least not charter schools.

Notably, however, no one in this volume argues or presents evidence that school boards are especially innovative, that they actively pursue creative public policies that immediately serve students. Instead, school boards defend a status quo that is quickly slipping out of their grasp. In part, this is due to a convergence of historical trends, most notably district consolidation, the expansion of choice initiatives, and the encroachment of state, federal, and judicial powers on district affairs. But it also is due to the political environment in which school boards operate—the interests that members are beholden to, the political constraints that they face, and the tensions that regularly arise between their own electoral incentives and those of state and federal officials. School boards may competently perform essential administrative functions, and they may also recommend and occasionally implement reasonable policy changes. Pockets of innovation and communities of local innovators certainly exist.[19] But if you

---

19. Glover, for instance, claims that "in Houston, Seattle, Sacramento, Charlotte-Mecklenburg, and Dayton, school boards have been the primary actors in reform. Likewise, the school boards in Aldine, Texas, and Long Beach, California, have been strong partners in maintaining a commitment to delivering better reform" (Glover 2004, p. 12). She also recognizes the exceptional nature of these cities' school boards, citing survey findings that more than 75 percent of the school boards in the nation's 120 largest districts generate exclusively "reactive" school reforms (p. 13).

believe that public education in the United States is in need of fundamental reform, it probably makes sense to look elsewhere for either policy recommendations or the independence and initiative to implement them.

References

Andrews, Matthew, William Duncombe, and John Yinger. 2002. "Revisiting Economies of Size in American Education: Are We Any Closer to a Consensus?" *Economics of Education Review* 21(3): 245–62.

Atkin, J. M. 1980. "The Government in the Classroom." *Daedalus* 109 (3): 85–97.

Bacharach, Samuel., ed. 1981. *Organizational Behavior in Schools and School Districts.* New York: Praeger.

Blumberg, Arthur. 1989. *School Administration as a Craft: Foundations of Practice.* Boston: Allyn and Bacon.

Campbell, Davis, and Diane Greene. 1994. "Defining the Leadership Role of School Boards in the 21st Century." *Phi Delta Kappan* 75 (5): 391–95.

Carver, John. 2000. "Toward Coherent Governance." *School Administrator* 57 (3): 6–10.

Cibulka, James, Rodney Reed, and Kenneth Wong, eds. 1992. *The Politics of Urban Education in the United States.* Washington: Falmer Press.

Cusick, Phillip. 1992. *The Educational System: Its Nature and Logic.* New York: McGraw-Hill.

Earley, Peter. 2000. "Monitoring, Managing, or Meddling? Governing Bodies and the Evaluation of School Performance." *Educational Management and Administration* 28 (2): 199–210.

Education Commission of the States. 1995. *The New American Urban School District.* Denver: ECS Publications.

First, Patricia, and Herbert Walberg, eds. 1992. *School Boards: Changing Local Control.* Berkeley, Calif.: McCutchan Publishing.

Flinchbaugh, Robert. 1993. *The 21st Century Board of Education.* Lancaster, Pa.: Techomic Publishing.

Gatlin, Douglas, Michael Giles, and Everett Cataldo. 1978. "Policy Support within a Target Group: The Case of School Desegregation." *American Political Science Review* 72 (3): 985–95.

Glover, Sarah. 2004. "School Boards as Leaders of Reform." *Education Next* 4 (3): 11–13.

Greene, Kenneth. 1992. "Models of School Board Policy-Making." *Educational Administration Quarterly* 28 (2): 220–36.

Guthrie, James. 1991. *Educational Administration and Policy: Effective Leadership for American Education.* Englewood Cliffs, N.J.: Prentice Hall.

Hannaway, Jane, and Martin Carnoy. 1993. *Decentralization and School Improvement.* San Francisco: Josey-Bass Publishers.

Hoxby, Caroline Minter. 2000. "Does Competition among Schools Benefit Students and Taxpayers?" *American Economic Review* 90 (December): 1209–38.

Institute for Educational Leadership. 1986. *School Boards: Strengthening Grass Roots Leadership.* Washington: IEL Publications.

———. 1992. *Governing Public Schools: New Times, New Requirements.* Washington: IEL Publications.

Kaestle, Carl F. 1983. *Pillars of the Republic: Common Schools and American Society, 1780–1860.* New York: Hill and Wang.

Lunenburg, Frederick, and Allan Ornstein. 1991. *Educational Administration: Concepts and Practices*. Belmont, Calif.: Wadsworth Publishers.

Lutz, Frank, and Laurence Iannaccone, eds. 1978. *Public Participation in Local School Districts*. Lexington, Mass.: Lexington Books.

Macedo, Stephen. 2003. "School Reform and Equal Opportunity in America's Geography of Inequality." *Perspectives on Politics* 1 (4): 743–55.

McAdams, Richard, and Brad Cressman. 1997. "The Roles of Pennsylvania Superintendents and School Board Members as Perceived by Superintendents and School Board Members." *Educational Research Quarterly* 21 (1): 44–57.

Meier, Kenneth, and Robert England. 1984. "Black Representation and Educational Policy: Are They Related?" *American Political Science Review* 78 (June): 392–403.

Meier, Kenneth, Joseph Stewart, and Robert England. 1991. "The Politics of Bureaucratic Discretion: Educational Access as an Urban Service." *American Journal of Political Science* 35 (1): 155–77.

Meier, Kenneth, J. L. Polinard, and Robert Wrinkle. 2000. "Bureaucracy and Organizational Performance: Causality Arguments about Public Schools." *American Journal of Political Science* 44 (3): 590–602.

Newman, Dianna, and Robert Brown. 1993. "School Board Member Role Expectations in Making Decisions about Educational Programs: Do Size of School and Region of Country Make a Difference?" *Urban Education* 28 (3): 267–80.

Reed, Doug. 2003. "Whither Localism?: No Child Left Behind and the Local Politics of Federal Education Reform." Paper presented at "School Board Politics," Program on Education Policy and Governance, Harvard University.

Rossell, Christine, and Robert Crain. 1982. "The Importance of Political Factors in Explaining Northern School Desegregation." *American Journal of Political Science* 26 (4): 772–96.

Sarason, Seymour. 1997. *How Schools Might Be Governed and Why*. New York: Teachers College Press.

Schneider, Mark. 1997. "Institutional Arrangements and the Creation of Social Capital." *American Political Science Review* 91 (March): 82–93.

Schneider, Mark, and others. 1997. "Networks to Nowhere: Segregation and Stratification in Networks of Information about Schools." *American Journal of Political Science* 41 (4): 1201–23.

Sergiovanni, Thomas, and others. 1992. *Educational Governance and Administration*. Boston: Allyn and Bacon.

Shannon, Thomas. 1992. "Local Control and 'Organizacrats.'" In *School Boards: Changing Local Control*, edited by Patricia First and Herbert Walberg, pp. 27–33. Berkeley, Calif.: McCutchan Publishing.

Streshly, William, and Larry Frase. 1993. "School Boards: The Missing Piece of the Reform Pie." *International Journal of Education Reform* 2 (2): 140–43.

Tyack, David. 1974. *The One Best System: A History of American Urban Education*. Harvard University Press.

Twentieth Century Fund. 1992. *Facing the Challenge: The Report of the Twentieth Century Fund Task Force on School Governance*. New York.

Wyman, Benjamin. 2000. "Decentralization Continued: A Survey of Emerging Issues in Site-Bound Decision Making." *Journal of Law and Education* 29 (2): 255–63.

2

The Local School District in American Law

RICHARD BRIFFAULT

The legal status of American school districts is shaped by the fundamental and long-standing tension between their formal subservience to the states and their de facto autonomy. A school district is a political subdivision of its state, entirely subordinate to the state and without constitutional rights of its own. Yet, in practice, in most states local school boards enjoy considerable power over the day-to-day operation and management of their schools, and this local school district autonomy has at times been recognized—and rewarded—by state and federal courts. The U.S. Supreme Court, in particular, has spoken frequently of the value of "local control" in the governance of American schools and has relied on the concept of local control in resolving constitutional questions involving the schools.

This chapter examines the tension between the "black letter" rule of local school district subordination to the state and the practice—and occasional legal recognition—of local school district autonomy. The chapter first presents a brief overview of the number and variety of school districts and their place in the U.S. federal structure. It then considers the formal legal status of the school district as a political subdivision of the state and, especially, as an agent of the state for the local provision of a critical state program—elementary and secondary education. The chapter next examines instances in which school district autonomy has received legal recognition. In concluding, it attempts to reconcile these conflicting approaches and considers the implications of recent developments for the legal status of school districts.

Local School Districts and School Boards in the U.S. Federal System

A school *district* is a territorial unit within a state that has responsibility for the provision of public education within its borders. A school district is a *corporate* body, that is, it exists as a legal entity separate and apart from its governing board and from the people who live within the district and utilize its programs. Like most corporate bodies, the school district can sue and be sued; acquire, hold, and dispose of real property; make and enforce contracts; hire employees; and adopt rules to govern its own operations.[1]

A school district is also a government, that is, a *public* body. The typical school district enjoys some of the perquisites of governments, such as the power to take property by eminent domain and to issue tax-exempt bonds. More important, school districts are subject to the constitutional constraints that apply to government bodies—and only government bodies—such as the protection of freedom of speech and of religion, the prohibition against unreasonable searches and seizures, and the requirements of due process and equal protection of the laws.[2]

Finally, a school district is a *local* government. This has both territorial and political significance. Territorially, the school district has authority over only the geographically defined portion of the state that falls within its boundaries. Politically, the district is created by the state government and can wield only those powers conferred upon it by the state. The nature of the school district as a local government will be examined more fully later in the chapter.

The school *board* is the governing body of the district, the body that exercises the district's corporate powers and carries out its public responsibilities. It, too, is a creature of state law, which determines the size of the board, the terms of board members, how board members are selected, and whether and how they may be removed.[3]

There are approximately 15,000 local school districts in the United States, accounting for more than one-sixth of all U.S. local governments.[4] These school

1. See, for example, Valente (1994, p. 25); Bolmeier (1973, p. 130), listing the corporate powers of school districts.

2. See, generally, Ryan (2000) for a discussion of the applicability of the establishment, free exercise, and free speech clauses of the First Amendment, the Fourth Amendment, due process, and antidiscrimination principles to public schools.

3. Bolmeier (1973, pp. 146–49).

4. U.S. Census Bureau (2002, p. vii), reporting 15,014 public school systems out of a total of 87,525 units of local government.

districts vary tremendously in territorial size, enrollment, organization, and legal powers and status; they even vary in name. A recent survey by the Education Commission of the States (ECS) found fifty-four legally distinct types of school district within the United States.[5] Part of this variation reflects the central role of state law in establishing and empowering school districts. With forty-nine different states providing for local school districts—Hawaii breaks the pattern by operating a single statewide school system—some interstate differentiation is inevitable. Moreover, there is often considerable variation in the types of school district within a state. The ECS study found that in fourteen states there were four or more types of district; three states had as many as six types; and only fifteen states had just one type.[6] Some of these variations may be just a matter of terminology, with different states using different terms—local district, city or municipal district, town district—to mean essentially the same thing. Others reflect differences in school district location (urban versus rural), territorial scope (running the gamut from neighborhood to metropolitan area), grade coverage (K–6, K–8, 9–12, K–12), and relationship to other local governments.

The vast majority of school districts—90 percent according to the U.S. Census Bureau—are legally and politically independent of general purpose local governments, that is, counties or municipalities.[7] Indeed, the boundaries of almost 80 percent of all school districts are not coterminous with the boundaries of other general purpose local governments, so that the districts either overlap more than one municipality or county or constitute only a subpart of the county.[8] Even most coterminous districts—which some states promote through the use of county or municipal school districts or by providing that a change in municipal boundaries also effects a change in school district boundaries—are legally independent of the corresponding local government.

The meaning of school district independence is not always clear. It certainly involves a separate legal existence.[9] The vast majority of school boards have also

5. Education Commission of the States (2002b).

6. Education Commission of the States (2002b).

7. According to the 2002 Census of Governments, of the 15,014 school systems in the United States in 2002, 13,506 were independent school district governments, while 1,506 were dependent systems. Of the dependent systems, 178 (including Hawaii's statewide school system) were categorized as state-dependent. The remainder were dependent on local governments. U.S. Census Bureau (2002, table 12, p. 17).

8. See U.S. Census Bureau (2002, table 15, p. 21). According to the Census Bureau, 2,712 school districts have the same boundaries as a county, municipality, town, or township; 5,722 are located within one county but are not coterminous with the county or any subdivision within the county; 4,329 districts overlap two or more counties; and 2,251 did not report boundary data. Of the reporting districts, then, only 21 percent are coterminous with a general purpose local government.

9. See, for example, *Rollins* v. *Wilson County Government*, 967 F. Supp. 990, 996 (M.D. Tenn. 1997): plaintiff's periods working for the county government and the county school board could not be aggregated for purposes of establishing coverage under the Family and Medical Leave Act because "a county board of education is a separate and distinct governmental entity from that

been made politically independent of other local governments by state laws providing for the election of school board members by school district voters, not for their appointment by a mayor or county governing board. In thirty-one states, all school districts are governed by independently elected governing boards; in another twelve states, nearly all districts are governed by elected boards.[10] However, in an important recent departure from this norm discussed in more detail below, some large urban school boards have been transformed into appointed bodies. Fiscal independence varies somewhat more. In some states, local school boards have the power, pursuant to state law and subject to state substantive and procedural limitations, to levy and collect taxes, usually an ad valorem tax on real property. In other states, school boards are fiscally dependent on other local governments. The board can frame the school district's budget, but it must turn to a county or municipal government to actually levy and collect the taxes needed to finance the school district's program.[11]

Given the enormous variation in laws dealing with school district organization, powers, and responsibilities, broad generalizations about the status of school boards must be hedged by some acknowledgment of the exceptions and departures from the norm. The legal status of any particular school district will turn on the laws of its state, which may include idiosyncratic provisions for that district. Still, painting with the broad brush necessary in a brief chapter, the following discussion lays out the two competing approaches that have shaped the legal status of school districts: the formal—and predominant—approach of treating the school board as a legally subordinate arm of its state; and the informal approach whereby many local school districts have enjoyed a de facto autonomy that has received intermittent legal recognition.

The Local School District as an Arm of the State

The legal status of school districts and school boards flows from two key facts. First, school districts are local governments, and thus, like all other local

---

county's government"; *Lanza v. Wagner,* 11 N.Y.2d 317 (N.Y. 1962): although New York City's Board of Education is connected to the City's government, board members are "officers of an independent corporation separate and distinct from the city." See, generally, Reutter (1994, p. 155): "It is essential . . . to stress the basic separateness of [school district and general local governments]. Even where boundaries of a municipal unit and a school district are coterminous, there is no merger of city affairs and school district affairs."

10. See Education Commission of the States (2002b). The ECS reports that in thirty-one states all school board members are elected. In another seven states, the members of all but one school board are elected; in five more states, the members of all but two to five school boards are elected. In only six states—Alabama, Indiana, Maryland, New Jersey, South Carolina, and Virginia—are more than a minimal number of school boards composed of appointed rather than elected officials.

11. See Hudgins and Vacca (1995, pp. 146–48), noting that local school boards are fiscally independent in Florida, Georgia, and Missouri, but are fiscally dependent in Virginia.

governments, they are subordinate to their states. Second, unlike general purpose local governments (counties and municipalities), school districts have a single function—the provision of public elementary and secondary education—which is, as a matter of state law, considered to be a state and not a local responsibility. As a result, school districts enjoy less formal autonomy and are subject to far more state mandates and oversight than other local governments. Indeed, for some purposes they are treated not simply as legally subordinate to the states but as essentially no more than an agency or arm of the state, rather than as an independent government.

The School District as Local Government

The formal status of a local government in relation to its state is summarized by the three legal concepts: "creature," "delegate," and "agent."[12] As a local government, a school district is a creature of the state. It exists only by an act of the state, and the state, as its creator, has plenary power to alter, expand, contract, or abolish it at will. The school district is a delegate of the state, possessing only those powers that the state has chosen to confer upon it. Absent any specific limitation in the state's constitution, the state can amend, abridge, or retract any power it has delegated, much as it can impose new duties or take away old privileges. The school district is also an agent of the state, exercising powers at the local level on behalf of the state in order to implement state policies.[13]

As a matter of federal constitutional law, local government boundaries, structures, rights, and powers are entirely for the states to decide. The U.S. Constitution recognizes only the federal government and the states; it is entirely silent concerning local governments. For American federalism, then, issues of local government power and organization are questions of state law. As a matter of federal constitutional law, local residents have no right to local self-government and certainly no right to be in any particular local government or to have a local government with any particular powers or independence from its state.[14]

Thus a school district's residents have no constitutional claim if the state redraws the district's boundaries, shifting them from one district to another. Nor can a district challenge the loss of its property to another district as an unconstitutional taking.[15]

12. See, generally, Briffault (1990, p. 7).

13. See, for example, Hazard (1971, p. 3): "Legally, school boards act as agents of the state legislature"; Bolmeier (1973, p. 129): "Local school districts are incorporated as agencies of the state for purposes of executing the state's educational policy."

14. *Hunter* v. *City of Pittsburgh*, 207 U.S. 161 (1907).

15. See, for example, Attorney General of Michigan ex. rel. *Kies* v. *Lowrey*, 199 U.S. 233 (1905). See also *Rousselle* v. *Plaquemines Parish School Board*, 633 So.2d 1235, 1241 (La. 1994): school board cannot claim that an amendment to the Louisiana Teacher Tenure Law that strengthened the rights of a teacher under an existing contract violates the Contracts Clause because as a state agency the board "is not protected by the constitutional prohibition against the legislature enacting laws which impair the obligation of contracts."

To be sure, state governments do not have unlimited authority to redraw school district boundaries or revise school district powers. The Supreme Court has held, for example, that New York state's creation of a school district for the specific benefit of the devoutly religious Satmar Hasidic Jewish community residing in the village of Kiryas Joel violated the establishment clause of the First Amendment.[16] Similarly, the Supreme Court held that a Washington state statute that prohibited local school boards from busing children to promote desegregation—but not from busing them for other purposes—was a racially charged action that violated the equal protection clause of the Fourteenth Amendment.[17] Similarly the provisions of the Voting Rights Act apply to the redistricting of elected school boards, much as they apply to other local governments.

In other words, federal constitutional norms and statutory requirements that generally constrain state government actions continue to apply when the state is dealing with local school districts. But school boards do not have federal constitutional rights against their states, and school district residents do not have any constitutionally protected interest in having a school district with particular boundaries and powers. As a result, state governments have broad authority to create, alter, or abolish school districts; revise their powers; and restructure or even eliminate their boards.[18] Indeed, some courts have found that school districts lack even the legal capacity to file lawsuits challenging state actions that would change their borders or dissolve them.[19] As a result, the dramatic reduction in the number of school districts during the twentieth century that is analyzed by Christopher Berry in chapter 3 of this volume was largely immune from judicial consideration.

The Special State Interest in Education

Federal constitutional law does not distinguish between school districts and other local governments, but at the state level, the legal status of school districts is typically weaker than that of counties, cities, towns, and townships. The position of school districts as disfavored local governments is a consequence of the fact that school districts are functionally specialized and their one activity—the local provision of public elementary and secondary education—is everywhere considered to be a state responsibility.

Virtually every state constitution contains a provision requiring the state legislature to provide for a system of free, nonsectarian public education. The existence of such a mandate is an unusual departure in American constitutionalism—

16. *Board of Education of Kiryas Joel Village School District* v. *Grumet,* 521 U.S. 687 (1994).
17. *Washington* v. *Seattle School District No. 1,* 458 U.S. 457 (1982).
18. Reutter (1994, p. 104); Valente (1994, p. 17).
19. See, for example, *Minnesota Association of Public Schools* v. *Hansen,* 178 N.W.2d 846 (Minn. 1970). See also *Unified School Dist. No. 335* v. *State of Kansas,* 478 P.2d 201 (Kan. 1970): one school district cannot sue to challenge the boundaries or validity of another district.

which has traditionally been far more focused on limiting government power and protecting people from government than on affirming government obligations to provide a public service—and it is a tribute to the central role of public education in American culture. As a matter of state constitutional law, courts have consistently held that due to the education mandate, public education is a matter of important state concern and a critical state responsibility. This has reinforced the subordinate position of school districts in the state-local hierarchy. It is not simply that school districts are of "lower rank" than their states. As a unit specializing in public education, a school district is often seen as an agency of the state—sometimes, rhetorically, as an "arm of the state"—responsible for implementing the state's education mandate locally. That conception is nicely illustrated by several state cases dealing with state laws transferring land or buildings from one school district to another. The courts have generally agreed that even if the losing district has formal legal title to the affected school building, the "beneficial interest" in the property lies really in the state itself or in the people of the state. Because the school district is little more than agency or "trustee" of the state, the losing district has no claim to compensation.[20]

The special state interest in education significantly affects the powers and status of local school boards. There is far greater state administrative oversight of school boards than of other local governments. Many state constitutions specifically address the administration of the educational system by providing for a state board of education with general supervisory authority over public education or for a chief state education officer, such as a superintendent of public instruction or a commissioner of education; sometimes they provide for both. Even when these state boards or officers are not provided for in the state's constitution, they are created by statute; all states have a state board of education, a chief education officer, or both.[21] Moreover, in twenty-three states, the constitution provides that either the board or the superintendent is to be elected, giving these state officials greater political clout and legitimacy.[22] These state administrators often have considerable supervisory authority with respect to local school districts and may promulgate extensive rules and regulations governing school

20. See, for example, *Pass School District of Los Angeles County* v. *Hollywood City School District of Los Angeles County*, 105 P. 122 (Cal. 1909): "the beneficial owner of the fee is the state itself," and school districts "are essentially nothing but trustees of the state, holding the property and devoting it to the uses which the state itself directs"; *City of Baker School Board* v. *East Baton Rouge Parish School Board*, 754 So.2d 291, 293 (La. App. 2000): "The ownership, management, and control of property within a school board's district is vested in the district, in the manner of a statutory trustee."

21. Reutter (1994, p. 113).

22. The superintendent of public instruction, or commissioner of education, is elected in fourteen states: Arizona, California, Georgia, Idaho, Indiana, Montana, North Carolina, North Dakota, Oklahoma, Oregon, South Carolina, Washington, Wisconsin, and Wyoming. Members of the state board of education are elected in Colorado, Kansas, Louisiana, Michigan, Nebraska, New Mexico, Ohio, South Dakota, and Texas.

board behavior and school district operations.[23] There is no comparable state administrative officer or body—other than the legislature itself—with similar powers over counties, cities, or other localities.

Besides being reflected in state administrative rules, the special state interest in education is typically manifested in extensive state legislative regulation of local schools, school districts, and school boards. The state regulates school district organization, elections, and governance; educational programs, instructional materials, and proficiency testing; attendance rules; length of the school day and school year; teacher credentialing, certification, tenure, and pensions; construction and maintenance of school buildings; school district finances and budgets; school safety; parents' and students' rights and responsibilities; and virtually every other aspect of school operations and policy. The California Supreme Court recently referred to the "voluminous regulations administered by the State's Department of Education and the Superintendent of Public Instruction."[24] In another recent case, the Louisiana Supreme Court found that the two volumes of the Louisiana Code devoted to the public schools "evinc[e] that public education in Louisiana is highly regulated by state law."[25] And Louisiana's laws concerning education are paltry compared with those of some other states. By my count, fourteen volumes of the California legislative code deal with education.

Finally, the strong state interest in education means that local school boards tend to have relatively limited power to initiate policies of their own. Under the legal norm known as Dillon's Rule—named after the nineteenth-century Iowa judge who first crystallized it—local governments may exercise only those powers expressly granted by the legislature, necessarily implied in the legislative grant, or essential to the accomplishment of the purposes of the locality. Dillon's Rule assumes that even when a state creates a local government and gives it powers, the locality has only very limited authority to act. Today, virtually all states have abandoned Dillon's Rule for at least some localities—particularly municipalities—and have instead provided them with some form of home rule. Although the forms vary from state to state—and among different types of localities within a state—home rule almost always provides localities with broader power to undertake new programs and initiate new policies with respect to "local" or "municipal" matters than would be permitted by Dillon's Rule. A few states go further and provide that local action with respect to local or municipal matters is immune from state legislative displacement. Due to the strong state interest in education, however, school districts have not been given home rule authority. Typically, the state constitutional provision for home rule refers only to municipalities or cities; some expressly disclaim any application to school

---

23. Reutter (1994, pp. 115–32).
24. *Butt v. State of California*, 842 P.2d 1240, 1254 (Cal. 1992).
25. *Rousselle v. Plaquemines Parish School Board*, 633 So.2d 1235, 1241 (La. 1994).

districts. Thus the Illinois constitution's home rule article expressly provides that the term "units of local government" "does not include school districts,"[26] and other language providing that school districts "shall have only those powers granted by law"[27] confirms that school districts continue to be subject to Dillon's Rule even though other local governments are not. The New York constitution's home rule article defines "local government" to mean "a county, city, town, or village" and then adds that nothing in the provision of home rule "shall restrict or impair any power of the legislature concerning the maintenance, support or administration of the public school system."[28] The Tennessee Supreme Court recently held that Dillon's Rule continues to apply to the determination of school board powers.[29] Without home rule, school boards may have to go to the legislature time and time again to obtain the authority to undertake specific actions. One recent study of school districts in Kansas found that they had to obtain express statutory authority to hire lobbyists, operate alternative schools, share guidance programs, enter into interdistrict agreements to share personnel or computer systems, pay dues to the Kansas Association of School Boards, educate military dependents, and obtain boiler, fire, auto, health, or student insurance.[30] To be sure, other commentators have found that courts have construed the implied powers of school districts broadly, particularly in recent years, permitting greater "freedom and experimentation" than the formal limitations of school board powers would suggest,[31] including the ability to add to the state-prescribed curriculum and supplement state-mandated materials.[32] Still, even though the scope of school boards' initiative may be broader in practice than it is in theory, school boards appear to enjoy less autonomy than other local governments.

The State Agency Model in Operation

The dominant paradigm of state-school relations is the state agency model. Under this model, the state has broad authority to command school districts, modify or displace their governing boards, and vest new powers in new local school bodies, like school councils and charter schools. Moreover, implicit in the state agency model are limitations on municipal power over local school districts. Broad state power over local schools may also carry with it special state responsibilities. As a result, school finance reform advocates have also relied on the state agency model when seeking to increase state financial support for local schools.

School Board Restructuring and State Takeover. One of the clearest illustrations of the state agency model is the freedom that the states enjoy to restructure

26. Ill. Const., art VII, sec. 1.
27. Ill. Const., art. VII, sec. 8.
28. N.Y. Const., art. IX, sec. 3.
29. *Southern Constructors, Inc.* v. *Loudon County Bd. of Educ.,* 58 S.W.3d 706 (Tenn. 2001).
30. See Benjamin (1996).
31. See Reutter (1994, p. 154).
32. See Valente (1994, pp. 60–61).

or displace locally elected school boards. New York state's reorganization of the New York City board of education in 1961 nicely demonstrates that the courts treat such a restructuring as something akin to an internal reorganization of a branch of state government rather than as an infringement of local autonomy. The legislature, at the request of the mayor, eliminated the existing board of education—thereby ousting incumbents in the middle of their terms—and authorized the mayor to appoint a new board from a list of nominees prepared by a committee designated by the legislature. The state's highest court rejected a claim by the ousted members that the legislature's action violated home rule. The court noted that "it has long been settled that the administration of public education is a state function to be kept separate and apart from all other local or municipal functions." Although the New York City board of education was connected to the city's municipal government—and New York law gave the city fiscal control over the board—board of education members were "officers of an independent corporation separate and distinct from the city, created by the State for the purpose of carrying out a purely State function and are not city officers within the compass of the constitution's home rule provision."[33] Even the mayor's central role in appointing the board did not change the state's authority: "The Mayor is acting by legislative direction as a State officer in support of the State system of education."

More recently, courts have upheld state laws eliminating the elected school boards in Cleveland and Detroit and giving each city's mayor the power to appoint all (Cleveland) or most (Detroit) of the restructured board's members. When such actions have been challenged as a violation of home rule or other provisions of state constitutions that limit a legislature's ability to target a single local government, the courts have determined that those limitations do not apply because of the special state concern with education.[34] Similarly, in a recent decision, the Pennsylvania Supreme Court upheld allowing the mayor of Harrisburg to appoint a board of control for his city's "failing" school district. Although the law was in tension with a state constitutional provision banning "special laws" dealing with individual localities, the court upheld it as "related to the Commonwealth's legitimate interest in, and the General Assembly's duty to ensure, the existence of a 'thorough and efficient system of education.'"[35]

To be sure, these restructurings were typically initiated by other local officials—usually the mayor—and resulted in the transfer of power to those officials. But state courts have been just as deferential to state laws displacing local school boards in favor of a state agency. As of 2002, a total of twenty-four

33. *Lanza* v. *Wagner*, 11 N.Y.2d 317, 326 (N.Y. 1962).

34. See *Spivey* v. *State of Ohio*, 999 F.Supp. 987 (N.D.Ohio 1998); *Mixon* v. *State of Ohio*, 193 F.3d 389 (6th Cir. 1999); *Moore* v. *School Reform Board of the City of Detroit*, 147 F.Supp.2d 679 (E.D. Mich. 2000), aff'd 293 F.3d 352 (6th Cir. 2002).

35. *Harrisburg School Dist.* v. *Zogby*, 828 A.2d 1079 (Pa. 2003).

states had adopted laws authorizing a state education agency to displace a school board and take over the operation of a school district in cases of protracted and severe problems with academic performance, fiscal mismanagement, or corruption. Although in some states the enabling legislation authorizes such a takeover only in a named school district, in many others state law provides general authority for a state takeover on a finding that the statutory criteria have been met. The Education Commission of the States found that since the late 1980s there have been nearly fifty school district takeovers (some involving multiple state interventions in the same district) in nineteen states.[36] While takeover laws differ from state to state, one recent study found that most follow the pattern set by the "pioneering" New Jersey law: "Upon a determination that a district is inadequate, the chief state education officer appoints a district superintendent, responsible to the state education department, who replaces (or at least exercises the powers of) the local superintendent and elected school board. Other states give their education officials the discretion to decide whether to take over or dissolve stubbornly deficient districts, with their territory, schools, students and teachers absorbed by neighboring districts."[37]

Courts that have assessed state takeover laws or considered challenges to state education departments' exercise of tighter control over local school systems have been deferential to the states and have found the laws or actions to be well within the state's plenary authority for education. They have held that local board challenges may be limited to requiring only that the state comply with the procedures and criteria spelled out in the takeover law, and they have found that school boards do not have broader rights to resist state displacement or close state monitoring.[38]

Local School Councils and Charter Schools. State laws shifting power from school district boards to individual schools within the district, either through site-based decisionmaking laws or through the authorization of charter schools, further reflect and reinforce the subordinate position of local school districts in the public school system.

The Kentucky Educational Reform Act (KERA) dramatically illustrates the potential impact of state-authorized, school-based councils to weaken the legal position of school boards. KERA requires that each local board of education "adopt a policy for implementing school-based decision making" by a school council composed of teachers, parents, and an administrator. The council "has the responsibility to set school policy consistent with district board policy,

36 See Education Commission of the States (2002a).
37 Saiger (1999, pp. 1848–49). See also Hyman (1995).
38 See, for example, *Contini* v. *Board of Education of Newark,* 668 A.2d 434 (N.J. Super. Ct. App. Div. 1995), upholding state takeover of the Newark school system; In re *Trenton Board of Education,* 431 A.2d 808 (N.J. 1981), upholding the state's appointment of a monitor to closely oversee Trenton public schools.

which shall provide an environment to enhance the students' achievement and help the school meet" the curricular and other goals set by the state board of education.[39] As one observer noted, such a school council has "far-reaching policy-making authority" for its school.[40]

One Kentucky county school board sought to constrain the school councils within its jurisdiction by requiring each council to submit to the school board for the board's review and *approval* the council's goals and objectives for the year, its implementation plan, and its method of evaluating the effectiveness of its implementation plan. When a council challenged this prior approval requirement, the Kentucky Supreme Court, in an opinion that laid out its understanding of the legislature's provision of a three-tiered governance structure for the state's schools (state–district–school council) agreed that the school board had gone too far. The court found that "decentralization" below the level of the school district was a "primary objective of KERA" and confirmed that the councils have broad authority over "site-based issues, including but not limited to, determining curriculum, planning instructional practices, selecting and implementing discipline techniques, determining the composition of staff at the school, and choosing textbooks and instructional materials." The requirement that council decisions be "consistent with district board policy" did not give the district board advance review and veto authority over council actions. Rather, all the requirement was intended to ensure was that the council's actions did not exceed the resources made available to it by district policy, since the district board was charged with managing school funds, property, and personnel for the district as a whole, including fixing the compensation for employees. Within the funds available to the district "the local board is *directed* to allocate funds that will enable the school to provide the materials and services determined necessary by the council. The primary limitation on the council's ability to determine what is to be acquired is the availability of resources. The resources that are available would be determined by district policy."[41]

The Kentucky Supreme Court found that KERA's considerable shift in power away from the local school board presented little legal difficulty given the state legislature's ultimate responsibility and "accountability for the overall success" of the state school system. Indeed, the court took a nice slap at the school boards, noting that "improper activities by the local boards occurring in some school districts"—including "problems associated with nepotism, favoritism, and misallocation of school funds"—had contributed to the need for the fundamental reforms contained in KERA.[42]

---

39. Kentucky Rev. Stat. 160.345.
40. Russo (1995, p. 612).
41. *Board of Education of Boone County* v. *Bushee*, 889 S.W.2d 809, 814, 816 (Ky. 1994).
42. *Board of Education of Boone County* v. *Bushee*, 889 S.W.2d 809, 816 (Ky. 1994).

The rise of charter schools also reflects the subordinate position of local school districts and to some extent further weakens their position. In many states, both the creation and the ongoing operations of a charter school challenge a school district's control over the public schools within its borders. Thus just twelve states provide that only a local school district has the authority to approve a charter school. By contrast, in twenty-three states various entities may approve charter schools, including the state board of education, a specially designated state board for charter schools, or specific universities, in addition to local school districts.[43] In twenty-six states (including ten of the twelve states that vest power to authorize a charter school solely in a local board of education), a local school board's initial denial of a charter school application may be appealed to the state board of education or another institution, thus curbing school district control of charter school approval even where school districts are given a role. Similarly, charter schools are considered to be part of the local school district in just twenty states, while in eleven states they are legally independent and in another eight states their legal status depends on how they were chartered, on negotiations between the school and the district, or on the decision of the school or its sponsoring organization.[44]

Relying on the plenary state power over public schools, state courts have rejected challenges to state legislation enabling charter schools. A California court found that charter schools easily fell within the legislature's "sweeping and comprehensive powers in relation to our public schools" and that the state's Charter Schools Act "represents a valid exercise of legislative discretion aimed at furthering the purposes of public education."[45] Similarly, the Utah Supreme Court rejected the school board association's claim that the statute authorizing the state board of education to authorize and supervise charter schools unconstitutionally expanded the state board's authority into the area of local schools. The state constitution's grant of "plenary authority" to the legislature "to create laws that provide for the establishment and maintenance of the Utah public school system" included the authority to enable the state board of education to supervise the charter school program.[46]

Courts have also been reluctant to entertain suits by school boards contesting decisions by chartering authorities to grant particular charter school applications. A Pennsylvania court held that a school district lacked standing to challenge the grant of a charter application, even though the school district had

43. Education Commission of the States (2003).

44. Education Commission of the States (2003). Charter schools are legally independent in Connecticut, Delaware, Florida, Illinois, Michigan, Missouri, New Hampshire, New Jersey, New York, Ohio, and Tennessee.

45. *Wilson* v. *State Board of Education,* 89 Cal. Rptr.2d 745, 751 (Cal. App. 4th 1999).

46. *Utah School Boards Association* v. *Utah State Board of Education,* 17 P.3d 1125, 1129 (Utah 2001).

alleged that the new school would draw students (and thus state funds) away from the district.[47]

State laws and court decisions involving school councils and charter schools demonstrate the power of state governments to create local school entities that operate with some independence from local school districts, and thus they both illustrate and contribute to the limited legal status of local school boards.

Exemption from Municipal Regulation. Not all examples of the subordinate legal status of local school boards involve limitations on their power. Local school districts may also benefit from being a mere arm of the state. An example of this is the freedom of local school boards from municipal regulation. State courts have held that school districts are not subject to a variety of municipal laws, ranging from building codes[48] to election procedures,[49] in the absence of state laws expressly authorizing municipal regulation.

As the California Supreme Court once explained, "the public schools of this state are a matter of statewide rather than local or municipal concern."[50] "School districts are agencies of the state for the local operation of the state school system."[51] As a result, they are not subject to local regulations when engaged in "such sovereign activities as constructing and maintaining buildings."[52] Home rule does not empower municipalities to regulate the schools within local borders. So, too, the Maine Supreme Court found that the municipal home rule power to regulate local election procedures did not extend to school board elections because of "the principle that local school boards are state agents or officers."[53]

Although state legislatures may waive the immunity of their local school districts from some forms of local regulation, in the absence of such a waiver the presumption is that the school district, as an arm of the state, is exempt from municipal regulation.

State Financial Responsibility. One final possible corollary of plenary state legal authority over local public education is state financial responsibility for local schools, which has often benefited individual school districts, even in the face of intense state opposition. Probably the most significant instance of a state court's finding that state constitutional power also entails state fiscal responsibility to a

---

47. *Pennsylvania School Boards Association* v. *Zogby,* 802 A.2d 6 (Pa. Comm. Ct.. 2002).

48. See, for example, *Hall* v. *City of Taft,* 302 P.2d 574 (Cal. 1956).

49. See, for example, *School Committee of Town of Winslow* v. *Inhabitants of Town of Winslow,* 404 A.2d 988 (Me. 1979). See also *Macauley* v. *Hildebrand,* 491 P.2d 120 (Alaska 1971): local school board operating a district coterminous with a municipality cannot be forced into the municipality's accounting system.

50. *Hall* v. *City of Taft,* 302 P.2d 574, 576 (Cal. 1956).

51. *Hall* v. *City of Taft,* 302 P.2d 574, 577 (Cal. 1956).

52. *Hall* v. *City of Taft,* 302 P.2d 574, 578 (Cal. 1956).

53. *School Committee of Town of Winslow* v. *Inhabitants of Town of Winslow,* 404 A.2d 988, 992 (Me. 1979)

particular district is the 1992 decision in *Butt* v. *State of California*, in which the California Supreme Court held that the state was constitutionally required to bail out a local school district which, due to acute financial difficulties, decided it would end the school year six weeks earlier than planned.[54]

The state had resisted the bailout, claiming that the district had been provided with an appropriate level of state support under California's equalized school funding system and that the district's problems were the result of its own financial mismanagement. The state contended that requiring additional state financial support would effectively enable a local district to "indulge in fiscal irresponsibility without penalty."[55] Moreover, the state contended that the bailout would be inconsistent with the value of local control.

The California Supreme Court sharply disagreed, finding first that the state had long previously departed from local control by giving itself an enormous role in school governance and decisionmaking, including setting standards for and assuming oversight of local school district budgets. Nor would a bailout create a moral hazard since the state has authority to "further tighten budgetary oversight, impose prudent, nondiscriminatory conditions on emergency State aid, and authorize intervention by State education officials to stabilize the management of local districts whose imprudent policies have threatened their fiscal integrity."[56] In any event, the state's "ultimate responsibility for equal operation of the common school system" meant that the "State is obliged to intervene when a local district's fiscal problems would otherwise deny its students basic educational equality."[57]

States have also been able to rely on their special responsibility for education to take unusual steps that benefit local school districts financially. Thus during the New York City fiscal crisis in the mid-1970s, the state legislature, concerned that the city would trim its support for schools, voted to bar the city from reducing the share of its budget devoted to the public schools. The New York Court of Appeals held that this did not violate home rule since education is a matter of state responsibility, which the state could fulfill in part by requiring the city's financial assistance.[58] Similarly, the New Jersey Supreme Court found that the state's commissioner of education could order a school board to issue the bonds necessary to fund an essential school building project even though local voters had refused to approve the bonds in a referendum—as required by state law before the bonds could be issued. The court found that the state constitution's education mandate fell on the legislature, which in turn had delegated

54. *Butt* v. *State of California*, 842 P.2d 1240 (Cal. 1992).
55. *Butt* v. *State of California*, 842 P.2d 1240, 1255 (Cal. 1992).
56. *Butt* v. *State of California*, 842 P.2d 1240, 1255 (Cal. 1992).
57. *Butt* v. *State of California*, 842 P.2d 1240, 1256 (Cal. 1992).
58. Matter of *Board of Education of the City School District of the City of New York* v. *City of New York*, 41 N.Y.2d 535 (N.Y. 1977).

responsibility to a combination of state and local entities, including the state department of education as well as local school boards. The state agency had been given legal authority to veto local capital projects. The court then found that the agency also had authority under the state constitution to determine that a capital project was essential to the educational mission of the local school district and to order the district to proceed with the necessary bond issue, the absence of local voter approval notwithstanding.[59]

Finally, the state constitutional proclamation of state responsibility for education provides the legal foundation for the repeated waves of court-ordered school funding equalization reforms over the last three decades. The topic of school finance reform litigation—including the various litigation theories reformers have advanced and the interstate differences in results—is far too broad and intricate to be discussed in this chapter. But it is appropriate to note that underlying nearly all the state court decisions that have ordered some form of funding reform is the finding that, under the state's constitution, the responsibility for securing the state's educational requirement is borne by the state. Whether the court has determined that the state constitution requires equal educational opportunities for pupils throughout the state or only an adequate basic education within each district, the burden of providing the necessary funding and administrative oversight for ensuring that the constitution's goals are met is the state's.[60] This may benefit some districts by requiring the state to provide more aid, hurt more affluent districts in the name of equalizing educational opportunities, or burden all districts in a state where the court's approach emphasizes the state's obligation to set standards, measure outcomes, and take steps to ensure that the state's educational goals are met throughout the state. But the legal theory of school finance reform is predicated to a significant degree on state responsibility for public education and on the vision of local school districts as essentially agencies of the states for providing the education mandated by the state's constitution.

School District Autonomy and the Value of Local Control

Although local school districts are nominally creatures and agents of the states, in practice local districts have traditionally enjoyed far more autonomy than the formal model would suggest. In some older states, many local school bodies were created locally and predate the formal establishment of a statewide system

59. Matter of *Board of Education of Upper Freehold Regional School District, Monmouth County,* 430 A.2d 905 (N.J. 1981).

60. See, for example, *Roosevelt Elementary School District No. 66 v. Bishop,* 877 P.2d 806, 813 (Ariz. 1994); *Tennessee Small School Systems v. McWherter,* 851 S.W.2d 139, 140–41 (Tenn. 1993); *Claremont School Dist. v. Governor,* 635 A.2d 1375 (N.H. 1993); *Rose v. Council for Better Education, Inc.,* 790 S.W.2d 186, 211 (Ky. 1989).

of school districts.[61] Even when state constitutions made education a matter of state concern, "[t]he actual governance of public schools in 19th century America . . . was a grassroots affair conducted by locally elected trustees, who had extensive powers and duties. They established curriculum, employed staff, chose textbooks, decided how many grades of school were to be offered, built the necessary schools, awarded diplomas and established the administrative structure needed to operate the schools."[62] State education establishments grew in the twentieth century, and state governments asserted far more regulatory authority over local school districts. But even in the mid-twentieth century, "the local school districts, through delegated powers from the state legislature, carr[ied] the major responsibility for day-to-day operations" so that "state control in most school matters" was considered "remote" in practice.[63]

The tradition of de facto local autonomy has had an impact on legal analysis, too. In some cases courts, particularly the U.S. Supreme Court, have found significant normative value in entrusting some measure of control over public education to local school boards. These decisions have not always benefited local school boards nor have they undermined the state's ultimate legal control. But, along with some recent state statutory developments, they complicate the assessment of the legal status of local school districts and school boards.

Federal Constitutional Law

The local autonomy paradigm has influenced federal constitutional law in a number of different and sometimes surprising ways. Concern for local district decisionmaking was central to the Supreme Court's rejection of the federal constitutional argument for school finance reform and of metropolitan area remedies for public school segregation. So, too, the importance of local governance in education led the Court to hold that elections to local school boards are governed by the "one person, one vote" principle. On the other hand, the finding that local school districts enjoy considerable de facto autonomy has led many federal courts to determine that school boards do not enjoy the sovereign immunity that the Eleventh Amendment confers on states and state agencies.

School Finance Reform. The Supreme Court's 1973 decision in *San Antonio Independent School District* v. *Rodriguez* illustrates the power and significance of the Court's recognition of the value of local control in public education. In *Rodriguez,* the Court to a considerable degree accepted the plaintiffs' contention that significant spending, taxing, and educational quality differences resulted

---

61. Griffey (1936, pp. 16–17). Griffey notes that the local school district of the late eighteenth and early nineteenth centuries was "a voluntary group"—"the direct offspring of the private school"—formed locally to receive state education appropriations.

62. Education Commission of the States (1999, p. 6).

63. Hazard (1971, pp. 3–4).

from the state's delegation of a substantial portion of the responsibility of funding public schools to school districts of unequal wealth and that the state had failed to provide revenues adequate to compensate for interlocal wealth differences. Nevertheless, the Court sustained the state's school financing system because it grew out of and supported a system of local control. The Court noted the many powers enjoyed by local school districts in Texas, including the power to take property by eminent domain; to hire and fire teachers and other personnel; to maintain order and discipline students; to decide whether to offer certain programs, such as kindergarten and vocational education; and to determine (within limits) policies regarding hours of attendance, grading, promotion, and recreational and athletic activities. As a result, it "cannot be seriously doubted that in Texas education remains largely a local function, and that the preponderating bulk of all decisions affecting the schools is made and executed at the local level."[64]

Local control is valuable, said the Court, because it facilitates "the greatest participation by those most directly concerned"[65] with school decisionmaking and because it builds public support for public schools, enables those communities that want "to devote more money to the education" of their children to do so, and provides "opportunity for experimentation, innovation, and a healthy competition for educational excellence."[66] The Court reasoned that requiring greater school funding equalization could undermine local control by increasing the state's power over school spending: "The people of Texas may be justified in believing that other systems of school financing, which place more of the financial responsibility in the hands of the State, will result in a comparable lessening of desired local autonomy. That is, they may believe that along with increased control of the purse strings at the state level will go increased control over local policies."[67] The Court determined that such a fear was reasonable and that local-based financing was constitutionally justified, notwithstanding the resulting inequalities, because the state could reasonably decide to promote local control in public education.[68]

To be sure, the Court did nothing to suggest that local districts were entitled to local control or that there was any basis for federal constitutional intervention if the state sought to reduce local autonomy. Rather, local control was the result of state decisionmaking. Nevertheless, in a case in which the state was not itself challenging local control but rather was relying on it, the Court gave the normative value of local control great weight in resolving the meaning of equal protection in the school funding context.

64. *San Antonio Independent School District* v. *Rodriguez,* 411 U.S. 1, 53 n.108 (1973).
65. *San Antonio Independent School District* v. *Rodriguez,* 411 U.S. 1, 53 n.108 (1973).
66. *San Antonio Independent School District* v. *Rodriguez,* 411 U.S. 1, 49–50 (1973).
67. *San Antonio Independent School District* v. *Rodriguez,* 411 U.S. 1, 51–53 (1973).
68. *San Antonio Independent School District* v. *Rodriguez,* 411 U.S. 1, 53 n.109 (1973).

School Desegregation. Perhaps an even more powerful departure from the model of the school district as state agency is *Milliken* v. *Bradley*, in which the U.S. Supreme Court rejected a lower court's order requiring interdistrict busing as a remedy for unconstitutional segregation in the Detroit school district.[69] The lower court had found that racial segregation in the Detroit schools was irremediable unless suburban school districts from the Detroit metropolitan area were included in the busing program. The lower court also took seriously the Michigan constitution's statement that public education is a state responsibility as well as Michigan case law's treatment of school districts as creatures and agents of the state. Accordingly, in the lower court's view Detroit and the suburban districts were merely different components of a single Michigan state school system, so that district boundaries could be ignored in developing an effective remedy for segregation.

The U.S. Supreme Court, however, sharply disagreed with both the result and the underlying analysis. The Court began by rejecting the district court's determination that the school district boundaries "are no more than arbitrary lines on a map." Rather, the Court asserted, "the notion that school district lines may be casually ignored or treated as a mere administrative convenience is contrary to the history of public education in our country."[70] The school district lines marked out distinct, independent local school systems. Extending the busing remedy beyond the Detroit system would undermine the autonomy of the suburban school districts.

Returning to the theme previously sounded in *Rodriguez*, the Court found that "[n]o single tradition in public education is more deeply rooted than local control over the operation of schools; local autonomy has long been thought essential both to the maintenance of community concern and support for schools and to the quality of the educational process."[71] Moreover, as in Texas, the Court found that "[t]he Michigan educational structure . . . in common with most states, provides for a large measure of local control." This would be disrupted by massive interdistrict busing, which would "require, in effect, consolidation of 54 independent school districts historically administered as separate units into a vast new super school district," which the Court considered to be utterly inconsistent with local control.[72]

Building from the practice (and value) of local control by an "autonomous political body corporate, operating through a Board of Education popularly elected" over "the day-to-day affairs of the school district,"[73] the Court held that the state and its school districts stood on independent legal footing despite the

69. *Milliken* v. *Bradley*, 418 U.S. 717 (1974).
70. *Milliken* v. *Bradley*, 418 U.S. 717, 741 (1974).
71. *Milliken* v. *Bradley*, 418 U.S. 717, 741–42 (1974).
72. *Milliken* v. *Bradley*, 418 U.S. 717, 742–43 (1974).
73. *Milliken* v. *Bradley*, 418 U.S. 717, 742 n. 20 (1974).

formal subordination of the districts to the state under Michigan law. The actions of the Detroit school board that had caused segregation within the Detroit school district meant that the Detroit district had violated the constitution and would have to implement a remedy. But there had been no lower court finding that any actions of the suburban school districts—or of the state in drawing school district lines—had contributed to segregation within Detroit. As a result there was no basis for extending the desegregation remedy beyond the boundaries of the Detroit district into other "separate and autonomous school districts."[74]

The four dissenting justices pointed to the considerable authority the state enjoyed over school districts, including the "wide-ranging powers to consolidate and merge school districts, even without the consent of the districts themselves or of the local citizenry."[75] Indeed, as the dissenters noted, between 1964 and 1972 Michigan had eliminated more than half of its school districts, cutting the number from 1,438 to 608. The prevailing view of the majority, however, was that the state's formal authority to consolidate school districts was irrelevant. Unless and until a state consolidation occurred, the suburban school districts could rely on their independent existence to insulate themselves from Detroit's problems. The federal courts had to respect the existing school district boundaries, even if that made an effective remedy for school segregation in the metropolitan area impossible.

One Person, One Vote. In considering the value of local control, the Court in both *Rodriguez* and *Milliken* gave great weight to the opportunity that local school district autonomy provided for popular participation in school district governance. The *Milliken* opinion specifically noted that Michigan school boards were popularly elected. In *Kramer* v. *Union Free School District No. 15*, the Court held that when a state provides for the election of a local school board, those elections must comply with the constitutionally required norms for federal, state, and general purpose local government elections: universal adult resident citizen suffrage—and one person, one vote. A state is under no obligation to make a school board elective, but when it does so, the broad, communitywide interest in "the quality and structure of public education" requires that all persons eligible to vote in general elections must also be allowed to vote in school district elections.[76] School districts thus differ from the many other special-purpose districts—like water storage or irrigation districts—in which, the Court has held, the franchise may be limited to those persons "disproportionately affected" by the district, such as landowners.[77] Instead, for purposes of the right to vote, school districts are treated as akin to cities and counties. Paradoxically, *Kramer's*

74. *Milliken* v. *Bradley*, 418 U.S. 717, 744 (1974).
75. *Milliken* v. *Bradley*, 418 U.S. 717, 796 (1974).
76. *Kramer* v. *Union Free School District No. 15*, 395 U.S. 621, 630 (1969).
77. See, for example, *Ball* v. *James*, 451 U.S. 355 (1981).

protection of the school district franchise subsequently operated to limit a state's experimentation with school-based governance. In *Fumarolo* v. *Chicago Board of Education*, the Illinois Supreme Court held that *Kramer* required it to invalidate the franchise and representation provisions of the 1988 Chicago School Reform Act, which provided for the creation of local school councils for each of Chicago's schools.[78] These councils were given powers to hire and retain the principal; make recommendations to the principal concerning textbooks and disciplinary and attendance policies; and review the principal's expenditure and school improvement plans.[79] Each council was to consist of ten members, with six elected by parents, two elected by the school's teachers, and two elected by community residents. The Illinois Supreme Court found that given a council's broad powers over education in its school, the one person, one vote norm applied. Due to the exclusion of nonparent residents from voting for most of a council's seats, the act was unconstitutional.

In response to *Fumarolo*, the Illinois legislature in 1991 revised the law to enable all residents to vote for all members of a council, although it reserved six of the eight seats on the board for parents. When this plan, too, was challenged, the federal appellate court that heard the case saved the councils by determining that their powers were sufficiently limited—they did not, for example, include the power to tax or even to set the size of the school's budget—to avoid the full force of the one person, one vote doctrine. According to the court, the councils did not really "govern" their schools: "The governing body of the public schools of Chicago is the Board of Education of the City of Chicago, not these local councils. Vital public education may be, but these councils, unlike the boards in *Kramer* . . . do not control it." The court also voiced sympathy for the underlying purposes of the statute: "There is a nationwide movement toward the decentralization and privatization of governmental functions, and the parent-centered local school councils are one manifestation of that movement. They are an experiment. . . . We will never be able to evaluate its success if we invalidate the law."[80]

The one person, one vote cases have three implications for thinking about the legal position of school boards. First, the decision of whether to have an elective board is entirely a matter for the state. This is consistent with the state agency model. Second, having decided to make a school board elective, the state cannot determine who can vote in the election; rather, the constitutional requirements of universal suffrage and one person, one vote apply. Third, this complicates efforts at decentralizing school governance to school-based councils controlled by parents and teachers. If the council is considered a governing body, the one

---

78. *Fumarolo* v. *Chicago Board of Education*, 142 N.E.2d 54, 566 N.E.2d 1283 (Ill. 1990).
79. *Fumarolo* v. *Chicago Board of Education*, 566 N.E.2d 1283, 1295 (Ill. 1990).
80. *Pittman* v. *Chicago Board of Education*, 64 F.3d 1098, 1103 (7th Cir. 1995).

person, one vote rule applies and all members of the community are entitled to vote and to equal representation on the board. However, if a court can be persuaded that the council has limited authority and that governance is still vested in the school district—with power over taxation and budgets a critical indicator of governance—then a parent-controlled council may be upheld.

Beyond the one person, one vote rule, the antidiscrimination provisions of the Voting Rights Act of 1965, as amended in 1982, also apply to school board elections, much as they apply to local elections generally. In many places, this has led to the replacement of at-large elections with district or ward electoral systems. As noted by Melissa J. Marschall in chapter 8 and by Kenneth J. Meier and Eric Gonzales Juenke in chapter 9 of this volume, such systems have resulted in the election of more racial minority representatives and in a greater minority role in school board governance.

It should be noted that although the courts are highly concerned with the formal rules that govern school board elections—such as the one person, one vote rule and regulations regarding at-large versus district elections—the courts do not appear to give much attention to the substance of school district democracy. Such issues as voter turnout, the level of campaign spending, the degree of competition, the role of teacher unions and other interest groups in school board elections, and the ability of school district voters to use elections to hold school board members accountable for the performance of their schools (which are dealt with in other chapters in this volume) rarely if ever come before the courts, although they are essential to the assessment of school board elections.[81] There is no evidence that the courts ever look at the underlying nature of school board elections—to the level of voter turnout or to their competitiveness, for example—in assessing the legal authority of school board actions. In other words, apart from the determination in Voting Rights Act cases of whether there is racial bloc voting in school board elections, the law regarding school district governance seems to pay little attention to the nature of school district politics.

Sovereign Immunity under the Eleventh Amendment. One area in which the Supreme Court's assumption of local school district autonomy has actually hurt districts involves liability to teachers and students for violations of federal rights. The Supreme Court has interpreted the Eleventh Amendment to bar federal courts generally from hearing damages actions against states and state agencies. However, the Court long ago concluded that local governments like cities and counties are sufficiently distinct from their states that they are not shielded by the Eleventh Amendment. In *Mount Healthy City School District* v. *Doyle*, the Court held that as a matter of Ohio law, which gives school boards extensive authority to issue bonds and levy taxes, an Ohio school district is "more like a

---

81. See the chapters by Frederick M. Hess and David L. Leal, Terry M. Moe, and Christopher R. Berry and William G. Howell.

county or city than it is an arm of the State" and thus enjoys no Eleventh Amendment immunity.[82] It is not clear whether *Mount Healthy* determined that all school districts are outside the Eleventh Amendment or only those in Ohio. On one hand, in a later case from Missouri, the Court observed in passing that the Eleventh Amendment "does not afford local school boards like the Kansas City Missouri School District immunity from suit," without presenting any analysis of Missouri law dealing with school boards.[83] On the other hand, the many lower courts that have considered the issue have engaged in a close critique of the laws of the state of the defendant school board in order to resolve the immunity question. For the most part, these courts have concluded that a local school district is not an "arm of the state" for Eleventh Amendment purposes and thus can be sued for damages for violating federal law.

In so doing, these courts have looked at such factors as the extent of school board autonomy, the degree to which state law treats a school district as a distinct legal actor, and the source of school district funding—which is particularly important in the context of the Eleventh Amendment since the purpose of the amendment is to protect state treasuries. Two cases illustrate the general approach. The U.S. Court of Appeals for the Second Circuit held that the Bridgeport, Connecticut, school board was not immune to a civil rights claim for damages growing out of a student's suspension because of the locally elected "board's authority and discretion" under state law concerning the "actual implementation of the goals and maintenance of the public schools" and because much of the district's funding came from local, not state, taxes.[84] Similarly, the U.S. Court of Appeals for the Fourth Circuit recently held that a North Carolina school board was not immune from a damages action under the Fair Labor Standards Act. The court ruled that the state was not obligated to pay any judgments obtained against a school board because the locally elected board was a legally distinct entity under state law—it could sue and be sued, buy insurance, retain counsel, and purchase, hold, and sell property—and because the board enjoyed considerable autonomy with respect to the "general control and supervision of all matters pertaining to the public schools in their respective administrative units." In short, "North Carolina law establishes local school boards with a sufficient degree of autonomy and independence that any judgment reached against a local school board would not in our judgment affect the dignity of the state."[85]

There have been two departures from this general approach. In a 1984 decision, the U.S. Court of Appeals for the Tenth Circuit ruled that local school boards in New Mexico were a mere arm of the state because the state

82. *Mount Healthy City School District* v. *Doyle*, 429 U.S. 274, 280 (1977).
83. *Missouri* v. *Jenkins*, 495 U.S. 33, 55 n.20 (1990).
84. *Rosa R.* v. *Connelly*, 889 F.2d 435, 437–38 (2d Cir. 1989).
85. *Cash* v. *Granville Co. Board of Educ.*, 242 F.3d 219, 226 (4th Cir. 2001).

constitution gave the state board of education broad powers of "control, management, and direction of all public schools," including authority over curriculums and teacher qualifications and certification. Moreover, the state provided the vast majority of school district funds. A decade later the New Mexico Supreme Court determined that the federal appellate court had underestimated the independent status of local school districts under New Mexico law. The state court found that state law defined the school boards as distinct "local public bodies" and that the locally elected school boards had significant autonomy concerning the control and supervision of their schools, including spending. Two years later the Tenth Circuit Court of Appeals reversed itself. Relying on the state supreme court's reading of New Mexico law, it concluded that New Mexico school districts, despite their heavy dependence on the state for funding, are not an arm of the state under the Eleventh Amendment.[86]

In California, however, the U.S. Court of Appeals for the Ninth Circuit has held that school districts are an arm of the state for Eleventh Amendment purposes. The court acknowledged that school districts have formal independent existence—for example, they can sue and be sued, hold property in their own name, and enjoy legally distinct corporate status. But the court emphasized that under California law public schooling is a state function and noted that because of California's school finance reforms plus the tight controls on local taxation following Proposition 13, the state effectively controls district revenues and budgets and so would ultimately be paying for any judgment against the school board. This approach has been followed subsequently by both federal and state courts in California. As one state court observed, although local school districts often are treated by California law as if they were the same as other local governments, "the state's pervasive involvement in school affairs makes its relationship with school districts qualitatively different from its relationship with entities such as cities and counties."[87] Another federal appellate decision found "the state so entangled with the operations of California's local school districts" that it described "the relationship between the State of California and California's local school districts [a]s analogous to the relationship between a corporate parent and its wholly owned subsidiaries."[88]

Thus, with California a distinct and important exception, the general rule has been that school districts, like cities and counties, are not state agencies for Eleventh Amendment purposes. This is due, in part, to their formally separate legal existence, to their de facto discretion over a range of school functions, and to their partial fiscal autonomy.

86. *Duke* v. *Grady Municipal Schools,* 127 F.3d 972 (10th Cir. 1997).

87. *Kirchmann* v. *Lake Elsinore Unified School District,* 100 Cal. Rptr 2d. 289, 299 (Cal. App. 4th. 2000).

88. *Association of Mexican-American Educators* v. *State,* 231 F.3d 572, 582 (9th Cir. 2000).

State Law

The local autonomy model has also had a significant impact on state law concerning local school districts. State judicial respect for the value of local control has affected how state courts respond to state school finance reform lawsuits. In one recent case, a state's constitutional provision for local school boards was the basis for a limiting judicial interpretation of the state's charter school law. Moreover, some state laws have given local school boards greater autonomy by providing for a measure of school district home rule.

School Finance Reform. Although a state legislature's responsibility under its state constitution for public education has played a critical role in providing some state courts with the legal underpinning for mandating school finance reform, the theme of local control has been significant in other state school finance cases. First, eight state supreme courts have agreed with the U.S. Supreme Court that the value of local control justifies relying on the local property tax–based system of school financing, notwithstanding the resulting interdistrict spending inequalities.[89]

Second, even many of the state courts that have held that their state constitution requires schools to meet a statewide standard of educational adequacy have also ruled that individual local districts are free to raise and spend above the basic level.[90] As the Arizona Supreme Court observed, in the course of finding that the state's school financing system failed to comply with the "general and uniform public school system requirement" of the Arizona constitution,

> [a]s long as the statewide system provides an adequate education . . . local political subdivisions can go above and beyond the statewide system. . . . Local control in these matters is an important part of our culture. Thus, school houses, school districts, and counties will not always be the same because some districts may either attach greater importance to education or have more wherewithal to fund it. Nothing in our constitution prohibits this. . . . Indeed, if citizens were not free to go above and beyond the state financed system to produce a school system that meets their needs, public education statewide would suffer.[91]

Finally, one state supreme court has looked to school district autonomy to invalidate a state plan that would have redistributed locally raised funds from

89. See, for example, *Lujan* v. *Colorado State Board of Education,* 649 P.2d 1005 (Colo. 1982). See Dayton (2001, p. 456, n. 4), citing decisions in Colorado, Georgia, Maryland, New York, Ohio, Oregon, Pennsylvania, and Wisconsin.

90. See, for example, *Edgewood Independent School District* v. *Meno,* 917 S.W.2d 717, 729-30 (Tex. 1995); *Roosevelt Elementary School District No. 77* v. *Bishop,* 877 P.2d 806, 814-15 (Ariz. 1994); *Rose* v. *Council for Better Education, Inc.,* 790 S.W.2d 186, 211–12 (Ky. 1989).

91. *Roosevelt Elementary School District No. 77* v. *Bishop,* 877 P.2d 806, 815 (Ariz. 1994).

affluent districts to poorer districts. The Wisconsin Supreme Court in *Buse* v. *Smith* found that the provision of the state's constitution mandating the "establishment of district schools" created a constitutional foundation for a measure of local school district autonomy:

> The power possessed by local districts to determine what educational subjects it will offer over and above those required by the state, and to raise funds therefore, is not merely a delegated power. Rather, the state-local control dichotomy in that regard is part and parcel of the constitution.[92]

As a result, the recapture provision of the Wisconsin school finance reform, which would have capped local district spending and redirected excess local revenues to other school districts, was held to violate the state constitution.

State Constitutions and Charter Schools. Buse v. *Smith* is the rare case that finds recognition of and protection for local school districts in the state constitution. Although virtually all state constitutions require the state legislature to provide for a public school system and many directly establish a state board of education or create the position of state superintendent of public instruction, only a relative handful expressly provide for local school districts or directly grant local school boards powers over local schools; even many of these also indicate that the state has authority over the powers and boundaries of such districts.[93] The 1999 decision by the Colorado Supreme Court in *Board of Education No. 1 in the City and County of Denver* v. *Booth*, which dealt with the process of approving charter schools, is the only state case besides *Buse* in which a constitutional reference to school districts led a state supreme court to recognize the interests of a local school board as well as those of the state in an important education policy conflict.[94]

92. *Buse* v. *Smith,* 247 N.W.2d 141, 151 (Wisc. 1976).

93. These states include Colorado (see Colo. Const., art. XX, secs. 2, 15: school district boards of education to "have control of instruction in the public schools of their respective districts"); Florida (see Fla. Const., art. IX, sec. 4, providing for county school districts and school boards that "shall operate, control and supervise all free public schools within the school district and determine the rate of school district taxes within the limit prescribed herein"); Georgia (see Ga. Const., art. VIII, sec. 5, para. I: "authority is granted to county and area boards of education to establish and maintain public schools within their limits," but the General Assembly may provide for the consolidation or combination of school districts); Kansas (see Kans. Const., art. VI., sec. 5: "local public schools under the general supervision of the state board of education shall be maintained, developed and operated by locally elected boards"); Louisiana (see La. Const., art. VIII, sec. 9: the legislature shall provide for parish school boards and provide for the election of their members); Montana (see Mont. Const., art. X., sec. 8: the supervision and control of schools in each school district shall be vested in a board of trustees to be elected as provided by law); and Virginia (see Va. Const., art. VIII, sec. 7: "The supervision of schools in each school division shall be vested in a school board, to be composed of members selected in the manner, for the term, and possessing the qualifications and in the number provided by law").

94. *Board of Education No. 1 in the City and County of Denver* v. *Booth*, 984 P.2d 639 (Colo. 1999).

The Colorado Charter Schools Act gives local school boards the authority to approve or disapprove a charter proposal. If the local board disapproves, the applicant may appeal to the state board of education, which may require the local board to reconsider the charter application. If the district board again denies the application, the charter applicant may again appeal to the state board of education. If on the second appeal the state board finds that granting the charter is in the public interest, it may reverse and remand to the district board "with instructions to approve the charter applicant." The Denver school board challenged the statute, asserting that it gave the state board of education more powers than the Colorado constitution permitted while infringing on the state constitution's provision that the local school board "shall have control of instruction." The Colorado Supreme Court rejected the Denver board's position, finding that the constitution's grant of "general supervision" over public education to the state board of education was broad enough to encompass the power to approve local charter schools. However, the local board's authority could not be entirely displaced. Rather, "as long as a school district exists, the local school board has undeniable constitutional authority," including "substantial discretion regarding the character of instruction that students will receive at the district's expense."[95]

The Colorado Supreme Court struck a compromise, finding that the state board of education could order the local school board to approve a charter application but could not require the local board to actually open a school or agree to all of the terms of the charter applicant's proposal. Rather, the state board's order is merely a directive to the local school board to negotiate with the applicant concerning the "issues necessary to permit the applicant to open a charter school," including questions regarding the site of the school and per-pupil funding. This would be "consistent" with the state board of education's "general supervisory authority regarding knowledge and dissemination of desirable improvements for the public education system" while ensuring that the local board's concerns would be "taken into account in final contract negotiations."[96]

School District Home Rule. In recent years, a number of states have acted to give their school boards greater autonomy, for example, by adopting school board home rule laws and laws enabling local boards to obtain waivers of state requirements; some states also have eliminated some of the burdens in state education codes.[97] Some state courts also have recognized that local boards may

95. *Board of Education No. 1 in the City and County of Denver v. Booth*, 984 P.2d 639, 646, 648 (Colo. 1999).

96. *Board of Education No. 1 in the City and County of Denver v. Booth*, 984 P.2d 639, 654 (Colo. 1999).

97. See, for example, *Board of Trustees of Hamilton Heights School Corp. v. Landry*, 638 N.E.2d 1261 (Ind. App. 1994), discussing the 1989 Indiana School Corporations Home Rule Act; *Eason v. Clark County School District*, 303 F.3d 1137, 1143–44 (9th Cir. 2002), discussing Nevada law giving school board trustees "such rights and powers as are necessary to maintain control of education

have greater authority to initiate new actions, including the contracting out of certain school operations, even if they are not specifically authorized to do so by state law.[98] To be sure, it is far from clear just how much real independence these state home rule or waiver measures have given local school boards.[99] Even in a state where a court has suggested that school districts may have broader discretion when acting to advance their educational mission, other courts have continued to adhere to an approach more consistent with Dillon's Rule by limiting school districts to those powers expressly granted to them or necessarily implied in the express legislative grants.[100] It is thus uncertain how much these recent developments have challenged the general subordinate status of local school boards.

Conclusion

The conflict between the state power and local autonomy models of school districts is not as great as it might appear. Most of the cases in which the rhetoric of local control has been invoked involved suits by individuals (parents or students) and some school boards against a state to force it to take on new and costly responsibilities. In these cases, local control has been asserted by the state defensively to relieve it from having to increase its school spending or take on undesired oversight responsibilities; local control also has been asserted by school districts that benefit from the status quo to resist the claims of other school districts seeking redistributive changes. To the extent that courts have accepted the local control argument, it has functioned as a shield to sustain state policy, not as a sword to alter policy in a more pro-local direction.

So, too, judicial recognition of school district autonomy in the Eleventh Amendment cases has exposed districts to liability to third-party plaintiffs (usually students or teachers), and it certainly has not strengthened districts relative to their states. Autonomy in these cases has meant only that districts in practice enjoy a measure of discretion in matters within their jurisdiction and operate relatively separately from their states; the districts, however, are still considered legally subordinate to their states. Similarly, the school district voting rights cases reflect the fact that the states have chosen to give their school boards

---

in their respective districts"; Goldner (1997), discussing school district home rule provisions of the Texas Public School Reform Act of 1995; Hosea, Colwell, and Thurston (1996), analyzing the Illinois Education Waiver of Mandates Act of 1995; Education Commission of the States (1999), discussing reductions in state education codes in South Carolina, Michigan, and Texas.

98. See *School District of Wilkinsburg* v. *Wilkinsburg Education Association,* 667 A.2d 5 (Pa. 1995).

99. See Goldner (1997); Hosea, Colwell, and Thurston (1996).

100. See, for example., *Giacomucci* v. *Southeast Delco School District,* 742 A.2d 1165 (Comm. Ct. Pa. 1999).

considerable responsibilities with respect to a fundamental public service, but they do not constrain the states from curtailing local board powers or eliminating local boards altogether.

Local control thus is significant primarily as a manifestation of state policy rather than as a federal or state constitutional constraint on the states. Although many states have delegated significant powers to their local school districts, they are not constitutionally compelled to do so and they remain relatively free to restructure local school governance. The extent of local autonomy, the powers of local boards, the scope of school district boundaries, the selection of school board members—all are matters for state determination even in states that provide for local control.

Indeed, local control does not mean or require independent school boards. In most states, the legislature would be free to abolish independent school boards and promote local control through other local institutions. Control of schools may be given to the general purpose local government or to the individual school. Nor is local control required at all. A state could govern its schools directly or develop new modes of state control. Judicial discussions of local control reflect an effort to integrate the state practice of school board autonomy into the legal interpretation of contested state constitutional and statutory provisions; they do not imply the legal recognition of an independent, grassroots-based limitation on state power.

To be sure, in some cases, like the Wisconsin *Buse* decision or the Colorado charter schools case, the concept of local control has been used against the state legislature, but these instances are rare. At the other extreme, perhaps because of the great role that state regulation and financing play in California schools, the California courts appear to give no weight to the concept of local school autonomy at all, treating local districts not merely as subordinates but as legally tantamount to a state agency. Most states lie somewhere between Wisconsin/Colorado and California. They probably lie closer to California on the question of school district legal subordination to the state but accord greater de facto autonomy to school boards.

Several recent developments have further challenged local control and the status of local school boards. The most obvious set of changes has involved the assertion of greater power by the state or the imposition of greater responsibility on the state with respect to education. Court-ordered school finance reforms—as well as reforms undertaken to forestall litigation—have increased the state share of education funding. Such reforms have often been accompanied by greater state control over the distribution of financial resources and the use of state dollars to affect school policies. Moreover, some judicial reform efforts—such as those in New Jersey, West Virginia, and Kentucky—have sought not simply to increase state aid to poorer districts but to require the state legislature or board of education to spell out the content of the education required by the state's constitution, to better monitor local school district performance, and to intervene when local school districts have failed to attain state educational goals.

Beyond court-ordered school finance reforms, in recent decades states have moved to set new content and performance standards for teachers and students. Through greater insistence on testing, the states have become more involved in shaping school curriculums; they also have raised high school graduation requirements and set higher teacher certification or minimum competency requirements. Some have extended the school day or school year and even set minimum homework requirements.[101] And, as already discussed, many states have adopted takeover laws, enabling state boards of education to take direct control of troubled school districts or schools.

The new federal No Child Left Behind Act (NCLB) reinforces the modern trend toward greater state specification and enforcement of the content of the education delivered at the local level. The NCLB, among other things, requires states to develop statewide standards for and assessments of local school districts. To be sure, the NCLB burdens the states as well as local districts, imposing obligations to develop academic standards, hire "highly qualified" teachers in core subjects, test all students annually in grades 3 through 8, and reconstitute persistently failing schools. Moreover, the act "imposes a slew of reporting requirements upon both state and local education agencies and contains literally hundreds of specific directives that states and localities must follow."[102] Although this chapter has focused almost exclusively on state-local relations in considering the legal status of local school districts, it is worth noting that federal laws such as the Elementary and Secondary Education Act, the Individuals with Disabilities Education Act, and now the NCLB also constrain local school districts and affect school board powers. The NCLB suggests that the federal role may grow, with implications for both local school boards and the states.

To be sure, greater state oversight, involvement in setting standards, and intervention in cases of poor local performance have been accompanied in some states with measures giving local school boards greater operational discretion in achieving state educational goals. States may conclude that their purposes may be better attained by a degree of school district home rule rather than by state-directed micromanagement of school operations. Yet that is consistent with plenary state authority; it is not a challenge to it.

Other changes have involved shifts in power at the local level and even efforts to decentralize control to below the school district level rather than increased control by the state or the federal government. As noted, in a number of states the governance of large urban school districts has shifted from an elected board to one appointed wholly or primarily by the mayor. New York state recently

101. See Briffault (1992, p. 781).
102. Ryan (2002).

went even further and abolished the New York City board of education altogether, vesting responsibility for the city's schools in the mayor and his appointee, the city commissioner of education. (The effects of mayoral control are assessed by Kenneth K. Wong and Francis X. Shen in chapter 4 of this volume.)

Some states, like Kentucky, have adopted site-based management programs that transfer power from school districts to individual school councils. So, too, many states have provided for charter schools, which operate with considerable independence from—and often in conflict with—local school districts. Although the actual role of both school councils and charter schools has been relatively limited to date, their emergence could change the nature of local control of schools. Certainly, the handful of cases involving contests between school districts and school councils or charter schools indicates that school districts may have to give way to these new local educational institutions.

These decentralizing moves may be as great a challenge to school boards as centralization. Not only do they create competing local school authorities, they also open alternative opportunities for the local participation in school governance that the courts have proclaimed to be the normative value at the core of local autonomy.

Taken together, the recent centralizing and decentralizing developments may operate to reduce the independent powers of school districts. As a matter of legal theory, they do not change the status of local school boards. Rather, they illustrate the formal view that this is an area of virtually plenary state power (although now subject to greater federal intervention) that can be reshaped by state legislatures through either centralization or decentralization or both simultaneously. Nevertheless, without changing the theory of state-local relations with respect to schools, these developments may be altering state-local relations in practice. If so, this could resolve some of the tension between the formal law of state control and the de facto autonomy of local school districts by bringing the practice of local autonomy into greater conformity with the legal theory of state power.

References

Benjamin, Charles. 1996. "Should There Be Home Rule for Kansas School Districts?" *Kansas Journal of Law and Public Policy* 5 (3): 175–85.

Bolmeier, Edward C. 1973. *The School in the Legal Structure.* 2nd ed. Cincinnati: W. H. Anderson.

Briffault, Richard. 1990. "Our Localism: The Structure of Local Government Law." *Columbia Law Review* 90: 1–115.

———. 1992. "The Role of Local Control in School Finance Reform." *Connecticut Law Review* 24: 773–811.

Dayton, John. 2001. "Serrano and Its Progeny: An Analysis of 30 Years of School Funding Litigation." *Education Law Reporter* 157: 447–64.

Education Commission of the States. 1999. *Governing America's Schools: Changing the Rules.* Report of the National Commission on Governing America's Schools. Denver.

———. 2002a. "Accountability—Rewards/Sanctions: State Takeovers and Reconstitutions." Policy brief. Denver.

———. 2002b. "Local School Boards: Types, Elected vs. Appointed and Number." *State Notes* (May). Denver.

———. 2003. "Charter Schools—Charter School Basics." *State Notes* (April). Denver.

Goldner, Charles W., Jr. 1997. "Home Rule School Districts: An Opportunity for Meaningful Reform or Simple Window Dressing?" *Southern Illinois Law Journal* 21: 255–74.

Griffey, Carl H. 1936. *The History of Local School Control in the State of New York.* Teachers College.

Hazard, William R. 1971. *Education and the Law: Cases and Materials on Public Schools.* New York: Free Press.

Hosea, Sonja, Brad Colwell, and Paul Thurston. 1996. "Increasing School District Autonomy through Waivers of Legislative Mandates: The Illinois Experience." *Education Law Reporter* 107: 443–55.

Hudgins, H. C., Jr., and Richard S. Vacca. 1995. *Law and Education: Contemporary Issues and Court Decisions.* 4th ed. Charlottesville, Va.: Michie.

Hyman, Ronald T. 1995. "State-Operated Local School Districts in New Jersey." *Education Law Reporter* 96: 915–35.

Reutter, E. Edmund. 1994. *The Law of Public Education.* 4th ed. Westbury, N.Y.: Foundation Press.

Russo, Charles J. 1995. "School Based Decision Making Councils and School Boards in Kentucky: Trusted Allies or Irreconcilable Foes?" *Education Law Reporter* 97: 603–17.

Ryan, James E. 2000. "The Supreme Court and Public Schools." *Virginia Law Review* 86: 1335–1433.

———. 2002. "The Legal Boundaries of Educational Governance." Public Law and Legal Theory Research Paper Series 02-21. University of Virginia School of Law.

Saiger, Aaron. 1999. "Disestablishing Local School Districts as a Remedy for Educational Inadequacy." *Columbia Law Review* 99: 1830–70.

U.S. Census Bureau. 2002. *Census of Governments,* vol. 1, no. 1: *Government Organization.*

Valente, William D. 1994. *Law in the Schools.* 3rd ed. New York: Macmillan.

3

School District Consolidation and
Student Outcomes: Does Size Matter?

CHRISTOPHER R. BERRY

In a quiet revolution in the middle of the twentieth century, the public education system in the United States was radically revised. As late as 1930, local
school districts, the governing units of American public education, were small,
informally organized institutions, most operating only one or two small schools.
From roughly 1930 to 1970, a rapid movement toward centralization and professionalization reduced the number of districts from 130,000 to only 16,000 as
about 90 percent of the districts that had existed were eliminated through consolidation. Over the same period, more than 100,000 schools were closed and average school size increased fivefold. In the process, school districts evolved into professionally run educational bureaucracies, some operating hundreds of schools
and educating hundreds of thousands of students. It is difficult to imagine a more
important change in the organization of public education in the past century.

Despite the dramatic scale and breakneck pace of these organizational
changes, little is known about the consequences of consolidation. Has the quality of public education risen commensurately as schools and districts have
become larger and more professional, as consolidation's proponents promised?
The small literature on the effects of school and district size on student outcomes that has emerged relatively recently speaks only obliquely to the pre-1970
consolidation movement.[1] A yet smaller literature addressing the effects of

1. See Andrews, Duncombe, and Yinger (2002) and Cotton (1996) for reviews of the literature
on school and district size.

56

school quality on student outcomes before 1970 has ignored issues of both school and district size—for example, Card and Krueger (1992a). Several case studies of consolidation—Reynolds (1999) is one—provide valuable historical details related to particular states or districts but offer few general findings. The aim of this chapter is to begin filling the gaps in our understanding of the consequences of consolidation, focusing on the effects of school and district size on student outcomes, specifically wages.

The chapter first presents background information on the consolidation of school districts and related trends in the number of schools and the state government's role in funding public education; this is followed by a review of the literature on consolidation as well as work related to the effects of district and school size on student outcomes. The chapter next describes my estimation strategy and data and presents the main results of the analysis. The final sections evaluate the consolidation movement in light of these results, discuss potential contemporary policy implications, and suggest directions for future research on consolidation and issues of school and district size generally.

Background on District Consolidation

The movement for district consolidation must be seen as part of a larger trend toward the professionalization of teaching that began in the late nineteenth century.[2] To the "administrative progressives" of the time, the concentration of authority over schooling in the hands of professional educators was seen as a cure for both the political corruption of city school systems and the parochialism of rural systems. Consolidation came first to urban areas, where one of the cornerstones of the Progressive attack on political machines was the effort to formally organize schooling under the leadership of professional superintendents. Reformers then turned their attention to rural areas, where they decried the inefficient, unprofessional, and "backward" practices of small community schools. Reformers drew the inspiration for their vision of a professionally run school system from the modern corporation, with its principles of "scientific" management by experts. Seen from this perspective, larger schools and districts were needed in order to minimize costs through economies of scale and to provide specialized training to prepare students for particular roles in society.

The school consolidation movement was about more than professional management, however. As Strang (1987) argues, school consolidation meant the centralization of authority for public education, along two dimensions. First, as school districts became larger and more complex, day-to-day authority over education gradually shifted from the school community to more distant

---

2. The discussion in this paragraph is based on Tyack (1974).

educational bureaucracies—that is, from elected school boards to superintendents and administrators—a shift Tyack has described as a "transfer of power from laymen to professionals."[3] Tellingly, over the period 1930–70, nine of ten school board members nationwide saw their position disappear. Meanwhile, the number of superintendents increased and the number of principals ballooned, even as the number of schools and districts dwindled.[4]

Second, state governments took an active role in consolidation. As part of broader efforts to expand state control over public education, professional educators linked to state departments of education often spearheaded initiatives to consolidate local school districts. In other words, not only was local control over education weakened by the elimination of most locally elected school boards, but the authority of the remaining boards was eroded as state governments gradually extended their authority over previously locally controlled issues, such as accreditation, curriculum, and teacher certification.[5] In short, school boards became more distant from local communities and lost authority to professional administrators and state government officials.

Local resistance to consolidation often was fierce, especially in rural areas where the school was the central community institution. As Reynolds observes, in the preconsolidation era, the local school district "was typically the key neighborhood institution binding neighbors and linking them to the larger social and cultural world around them."[6] Thus consolidation of the local district and in particular the loss of the local school often threatened a community's social cohesion and economic vitality. For these reasons, the impetus for district consolidation seldom appears to have come from local communities in the absence of state initiatives; rather, state governments often induced consolidation by offering fiscal incentives or forced consolidation by redrawing district boundaries.[7] In response to state pressures, "defensive consolidation" also was common, in which districts rushed to consolidate in anticipation of an even less desired forced consolidation by the state government.[8] In the long run, few districts withstood the financial and political pressures of the state government and professional educators for long.

Vanishing Act

The informal nature of school districts early in the twentieth century is evidenced by the fact that many states did not even keep a count of the number of

3. Tyack (1974, p. 25).
4. The number of school districts declined by 90 percent from 1930 to 1970. Assuming a constant board size, nine of ten elected board positions were eliminated. Strang (1987) shows that the number of superintendents increased slightly over this period and the number of principals grew several fold.
5. Strang (1987).
6. Reynolds (1999, p. 61).
7. Hooker and Mueller (1970).
8. Reynolds (1999).

Figure 3-1. *Number of School Districts, 1931–99*

School districts (thousands)

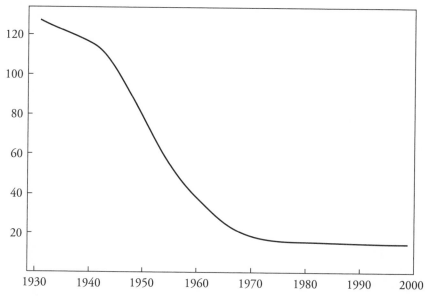

Source: National Center for Education Statistics, *Digest of Education Statistics* (U.S. Department of Education).

districts before 1930. The 1931–32 edition of the *Biennial Survey of Education* was the first to report school district statistics for each state.[9] As figure 3-1 shows, the data soon revealed a decline in the number of districts, which fell by half between 1931 and 1953 as more than 60,000 districts were dissolved by consolidation. The number of districts declined by half again between 1953 and 1963 and by roughly half again by 1973. The number of districts stabilized in the early 1970s and has not changed appreciably over the last thirty years.

Coincident with the consolidation of school districts, the number of schools declined dramatically beginning in the 1920s.[10] Figure 3-2 shows that the number of public schools grew from 116,000 in 1869 to peak at 217,000 in 1920. The number of schools declined rapidly over the succeeding fifty years, as district consolidation made it possible to merge schools. The pace of decline slowed in the 1970s, and the number of schools reached a nadir in the late

9. The *Biennial Survey of Education* was the first federal government publication to systematically track statistics related to state and local education. The *Biennial Survey* began publication in 1869, changed its title to the *Digest of Education Statistics* in 1960, and continues publication under that name to this day.

10. Although data on the number of school districts prior to 1931 are not available, if districts followed a trajectory comparable to that of schools, we can infer that the number of districts was at its apex around that time.

Figure 3-2. *Number of Public Schools, 1869–1999*

Schools (thousands)

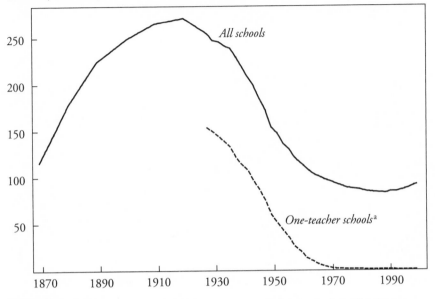

Source: National Center for Education Statistics, *Digest of Education Statistics* (U.S. Department of Education).
a. Data for one-teacher schools available only after 1927.

1980s at around 83,000. Since then, approximately 10,000 schools have been added nationwide, in the first significant burst of net new school construction in more than sixty years. Also notable over the period was a pronounced shift away from one-teacher schools. In 1927, the first year for which data on one-teacher schools are available, they composed 60 percent of all public schools. By 1970, one-teacher schools had all but died out, and only about 400 remained as of 1999.

At the same time that schools and districts were consolidating to form larger units, the number of pupils attending public schools was on the rise. Average daily attendance (ADA) in public elementary and secondary schools roughly doubled from 1929 to 1969, rising from approximately 21 to 42 million students.[11] These two forces—declining numbers of schools and districts coupled with rising attendance—produced substantially larger educational institutions

11. Average daily attendance is a better indicator of size than is enrollment. Early in the century, there often were substantial discrepancies between the number of students nominally enrolled in schools and those who actually attended regularly. Today, the two are nearly identical. For a comparison of average daily attendance and enrollment over time, see Heckman, Layne-Farrar, and Todd (1996).

Figure 3-3. *Average District Size, 1931–99*

Average daily attendance per district (thousands)

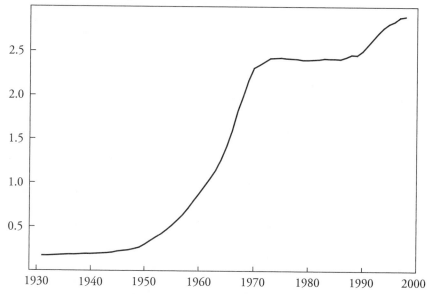

Source: National Center for Education Statistics, *Digest of Education Statistics* (U.S. Department of Education).

over the course of the twentieth century. Figures 3-3 and 3-4 show the average size of schools and districts over the periods for which data are available. Over the period of rapid consolidation, 1930 to 1970, ADA per school district increased from approximately 170 students to 2,300.[12] At the same time, ADA per school increased from 87 to 440. In other words, the average school district was fourteen times larger in 1970 than in 1930, and the average school was five times larger. Both schools and districts witnessed their most rapid growth in the years from 1950 to 1970, as increasing attendance rates, the baby boom, and institutional consolidation coincided.

If the growing size of schools and districts represents one dimension of centralization of authority over public education, the second was evident in the increasing role of state governments in what traditionally had been a strictly local matter. As demonstrated in figure 3-5, the state share of funding for public education grew considerably from about 1930 to 1950 and made a smaller jump again in the late 1970s. The local share of revenue, meanwhile, declined from more than 80 percent early in the century to less than half by the mid-1970s. For about the last twenty-five years, state and local governments have

12. From 1970 to 2000, average district size continued to increase, reaching 2,900 students.

Figure 3-4. *Average School Size, 1869–1999*

Average daily attendance per school (thousands)

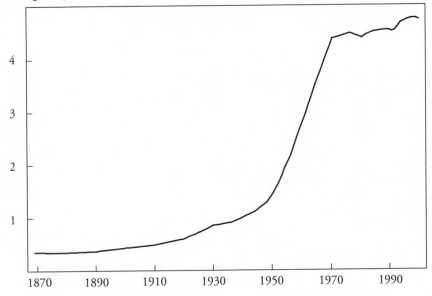

Source: National Center for Education Statistics, *Digest of Education Statistics* (U.S. Department of Education).

contributed nearly equal shares of funding for public education. The federal share has risen noticeably from its starting point of next to nothing in 1920, but it still remains at less than 10 percent. As discussed below, the growing state role in funding public education is related to some degree to school district consolidation.

Related Literature

Disappointingly few studies have attempted to explain systematically the consolidation of school districts over time and across states. Indeed, the literature on the subject is sparse enough—three studies—that it can be reviewed here in its entirety. David Strang (1987) was the first to develop and test a model of district consolidation. Strang argues that consolidation was primarily the result of efforts by state politicians and professional educators to centralize and professionalize the administration of public education. These reformers were able to overcome widespread opposition from local communities and interest groups by providing fiscal inducements for district consolidation. Specifically, by expanding their share of funding for public education, state governments were able to gain leverage over local decisionmakers by awarding or withholding funds in response to local consolidation efforts. Empirically, Strang found that school districts were consolidated more quickly and extensively where the state

Figure 3-5. *Sources of Public Education Funding, 1919–98*

Share of revenue (percent)

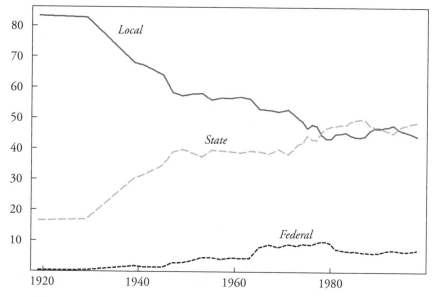

Source: National Center for Education Statistics, *Digest of Education Statistics* (U.S. Department of Education).

government's share of education funding was higher. Indeed, according to his point estimates, a 50 percent increase in state revenue reduced the predicted number of districts by half.[13]

Kenny and Schmidt (1994) were the next to examine the causes of school district consolidation, focusing on the period from 1950 to 1980. They argue that decisions about consolidation present a trade-off between the benefits of having many districts to satisfy the diverse preferences of a heterogeneous population and the benefits of having large districts to take advantage of the cost savings arising from economies of scale. They found that declining farm employment, increasing population density, and the falling cost of transporting students were among the most important factors in the decline in the number of school districts. Interestingly, they also found that the rate of teacher unionization was positively associated with consolidation, although they were not able to distinguish whether increasing unionization was a cause or an effect of increasing consolidation.[14]

13. Strang (1987, p. 362).

14. Unfortunately, because Kenny and Schmidt (1994) examine consolidation after 1950, some of their findings may not apply to the wider period under study in the present chapter. For example, teacher unionization was trivial prior to 1960 (see Peltzman 1993) and so is an implausible explanation for district consolidation over most of the study period.

Like Strang, Kenny and Schmidt found that the increasing role of state governments in school funding was positively associated with district consolidation. A few state governments (for example, Florida, Maryland, and Nevada) influenced consolidation more directly by mandating the consolidation of school districts to conform to county boundaries. Finally, Kenny and Schmidt found that states with greater income heterogeneity experienced less consolidation but that this relationship was tempered by state funding of public education. Presumably, state funding reduced the variation in quality among districts and hence removed opportunities for local communities to tailor schools to local tastes.[15]

The final study to examine district consolidation is Alesina, Baqir, and Hoxby (2000). This study is more general than the others in that it examines not only school districts but all types of local governments and attempts to explain the formation as well as consolidation of local jurisdictions. An additional advantage of this study is that it was conducted at the county level, thus possibly identifying additional sources of variation in the number of local jurisdictions. As did Kenny and Schmidt (1994), Alesina and others studied the period after 1950, meaning that they missed the era of greatest school district consolidation. Focusing their attention on population heterogeneity as a possible explanation for jurisdictional creation and dissolution, they found that less consolidation took place in counties that were more racially, ethnically, or religiously diverse. Alesina and others thus argue that citizens seek to avoid racial heterogeneity within local school districts. These results are generally concordant with Kenny and Schmidt's finding that *income* heterogeneity made consolidation less likely, suggesting generally that population diversity has been one of the few significant barriers to the consolidation of local school districts.

If relatively little is known about the causes of district consolidation, even less has been written about the consequences of pre-1970 consolidation for student outcomes. Although a sizeable literature has developed on the relation of student outcomes to school and district size, few studies address consolidation directly, most are limited to a single state or district, and all rely on data too recent to speak directly to the period of greatest consolidation.[16] One of the earliest and most influential studies of school size was the "Conant Report."[17] James Conant, a former Harvard University president, studied questionnaires from more than 2,000 high schools nationwide and concluded that large "comprehensive" high schools were more cost efficient and provided higher-quality schooling through a wider range of course offerings. Although the Conant Report received great publicity at the time and has been credited with spurring district consolidation, most consolidation had already taken place before the

15. Kenny and Schmidt (1994, pp. 9–10).
16. Andrews, Duncombe, and Yinger (2002), Cotton (1996), Fox (1981), and Walberg (1993) provide reviews of the literature on the effects of school and district size on student outcomes.
17. Conant (1967).

report was released. A little-noted irony of the Conant Report was that there were no small schools in Conant's data set. The smallest school he examined had 750 students, well above the average high school size at the time.[18]

More recent and more rigorous studies generally have not supported Conant's argument that larger schools produce better student outcomes at lower cost. Of the seven studies of school size and student performance reviewed by Andrews, Duncombe, and Yinger (2002), only one, Kenny (1982), found increasing returns to scale; the remaining six studies found decreasing returns.[19] Four of these studies also identified constant returns to scale over at least some of the data's range, suggesting that returns to scale in school size are nonlinear.[20] Summers and Wolf (1977) found that African American students were particularly harmed by large school size, while Lee and Smith (1997) found that students of low socioeconomic status did particularly poorly in large schools.

The empirical literature on the effects of *district* size on student outcomes is smaller and less consistent in its findings. Controlling for student and teacher characteristics, Walberg and Fowler (1987) and Ferguson (1991) found a negative relationship between student achievement and district size in New Jersey and Texas, respectively. On the other hand, Sebold and Dato (1981) found increasing returns to district size for California high schools, while Ferguson and Ladd (1996) found increasing returns to district size for elementary schools in Alabama. Unfortunately, as each of these studies focuses on a different state, it is difficult to identify the reasons for the discrepancies in their conclusions. As Andrews, Duncombe, and Yinger concluded from their review of the literature, "Mixed results emerge from those studies estimating returns to size at the district level. The results from estimates of returns to size at the school level are more consistent. Generally, larger schools are associated with lower student performance holding school and nonschool inputs constant."[21]

As noted above, most of the existing literature speaks at best indirectly to questions of the effects of district and school consolidation from 1930 to 1970. Moreover, if returns to size in education are indeed nonlinear, then results of recent studies may differ substantially from results that would be obtained from analysis of earlier data. For instance, if returns to size increase up to some threshold size and decrease thereafter, studies that were conducted after consolidation had eliminated the smallest districts and schools may observe only cases

18. Walberg (1993).

19. Usefully, Andrews, Duncombe, and Yinger (2002) restrict their survey to studies that meet minimum standards of methodological rigor.

20. Andrews, Duncombe, and Yinger (2002)

21. Andrews, Duncombe, and Yinger (2002, p. 20). Cotton (1996) reaches a similar conclusion in her review of more than 100 articles on the effects of school size on student outcomes. Cotton's review is more comprehensive than that of Andrews, Duncombe, and Yinger, but it is less attuned to methodological issues. It is encouraging that the two surveys come to roughly similar conclusions.

in the range of decreasing returns. Analysis of data from before 1970, when the range of observed values for school and district size was wider, could reveal a substantially different picture. The remainder of the chapter explores the effects of consolidation using data from the era of consolidation.

Empirical Analysis

It is not possible to test the effects of consolidation on conventional measures of student achievement, such as standardized test scores, because they were not in wide use until after consolidation had largely come to an end. Instead, using the Public-Use Micro-Sample (PUMS) of the U.S. Census Bureau, it is possible to relate aspects of consolidation to the returns to education in the labor market. I follow the methodology established by David Card and Alan Krueger in a pair of influential papers on school quality and earnings.[22] A brief outline of the statistical model follows.[23]

Let y_{ijkc} represent the (natural logarithm of) weekly earnings for individual i, born in state j in cohort c and currently working in state k of region r. Let E_{ijkc} represent the years of education completed by individual i, who is assumed to have been educated in the public school system of the same state in which he was born. Card and Krueger postulate a linear function of log weekly earnings of the form

$$(1) \qquad y_{ijkc} = \delta_{jc} + \mu_{kc} + \beta_c \cdot X_{ijkc} + (\gamma_{jc} + \rho_{rc}) \cdot E_{ijkc} + \varepsilon_{ijkc},$$

where δ_{jc} represents a cohort-specific fixed effect for each state of birth, μ_{kc} represents a cohort-specific fixed effect for each state of residence, and ε_{ijkc} is a stochastic error term assumed to be identically and independently distributed across individuals. X_{ijkc} is a set of demographic variables, including marital status, labor market experience, labor market experience squared, and an indicator of whether the individual lives in a metropolitan statistical area. The model also allows a cohort-specific region-of-residence effect (ρ_{rc}) and a cohort-specific state-of-birth effect (γ_{jc}) on the return to education—that is, returns to education may differ across different regional labor markets, and they may differ for individuals educated in a particular state regardless of their labor market.

Because the model includes interactions between state-of-birth dummies and education and a second set of interactions between region-of-residence dummies and education, the component of the return to education that is specific to the state of birth is identified by individuals who are born in one state and move to another. These cohort-specific and state of birth–specific rates of return to

---

22. Card and Kruger (1992a, 1992b).
23. A more detailed methodological discussion can be found in Card and Krueger (1996) and Heckman, Layne-Farrar, and Todd (1996).

education, γ_{jc}, are the key parameters of the model, which Card and Krueger seek to explain through differences in school quality. Specifically, Card and Krueger allow the returns to education for each state of birth and cohort to depend on the characteristics of the public schools as well as on state-of-birth and cohort fixed effects:

$$(2) \qquad\qquad \gamma_{jc} = a_j + a_c + \varphi Q_{jc},$$

where a_j and a_c are state-of-birth and cohort fixed effects, respectively, and Q_{jc} is a set of characteristics of public schools in state j during the education of cohort c. Card and Krueger (1992a) use class size, term length, and relative teacher salaries as their measures of school quality. I aim simply to extend the model by incorporating variables related to consolidation, such as district and school size and the state share of education funding, into Q_{jc}.[24]

Several features of this modeling strategy are noteworthy. First, the model is designed to identify the effect of school characteristics on the *slope* of the return to education—that is, the increase in earnings associated with an additional year of schooling. In addition, permanent differences in the rate of return to education across states are absorbed by the state-of-birth dummies in the second stage. Second, the first-stage model controls for variation across labor markets in the level of earnings through the state-of-residence intercepts; regional variation in the rate of return to education through interactions between region-of-residence dummies and years of education; and differences in the average earnings of individuals born in different states through state-of-birth dummies. These features of the model obviate some common criticisms of studies that attempt to estimate the relationship between school characteristics and student outcomes. For instance, to the extent that family background characteristics (or other omitted variables) affect the level of earnings, rather than the rate of return to education, the estimated rates of return are cleansed of the effects of family background (more on this below).

Data

The data used to estimate rates of return to education are from the PUMS A Sample of the 1980 census. Following Card and Krueger (1992a), subjects were restricted to white men born in the forty-eight mainland states and the District

---

24. Although this model can be estimated in one step, Card and Krueger argue in favor of two-step estimation, primarily for computational convenience. In the first step, equation (1) is estimated and the state-of-birth-by-cohort returns to education, γ_{jc}, are obtained. In the second stage, these estimated returns are used as the dependent variable and equation (2) is estimated by generalized least squares (GLS). The two-step estimates are asymptotically unbiased and efficient if proper weights are used in the second stage; specifically, the second-stage observations are weighted by the inverse sampling variance from the first stage.

of Columbia between 1920 and 1949. The sample was divided into three ten-year birth cohorts. Three separate cohort-specific first-stage regressions were then run, as per equation (1) above, to obtain 147 separate cohort-by-state-of-birth estimates of the rate of return to education. These 147 slope estimates became the dependent variable in the second-stage models reported below. In the second stage, the estimated rates of return to education were matched to state-level characteristics of schools at the time each cohort attended school. Data on the pupil-teacher ratio, term length, and relative teacher wages (that is, normalized by the average state wage) were obtained from Card and Krueger (1992a). In addition, I included data on average daily attendance per school district and per school, as well as the state government's share of funding for public education. All data on school characteristics, including those of Card and Krueger (1992a), were obtained from various issues of the *Biennial Survey of Education* (later renamed the *Digest of Education Statistics*). Additional details on the data are contained in the appendix to this chapter.

Consolidation and the Rate of Return to Education

I began by estimating equation (1) using the 1980 census PUMS data, following the specification of Card and Krueger (1992a). Rates of return to education were estimated using three cohort-specific regressions of log weekly earnings on a set of state-of-residence indicators, forty-nine state-of-birth indicators, nine region-of-residence indicators interacted with completed years of education, and forty-nine state-of-birth indicators interacted with completed years of education.[25] The models also included controls for labor market experience and its square, an indicator for current residence in a metropolitan statistical area, and an indicator for being married with a spouse present. The cohort-specific interactions between state of birth and years of education become the observations for the dependent variable in the second-stage models. Because my first-stage model results are virtually identical to those reported by Card and Krueger (1992a), I do not discuss them further here.[26]

Table 3-1 presents the results of a series of regression models representing versions of equation (2) based on the estimated rates of return generated in the first-stage model. The first model reproduces the primary specification of Card and Krueger (1992a).[27] Consistent with their results, increasing class size had a

25. There are forty-nine states of birth because Alaska and Hawaii are excluded (they were not states until 1959) and Washington, D.C., is included as a state of birth.
26. The appendix to this chapter provides additional details.
27. Card and Krueger (1992a) report two versions of their model. In one, the rates of return to education in the first stage are estimated to be linear in log earnings. In the other, they use an ad hoc nonlinear model in which the years-of-education variable is coded relative to the 2nd percentile of the distribution for each state. They find little difference between the two models. Heckman, Layne-Farrar, and Todd (1996), in their replication of the Card and Krueger (1992a) model, ignore the 2 percent nonlinear model. I do the same here and simply estimate the first stage as

Table 3-1. *Determinants of the Return to Education (GLS), Dependent Variable: Percentage Return to Education*[a]

Independent variable	Base models					With quadratic terms		Without Washington, D.C.	
	(1)	(2)	(3)	(4)	(5)	(6)	(7)	(8)	(9)
Pupil-teacher ratio/100	-7.368	-7.449	-8.110	-7.269	-8.02	-8.028	-7.319	-7.487	-7.054
	(2.507)***	(2.507)***	(2.436)***	(2.502)***	(2.43)***	(2.355)***	(2.354)***	(2.484)***	(2.371)***
Term length (hundreds of days)	0.320	0.399	0.221	0.227	0.14	-0.060	0.106	0.003	0.301
	(0.779)	(0.787)	(0.754)	(0.783)	(0.77)	(0.736)	(0.740)	(0.905)	(0.744)
Relative teacher wage	0.788	0.753	0.567	0.779	0.56	-0.005	0.261	0.261	0.196
	(0.360)**	(0.364)**	(0.355)	(0.359)**	(0.36)	(0.378)	(0.355)	(0.377)	(0.360)
District size (thousands)		-0.015			-0.00	0.109	0.098	0.116	0.074
		(0.024)			(0.02)	(0.037)***	(0.037)***	(0.080)	(0.032)**
School size (hundreds)			-0.208		-0.21	-0.017	-0.313	-0.321	-0.306
			(0.065)***		(0.07)***	(0.171)	(0.072)***	(0.075)***	(0.071)***
State share of funding				0.006	0.01	0.001	0.002	0.001	0.002
				(0.006)	(0.01)	(0.006)	(0.006)	(0.006)	(0.006)
District size squared						-0.001	-0.001	-0.002	0.006
						(0.000)***	(0.000)***	(0.003)	(0.006)
School size squared						-0.047			
						(0.025)*			
Dummy for those born 1930–39	0.905	0.905	0.984	0.852	0.93	0.951	1.007	1.018	1.017
	(0.073)***	(0.073)***	(0.075)***	(0.092)***	(0.09)***	(0.096)***	(0.092)***	(0.093)***	(0.093)***
Dummy for those born 1940–49	1.854	1.865	2.150	1.802	2.10	2.096	2.236	2.243	2.247
	(0.098)***	(0.099)***	(0.132)***	(0.112)***	(0.14)***	(0.160)***	(0.144)***	(0.145)***	(0.145)***
Constant	5.619	6.994	7.287	5.512	7.46	7.916	7.773	6.797	6.244
	(1.700)***	(2.618)***	(1.667)***	(1.696)***	(2.54)***	(2.420)***	(2.449)***	(1.871)***	(1.609)***
Summary statistic									
N	147	147	147	147	147	147	147	144	144
R^2	0.95	0.95	0.96	0.95	0.96	0.96	0.96	0.96	0.96

Source: Author's calculations.

a. Standard errors in parentheses. All models include state-of-birth fixed effects. Equations are weighted by the inverse sampling variance of the dependent variable. $*p < .10$; $**p < .05$; $***p < .01$.

negative effect on the return to education, while increasing teacher salaries had a significant positive effect. Next, district size, school size, and the state's share of funding for public education were added to the model sequentially. Of these three consolidation-related variables, only school size showed a statistically significant relationship with the estimated returns to education. The results indicate that increasing school size is associated with a decline in the return to education. When all three variables were added to the model as a group, school size remained the only one to achieve statistical significance. For both district size and state share of funding, the standard errors were larger than the point estimates. It is worth noting that school size remains significant, while district size and state share of funding remain insignificant, when models (2) to (5) are run without the three Card and Krueger school quality measures (not shown). Also notable is that school size appears to absorb some of the effect of teacher salary, as the latter variable falls to insignificance in all of the models that include school size. The effect of class size, on the other hand, is robust across all of the models.

As discussed above, several recent studies have identified nonlinear effects of school and district size on student outcomes. In the context of consolidation, it may be the case that an increase in school and district size initially has a positive effect on returns to education, but that once schools or districts become "too big," diseconomies of scale dominate and returns to education diminish. In order to explore this hypothesis, I added quadratic terms, school and district size squared, in model (6). Interestingly, with the addition of the quadratic term, district size becomes significant, suggestive of an inverted U-shaped pattern in the returns to district size. The quadratic for school size, on the other hand, is not significant, and in model (7) it is dropped. Model (7) thus shows that school size has a uniformly negative effect on the returns to education, while returns to district size first increase in district size and then decrease.

However, the nonlinear effect of district size in model (7) is not robust. Sensitivity analysis revealed that the significance of the quadratic term for district size depends exclusively on the effect of Washington, D.C. (hereafter referred to as D.C.). With only one school district throughout the study period, D.C. has the largest average district size in every cohort.[28] For example, the average size of the D.C. district is 79,000, 85,000, and 98,000 students for the 1920–29, 1930–39, and 1940–49 cohorts, respectively. The second-largest state average district size in each of the three cohorts was 11,000, 13,000, and 20,000, respectively.[29] Thus D.C. appears to be a substantial outlier in district size for

---

linear in log earnings. Thus the second-stage results presented here should be compared with the equivalent estimates of Card and Krueger (1992a) in table 5, column 10. I am nearly, but not perfectly, able to replicate their results. See the appendix for further discussion.

28. Recall that Hawaii, which also has only one district, is excluded from the analysis.

29. Maryland had the second-largest average district size in every cohort.

every cohort. Model (8) shows that when D.C. is excluded, district size and district size squared are no longer significant. However, when the quadratic term is dropped in model (9), district size becomes significant and positive with D.C. excluded. Interestingly, although D.C. also has the largest average school size for every cohort, the estimated effect of school size is essentially unaffected when D.C. is dropped from the model. If D.C. is excluded as an outlier, model (9) is the preferred specification and the results indicate increasing returns to scale in district size, but decreasing returns in school size.[30]

The point estimates from model (9) reveal substantively consequential effects of consolidation on the returns to education. An increase of 1 standard deviation in school size (equivalent to about 100 students) is associated with a decrease of one-third of a standard deviation in the rate of return to education. On the other hand, an increase of 1 standard deviation in district size (about 2,800 students) is associated with an increase of about one-fifth of a standard deviation in the rate of return to education. For comparison, note that an increase of 1 standard deviation in class size (four students) is estimated in model (9) to increase the return to education by about one-quarter of a standard deviation. Put more directly, an increase in school size of 100 students is associated with a 3.7 percent decline in earnings for high school graduates (those with exactly twelve years of education). An increase in district size of 2,800 students is associated with a 2.5 percent increase in earnings for high school graduates.

Sensitivity Analysis

Heckman, Layne-Farrar, and Todd (1996) provide a thoughtful critique of the Card and Krueger (1992a) study and its methodology.[31] The most important issue raised by the Heckman team is that Card and Krueger were not able to separate the effects of school characteristics from family background or other early community influences. Card and Kruger merely posit that family background affects the level of earnings rather than the rate of return to education. Heckman, Layne-Farrar, and Todd challenge this assumption as arbitrary and point out that if it does not hold, even Card and Krueger's state-of-birth fixed-effects strategy provides no guarantee that estimated effects of school quality are not merely proxies for the effects on earnings of other early environmental

30. Another case for excluding the District of Columbia is that it is not actually a state. Practically, however, the inclusion or exclusion of D.C. is of little consequence. For model (7), the quadratic in school size is maximized at 48,000 students, well over twice the average size for every state except D.C. Thus even under this specification, returns to education are increasing in district size over the practically relevant range of the data. Nevertheless, the fundamental question of whether district size ever reaches a point of decreasing returns to scale is an important one. Analysis of more recent data, which offer more observations comparable in scale to those for D.C., may help to resolve this issue.

31. Card and Krueger (1996) provides a response to this critique.

factors. Because my analysis closely follows the Card and Krueger empirical methodology, these issues warrant attention here.[32]

Note first that school size and district size are positively correlated but show opposing effects on returns to schooling. Thus the argument that they are both merely proxies for unobserved early environmental characteristics is not straightforward. For instance, if it were the case that small schools were positively correlated with "good" family background characteristics, then the observed effects of school size in table 3-1 might merely be proxies for these (unobserved) background variables. If this were the case, then one would also expect district size to be correlated with the same background characteristics. Yet district size is negatively related to schooling returns, so it must not be a proxy for the same unobserved background variables represented by school size. Of course, background characteristics could conceivably be correlated only with those components of school size that are orthogonal to district size—the two size variables, after all, are not *perfectly* correlated. For instance, perhaps students who attended small schools in large districts had especially strong family environments, or students who attended large schools in small districts had poor unobserved background characteristics. In short, while it is conceivable that school and district size merely proxy for unobserved early environmental variables, explaining the observed effects in this way is not as easy as it may first seem.

One can do better than speculate on the relationship between consolidation and early environmental characteristics, however. Although individual-level data on parental characteristics and other early environmental variables are not contained in the census, information can be obtained about the characteristics of the population in the state at the time when the men in the sample were in school. Accordingly, I collected two relevant variables: the real per capita income in the state at the time each cohort entered school and the corresponding percentage of the population classified as *rural* by the census. Spearman rank correlations between these two variables and school size, district size, and class size are shown in table 3-2. Income is negatively related to the pupil-teacher ratio, indicating that more affluent states provided smaller classes, and this correlation increases over time. Thus parental income presents itself as a

---

32. Heckman, Layne-Farrar, and Todd (1996) suggest several refinements to Card and Krueger's analysis. First, the Heckman group suggest that returns to education are nonlinear, finding evidence of significant "sheepskin effects" in the first-stage model at twelve and sixteen years of education. Second, they suggest that school characteristics may influence the first-stage state-of-birth intercepts, in addition to the slopes, and that these effects can be modeled in a second-stage regression analogous to equation (2) above. Third, they show that school characteristics affect educational attainment (years of schooling completed). Fourth, Heckman, Layne-Farrar, and Todd argue that returns to education are region-of-residence specific. I plan to pursue each of these issues, as they pertain to the consolidation effects, in future work.

Table 3-2. *Spearman Rank Correlations between School Characteristics and Population Characteristics*[a]

| | Birth Cohort | | | | | |
| | 1920–29 | | 1930–39 | | 1940–49 | |
School characteristic	Real per capita income of parents' generation	Percent rural	Real per capita income of parents' generation	Percent rural	Real per capita income of parents' generation	Percent rural
Percent rural	−0.863		−0.849		−0.631	
	0.000		0.000		0.000	
Pupil-teacher ratio	−0.348	0.068	−0.339	0.177	−0.500	0.111
	0.014	0.643	0.017	0.224	0.000	0.449
District size (ADA)	0.070	−0.294	0.059	−0.207	−0.145	−0.235
	0.631	0.037	0.689	0.145	0.311	0.097
School size (ADA)	0.380	−0.610	0.500	−0.624	0.349	−0.720
	0.007	0.000	0.000	0.000	0.012	0.000

Source: Author's calculations.

a. Numbers in italics are p values. ADA = average daily attendance.

possible partial explanation for the observed effect of class size. However, income is unrelated to district size for all three cohorts and *positively* related to school size; that is, more affluent states had larger schools. On the basis of these simple correlations at least, it appears unlikely that school or district size is merely a proxy for parental income. On the other hand, school size is strongly negatively correlated with the proportion of the population classified as rural, and this correlation increases somewhat across the cohorts. So if it is not family income but rather some factor associated with being raised in a rural community that is associated with returns to education, then the estimated effects of school size in table 3-1 may be confounded.

In order to get at these issues more directly, I ran a series of models incorporating the income and rural variables, reported in table 3-3. As seen from model (1), the income of the parents' generation actually shows a statistically significant *negative* relationship with returns to education. This result suggests that children raised in less affluent states derived greater returns from a year of education. That the income of the parents' generation is significant here challenges Card and Krueger's (1992a) assumption that family background variables influence the level of earnings but not the rate of return to education. Nevertheless, the estimated effects of school and district size are largely unaffected by the inclusion of the income variable. The rural variable, on the other hand, shows no significant association with returns to education. In fact, even when all of the

Table 3-3. *Population Characteristics and Return to Education (GLS)* [a]

Population characteristic	(1)	(2)
Pupil-teacher ratio/100	−6.358	−7.070
	(2.366)***	(2.370)***
Term length (hundreds of days)	−0.061	0.361
	(0.754)	(0.742)
Relative teacher wage	0.670	0.295
	(0.427)	(0.430)
District size (thousands)	0.062	0.076
	(0.032)**	(0.031)**
School size (hundreds)	−0.287	−0.301
	(0.070)***	(0.072)***
Real per capita income of parents' generation (thousands of dollars)	−0.790 (0.394)**	
Percent of population that is rural		0.396
		(0.914)
Dummy for those born 1930–39	1.159	1.031
	(0.096)***	(0.074)***
Dummy for those born 1940–49	2.779	2.284
	(0.288)***	(0.139)***
Constant	7.107	5.854
	(1.711)***	(1.833)***
Summary statistic		
N	144	144
R^2	0.96	0.96

Source: Author's calculations.
a. *p < .10; **p < .05; ***p < .01.

school characteristics are removed from the model (not shown), rural population does not approach statistical significance. Thus it appears unlikely that school or district size are merely proxies for unobserved factors associated with a rural upbringing.[33]

In summary, although income and rural status are correlated with school size, neither background variable appears to account for the effect of school size on returns to education. District size is unrelated to background income and only modestly correlated with rural status. Hence it is unsurprising that these variables do not absorb the effects of district size when included in the model. The attendance rate is essentially unrelated to school or district size and exhibits little influence in either of the models in which it is present. Taken together, the

33. The preceding analyses have considered each of the environmental variables individually. When all of the background variables are included jointly (not shown), only the income variable is statistically significant. It is important to note that the estimated effects for school and district size are unperturbed.

results reported in table 3-3 suggest that school and district size are unlikely proxies for early environmental characteristics.

An additional issue that has dogged Card and Krueger's analysis deserves comment. Their finding of a positive effect of school quality on earnings—in particular, the effect of class size—runs counter to many studies using individual-level data and has led others—for example, Hanusheck, Rivkin, and Taylor (1996)—to question whether the result is an artifact of "aggregation bias." Without delving into the aggregation bias debate, it is reassuring that the present findings related to school size are broadly consistent with other studies using individual-level data, such as those reviewed in Andrews, Duncombe, and Yinger (2002) and Cotton (1996). While the literature on district size is smaller and less consistent in its results, the finding of a small positive effect is not out of line with those of some other studies using individual-level data, for example, Ferguson (1991) and Walberg and Fowler (1987).

Directions for Future Research

As indicated above, Heckman, Layne-Farrar, and Todd (1996) suggest several important extensions to Card and Krueger's (1992a) empirical strategy. Pursuing these lines of analysis in relation to the school and district size variables introduced here is an essential next step. In particular, gaining a better understanding of nonlinearity in the return to education, the relationship between size and educational attainment, and region-specific returns to education would go far toward solidifying the basic conclusion reached here that size has an important effect on returns to education. Analyzing whether district or school size influences educational attainment, in particular, is an important complement to the analysis presented here related to the returns to a year of schooling.

In addition, future work should distinguish the effects of size for elementary and secondary schools. Because the *Biennial Survey* did not begin reporting enrollment for secondary schools separately until the early 1940s, I was not able to differentiate size by level of education. However, such analysis could easily be conducted with the individual-level data used in more recent studies.

Most of the work exploring the relationship between school characteristics and earnings has focused on average earnings across students. Perhaps an equally important question is whether school characteristics influence the variance in earnings across students. In the present context, one effect of district consolidation presumably was to reduce the variance in educational quality across students.[34] In other words, if equality of educational opportunity is a policy goal, consolidation may have benefits (or costs) that are not observed in an analysis of mean earnings, such as that presented here.

34. Kenny and Schmidt (1994).

Finally, the results presented here do little to explain what it is about small schools or large districts that affects student outcomes. Potential explanations for the positive effects of school size range from participation in extracurricular activities and attachment to community to parental involvement and self-esteem.[35] Benefits of district size are typically seen to include cost reductions due to economies of scale.[36] Narrowing the analysis from considering general effects of size to identifying the specific mechanisms by which size matters will be essential in making effective policy.

Discussion

The analysis presented above represents the first attempt to assess the effects of the consolidation movement across states and over time during the period of greatest consolidation, 1930–70. The results would not please Elwood P. Cubberley and other early-twentieth-century "administrative progressives." I find that the modest gains associated with larger *districts* are likely to be outweighed by the harmful effects of larger *schools*. From the estimates reported above, it appears that a change of 1 standard deviation in school size has about one-and-a-half times as large an effect as a change of 1 standard deviation in district size. Perhaps equally dismaying to the proponents of consolidation would be just how meager the estimated district-size effects turned out to be. After decades of political struggle to centralize control over public education, the elimination of more than 100,000 districts, and a fourteenfold increase in average district size, the observed effects of district size amount to about one-fifth of a standard deviation in earnings.

If the results indicate that the combination of larger districts with smaller schools provides the greatest returns for students, policymakers historically have not followed that recipe. The Spearman rank correlation between school and district size across states remained nearly constant at about 0.70 from 1930 to 1970—that is, larger districts tended to operate larger schools. Indeed, the mix of school and district size is central to issues of authority and governance in education. The number and size of schools within a district directly influence the extent to which central authorities, such as superintendents and school boards, can be directly involved in the operations of the schools. In other words, school board members may face a conflict of interest between implementing good education policy and maintaining their own authority over schools. For instance, given a district of 10,000 students, it will be less costly for the central authority to monitor the operation of ten schools with 1,000 students each than to monitor twenty-five schools with 200 students each. A shift toward smaller schools

35. Cotton (1996).
36. Andrews, Duncombe, and Yinger (2002).

would require central authorities either to spend more time and money on oversight or to become less directly involved in the operation of individual schools. Thus any move toward smaller schools is intertwined with the decentralization of authority within school districts.

After professional educators and centralized education bureaucracies have struggled long and hard to centralize power, would it be in their interest to give some control back in the form of smaller schools? Although the evidence points to the benefits of smaller schools, education policy is seldom made on the basis of good research alone, especially policy that would involve transfers of power. Other contributors to this volume offer clues about the likely politics of decentralization in large school districts. The chapters by Hess and Moe agree that unions are most active in large school districts.[37] Campbell finds that ordinary citizens, in contrast, are least likely to attend school board meetings in large districts. Thus, as in so many areas of education policy, proposals for decreasing school size must confront the power of the teacher unions. The high correlation between school size and teacher salaries suggests that unions may be at least skeptical of, if not downright hostile toward, decreasing the size of schools. On the other hand, teachers, like students, may appreciate the intangible benefits of community attachment and individual participation associated with small schools.[38] In either case, there can be little doubt that decentralization proposals that attain union support will go farther faster than plans that raise union ire.

Despite the long history of centralization and professionalization in education—and the undoubted influence of teacher unions—ultimate authority still lies with voters, although their channels of influence may be less direct than in the past. Limited survey research suggests that voters generally support smaller schools, and as additional evidence accumulates in their favor, public sympathy could grow.[39] Even if voters in large districts are less likely to attend school board meetings (Campbell, chapter 12 of this volume), they still rule at the ballot box, where board members are regularly voted in and out of office. And, encouragingly, Berry and Howell suggest in chapter 7 of this volume that voters do, in fact, reward and punish school board members at the polls. Thus whether smaller schools and the decentralization of power that they represent have the potential to become anything more than policy prescriptions will depend on voters' appetite for challenging what William Fowler has described as "the natural predilection in American education toward enormity."[40] If history is any guide, it will be an uphill battle.

37. Terry Moe, in chapter 11 in this volume, provides a more detailed analysis of how union activity translates into political influence and suggests that unions may be equally influential in small districts, even though they are less active politically.
38. Cotton (1996).
39. Cotton (1996).
40. Fowler (1992).

Implications for contemporary education policy, however, must be drawn only with caution from the analysis presented here, for several reasons. First, I have not examined any school or district size data more recent than 1966. Much can change over thirty-some years. Second, the findings pertain to state *average* school and district size. One must therefore be cautious in trying to ascertain the "right" size for any individual school or district. Third, the analysis focuses on only one of the channels by which school and district characteristics influence earnings: the rate of return to a year of education. As Heckman, Layne-Farrar, and Todd (1996) point out, there are at least two additional channels to be considered: effects on the level of earnings and effects on educational attainment, which in turn affects earnings. Finding that school or district size influences earnings differentially through these various channels could lead to a more complex picture than that presented here.

Appendix

1980 Census Data

Samples were taken from the 5 percent PUMS A Sample, which is a self-weighting sample of the U.S. population. To maintain comparability with Card and Krueger (1992a), I followed their case selection criteria. Specifically, cases were restricted to white men born between 1920 and 1949 in the forty-eight mainland states and the District of Columbia.[41] Cases with imputed data for age, race, sex, education, weeks worked, or earnings were dropped. Individuals who reported no weeks of work, annual wage and salary income of less than $101, or average weekly wage and salary income of less than $36 or more than $2,500 were excluded. Using these selection criteria, reported by Card and Krueger, I was not able to reproduce their exact sample: they reported a total sample size of 1,019,746,[42] while I obtained a total sample size of 994,883. Nevertheless, the discrepancy does not appear consequential. The correlation between my first-stage estimates of the rates of return to education and those reported by Card and Krueger is 0.99. The correlation between my estimates of first-stage errors and theirs is 0.99. When I used my estimated rates of return and their school quality variables, I was able to reproduce their main results very closely.

School Characteristics

Data on the pupil-teacher ratio, term length, and relative teacher wages were obtained from table 1 of Card and Krueger (1992a). Data on average daily

41. Year of birth was estimated from information on quarter of birth and age.
42. This is the sample size reported in the original article (Card and Krueger, 1992a). However, in a later paper summarizing that article, they reported the sample size as 1,018,477 (Card and Krueger, 1996).

attendance, the number of public schools, the number of school districts, and the state share of funding for public education were obtained from various issues of the *Biennial Survey of Education* and, after 1960, the *Digest of Education Statistics*. Because data from the *Biennial Survey* are available only every two years, I coded each estimate to the odd year of the issue and linearly interpreted values for the even year. For instance, the values reported in the 1931–32 and 1933–34 editions were assigned to 1931 and 1993, respectively. The value for 1932 was then computed as the average of the 1931 and 1993 values. Each cohort was assigned the average of the school characteristics during the years that people born in that cohort would have attended school. Following Card and Krueger (1992a) and Heckman, Layne-Farrar, and Todd (1996), I assumed that all individuals completed twelve years of schooling.[43] For instance, a high school graduate born in 1920 would have entered school in 1926 and graduated in 1937. So school characteristics were averaged over 1926–37 for individuals born in 1920. For the 1920–29 cohort, averages were taken for years of birth from 1920 through 1929, weighted by the number of births in each year.

Other Variables

The income of the parents' generation for each cohort is per capita income from the State Personal Income Estimates of the Bureau of Economic Analysis. The state-level per capita income from 1930 was assigned to the 1920–29 cohort, from 1940 to the 1930–39 cohort, and from 1950 to the 1940–49 cohort. I used the consumer price index to convert all of the estimates into 1950 dollars. The percent of the population classified as rural was taken from the 1930, 1940, and 1950 U.S. censuses. As with the income estimates, the 1930 value was assigned to the 1920–29 cohort, the 1940 value to the 1930–39 cohort, and the 1950 value to the 1940–49 cohort.

References

Alesina, Alberto, Reza Baqir, and Caroline Hoxby. 2000. "Political Jurisdictions in Heterogeneous Communities." Working Paper 7859. Cambridge, Mass.: National Bureau of Economic Research.

Andrews, Mathew, William Duncombe, and John Yinger. 2002. "Revisiting Economies of Size in American Education: Are We Any Closer to a Consensus?" *Economics of Education Review* 21 (3): 245–62.

Card, David, and Alan Krueger. 1992a. "Does School Quality Mattter? Returns to Education and the Characteristics of Public Schools in the United States." *Journal of Political Economy* 100 (1): 1–40.

43. Both Card and Kruger (1992a) and Heckman, Layne-Farrar, and Todd (1996) reported estimating models using individual-specific averages of the quality variables and finding that the results did not change.

————. 1992b. "School Quality and Black-White Relative Earnings: A Direct Assessment." *Quarterly Journal of Economics* 107 (1): 151–200.

————. 1996. "Labor Market Effects of School Quality: Theory and Evidence." In *Does Money Matter?* edited by Gary Burtless. Brookings.

Conant, James. 1967. *The Comprehensive High School.* New York: McGraw Hill.

Cotton, Kathleen. 1996. "School Size, School Climate, and Student Performance." School Improvement Research Series. Washington: Office of Educational Research and Improvement.

Ferguson, R. F. 1991. "Paying for Public Education: New Evidence on How and Why Money Matters." *Harvard Journal of Legislation* 28: 466–98.

Ferguson, R. F., and H. F. Ladd. 1996. "Additional Evidence on How and Why Money Matters: A Production Function Analysis of Alabama Schools." In *Holding Schools Accountable: Performance-Based Reform in Education,* edited by H. F. Ladd. Brookings.

Fowler, William. 1992. "What Do We Know about School Size? What Should We Know?" ERIC Document Reproduction Service ED 347 675. Paper presented at the annual meeting of the American Educational Research Association.

Fox, W. F. 1981. "Reviewing Economies of Size in Education." *Journal of Education Finance* 6 (Winter): 273–96.

Hanushek, Eric, Steven Rivkin, and Lori Taylor. 1996. "Aggregation and the Estimated Effects of School Resources." *Review of Economics and Statistics* 78 (4): 611–27.

Heckman, James, Anne Layne-Farrar, and Petra Todd. 1996. "Human Capital Pricing Equations with an Application to Estimating the Effect of School Quality on Earnings." *Review of Economics and Statistics* 78 (4): 562–610.

Hooker, Clifford, and Van Mueller. 1970. *The Relationship of School District Reorganization to State Aid Distribution Systems.* National Education Finance Project Special Study 11. Minneapolis: University of Minnesota, Educational Research and Development Council of the Twin Cities Metropolitan Area.

Kenny, Lawrence. 1982. "Economies of Scale in Schooling." *Economics of Education Review* 2 (Winter): 1–24.

Kenny, Lawrence, and Amy Schmidt. 1994. "The Decline in the Number of School Districts in the U.S.: 1950–1980." *Public Choice* 79 (April): 1–18.

Lee, V. E., and J. B. Smith. 1997. "High School Size: Which Works Best and for Whom?" *Educational Evaluation and Policy Analysis* 19 (3): 205–27.

Peltzman, Sam. 1993. "The Political Economy of the Decline of American Public Education." *Journal of Law and Economics* 36 (1): 331–70.

Reynolds, David. 1999. *There Goes the Neighborhood: Rural School Consolidation at the Grass Roots in Early Twentieth-Century Iowa.* University of Iowa Press.

Sebold, F. D., and W. Dato. 1981. "School Funding and Student Achievement: An Empirical Analysis." *Public Finance Quarterly* 9 (1): 91–105.

Strang, David. 1987. "The Administrative Transformation of American Education: School District Consolidation, 1938–1980." *Administrative Science Quarterly* 32 (September): 352–66.

Summers, A. A., and B. L. Wolfe. 1977. "Do Schools Make a Difference?" *American Economic Review* 67 (4): 639–52.

Tyack, David. 1974. *The One Best System: A History of American Urban Education.* Harvard University Press.

Walberg, Herbert J. 1993. "Losing Local Control of Education." Heartland Institute Policy Study 59. Chicago: Heartland Institute.

Walberg, Herbert J., and W. J. Fowler. 1987. "Expenditure and Size Efficiencies of Public School Districts." *Educational Researcher* 16 (7): 5–13.

4

When Mayors Lead Urban Schools: Assessing the Effects of Takeover

KENNETH K. WONG AND FRANCIS X. SHEN

I n an arrangement facilitated over time by both institutional and structural factors, city government and the urban school system in the United States traditionally have existed as two independent jurisdictions.[1] The American public has endorsed the authority of the school board in part because of its belief in strong local control over schools, and this creed of local control is frequently equated with an independently elected, nonpartisan school board. Since the mid-1990s, however, several of the nation's large urban school districts have made significant changes in school governance by shifting from elected to mayor-appointed school boards. In these "mayoral takeover" governance structures, mayors have taken over citizens' authority to select school board members directly.

In 2002, the largest school district in the nation was taken over by a mayor when Michael Bloomberg was given control of the New York City public schools. With the addition of New York to a list of cities that includes Boston, Chicago, Philadelphia, Cleveland, Baltimore, and Washington, D.C., nearly 2,000,000 students now receive their education in a mayoral takeover school district. Mayoral takeover gained further prominence in 2002 when voters in Cleveland strongly supported the continuation of the mayor-appointed board.

We acknowledge funding support provided by "School Takeover by City and State Government as a Reform Strategy," a research project of the Mid-Atlantic Regional Educational Laboratory.
    1. Tyack (1974).

Although the trend toward mayor-appointed school boards is still emerging, it is important to gauge its initial effects because other urban districts are looking to mayoral takeover as a promising policy option.[2]

The analysis in this chapter is guided by a theory of "integrated governance" under mayoral leadership.[3] As understood in this theory, the shift to mayor-appointed school boards is not simply a recentralization of power nor solely a question of "Who governs?" (Dahl 1961). Rather, the move to mayor-appointed school boards fundamentally redefines the responsibilities of the education leadership districtwide. In the current climate of accountability, mayors and their appointed school district leaders not only are given more power, they also take on greater responsibility to turn around the entire city school system. Mayors may be motivated to accept such responsibility when they recognize that their city's economic health and its middle-class tax base are linked to the performance of its schools. To be sure, mayoral control may not necessarily turn into integrated governance reform. In some instances, mayors may be reluctant to play an active role even though they are granted the legislative authority to do so. In other instances, mayoral control may be constrained by state legislative compromises. Mayors also confront complex, multilevel urban school systems with multiple points of control. Unilateral action by the mayor's office may not be possible in the face of much inertia. Civic leaders and other interest groups may also be pushing for reforms independent of the mayor.

In light of the emerging trend toward mayor-appointed school boards, this chapter is intended to provide a systemic assessment of the multifaceted effects of mayoral takeover.[4] The chapter adds to the literature by examining the effects

2. St. Louis and Pittsburgh are two examples of districts moving in this direction. In St. Louis, Mayor Francis Slay has not officially taken over the schools, but the slate of four candidates that he backed in 2003 all won, providing him with significantly more power to reform the schools. Taking advantage of his position, he hired an outside team of turnaround specialists, including former New York City chancellor Rudy Crew. Pittsburgh's mayor, Tom Murphy, received a report from his appointed citywide commission that recommended mayoral takeover of the school district. The full report, "Keeping the Promise: The Case for Reform in the Pittsburgh Public Schools," is available at www.educationcommission.org/KeepingthePromise-Full2.pdf [September 28, 2004]. For several commentaries on this report, see the *Pittsburgh Post-Gazette*'s special forum, "The Mayor's Commission on Public Education: Three Perspectives," September 28, 2003. See also C. J. Lee and E. Chute, "Mayors in the Schools: Will City Join in Trend to Give More Control over Board Members?" *Pittsburgh Post-Gazette,* April 27, 2003.

3. Wong (2000).

4. This study builds on Wong and Shen (2002, 2003). Two preliminary notes should be made about mayoral takeover and its effects. First, mayor-appointed school boards remain in the minority, and they are relatively new on the scene. The attention that has been paid to them has less to do with their pervasiveness than with the prominence of two examples of this policy in action: Chicago and Boston. In analyzing the effects of mayoral takeover, then, it is important to remember that we have neither a great many years to look at nor a great many cities to consider. Evaluation of takeover necessarily relies at this time on the experiences of a limited number of localities. The second preliminary point to consider is that mayoral takeover is intended to have far-reaching, systemic effects beyond improving teaching and learning in the classroom. As is clearly evident in

of mayoral takeover on resource allocation. Although student achievement outcomes dominate policy discussion, the data currently available make it quite hard to generalize across districts about the effect of mayoral takeover on student achievement.[5] The data on resources and staffing, however, are remarkably consistent over time and across districts. We were able to construct reliable fiscal and staffing indicators from data across all school districts from 1992 to 2001 provided by the U.S. Census Bureau's *Annual Survey of Government Finances* and the National Center for Education Statistics Common Core of Data.

Our analysis suggests that at this relatively early reform phase, mayoral takeover had yet to show a consistent significant impact on fiscal and staffing outcomes across the nation. We find that the duration of the mayoral takeover regime is significantly related to several outcomes, suggesting that mayors do in fact face much inertia in setting up an integrated governance structure for the city school district.

The chapter first provides a brief background on the political dynamics of mayoral takeover and summarizes the relevant research. Next, we lay out our theory of integrated governance, developing a set of hypotheses about both the positive and the negative effects that may result from mayoral takeover. We then discuss the data and analytic approach that we used to test our hypotheses and report the results. We conclude with an overall evaluation of what mayoral takeover has produced thus far, what one might be likely to see in the years to come, and what researchers can do to improve public knowledge about this governance strategy.

Political Economy of Mayoral Control

Mayoral appointment of school board members gained national prominence in the mid- to late 1990s as a host of cities adopted this approach to reform, and it did not relinquish its place in the national spotlight in the first few years of the twenty-first century. In an increasing number of urban districts, the mayor assumed control of schools by appointing a school board. Currently, twenty-four states have passed legislation authorizing the management of school districts by

---

Chicago, mayoral takeover is designed in part to help retain and recruit middle-class residents; integrate educational services with those of other social service providers; strengthen both the school district and citywide budget; and perhaps most important, restore the general public's confidence in the city school system. Given that the aims of takeover are so broad, any single effort to measure the policy's "effectiveness" will ultimately fail to consider all the policy's intended effects. Scholars, recognizing this challenge, are currently employing a number of methods to study mayoral takeover. Henig and Rich (2004), as well as Cuban and Usdan (2003), have compiled case studies on the topic of increasing mayoral influence in urban education.

5. We have explored achievement effects in several other studies. In Wong and Shen (2003), although we find some mixed evidence on recent student achievement, we find no evidence to suggest that mayoral takeover will leave the worst schools behind in the wake of reform.

either mayors or state officials.[6] Mayoral control has occurred in New York, Philadelphia, Chicago, Boston, Baltimore, Cleveland, Detroit, Washington, D.C., and Oakland, California. Because the No Child Left Behind Act identifies takeover as a corrective action to turn around failing districts, it is likely that a growing number of mayors will seek control of the local school board.

Mayoral takeover is attractive because it recognizes that existing political structures are not easily altered; it empowers the district-level administration to intervene in failing schools; it enables city hall to manage conflicting interests and reduce fragmentary rules; and it integrates electoral accountability and educational performance standards at the systemwide level.[7]

In the context of intercity competition for economic gains, city leaders find schools an important revitalization tool,[8] and as cities began to make an economic comeback in the 1990s, retaining middle-class families became a major task for mayors. Concerns about crime and the quality of education often contribute to the out-migration of the urban middle class, so in order to help maintain a taxpaying labor force in the cities, public schools have to be improved to attract middle-class families. Businesses also choose cities that have a good record of school performance so that they can attract a pool of talented employees. These interrelated factors suggest that pressure has been building on city mayors to tackle the problems of their educational systems. Mayors, in other words, can no longer afford an educational system that is largely isolated from the economic future of their cities.

Mayors have turned to three distinct legislative processes to gain the power to appoint city school board members.[9] First, they have worked with state legislators and governors to pass state legislation granting mayors the authority to replace an elected board with an appointed board. Chicago and New York are examples of this process. A second option has been state legislation that calls for a referendum to allow city residents to vote on whether the mayor should have the authority to appoint the school board;[10] this was the route taken by Boston and Cleveland.[11] Finally, a city can vote to change the city charter, allowing the mayor more control over the school board. Oakland held such a vote, changing its charter and granting the mayor the power to appoint three board members.

6. Cibulka (1999); Ziebarth (2002).

7. Wong (1992, 1999).

8. Peterson (1981).

9. For a detailed legal analysis of state-local legal relationships, see Saiger (2004).

10. In practice, the state has allowed the mayor to appoint board members immediately. The referendum follows a few years later, allowing city residents to vote "no" if they do not want the mayor-appointed board to continue.

11. The Michigan legislature held a referendum in Detroit in November 2004. Voters rejected mayoral appointment of a CEO for the school system, choosing instead to have the school district governed by a superintendent chosen by a traditional eleven-member elected school board.

Just as there are different methods of gaining legal authority to appoint a board, the resulting power structures also vary city by city. As Kirst points out, mayors may have low, low-moderate, moderate, or high influence.[12] In Oakland, for instance, Mayor Jerry Brown can appoint three of seven board members, which is not a majority. In Washington, D.C., Mayor Anthony Williams currently appoints only four of the nine members.[13] In these "partial" or "hybrid" governance systems, the mayor has greater (but not absolute) control over the board's activities. In Baltimore, a city-state partnership complicates the politics of control.[14]

At the outset then, there is a question about the precise definition of "mayoral takeover," particularly about how to model it for the purposes of the empirical analysis to follow. In this study, we measure takeover as the percentage of school board seats appointed by the mayor. This measure does not capture the nuances of the power dynamics between city hall and the school board in each city, and it is further complicated by the fact that mayors have discretion over how to use their new powers. Of the seven school districts in our sample that allow mayors to appoint school board members, Oakland and Washington restrict their mayors to less than 100 percent of the school board appointments. In Baltimore and Philadelphia, board members are jointly appointed by the mayor and governor. In Detroit too, coordination with the state legislature is a prerequisite for some major reform proposals, for example, to abolish unions for principals.[15] The personal and political preferences of mayors also interact with reform. In Baltimore, for instance, former mayor Kurt Schmoke showed more of an interest in directing the school district than did his replacement, Mayor Martin O'Malley, who has been more intently focused on crime reduction.[16]

Although nuances such as these pose a challenge to accurately quantifying the takeover phenomenon, we believe that the percentage of school board seats appointed by the mayor is a fundamental indicator of the city's school governance structure. We recognize, however, that the prominent examples of takeover in Chicago, Boston, New York, and Cleveland may be different from the rest in the sense that they provide the mayor with 100 percent control over the school board. If appointing 100 percent of school board members is markedly different from appointing a smaller majority (for example, 66 percent or 75 percent), then we would expect these four cities to perform more effectively.

---

12. Kirst (2002).
13. Mayor Williams has pushed to gain full control of the schools, commenting that "the schools ought to be under the mayor and the council. I'm ultimately accountable for what happens to the students." Craig Timberg and Justin Blum, "Williams Seeks School Takeover," *Washington Post*, September 25, 2003, p. A1.
14. Orr (1999).
15. Mirel (2004).
16. Cibulka (2003).

There is a growing literature on the politics of mayoral takeover and changing urban school board dynamics. Recognizing the need for a detailed understanding of this complicated reform measure, much of the work involves case studies of mayoral takeover cities. A volume edited by Henig and Rich includes contextually rich case studies of the politics of mayoral control. Cuban and Usdan have compiled studies from Chicago, Boston, Seattle, San Diego, Philadelphia, and Baltimore. Henig, Hula, Orr, and Pedescleaux include detailed case studies of cities led by black mayors, including Atlanta, Detroit, Baltimore, and Washington, D.C. Orr provides a detailed look at the interplay of social capital and civic capital in Baltimore schools. In previous studies we have discussed the theory of mayoral takeover at greater length and attempted to complement the case study approach with more quantitative analyses. As noted by Cuban and Usdan, no general consensus is emerging about the overall effectiveness of mayoral takeover. Although Chicago often is noted as a success, its success has been qualified, and the success of other localities has not been as strong. There remains a need for more systematic analysis of the effects of mayoral takeover.[17]

Predicted Effects of Integrated Governance

If mayors are able to overcome existing political barriers and establish a functioning integrated governance regime, we would expect to see mayoral takeover produce changes along three dimensions:

—political will (the degree to which mayors are willing to take charge and shift their political weight to support schools)

—electoral incentives (mayors' recognition that public education is an important aspect of public concern about quality-of-life issues)

—institutional capacity (management efficiency, human capital, fiscal prudence, and a more diverse pool of expertise).

In this chapter, we focus on several aspects of the third dimension, institutional capacity. We also pay close attention to the possibility that mayors may *not* be able to overcome existing barriers to reform. Entrenched interest groups such as teacher unions, established district leaders who are used to operating without interference from city hall, and citizen groups opposed to centralized management may all serve as checks against a comprehensive mayoral reform strategy. To the extent that these multiple "veto points" serve to keep the school district insulated from mayoral encroachment, the promise of integrated governance may not be fully realized.

17. Henig and Rich (2004); Cuban and Usdan (2003); Henig and others (1999); Orr (1999); Wong (1999); Wong and Shen (2002).

Management

The increase in mayors' involvement in schools is closely related to the politics of public schools at the local level and the functions that they perform. From a fiscal perspective, public schools constitute one of the largest local employers; the Chicago public school system, for example, is the second-largest public employer in the state. Furthermore, education dominates the local budget. Though in a technical sense they are not a part of the city budget in most cities, education expenses often consume roughly half of the total city tax revenues. Schools' heavy reliance on local property taxes strongly affects a city's capacity to tax and to spend. Thus when mayors take over schools, management and budget issues become a top priority. Business communities in the mayoral takeover districts have all played an instrumental role in the transformation to appointed school boards.[18]

If business leaders see mayoral takeover as analogous to a corporate takeover, it also must be acknowledged that taking over an underperforming firm does not necessarily produce a turnaround. If the fundamentals remain unchanged, mayors may not be able to generate the change they promise. In the context of the school district and the "education marketplace," if the tax base, student population, and parents (or consumers) are relatively fixed, it may be difficult to bring about systemic change. Whether mayors were able to overcome such challenges is for our analysis to answer.

In our study we consider per-pupil revenues and capital outlays; the distribution of revenue streams among federal, state, and local sources; and the overall fiscal health of the district (measured as total revenues minus total expenditures divided by total expenditures). We also track the overall level of expenditures per student, which we predict should be greater under mayoral takeover regimes, as mayors attempt to protect education budgets and demonstrate their commitment to education.[19] All the financial indicators discussed in the chapter are drawn from data collected through the Annual Survey of Government Finances.[20] The integrated governance theory predicts that mayoral takeover should be positively associated with each of these indicators.

Human Capital

In addition to improving fiscal stability, integrated governance allows central decisionmaking authorities more flexibility in terms of resource allocation. In

18. Cuban and Usdan (2003).

19. A business model of school governance will also emphasize efficiency in the educational production process, but we do not directly measure "efficiency" in our data set beyond the fiscal responsibility indicator.

20. The Annual Survey of Government Finances is conducted by the Census Bureau. The financial data for the analysis were downloaded from the bureau's website (www.census.gov/govs/www/school.html [December 1, 2004]).

particular, mayors may be able to reduce central office inefficiencies, thereby allowing for greater investments in teaching, learning, and provision of student services.[21] In terms of upgrading human capital, mayors are likely to desire greater investment in employees who have the most direct contact with students and less investment in noninstructional personnel. Like changes in the budget, successful changes in staffing allocations also must overcome significant inertia.

In particular, since mayoral takeover involves an external authority trying to permeate an existing power structure, it may be difficult to move beyond changes at the top—for example, in central office management. Washington, D.C., illustrates this inertia effect. As part of the central office transformation plan of then superintendent Paul Vance, every central office employee was given a pink slip and required to be interviewed in order to be rehired. While the district was able to bring in a new leadership team with broad experience, it ended up rehiring a majority of the rest of the middle- and lower-level central office employees. Anecdotal evidence suggests that a large number of these employees believed that they would outlast this latest wave of reform. Once again, whether a mayor can surprise such employees and bring about substantial aggregate change is a question for the analysis to address.

In this study, we looked for evidence of shifts in human capital investments in two ways. First, in terms of expenditures, if mayoral takeovers were successful in changing budgeting practices, we should see more per-pupil expenditures on instruction, student support services, and school administration services. Conversely, we would expect to see an inverse relationship with expenditures on central office and general administration services. If the budget was too unwieldy or if existing power brokers in the district could not be overcome or persuaded to cooperate, such positive effects may not have arisen. Second, we looked at staffing distributions (the actual number of employees in particular positions).[22] Here, we expected to find a successful mayoral takeover to be positively associated with the district's percentage of teachers, aides, and student support. We expected to see an inverse relationship between takeover and the percentage of administration employees and supervisors. The absence of such effects would lend credence to the alternative theory that district inertia is too much to overcome, even for mayor-appointed regimes.

---

21. Again, Chicago illustrates how this theory is put into practice. Once appointed and granted new discretionary powers, the Chicago school board eliminated the Bureau of Facilities Planning in the central office (resulting in the elimination of ten jobs), reduced the number of positions in the Department of Facilities Central Service Center by half (twenty-six of fifty positions), and reduced the number of positions related to the administration of facilities citywide from 441 to thirty-four. Contracts for providing these services are now with private companies.

22. All staffing data are supplied by the U.S. Department of Education's Common Core of Data. The CCD reports, for each district, the number of full-time equivalent employees in a number of positions: teachers, aides, instructional coordinators and supervisors, guidance counselors, librarians/media support staff, local education agency (LEA) administration, and school administration.

Confounding factors

In examining management and human capital outcomes, it is important to consider a host of confounding factors (other than mayoral takeover) that may explain the variation. The results may depend not simply on the change to a mayor-appointed board, but also on the length of time that the appointed board has been in place, especially when implementing longer-term programs. We assume that there are decreasing marginal returns associated with the duration of an appointed school board. Getting through the first two years, for instance, is likely more of an accomplishment than maintaining through years seven and eight. We therefore control for duration by including the square root of the number of years that a district has been under an appointed board.[23]

There are other factors that we do not control for but that are important to note. First, while mayoral takeover is an important aspect of city and school district governance, it is by no means the only way to characterize districts. Urban school districts also vary by school board size, at-large versus single-member district elections, and tenure of the mayor, superintendent, and board members. We performed analysis using the percent of school board members that were elected at-large, but that was not consistently significantly related to our series of outcome measures. There may also be underlying city or school district characteristics (for example, a history of strong mayors) that make a district more likely to adopt takeover. To the extent that these underlying factors also had an independent effect on the financial outcomes we consider here, our analysis would suffer in its explanatory power.

Second, even if takeover is found to have been a significant factor in explaining variations in these outcomes, it is not clear whether it is takeover per se or a particular policy that was instituted by a takeover regime. The question to consider is whether the successful policy could have been implemented just as well by an elected school board. Alternatively, it may be that the changes came not from takeover specifically but simply from the fact that takeover represents a new policy. To the extent that "just shaking up the system" would produce the same outcomes, the effects attributed to takeover would again be overstated.

As discussed later, we employed a fixed-effects model with controls for unobserved differences between districts and years. While this captures the between-district variation, we did not control for unobserved changes within the district over time. We also introduced four measures that we suspected of affecting management and human capital levels in school districts. First, we controlled for size (measured as district student enrollment). Larger districts are likely to

---

23. We do not have comparable data from non-takeover districts to estimate the number of years that alternative reform strategies have been in place. In an alternative analysis, using the simple number of years as the counter did not change the substantive results of the analysis.

enjoy economies of scale that smaller districts cannot. We would expect higher revenues. Larger districts, however, also face unique challenges and may require more assistance than provided by their local tax base. We thus would expect more revenues to flow from state and federal sources. Due to their more complex service delivery systems, larger districts may also require that a greater percentage of their resources be allocated to central office and administrative personnel. Moreover, we controlled for poverty and unemployment. School districts serving larger populations of at-risk students or operating in worse economic conditions should receive a greater percentage of their revenue from federal funds, which are frequently earmarked for redistribution. Worse-off districts may also need to allocate more resources to student services and may have a more difficult time maintaining fiscal stability. Finally, we controlled for the percentage of African American students in the school district. This helps by serving as a proxy for the high concentrations of minorities that present a special challenge to some districts, especially the older, Northern industrial cities.

Data and Methodology

To consider the relationship between mayor-appointed school boards and measures of effective management and improvements in human capital, we employed a panel data approach. Before discussing the specifics of the model, however, we must explain how we selected the districts in the sample. Determining the appropriate sample is an especially important step in the context of mayoral takeover, because it is not a policy reform designed for all school districts. Specifically, mayor-appointed boards have gained prominence as policy options in large, urban districts. Our takeover cities are dispersed throughout the hundred largest districts in the nation.[24] To determine a set of peer districts, we made use of two classifications established by the National Center for Education Statistics. First, we focused on school districts that are designated as serving "primarily the center city of a Metropolitan Statistical Area."[25] Second, we looked at large cities. Thus we restricted our analysis to the 100 largest school districts serving central cities.

We also included in this sample two school districts that had more long-standing appointed boards. In Norfolk, Virginia, the school board is appointed by the city council. In Jackson, Mississippi, the school board is appointed by the mayor in the same fashion as the construction board of adjustment or the civil commission. In our data set, we coded both of these as appointed boards, since

24. The national ranks for the districts are, in descending order: Chicago (4), Detroit (12), Baltimore City (23), Cleveland (41), Washington, D.C. (48), Boston (53), and Oakland (80). Although not in our takeover subset for the 1992–2001 period, newcomer New York City ranks first.
25. This classification is reported in the Common Core of Data, various years.

they are similarly subject to electoral accountability from the citywide electorate. City council elections, particularly at-large elections, encourage politicians to pay attention to the preferences of those who are most likely to vote. Often these preferences reflect taxpayers' concerns on fiscal and policy accountability.

If we focus on only the mayoral takeover districts, it is evident from even a comparison of summary statistics that they were different in some important regards from the rest of the cities in our dataset (table 4-1). When averaging across the mayoral takeover districts in our sample, it is evident that they were larger and spent more in order to serve student populations that were less well off and more heavily African American. We now considered whether these and other relationships hold up under a more rigorous statistical analysis.

As mentioned, the bulk of the data used for cross-sectional analysis came from the *Annual Survey of Government Finances*, conducted by the U.S. Bureau of the Census, which gathers data on revenues, expenditures, and debt from more than 15,000 school districts.[26] In addition to these financial data, we used the National Center for Education Statistics's Common Core of Data (CCD) as a source for our demographic control variables as well as data on district staffing patterns.[27] Both data sources provide data that are comparable across time and across districts.

We were thus able to construct a data set containing data from the 100 largest urban school districts, from 1992 through 2001. The timing of the first mayoral takeover (Boston in 1992) coincides well with the starting points for the two national data sets. We made adjustments for inflation, using the Bureau of Labor Statistics's constant dollar employment cost index, in order to make all dollar figures constant in 2001. Because the majority of school district expenditures are on salaries and wages, we used the index for state and local governments' educational services.[28] To adjust for geographic cost differentials, we used the geographic cost of education index (GCEI) developed by Chambers,[29] which appears to be the most applicable adjustment measure currently available.[30] The index is currently available only for three years: 1987, 1990, and 1993. On one hand, this presents a problem since our financial data are from later years. On the other hand, if the relative costs between geographies remain relatively constant over time, we should not seriously bias our findings by incorporating this index. Luckily for our analysis, one of the conclusions from

26. All of these financial data were downloaded for analysis from the Census Bureau's website (www.census.gov/govs/www/school.html [September 28, 2004]).

27. All of the CCD data were downloaded for analysis from the NCES website (http://nces.ed.gov/ccd/ccddata.asp [September 28, 2004]).

28. We also used the general CPI-U inflator produced by the Bureau of Labor Statistics, but the results of the analysis remained substantively the same.

29. Chambers (1998).

30. Fowler and Monk (2001).

Table 4-1. *Summary of Selected Variables for Takeover and Non-Takeover Districts, 2001*

District characteristics	All (N = 100)	Takeover (N = 7)	Non-takeover (N = 93)	Boston	Chicago	Cleveland	Detroit	Baltimore	Washington	Oakland
Basic demographics										
Enrollment	77,915	137,116	73,459	63,024	435,261	75,684	162,194	99,859	68,925	54,863
Percent unemployment	5.5	7.3	5.4	4.1	7.0	8.7	9.8	7.9	6.4	7.2
Percent free lunch	45.1	64.3	43.6	64.2	65.2	76.6	65.8	63.5	59.6	55.3
Percent African American	37.6	69.5	35.2	48.9	53.1	71.3	91.3	86.4	85.9	49.8
Revenue source										
Percent federal	9.4	12.5	9.1	6.4	16.7	15.7	12.2	14.9	11.0	10.5
Percent state	49.3	45.7	49.6	35.5	41.7	47.8	74.9	60.2	0.0	60.0
Percent local	41.3	41.8	41.3	58.1	41.6	36.5	12.9	24.8	89.0	29.5
Expenditures and staffing allocations										
Percent expenditures on central office	3.2	3.4	3.1	2.3	2.4	4.9	4.9	4.1	2.0	3.4
Percent of teachers on staff	51.4	55.8	51.1	52.2	84.6	53.6	44.9	59.1	43.5	52.8
Per-pupil expenditures on instruction ($)	4,912	6,853	4,766	10,718	5,421	5,669	6,599	6,108	6,880	6,576
Per-pupil expenditures on central office ($)	308	427	299	415	256	537	552	464	344	422

Source: Authors' calculations based on data from the U.S. Bureau of the Census, *Annual Survey of Government Finances*, and the National Center for Education Statistics's Common Core of Data.

Chambers's analysis is that "the patterns of geographic variations in cost do not change substantially over time and that the GECI estimated for any given year provides a reasonable estimate of the GECI for adjacent years."[31] Given this consistency across years, we did not believe that adjusting our figures with the 1993 index would seriously jeopardize the validity of our results. Put another way, by relying on this index we worked under the assumption that cities in which it was more expensive to live in 1993 remained, by and large, just as expensive in the late 1990s.

We employed a fixed-effects model, dividing our time-series (N = 10) data by cross-sectional (N = 100) data.[32] The fixed-effects model was appropriate since we believed that the fixed effects were not independent of our regressors, in particular the measure of mayoral takeover. We could control for the between-district differences that were not captured by our covariates, as well as the between-year differences that were not captured in our controls. Thus our model with district- and year-fixed effects is

$$Y_{ti} = \beta_0 + \beta_1 TAKEOVER_{ti} + \beta_2 ENROLL_{ti} + \beta_3 UNEMPLOYMENT_{ti} + \beta_4 FREE\_LUNCH_{ti} + \beta_5 AFR\text{-}AMERICAN_{ti} + \beta_6 DURATION_{ti} + \delta_t + \delta_i + \varepsilon_{ti},$$

where Y_{ti} is the management or human capital outcome measure for school district i in year t. We controlled for enrollment, student poverty level, citywide unemployment level, the percentage of African Americans in the school district, and the duration of the takeover. The effects of year and district effects are captured by δ. We also used robust standard errors, as recommended by Kezdi.[33]

Results

Given the large number of indicators used in this analysis, it is useful to begin by laying out the overall picture (table 4-2). Assessing the effects of mayoral takeover in terms of the frequency of significant relationships with either management or human capital outcome measures, it seems that there are relatively few significant relationships when we include district fixed effects. The relative lack of impact from mayoral takeover regimes on these management and staffing outcomes provides support for the theory that existing power structures within the school district may make it difficult for integrated governance to fully occur.

Although top management may be integrated, the middle and lower strata of district operations may remain insulated from city hall and the changes that the

31. Chambers (1998, p. x).
32. Discussion of the model follows that provided by Davidson and MacKinnon (1993, pp. 320–25).
33. Kezdi (2002).

Table 4-2. *Summary of Significant Relationships between Mayoral Takeover and Selected Indicators of Management and Human Capital* [a]

District characteristics	Mean	Standard deviation	Base	Year fixed effects	Year and district fixed effects
Takeover and control variables					
Percent board members appointed	7.74	25.87			
Enrollment	75,917	124,454			
Percent unemployment	6.15	2.96			
Percent free lunch	44.88	16.80			
Percent African American	36.35	25.74			
Fiscal stability					
Fiscal health	0.01	0.07	–	–	–
Cash funds (thousands of dollars)	1,496	1,427			
Revenue source					
Percent federal	8.78	2.96			
Percent state	49.64	15.22			
Percent local	41.59	16.21			
Per-pupil expenditures					
Instruction	3,858	1,348	+	+	–
Capital outlay	708	548	–	+	–
General administration	101	87			
School administration	374	143	+	+	
Central office	221	181	+	+	
Staffing allocation (percentage of all district employees)					
Teachers	53.98	9.99			
Aides	10.20	4.58			
Student support	2.29	2.31			
Administration	3.30	3.00			
Supervisors	0.78	0.83			
Expenditure distribution (percentage of all district expenditures)					
Instruction	52.45	5.12	+	+	
Capital outlay	9.30	5.84	–	–	–
General administration	1.36	0.99			
School administration	5.12	1.15			
Central office	2.92	2.25			

Source: Author's calculations based on data from the U.S. Bureau of the Census, *Annual Survey of Government Finances,* and the National Center for Education Statistics's Common Core of Data.

a. $N = 100$. "+" indicates a statistically significant and positive relationship, at least $p < .10$. "–" indicates a statistically significant and inverse relationship. Blank cells indicate no statistically significant effects.

mayor wishes to bring about. Keeping in mind that mayor-appointed boards have generally been introduced to districts that are at or near "bankruptcy," it may be unrealistic to expect to see sizeable changes in the aggregate figures so quickly. In our data set, only Chicago and Boston had more than five years of governance under mayor-appointed boards. It may be too early to see differences. Despite the prevalence of null findings, we do find several intriguing significant relationships, which we now discuss in more detail.

Management

When assessing management, we find that there is an inverse relationship between appointed school boards and district fiscal health (table 4-3). Although the magnitude of the effect is quite small, it appears that mayoral takeover did not bring with it the increased financial stability it promised. Perhaps one explanation for the diversion from our prediction is that mayoral takeover regimes are interested in increasing expenditures, focusing on long-term school district goals rather than matching revenues and expenditures each year. It may also be that it takes these districts more than a few years to get their books in order. Both of these explanations find some support in the fact that the duration variable is positively related to fiscal health: the longer a takeover regime is in place, the better the district's fiscal health. That the duration measure is consistently significantly related to additional management outcomes suggests that it takes time for organizations to adjust to the new governance arrangements.

Related to revenue streams, when we control for duration of the appointed board, it is not takeover per se but the duration of the takeover that is positively related to state funding and inversely related to revenue from local funding (table 4-3). The magnitude of this change is rather small. One plausible explanation for both the small magnitude and direction of these revenue effects is that mayors would like to avoid local property tax increases and shift education burdens to the state, but state legislatures (the other half of the takeover political dynamic) are not willing to go along with such efforts. Although mayors may pursue a "politics of grantsmanship" at the state level, attempting to demonstrate to state officials that mayor-appointed boards can be successful, these mayors may need more time to make their arguments convincing.

When we examine the level of expenditures on instruction, capital outlay, general administration, school administration, and the central office, we find that there are inverse relationships with spending levels on both instruction and capital outlays (table 4-4).[34] Our results predict that increasing the proportion of appointed board members from 0 percent to 50 percent will reduce spending on

---

34. When we look at the allocation of expenditures and not just the level amount, we see a similar relationship (also small in magnitude) between mayor-appointed boards and spending on capital outlay.

Table 4-3. *Relationship between Mayoral Takeover and School District Fiscal Health and Revenue Sources, Fixed Effects Model, Including Duration*[a]

District characteristics	Fiscal health	Percent of revenues from federal sources	Percent of revenues from state sources	Percent of revenues from local sources
Mayoral takeover	−0.092**	0.008	−0.003	−0.005
	(0.042)	(0.007)	(0.011)	(0.011)
Enrollment	2.87E-07	−5.7E-08	2.67E-07	−2.1E-07
	(2.52E-07)	(5.93E-08)	(1.88E-07)	(1.86E-07)
Unemployment	0.0006	0.001***	−0.002	0.000
	(0.0024)	(4.90E-04)	(2.10E-03)	(2.20E-03)
Percent free lunch	−0.104**	−0.012	0.146***	−0.133***
	(0.044)	(0.009)	(0.026)	(0.025)
Percent African American	0.014	0.048**	0.073	−0.121
	(0.083)	(0.023)	(0.083)	(0.074)
Duration of takeover	0.054***	0.00	0.007***	−0.007***
	(0.020)	(0.002)	(0.002)	(0.002)
Constant	.029	0.066***	0.396***	0.539***
	(.038)	(0.009)	(0.033)	(0.031)
Summary statistic				
N	1,000	1,000	1,000	1,000
R^2	.2908	0.8451	0.929	0.9348
F statistic	2.07	5.48	6.96	6.52

Source: Authors' calculations.

a. *** $p \leq .01$; ** $p \leq .05$; * $p \leq .1$. Robust standard errors are reported in parentheses. District and year fixed effects included for all models. N represents "district years" (ten years by 100 districts).

capital outlay by about $225, or 0.4 of a standard deviation. Our results also predict that moving from a 0 percent to a 50 percent share of appointees will result in a drop of more than $2,200 per pupil on instructional expenditures, a change of 1.5 standard deviations. At the same time, however, both measures of spending are positively related to the *duration* of the mayor-appointed board. This may again raise the possibility that it is the stability ushered in by mayor-appointed boards that offers the greatest promise for reallocation of funds. It may also be related to the fact that state legislatures are willing to give the mayor more control but not necessarily more funds in the initial phase of reform. When the Illinois legislature passed a bill in 1995 giving Mayor Richard Daley control of Chicago's school system, it was clearly communicated that no additional dollars would be attached. In other words, takeover has been seen as a fiscally neutral reform from the state perspective. Some state lawmakers also argue that it is up to the mayors to provide evidence of improvement before they will give a district more money.

Table 4-4. *Relationship between Mayoral Takeover and Per-Pupil Spending by Spending Category, Fixed-Effects Model, including Duration*[a]

District characteristics	Instruction	Capital outlay	General admin-istration	School admin-istration	Central office
			Per-pupil expenditures		
Mayoral takeover	−1.163***	−0.635***	0.030	−0.052	−0.029
	(0.377)	(0.221)	(0.057)	(0.043)	(0.078)
Enrollment	2.51E-06	2.60E-06*	−6.29E-07**	−7.04E-07***	1.84E-07
	(2.65E-06)	(1.45E-06)	(2.71E-07)	(2.63E-07)	(4.76E-07)
Unemployment	−0.056***	−0.028*	−0.0001	0.001	−0.008*
	(0.015)	(0.016)	(0.0022)	(0.003)	(0.005)
Percent free lunch	−0.362*	0.115	0.125***	−0.046	0.022
	(0.191)	(0.266)	(0.031)	(0.034)	(0.060)
Percent African American	1.658***	−2.003***	0.064	0.135**	−0.764***
	(0.385)	(0.568)	(0.065)	(0.061)	(0.194)
Duration	0.845***	0.495***	−0.005	0.032	−0.024
	(0.201)	(0.150)	(0.034)	(0.022)	(0.043)
Constant	3.019***	1.179***	0.075**	0.319***	0.473***
	(0.246)	(0.291)	(0.035)	(0.042)	(0.079)
Summary statistic					
N	1,000	1,000	1,000	1,000	1,000
R^2	0.9589	0.5023	0.6899	0.8735	0.6478
F statistic	195.37	16.59	3.98	64.28	13.84

Source: Authors' calculations.

a. *** $p \le .01$; ** $p \le .05$; * $p \le .1$. Robust standard errors are reported in parentheses. District and year fixed effects included for all models. N represents "district years" (ten years by 100 districts).

Human Capital

Switching to our human capital indicators, it appears that district employees also may be insulated from sweeping changes brought about in a mayoral takeover. We find that mayor-appointed school boards are not significantly related to increases in the percentage of district staff who are teachers, aides, supervisors, or administrative or student support staff (table 4-5). Although takeover districts hope to adopt a corporate model of school governance and to "transform" the central office, these findings may suggest that the mayor has diminishing direct effects on human capital as we move down the organizational structure and out of the district's central offices. These organizational constraints are not a surprise, as large urban school systems are complex, multilayered institutions with existing cultures and practices. The duration of the takeover reform is likely to be important in changing long-standing practices.

These null findings on human capital impact are in contrast to the expectations generated by our theory on integrated governance regimes. The mayor's

Table 4-5. *Relationship between Mayoral Takeover and Staffing Allocations, Fixed-Effects Model, including Duration*[a]

District characteristics	Percent of staff allocations				
	Teachers	Aides	Super-visors	Admin-istration	Student support
Mayoral takeover	0.034	0.006	0.007	0.013	0.009
	(0.035)	(0.016)	(0.006)	(0.008)	(0.008)
Enrollment	3.96E-07	1.79E-07	–4.2E-08	8.07E-08	–1.98E-07***
	(4.26E-07)	(1.94E-07)	(2.66E-08)	(9.91E-08)	(6.18E-08)
Unemployment	0.004	0.002 *	0	–0.001**	–0.001
	(0.003)	(0.001)	(0)	(0.001)	(0.001)
Percent free lunch	0.025	0.01	–0.004	–0.003	0.014**
	(0.052)	(0.02)	(0.004)	(0.01)	(0.007)
Percent African American	–0.15	0.02	0.006	0.046**	0.014
	(0.094)	(0.032)	(0.006)	(0.018)	(0.014)
Duration	0.018***	–0.005	0.001	–0.004**	0.002
	(0.006)	(0.003)	(0.001)	(0.002)	(0.002)
Constant	0.551***	0.070***	0.007**	0.023**	0.029***
	(0.051)	(0.019)	(0.003)	(0.01)	(0.01)
Summary statistic					
N	1,000	1,000	1,000	1,000	1,000
R^2	0.4059	0.6182	0.7571	0.7571	0.7598
F statistic	6.41	3.36	1.65	2.08	4.99

Source: Authors' calculations.

a. *** $p \leq .01$; ** $p \leq .05$; * $p \leq .1$. Robust standard errors are reported in parentheses. District and year fixed effects included for all models. N represents "district years" (ten years by 100 districts).

office takes into consideration the interest of the city as a whole, and schools are constrained by the broad community and institutional context, such as gangs, crime, health, and so forth. We therefore would expect that in order to turn around failing schools, mayor-appointed school boards would be more likely to allocate more supportive staff to combat social problems in the immediate school environment. For example, mayor-appointed school boards instituted vision tests in inner-city schools when they found that many elementary students could not follow the materials presented on the blackboard. That such anecdotes do not correspond to shifts in the aggregate staffing numbers may again suggest that, to borrow Hess's description, mayors may find themselves swinging a pick-axe rather than driving a bulldozer.[35] In other words, policy improvement in a particular locale may not provide sufficient evidence to enable us to confidently generalize about the impact of the reform nationwide.

35. Hess (2002).

Conclusion

This chapter set out to introduce the emerging policy of mayor-appointed school boards, focusing on some of its expected effects under the theory of integrated governance. In this chapter, we have updated our previous study of the effects of mayoral takeover. Now, as then, we must point out that there is an evidence gap in fully addressing the question of reform effects. The empirical tests are always in need of further refinement and more years of observation of data under a takeover regime. With that caveat out of the way, however, the analysis using our updated and expanded takeover database suggests to us that there are several noteworthy trends.

The lack of a consistent, significant relationship between mayoral takeover and our host of management and staffing outcome measures suggests that mayors are facing significant barriers as they attempt to introduce integrated governance into their city school districts. Although district managers put in place by mayors may speak with much enthusiasm about their work—and although there certainly are anecdotal examples of positive change—our analysis suggests that when aggregated across districts at the national level, takeover has not yet changed fundamental district operations. It may be that mayoral takeovers have not yet been able to fully integrate city hall and school district operations.

This leads us to the other notable finding that emerges from the analysis: the importance of the duration variable on several outcomes. That the length of the takeover regime is significantly related to expenditure and staffing outcomes suggests that mayors may be able to bring about change if they have the time they need to form the type of broad-based support required for sustained reform efforts.[36]

It is also likely that our measurement of takeover has glossed over some important management details. One aspect of mayoral takeover that likely bears on the outcomes that we measure but that we cannot adequately quantify is the management style of the CEOs that mayors put in charge of their districts. Many have anecdotally observed that big cities have turned to "outsiders" to run their school systems.[37] But in Chicago, former CEO Paul Vallas was successful in part because he was a political insider.[38] To the extent that our findings suggest that inertia may prevent mayors and their appointed managers from introducing sweeping changes in district staffing and expenditures, political bargaining may be an important prerequisite for success.

There remains much work for educational policy analysts on the mayoral takeover front. As more mayors turn to this policy reform as a tool to improve

36. Henig and others (1999).
37. See, for example, Hurwitz (2001).
38. Russo (2003).

schools, it is our hope that more educational policy analysts will also begin to investigate the effects of mayor-appointed boards. Specifically, we feel that more attention should be paid to student achievement outcomes and the specific nature of the governance structure in practice:

Develop cross-district achievement measures. The most important task for researchers is to establish credible methods for determining the relationship between mayoral takeover and achievement. This is all the more important given that our results here suggest that management changes seem to be mixed. While one method is to continue to track district performance (as we have done in previous studies), we would like to see takeover included as an independent variable to explain achievement levels across different districts. This would require a comparable cross-district achievement measure.

Determine additional political measures of takeover. It is apparent that although mayors may be given more control of the schools on paper, not all mayors take full advantage. While Mayor Thomas Menino in Boston and Mayor Daley in Chicago are seen as the exemplars, not all mayors have been such power brokers. In Cleveland, for instance, former mayor Michael White allowed district superintendent Barbara Byrd Bennett much autonomy. Further classification of the actual mayor-district relationship would enable researchers to uncover more nuanced relationships between governance structure and outcomes. To make these data useful for multivariate, cross-district analysis, we would need to evaluate the mayor-schools relationship in all of the largest urban districts, not simply those where the most changes in governance structure have occurred.

As more data continue to become available, we believe that our framework for evaluation will produce more interesting results. Especially if duration of the takeover is a key explanatory variable, we would expect to see more substantive results in subsequent analyses. Isolating the specific effects of mayoral takeover is a difficult task, but given that so many urban systems continue to turn to their mayors for help, researchers need to develop better tools to evaluate precisely what it is that those mayors have contributed to improving education.

References

Chambers, Jay G. 1998. *Geographic Variation in Public Schools' Costs.* NCES Working Paper 98-04. Washington: National Center for Education Statistics.

Cibulka, James. 1999. "Moving toward an Accountable System of K–12 Education: Alternative Approaches and Challenges." In *Handbook of Educational Policy,* edited by Gregory Cizek. San Diego: Academic Press.

———. 2003. "The City-State Partnership to Reform Baltimore's Public Schools." In *Powerful Reforms with Shallow Roots: Improving America's Urban Schools,* edited by L. Cuban and M. Usdan. Teachers College Press.

Cuban, L., and M. Usdan, eds. 2003. *Powerful Reforms with Shallow Roots: Improving America's Urban Schools.* Teachers College Press.

Dahl, R. A. 1961. *Who Governs? Democracy and Power in an American City.* Yale University Press.

Davidson, Russell, and James G. MacKinnon. 1993. *Estimation and Inference in Econometrics.* New York: Oxford University Press.

Fowler, W. J., Jr., and D. H. Monk. 2001. "A Primer for Making Cost Adjustments in Education: An Overview." In *Selected Papers in School Finance, 2000-01,* edited by William J. Fowler Jr. Washington: National Center for Education Statistics.

Henig, J. R, and others. 1999. *The Color of School Reform: Race, Politics, and The Challenge of Urban Education.* Princeton University Press.

Henig, J. R., and W. C. Rich, eds. 2004. *Mayors in the Middle: Politics, Race, and Mayoral Control of Urban Schools.* Princeton University Press.

Hess, F. M. 2002. *Revolution at the Margins: The Impact of Competition on Urban School Systems.* Brookings.

Hurwitz, S. 2001. "The Outsiders." *American School Board Journal* 188 (6): 10–15.

Kezdi, G. 2002. "Robust Standard Error Estimation in Fixed-Effects Panel Models." Working paper. University of Michigan, Department of Economics.

Kirst, M. W. 2002. *Mayoral Influence, New Regimes, and Public School Governance.* CPRE Research Report Series RR-049. Consortium for Policy Research in Education, University of Pennsylvania Graduate School of Education.

Mirel, J. 2004. "Detroit: 'There Is Still a Long Road to Travel, and Success Is Far from Assured.'" In *Mayors in the Middle: Politics, Race, and Mayoral Control of Urban Schools,* edited by J. R. Henig and W. C. Rich. Princeton University Press.

Orr, M. 1999. *Black Social Capital: The Politics of School Reform in Baltimore, 1986–1998.* University Press of Kansas.

Peterson, P. E. 1981. *City Limits.* University of Chicago Press.

Russo, A. 2003. "Political Educator." *Education Next* 3 (1): 38–43.

Saiger, A. J. 2004. "Taking Over: Federalism, Deterrence, and the Search for Educational Accountability." Ph. D. dissertation, Princeton University (January).

Tyack, David. 1974. *The One Best System: A History of American Urban Education.* Harvard University Press.

Wong, K. K. 1992. "The Politics of Urban Education as a Field of Study: An Interpretive Analysis." In *The Politics of Urban Education in the United States: The 1991 Yearbook of the Politics of Education Association,* edited by James Cibulka, Rodney Reed, and K. K. Wong. Washington: Falmer Press.

———. 1999. *Funding Public Schools: Politics and Policy.* University Press of Kansas.

———. 2000. "Big Change Questions: Chicago School Reform: From Decentralization to Integrated Governance." *Journal of Educational Change* 1 (1): 97–105.

Wong, K. K., and F. X. Shen. 2002. "Does School District Takeover Work? Assessing the Effectiveness of City and State Takeover as a School Reform Strategy." *State Education Standard* (Spring): 19–23.

———. 2003. "Measuring the Effectiveness of City and State Takeover as a School Reform Strategy." *Peabody Journal of Education* 78 (4): 89–119.

Ziebarth, T. 2002. "State Takeovers and Reconstitutions." Policy Brief. Prepared for the Education Commission of the States. Available at www.ecs.org.

5

Desegregation and School Board Politics: The Limits of Court-Imposed Policy Change

LUIS RICARDO FRAGA, NICK RODRIGUEZ, AND BARI ANHALT ERLICHSON

It is difficult to imagine a Supreme Court decision more consistent with the promise of American democracy than *Brown* v. *Board of Education of Topeka, Kansas,* in 1954.[1] By finally declaring unconstitutional the overwhelming disparity between the educational opportunities offered to many African Americans and those offered to whites, the United States was given yet another chance to make available to all its citizens the unlimited prospects for upward mobility and political incorporation that are the foundation of any meaningful understanding of inclusive citizenship. Not since Reconstruction had a major institution of national government forced America to take such a hard look at itself in the mirror of history.

Nonetheless, it took less than a year for this promise to come up against the overwhelming challenge of implementation, which has always been the key to making any meaningful shift in public policy.[2] Courts decide cases and legislators

---

1. We are not, of course, suggesting that the United States was founded solely on the basis of principles of individual liberalism and civic republicanism, which historically have served as the means through which inclusive citizenship has applied to more and more Americans over the course of history. We are informed by Rogers Smith that "ascriptive inegalitarianism" is just as significant a founding principle and factor in the continuing evolution of American democracy (Smith 1996). In fact, *Brown* v. *Board of Education* can be understood as a major attempt by the United States to overcome the application of ascriptive inegalitarianism in regard to race; *Brown* v. *Board of Education of Topeka, KS,* 347 U.S. 483, 74 S. Ct. 686, 98 L. Ed. 873 (1954).

2. *Brown* v. *Board of Education of Topeka, KS.* 349 U.S. 294, 75 St. Ct. 753, 99 L. Ed. 1083 (1955).

enact laws, but in the American federal system, administrators must implement policy in order to make it a reality for all citizens. Disappointingly, recent data regarding the resegregation of public schools on the basis of race—made even more dramatic by the concomitant rise of social class segregation—demonstrate that U.S. public schools may be just as vulnerable today as they were in 1954 to the charge of institutionalizing inequality of educational opportunity.[3] Why has it been so difficult for the United States to maintain the consensus necessary to achieve inclusive citizenship, the concept at the heart of *Brown v. Board of Education*? Why has finding the most effective way to promote equal educational opportunity for all racial and ethnic groups been such an elusive goal?

One reason that has received little attention from legal scholars and social scientists is electoral politics and the implementation of post–court order school board policy. The success of any attempt to enhance educational opportunity through desegregation depends on the commitment of direct service providers like superintendents, principals, and teachers.[4] No other official is as directly responsible for determining the tone, direction, and expectations of the school system—especially those of its principals and teachers—as the superintendent of schools. Whatever the commitment of judges, plaintiffs and their attorneys, scholars, and community leaders to the laudable goal of enhancing educational opportunity for African American, Hispanic, and other historically segregated students, achieving that goal is fundamentally dependent on the corresponding commitment of a school district superintendent and the administrators, principals, and teachers to whom the superintendent assigns responsibility for policy implementation. Moreover, in most school districts across the country it is the school board that appoints the superintendent.[5] Even more important, the superintendent serves at the pleasure of the board. As a result, the policy and related electoral politics of the school board can greatly influence the likelihood that an entire district will or will not commit itself to the broad educational goals underlying the court-ordered desegregation of schools.[6]

In this chapter, we use school desegregation in the San Francisco Unified School District (SFUSD) to demonstrate both the great promise of *Brown v. Board of Education* and what have become overwhelming obstacles to its full realization. Key among those obstacles have been the evolving policy and electoral factionalism of the San Francisco board of education. The focus on San

3. Orfield (2001).

4. Tyack and Cuban (1995).

5. A new trend is for city mayors to have sole authority to appoint superintendents, a relatively new phenomenon in school politics in the United States. See chapter 4 of this volume, by Kenneth K. Wong and Francis X. Shen.

6. This point is in noticeable contrast to recommendations made by Sandler and Schoenbrod (2003) in their critique of court-ordered decrees. We assess the validity of these authors' assumptions in our conclusion.

Francisco as a foundational case study is appropriate because this city, like few other places in the country, represented one of the greatest opportunities to finally implement desegregation in a way that was fully consistent with the expectations of *Brown.* A judge who was sympathetic to desegregation pushed the parties in *NAACP* v. *San Francisco Unified School District et al.* (1978)— which included the San Francisco chapter of the National Association for the Advancement of Colored People (NAACP), the SFUSD, and the California Department of Education—to reach agreement on important elements associated with the desegregation of San Francisco's schools.[7] Although enrollment desegregation was a key goal of the consent decree ultimately accepted in 1983, a parallel goal was to enhance the academic achievement of all students, especially African Americans, in the district. Moreover, the policy mechanism of reconstitution, directed by the superintendent, was the means used to promote the school reform necessary to increase academic achievement.[8] In addition, a majority of the SFUSD school board agreed to the decree, as did the superintendent.

The comprehensive scope of desegregation in San Francisco did not develop by chance. The suit that led to the consent decree was originally filed twenty-five years after *Brown* v. *Board of Education,* and attorneys for both the NAACP and the SFUSD had learned from failed desegregation attempts in other cities. These attorneys appreciated that if desegregation efforts in San Francisco led to white flight and perpetuated in-school segregation, for example, through tracking of educational achievement, the position of African American children in San Francisco would not improve substantially.[9] Clearly a type of political learning had occurred that led to policy innovations that had rarely been tried.[10] In addition, the funding for both desegregation and enhancement of academic achievement was to be provided by the state of California. Substantial resources were available to make the hope of desegregation and the expected increase in academic achievement a reality. However, it is noteworthy that the court-imposed policy change did not specify collaborative roles for either the board of education or the teacher unions. We will demonstrate that this was, perhaps, a fatal omission.

---

7. *NAACP v. SFUSD et al.,* No. C-78-1445 WHO; 484 F. Supp. 657 (1978). In 1962 the NAACP filed *Brock v. Board of Education,* 71034 (N.D. Calif., October 2, 1962). It did not pursue the case when the SFUSD made some initial attempts to desegregate schools.

8. Reconstitution refers to the practice of changing the administration and teaching staff at a school that is identified as low performing. In San Francisco this occurred most often one year after a school had been put on notice that it was a target for reconstitution. Reconstitution can also be referred to as zero-based staffing. For a full discussion of the scope of reconstitution in the SFUSD, see Erlichson and Fraga (2004).

9. On white flight, see Orfield (1987); on tracking, see England, Meier, and Fraga (1988).

10. Heclo (1994).

The 1983 Consent Decree

The 1983 consent decree has been the driving force behind desegregation efforts in San Francisco. However, the lawsuit that resulted in the decree, *NAACP* v. *San Francisco Unified School District et al.,* was the culmination of efforts that began as early as 1962 to address the concerns of civil rights groups and civic associations regarding several city schools whose enrollment was almost 100 percent African American.

In response to a lawsuit spearheaded by then Mayor Joseph Alioto to end all efforts to desegregate schools on the basis of race,[11] the NAACP filed *Johnson* v. *SFUSD.*[12] In May 1971, Judge Stanley A. Weigel issued an order to desegregate San Francisco's elementary schools within sixteen months. The district's Horseshoe Plan was implemented on time during the 1971–72 school year.[13]

In 1975, Robert Alioto—no relation to the mayor—was appointed superintendent of SFUSD. Alioto designed a new plan to desegregate the schools that focused on restructuring the grade levels, capping at 40 to 45 percent the proportion of a school's student population composed of any one ethnic or racial group, and requiring the enrollment in each school to include at least four ethnic groups. Judge Weigel dismissed the NAACP's suit in *Johnson* without prejudice on June 22, 1978, without ruling on the constitutionality of Alioto's desegregation plan. Weigel decided that both sides had been lax in their oversight of the implementation of his court order. He also stated that too many other factors, including student enrollment, school governance, school administration, and legal standards, had changed since his first judgment in 1971.[14]

Eight days after Judge Weigel dismissed the NAACP's *Johnson* case, lawyers from the national office of the NAACP filed *NAACP* v. *San Francisco Unified School District et al.* on behalf of three African American students residing in the still-segregated Bayview–Hunter's Point neighborhood. The case was assigned to Judge William Orrick. The plaintiffs in the case argued that the district's enrollment process was to blame for the continued school segregation in Hunter's Point despite some success in desegregating schools in other parts of the city.

In May of 1982, after several years of legal maneuvering, the court appointed a group of eight people to make plans for a settlement and to submit its recommendations to the court. After six months of negotiating, the parties finally submitted a consent decree to the court, and in May 1983 the court declared it to be "fair, reasonable, and adequate."[15]

11. *Nelson* v. *San Francisco Unified School District*, No. 618-643, San Francisco Superior Court, June 15, 1970.
12. *Johnson* v. *SFUSD*, 339 F. Supp. 1315, 1325–27 (N.D. Calif. 1970, 1971).
13. Kirp (1982, p. 108).
14. Kirp (1982, p. 113).
15. Consent Decree, *NAACP* v. *SFUSD*, Civ. No. C-78-1445 WHO, 576 F. Supp. 34 (1983).

The consent decree was extensive, detailing a wide range of areas that required action, including student segregation, faculty segregation, school discipline, and academic achievement. However, two elements of the decree were most important. First, enrollment desegregation was to be achieved by categorizing students into nine racial groups (Spanish-surname, Other White, Other Non-White, Japanese, Chinese, Filipino, Korean, African American, and Native American) and making sure that each school in the district contained students from four of these groups and that no school had more than 40 to 45 percent of any one group.[16] The district maintained a great deal of flexibility in the specific design of the desegregation plan. The second major element of the decree was the goal of enhancing the academic achievement of African American students. This was equal to the goal of enrollment desegregation, and it was considered the major innovation of the desegregation plan. The decree even specified the mechanism through which academic enhancement was to be achieved:

> The S.F.U.S.D. shall declare all staff and administrative positions in the Bayview–Hunter's Point schools open, and shall reconstitute the staff and administration of those schools on the basis of a desegregation plan developed by the S.F.U.S.D. and submitted to the court. The plan shall specify changes in attendance boundaries and methods for selecting staff and administrators appropriate to the new educational programs. The plan shall provide for the assignment of administrators who are strong instructional leaders, with sufficient administrative support.[17]

Initially five schools in Bayview–Hunter's Point and one in the Mission, an area of the city heavily populated by Hispanics, were targeted for the reform mechanism that became known as *reconstitution*. Four schools were reconstituted: Charles Drew Elementary, Sir Francis Drake Elementary, George Washington Carver Elementary, and Horace Mann Middle School. Two new schools also were opened: Martin Luther King Jr. Middle School and Philip Burton High School.

The decree sought to incorporate lessons learned from other cities' efforts at desegregation. It required state officials to prevent students from transferring to suburban schools as a way to avoid attending desegregated city schools, and it prevented the U.S. Department of Defense from providing transportation to military dependents to attend private schools. The decree also required the district to collaborate with housing officials to promote integration in public housing, and it obligated the state to fund substantial portions of the costs associated with desegregation.[18]

16. The percentage varied depending on whether the school was designated an alternative school or simply a neighborhood school. The limit was placed at 40 percent for alternative schools and 45 percent for neighborhood schools.

17. Consent Decree, p. 17.

18. Consent Decree, pp. 24–25, 29–33.

In sum, the consent decree was comprehensive in that it made enrollment desegregation and enhancing academic achievement equal goals and also in that it empowered all of the parties to the decree to feel that they could affect the overall development of the desegregation process in San Francisco. Attorneys for the NAACP would now be players in the development and evaluation of the decree. The state department of education would pay for most of the expenses incurred under the decree, but payment would be on a reimbursement basis, giving the department the opportunity to fully review all that the SFUSD did. The district received the additional funding from the state (which throughout the 1990s averaged approximately $30 million a year). Most important, the superintendent was allowed to promote school reform in targeted schools through school reconstitution and thereby was given considerable discretion to reassign principals and teachers as he or she saw fit. Notice that neither the school board nor the teacher unions were explicitly included as participants in implementing the decree.

Desegregation and School Board Politics

How did the implementation of the consent decree evolve? What specific role did the school board play in affecting the course of that evolution? Our analysis of the relationship between the politics on the board of education and implementation of the consent decree from 1983 to 2003 reveals that there were nine years of clear commitment to the goals of the decree and eleven years of very weak support. Two superintendents, Robert Alioto (1975–85) and Waldemar "Bill" Rojas (1992–99) were active supporters; Carlos Cornejo (1985–86), Ramon Cortines (1986–92), and superintendent Arlene Ackerman (2001–03) displayed weak support and at times made pointed criticisms of the decree.[19]

In a way largely beyond the reach of court authority, the decree led to significant divisions among members of the school board that structured board politics. Most interesting was the support provided by the San Francisco branch of the California Federation of Teachers (CFT) and later by the combined United Educators of San Francisco (UESF), which was key to maintaining a consistent block of school board members who were critical of important elements of the decree.[20]

We are not suggesting that board members and teacher unions that gave the greatest support to board members who were most critical of the decree worked

19. Throughout this period, the SFUSD has been governed by a seven-member board, elected at large, for four-year terms. These terms are staggered; three members are elected at one two-year interval and four others are elected at the next two-year interval. There are no term limits. Arlene Ackerman is still the SFUSD superintendent. Our study goes only through 2003.

20. In 1990 the San Francisco branches of the California Teachers' Association and the California Federation of Teachers combined to become the United Educators of San Francisco (UESF). This is discussed in more detail later in the chapter.

to promote the increased segregation of racial and ethnic minority students in San Francisco schools. They were, however, very much against those provisions that gave great authority and effective power to the superintendent to make decisions on important matters involving the assignment of administrators, teachers, and students. The strategic decision in the decree—to secure the support of district administrators by enhancing the superintendent's powers—provided the superintendent with more opportunities to be creative in implementing the decree. However, this provision also gave the superintendent the capacity to limit responsiveness to the decree when that seemed to be the direction desired by a majority of the board.

What follows is an analysis of the politics of the San Francisco board of education as they relate to support for the superintendent and to his or her commitment to the provisions of the consent decree.[21] We ordered the analysis according to the terms of the five superintendents who have served in San Francisco since the decree was adopted in 1983. We did this for several reasons. First, although one can generalize about board politics over time, board politics is specific to the particular superintendent in office. A superintendent's personality and leadership style set parameters within which issues are negotiated between the board (and its varying majorities) and the superintendent. Second, boards operate in a path-dependent reality. Decisions made in earlier periods of time can largely define both the opportunities and the constraints that exist in the current context. This is especially so in the case of board electoral politics, in which candidates often run in favor of or in direct opposition to decisions made in the immediate past by previous board members. Third, perhaps the most significant policy decision made by any board is who the superintendent—the chief implementer of policy—will be. No other policy decision is as likely to set the direction of educational policy. In sum, this analysis allows us to appreciate the consistent power of the San Francisco board, as structured by its relationship with its superintendent, and to see how, despite court expectations, it was able to control much of the pace and scope of the implementation of the decree without any substantial court review.

Robert Alioto, 1975–85

The 1983 consent decree had arisen in part because of allegations that Robert Alioto, along with other district leaders, had largely neglected the segregated schools in the city's Bayview–Hunter's Point area. Community leaders blamed Alioto, and he, in turn, blamed community leaders for their unwillingness to

21. The following discussion is based on a thorough review of all online newspaper articles in the *San Francisco Chronicle* and the *San Francisco Examiner* from 1980 to 2003 (articles from the *Examiner* have not been cited in this chapter). It is supplemented by interviews with major decisionmakers active at various periods of time. A fuller discussion of the methodology used to identify and categorize the articles is available from the senior author.

engage in dialogue. Still, Alioto reached an understanding with NAACP leaders in negotiations over the suit, and many observers said that the settlement was reached only because NAACP leaders had come to "trust" Alioto.

In the early part of 1983, the final consent decree was approved. Alioto claimed that it would solve the problems regarding desegregation and the racial achievement gap while holding mandatory busing to a minimum. The essential mechanism for education reform was to be reconstitution, which would be applied to the Hunter's Point schools in an effort to make them more attractive to white and other non–African American students.

After a successful negotiation to increase teacher salaries by 6 percent, Alioto committed himself to the full implementation of the consent decree in March 1983. The initial plan was to use money provided by the state to reconstitute and improve the quality of several Hunter's Point schools and to start new schools in the area. Nonetheless, after Governor George Deukmejian (R) vetoed state money for desegregation, the NAACP filed contempt of court charges against both the district and the state for implementing the plan too slowly, stating that the district had a mandate, with or without the money, to move faster.[22]

Despite this setback, Alioto persisted in his commitment to the Hunter's Point schools. It would later be asserted by critics that he ran the schools under the consent decree "like a separate district."[23] He took liberties in their management, cutting through much of the usual red tape to ensure that they were provided with the resources they needed to improve. Alioto's management approach was, for detractors like board member Myra Kopf, a further sign of an arrogant style of leadership. His actions also had a negative impact on one of his long-time supporters, board member Rosario Anaya. Alioto rarely consulted the board regarding his plans for the Hunter's Point schools.[24]

That alone might not have been enough to turn Anaya against Alioto. However, Anaya also had a very strong interest in protecting her Hispanic constituency and other students in socioeconomically disadvantaged neighborhoods. To the extent that Alioto focused primarily on schools in an area that served a limited population of mostly African American students, Anaya would come to fault him for failing to try to correct overall academic disparities between rich and poor students throughout the district.

Alioto's work on reconstitution clearly gave his opponents ammunition with which to attack him during the election cycle of 1984. In particular, Libby Denebeim and Myra Kopf, his two most consistent critics on the board, worked with a coalition of disgruntled, mostly white parents and teachers to support a challenger, JoAnne Miller, to oust aging board member Eugene Hopp. Miller, a white parent in the district, ran hard as the only potential board member who

22. *San Francisco Chronicle* (hereafter, SFC), May 10, 1983.
23. SFC, May 21, 1983.
24. SFC, June 13, 1984.

had children in the SFUSD schools. She ducked the issue of support for Alioto, claiming that she was unaligned even as the press speculated about her potential to tip the board against the embattled superintendent. In the end, her work paid off: in November, she managed to take Hopp's seat on the board. Incumbents Ben Tom, Richard Cerbatos, and Libby Denebeim were reelected. Going into office, Miller claimed that she would not join the anti-Alioto faction, but she did say that she had "reservations about how he deals with people." Within six months, those "reservations" would help to polarize board factions more than ever before, souring relationships among the district leadership to the breaking point.[25] Board support for and against Alioto was now balanced at 3-3, with one swing vote, Rosario Anaya's.

Bad news for Alioto came in January 1985, when Myra Kopf was elected board president with the support of Denebeim, Miller, and Anaya. Even the press pointed out that this signaled a power shift on the board: whereas Kopf had been one of a two-person minority three years earlier, she had built a coalition that carried her to power. Anaya's membership in this coalition, which came early in the term, made it clear that she favored Kopf over Alioto, although she was not quite ready to fire him.[26]

However, Anaya was offered a unique incentive that led her to break entirely with Alioto: in exchange for Anaya's vote, the Kopf coalition promised to appoint Carlos Cornejo, a district administrator whose career had suffered under Alioto, as acting superintendent. The deal was done, and in late July, Alioto was fired in a closed-door meeting without so much as a formal public vote; as Alioto's supporters on the board would later complain, they were not even present at the meeting. The cost to the district of buying out Alioto's contract was more than $900,000—a point on which the Kopf coalition would be later criticized.[27]

Only after Alioto's firing did his supporters surface in the press. An editorial in the *Chronicle* asserted that Alioto deserved better than "a firing in the night."[28] Bill Honig, the state superintendent of public instruction, criticized the board for its overtly political firing of a well-qualified superintendent. California Teachers' Association (CTA) president Judy Dellamonica praised Alioto for standing up to Kopf and her "old guard" of "do-nothing cronies."[29] Others praised Alioto for his leadership and his effectiveness: by any measure, wrote one columnist, Alioto had been a good superintendent, scaling down the busing plan, gaining the support of the black community on desegregation, and raising test scores in the district.[30]

25. SFC, November 7, 1984.
26. SFC, January 9, 1985.
27. SFC, July 25, 1985.
28. SFC, July 25, 1985.
29. SFC, August 15, 1985.
30. SFC, July 30, 1985.

Perhaps even more indicative of the potential impact of the firing on the implementation of the consent decree was the radically different characterization of the dispute between Kopf and Alioto in the wake of the firing. In the months leading up to July 1985, most of the news had focused on bad relationships, ego issues, political bickering, and questions over leadership style. However, the response to the firing from communities of color—and those who followed issues that affected communities of color—revealed a different side of the debate. The NAACP warned that the new administration would set back progress on the consent decree.[31] State superintendent of public instruction Honig asserted that newly appointed superintendent Cornejo was "a puppet" of Kopf who would do her bidding and dismantle Alioto's work on desegregation. Board members Sodonia Wilson, the only African American member, and Richard Cerbatos, a Filipino American, went further, suggesting that Alioto's firing was racially motivated, done in secret without three board members of color present.[32] CTA president Dellamonica put it best when she wrote that Kopf "never forgave the Superintendent for negotiating the Consent Decree that resolved San Francisco's desegregation problems."[33] These criticisms gave new meaning to the nickname that the *Chronicle* had created for Kopf, Miller, and Denebeim: the "three white ladies."[34]

These criticisms did not go unanswered. In what would become a huge battle for upcoming elections, the local president of the California Federation of Teachers, Joan-Marie Shelley, wrote an editorial blasting Alioto, saying that he had run roughshod over the rights of teachers and that his departure had come not a moment too soon.[35] Anaya defended her decision to oust Alioto, citing the reasons listed earlier: his neglect of poor schools outside the consent decree's mandate and his spotty record on Hispanic issues.[36] Kopf defended her leadership of the coalition against Alioto as well, repeating the criticisms of his management style and asserting that he ran the consent decree schools like a separate district under his own fiat.[37]

Alioto had poured resources into the revitalization of Hunter's Point schools at the alleged cost of the constituents of the board members who ousted him. The bottom line was simple: Kopf and her constituency had no stake in desegregation or the narrowing of the achievement gap, much less a singular focus on any actions that weakened the protections enjoyed by teachers in targeted schools. But she and her allies managed to bring Alioto down with criticisms that were, on their face, race neutral. It was only after Alioto's sudden firing that his supporters couched the debate in terms explicitly related to the consent decree.

31. SFC, July 27, 1985.
32. SFC, July 30, 1985.
33. SFC, August 15, 1985.
34. SFC, July 26, 1985.
35. SFC, August 1, 1985.
36. SFC, July 31, 1985.
37. SFC, August 9, 1985.

Despite the authority provided to Alioto by the consent decree and the support he had from three members of the school board, a majority developed—with the sole Hispanic on the board as the swing vote—that severely disagreed with the direction he took in implementing the consent decree. In two short years, board politics had evolved to remove a superintendent who was highly supportive of important elements of San Francisco's plan to limit the detrimental effects of its history of school segregation.

Carlos Cornejo, 1985–86

To a large extent, Carlos Cornejo lived up to the assessment that he was a puppet of Kopf and her allies. He paid attention to personnel evaluations that Alioto had never examined and reorganized the district around the wishes of the board majority.[38] He even asked the San Francisco district attorney to investigate charges of wrongdoing in Alioto's dealings with the CTA, a prospect that delighted both the Federation of Teachers and their staunch supporter, Myra Kopf.[39] Perhaps the greatest sign of the malleability of the new superintendent was his negotiation of a 9.5 percent increase in teacher salaries in September 1985, *contingent on the reimbursement of $5.8 million from the state for desegregation costs.* This was to be the beginning of a long-term dependence of the SFUSD on desegregation money, portions of which it allegedly used to cover general operating expenses rather than the specific purposes for which it was earmarked.[40] Cornejo was supported by a split on the board of 4-3.

Cornejo also had ambitions of his own. Under Alioto's leadership, he had chafed at the bit; now was his time to shine, and in a sense, he was doing his best to make a great impression in the short time he had as interim superintendent. His ambitions were confirmed when, despite a promise to the contrary, he applied for the permanent position when the board began its selection process.[41] Several in the coalition against him, particularly Cerbatos, criticized him for breaking this promise, and even Kopf was described as "furious" at him for misleading the board.[42]

In the end, however, it was Cornejo's presence that determined the final outcome. As the selection process heated up, three candidates emerged, Cornejo, San Jose superintendent Ramon Cortines, and St. Louis superintendent Robert Jones. Jones, the only African American candidate, won wide support from the African American community; he also had the votes of Cerbatos, Tom, and Wilson. The four-member Kopf coalition, however, favored Cortines. The board had agreed that they would not pick a superintendent without at least five votes.

38. SFC, August 28, 1985.
39. SFC, November 16, 1985.
40. SFC, January 15, 1986.
41. SFC, January 22, 1986.
42. SFC, March 14, 1986.

Board member Ben Tom later told the story of how, seeking to break the impasse, Libby Denebeim had proposed keeping Cornejo for an additional year. The prospect was so unacceptable to Tom that he threw his support to Cortines in order to keep Cornejo out of power.[43] The African American community was naturally angry, asking why any superintendent would take such a job with such a lack of consensus on the board.[44]

Cornejo's tenure as superintendent revealed that the Kopf majority, however slim, clearly controlled school politics, including the policy goals of the 1983 consent decree. No innovations involving the decree occurred under Cornejo. Although resources continued to be devoted to the six schools originally targeted for reform, desegregation monies were spread out among many different schools and used for other district purposes. Nonetheless, it must be acknowledged that there were no allegations that schools in San Francisco were still segregated by race and ethnicity. Enrollment desegregation had been largely attained. Nonetheless, the same board majority would continue to push the subsequent superintendent to focus on issues apart from those identified in the consent decree.

Ramon Cortines, 1986–92

Cortines was a consensus builder. Starting in April 1986, when he assumed his responsibilities, he made a point of visiting schools, meeting with stakeholders, and doing all of the things that neither Alioto nor Cornejo had done to win widespread support. His leadership style was like a breath of fresh air after more than a year of bickering and distrust in SFUSD politics, and he quickly won over other members of the board.

However, Cortines began as and remained the darling of the Kopf coalition. Almost echoing Kopf's language, in May 1986 he stated that there was a problem when SFUSD was run as a divided district, with a separate mandate and management for the consent decree schools. Right out of the gate Cortines made his position clear: he wanted to see SFUSD become "one school district."[45] In December 1986 he criticized the magnet and alternative schools that had been the hallmark of Alioto's desegregation reforms, saying that the desegregation plan needed to be reworked to ensure that students attended neighborhood schools. He did not favor targeting African American and Hispanic students for access to magnet and alternative schools either; in the same month he proposed admitting students to these schools by lottery, rather than allowing them to serve students from low-performing schools.[46]

43. SFC, April 6, 1986.
44. SFC, May 1, 1986.
45. SFC, May 9, 1986.
46. SFC, December 17, 1986.

The 1986 election was described everywhere as one of the most contested in the district's history. Kopf had angered many education officials and interest groups with her power politicking on the board; at the same time, her success in dumping Alioto had won her fervent support from parent groups and the San Francisco branch of the California Federation of Teachers. Other politicians got involved: Willie Brown, speaker of the California State Assembly, and Bill Honig, state superintendent of public instruction, helped to form and fund an anti-Kopf coalition.[47] They ran a slate with three members: Sodonia Wilson, the incumbent African American on the board, the relatively unknown Leland Yee, a Chinese American, and, surprisingly, Jule Anderson, a former board member whose relationship with Kopf had been quite good. Anaya had been asked to join the slate but declined because she would not accept the conditions, which included actively working for Kopf's defeat and promising to vote with the former pro-Alioto minority on the board.

Kopf's supporters, however, were also very active. When Honig called a press conference to attack her, he was criticized for abusing his office by a PTA activist named Jill Wynns, who would later be elected to the board herself and, in a very large sense, follow in Kopf's footsteps. The Federation of Teachers bucked a CTA walkout, saying it was an election gimmick to fuel rumors that Kopf had caused chaos in the schools. The election was divided and close: the *San Francisco Chronicle* endorsed Anaya, the little known Leland Yee, and Wilson, while the *Examiner* endorsed Anaya, the same unknown challenger, and Kopf.

In the end, Anaya took the most votes, followed by Sodonia Wilson. Kopf came in third but finished comfortably ahead of Yee. Triumphant in her victory, she sharply criticized Honig and other power brokers who had tried to unseat her, saying that her victory was a sign that such meddling was not appreciated by San Francisco voters.[48]

The Cortines honeymoon with the board and the community generally began to fade in 1987. The district again faced significant financial shortfalls, at a time when it needed to close one major high school, McAteer, because of asbestos contamination. Moreover, new tensions emerged over the consent decree. They arose in multiple places—at the district's prestigious Lowell High School, in the McAteer controversy, and in the alternative schools that had been built by Alioto. These tensions reenergized the power struggle on the board between the members of color and the Kopf coalition's "three white ladies." The events that ensued showed how differently a situation similar to that in 1985 could play out when the superintendent's inclinations ran counter to important elements of the consent decree.

In this period, Cortines took two significant steps that weakened the decree.

47. SFC, October 8, 1986.
48. SFC, November 6, 1986.

First, amid criticism that Lowell High School had a Chinese enrollment of 44 percent (4 percent above the original maximum allowable percentage of any one race under the district's desegregation plan), Cortines suggested in June 1987 that the solution might be to raise the enrollment cap to 45 percent, thus weakening a key provision of the decree.[49] This suggestion was followed up in July 1987 by a plan to save the district money on busing by raising enrollment caps to 45 percent at a number of the alternative and magnet schools.[50]

Second, Cortines pushed for students to be assigned to the alternative schools by lottery rather than by the system in place, which took demographic factors into account in admitting students. Irrespective of how well funded the consent decree schools were, this system effectively barred the district from being able to concentrate resources on any one group of students.[51] The result was that while desegregation continued (in its weakened form, given new enrollment caps), the consent decree's unique second goal—to close the achievement gap between students of color and white students—was further neglected.

However quietly Cortines managed to make these changes, the overall fate and interpretation of the consent decree was brought into the limelight through the proposed McAteer closing. The challenges to student displacement were not rooted simply in community discontent with the closing; the NAACP had something to say about the implications of various moves affecting enrollment caps, school assignment, and the McAteer closing for the desegregation goals of the decree. In August 1987, Cortines had to appear in court to explain how the McAteer closing did not constitute a violation of the consent decree. The plan for student reassignment resulting from the closing, the NAACP contended, both devastated the population of an integrated school and failed to respect the agreement that all parties to the consent decree be consulted before major changes in school attendance policies were implemented. Judge William Orrick agreed and halted work on the plan until the district was able to broker a settlement with the NAACP and the state.[52] Cortines was furious with the court's intervention in his job as chief administrative officer of the district, but he swallowed his objections and went forward with the newly negotiated plan, which would cost the district an additional $1.5 million and led to additional battles with the state over reimbursement for desegregation costs.[53]

The issue of academic achievement at James Lick Middle School also reenergized the debate over reconstitution. With test scores slipping, educators at Lick voiced fears in October 1987 that the school would be reconstituted. They claimed that such a move would be unfair, given the tumult through which the

49. SFC, June 18, 1987.
50. SFC, July 17, 1987.
51. SFC, December 17, 1986.
52. SFC, August 20, 24, and 26, 1987.
53. SFC, September 2, 1987.

entire school had gone in recent months related to the McAteer relocation.[54] In a nod to the powers that backed him, Cortines promised that he had no intention of reconstituting the school; he had responded in the same way to a similar situation at Balboa High School in 1986.[55] However, in April 1987, Judge Orrick, citing its low test scores, ordered the reconstitution of James Lick Middle School.[56]

Another important development occurred that would have dramatic consequences for the implementation of the consent decree. After many years of domination by the CTA, which first came to power in 1981, the local affiliate of the American Federation of Teachers (AFT) managed to win the support of a majority of the teachers in May 1989. Some of that support had come from the AFT's endorsement of a proposal to merge the two unions.[57] The following year, the proposal resulted in the creation of the United Educators of San Francisco (UESF), which bargains on behalf of San Francisco's teachers to this day. The shift in power over collective bargaining was significant because, during nearly the entire period that is studied here, the CTA had represented teachers' interests in a manner that was sympathetic to the letter and spirit of the consent decree. Recall that at the time that Alioto was fired, the CTA condemned the power grab by the Kopf coalition, while the AFT expressed its satisfaction at the superintendent's departure.[58]

The takeover of collective bargaining by the arguably "anti–consent decree" forces among San Francisco's teachers (or, at the very least, the inclusion of these forces at the bargaining table) would bring a powerful new element to the coalition that had an interest in undercutting the district's desegregation efforts. At this time, when the superintendent was already hostile to the decree, this shift manifested itself in small ways. For example, by September 1990, the district had adopted a method of school administration known as "restructuring"—a process that empowered teachers, principals, and other staff to share in decisions made about school governance. The new union fought hard for this and other similar reforms that ran counter to the type of top-down authority granted to the superintendent by the consent decree.[59]

In what might be termed an anti-incumbent trend, the election of 1990 led to the ouster of three board members, Sodonia Wilson (African American), Myra Kopf (Caucasian), and Rosario Anaya (Hispanic), and three new, relatively unaligned members joined the school board.[60] Cortines announced his intention to leave soon after these new board members were seated; nonetheless,

54. SFC, October 5, 1987.
55. SFC, April 12, 1988.
56. SFC, September 2, 1987.
57. SFC, May 27, 1989.
58. SFC, May 27, 1989.
59. SFC, September 4, 1990.
60. SFC, November 8, 1990.

in his last few months in office, he continued to show limited concern for the goals of the consent decree. In January 1991 he announced a plan to offer "more choice for parents" in deciding where their children would attend school. Some described this as a parting shot at the goals of the decree.[61] Whatever the purpose of his statement, Cortines left early in 1992.

Cortines's tenure as superintendent clearly demonstrated the power of a majority of the board to limit the district's responsibility to comply vigorously with the consent decree. Again, it was not that the board demanded that schools be resegregated or that the district file for removal from the supervision of Judge Orrick. Rather, in responding to the provisions of the decree, Cortines set a tone that was weak at best and dismissive at worst. Whether responding to the concerns of African American and Hispanic parents, planning the reassignment of students from a middle school, or responding to calls to hire more teachers of color, in every instance his preferences seemed to differ from those in the original goals of the decree. In each of these instances, however, he was reflecting the preferences of a majority of the school board.

Waldemar "Bill" Rojas, 1992–2001

Although there was some controversy over the selection of Waldemar Rojas over Rudy Crew, a prominent African American superintendent in Sacramento, Rojas soon pledged support for the consent decree and met with leaders of the African American community. However, he also developed a reputation for having a combative style in his approach to education reform.[62]

The elections of November 1992 created as large a transition on the board as did those of November 1990, but this time, it was peaceful and voluntary. Three incumbents chose not to run for reelection. There was no anti-incumbent fever, the board's reputation was in fair shape, and the election was simply a contest between newcomers. In the end, Yee was reelected to the board, and the three victorious challengers were Jill Wynns, Angie Fa, and Steve Phillips. Jill Wynns had been an active parent in the district for several years, serving as president of Parents' Lobby, a group that had been aligned with the Kopf coalition. Angie Fa, the chair of Asian American studies at City College, was a member of the Asian American community who shared its somewhat ambiguous but increasingly critical stance toward the consent decree. Steve Phillips, the first African American to serve on the board since Sodonia Wilson, was very much in touch with his community and in the camp of a reformer like Rojas.[63]

The election of this new group completed the transition that had been taking place since November 1990. Leland Yee was the only person who remained on the board from before that time, and Rojas had just been hired. The position of

61. SFC, October 7, 1991.
62. SFC, April 13, 1992.
63. SFC, November 4, 1992.

Rojas on the decree would rekindle considerable conflict, and the makeup of the new board was equally important in defining new cleavages. The board was now composed of two progressive Caucasians (Tom Ammiano and Dan Kelly), two ethnic advocates (Carlota del Portillo and Steve Phillips), two Asian Americans (Leland Yee and Angie Fa), and one member of the Kopf old guard (Jill Wynns).

Rojas became superintendent just as a court-appointed committee of experts submitted its review of the first ten years of implementation of the consent decree. Judge Orrick had ordered the report out of concern that the district's commitment to the decree had waned over the several years preceding his order. The committee, headed by Gary Orfield, found that the district had largely met the goals of enrollment desegregation but that the goal of higher achievement for all students was still unfulfilled.[64] They found that phase one schools—those that had been fully reconstituted in the early 1980s—demonstrated substantial achievement gains. Building on this finding and the mandate of the court, Rojas began to develop a plan, the Comprehensive School Improvement Program (CSIP), to expand the efforts begun in phase one schools. The plan specified both quantitative and qualitative criteria to identify low-performing schools. Although the list of criteria was broad, among the most important factors was the trajectory of student performance on standardized tests over the previous three years. Nine schools were initially declared to be low achievers and were put on CSIP probation for a period of one school year, during which the school had an opportunity to develop a plan and demonstrate improvement. Failure to improve—or the district's determination that the school did not have a reasonable chance of improving—meant that the school would be reconstituted at the end of the probation period.

Of the nine schools placed on probation in 1993, five schools were reconstituted by the 1995–96 period and four schools eventually "graduated" from CSIP probation. Rojas, however, continued to expand the CSIP process, using reconstitution as a major school reform strategy. In 1994, four additional schools were put on CSIP probation; all would leave probation without being reconstituted. In 1995, six additional schools entered probation, three of which were reconstituted during the 1996–97 school year, and in 1996, five schools were placed on probation, two of which were reconstituted. In sum, under Rojas's leadership, nearly twenty-five schools were included in the CSIP reform process, resulting in ten schools being reconstituted in addition to the original phase one schools. These actions created a great deal of controversy in the district, which began to be reflected in increasing factionalism on the board.[65]

For example, students, parents, and teachers at Mission High School erupted in protest when Rojas made the decision to reassign three popular administrators

64. Orfield (1992).
65. SFC, March 4 and 23 and May 11, 1994.

there in April 1996, under the guise of reconstitution.[66] The board quietly approved Rojas's recommendation. Mission High School was, at the time, the worst-performing high school in the SFUSD, but many said that the administrators who had been removed, who had been there only a few years, were turning it around. Some accused Rojas of using reassignment as a tool in a strategy to reduce the length of administrators' contracts, and there had been complaints that Rojas tended to use his own criteria to pick the targets of his reforms rather than any objective, measurable standard.

The same went for Rojas's proposal to reconstitute three additional schools—Starr King Elementary, Aptos Middle, and Balboa High—in May 1996. As at Mission High School, the proposals drew strong criticism from the communities served by the targeted schools. In both cases, Rojas was supported by a slim majority on the board: del Portillo, Kelly, Phillips, and Keith Jackson. The other three members—Wynns, Fa, and Yee—either voted against the proposals or abstained from voting. Of those opposed, Jill Wynns was the most adamant; in fact, she was the only board member who can be said to have uniformly opposed Rojas at this time.

As the Asian American community continued to grow, it began to feel the strain on enrollment caps at San Francisco's academic high schools and its better elementary and middle schools. The cap of 40 percent made it much more difficult for Asian Americans to gain admission to schools like Lowell and Wallenberg than students from other ethnic groups. Charging reverse discrimination, Asian American parents filed a lawsuit against the district, *Ho v. SFUSD*, and asked that the quotas be eliminated.[67] Though the case would not be resolved for another four years, the district felt the criticism immediately. Under pressure from members like Leland Yee, the board changed Lowell's admissions policy in February 1996. The school had had separate standards for members of different ethnic groups, but with this change, that system was replaced with an comprehensive assessment process of the type used by some universities—a move which, while somewhat conciliatory to the Asian American community, allowed the district to preserve affirmative action at schools like Lowell.[68]

The consensus in favor of the consent decree continued to weaken. The proponents of the neighborhood school movement in the Tenderloin, for example, began to complain that, after all of their hard work to build a new school, not everyone in the neighborhood would attend it because of the busing and enrollment requirements imposed by the decree.[69] Statewide class-size reduction

66. SFC, May 19, 1996.
67. *Ho v. SFUSD*, No. C-78 1445 WHO. First Amended Class Action Complaint (1995).
68. Office of Superintendent Bill Rojas (1996).
69. Lisa Davis, "Bus to Nowhere: Why San Francisco's Byzantine School Desegregation Program Systematically Fails the Children It Was Designed to Help," *San Francisco Weekly,* April 2, 1997.

efforts also exacerbated the need for busing and made it more unpopular.[70] The plaintiffs in the *Ho* case were now asking Judge Orrick to put an end to the consent decree altogether.[71]

As people continued to question the need for the consent decree—and the powers it granted the superintendent—Rojas took steps to institutionalize his reforms, placing them beyond the power of the consent decree. Facing a lawsuit that challenged the consent decree itself and knowing that there was a nationwide trend against desegregation court orders, Rojas began to seek other ways to circumvent the education bureaucracy and fix schools. He found them in the state's charter school law and in the Edison Project, a private, for-profit school management company that contracted with districts to manage school sites and operated free of most of the traditional restrictions on school governance.[72] If Rojas's heavy use of reconstitution had angered the teachers and community members it displaced, his embrace of the Edison Project—a move labeled as "school privatization" by its detractors—raised the anger another notch and caused some of his allies to turn away.[73]

In the end, the board voted 5-2 to enter a contract with the Edison Project, to take over Edison Elementary School. However, the strength of the anti-Edison sentiment was evident when the two dissenters, Wynns and Kelly, attempted to reopen the discussion by challenging the legality of the vote that had taken place. In June of 1998, Keith Jackson, then the board president and a member of Rojas's coalition, resigned over allegations that he had unpaid child support obligations. His resignation took effect at midnight on the evening of the vote on Edison, but Jackson voted anyway. The challenge was largely symbolic, since even without Jackson's vote the board had a 4-2 majority in favor of Edison. However, it represented an escalation of the conflict on the board, which had been relatively quiet up to this point.[74] True to form, Rojas used the Edison contract to do what he had always done with reconstitution: he negotiated the entire contract and helped to determine how the school would be run without input or advice from the teachers' union.[75]

The anger over Edison was part of the growing sentiment against Rojas himself, particularly in his fiscal management of the district. In June 1998, Rojas also announced huge budget cuts due to a $13 million desegregation reimbursement dispute with Sacramento.[76] He used the threat of fiscal insolvency to pressure the state to reimburse the entire shortfall. Of course, what may have been

70. Ibid.
71. SFC, August 21, 1997.
72. SFC, April 29 and October 18, 1998.
73. SFC, November 5, 1998.
74. SFC, June 25, 1998.
75. SFC, October 18, 1998.
76. SFC, June 22, 1998.

viewed as a daring and risky strategy of brinksmanship to the outside viewer appeared to some within the district as a fiscal crisis that had been engineered by the superintendent. Jill Wynns was outraged: the state was running a multibillion dollar surplus, and the district was nevertheless in deficit.[77]

There was an important political undercurrent to these events that resulted in a crucial shift of power on the board: the defection of Dan Kelly from the Rojas camp. Kelly was to Rojas what Rosario Anaya had been to Alioto. A board member who put the interests of San Francisco's children first, Kelly had supported Rojas as recently as April 1997, when he voted for a salary increase for the superintendent. Kelly was not bound to one constituency or ideology, as can be argued in regard to other board members, and his support lent legitimacy to a Rojas coalition. That changed in 1998. The Edison proposal and Rojas's fiscal management of the district were enough to turn Kelly away from Rojas. He stood with Jill Wynns on the Edison issue, and he ultimately became a part of the coalition against the superintendent. Jackson's resignation also weakened Rojas's coalition. Mayor Brown filled the seat with Frank Chong, an Asian American who was a lukewarm supporter of the superintendent.[78] Chong had far less appeal, and he would become a prime target for campaigns that opposed Edison in the following election.

The election of 1998 was a referendum on Edison and Rojas's leadership, plain and simple.[79] The ruling coalition had been criticized for its lack of independence from the superintendent, and that showed in the election returns. Carlota del Portillo lost her seat to newcomer Eddie Chin, an avowed opponent of the Edison contract who promised to work to rescind it once in office. Frank Chong, a moderate supporter of Rojas, came close to losing his seat to challenger Mauricio Vela, another outspoken opponent of Edison.[80]

The board that emerged still contained a fragile majority—Chong, Juanita Owens, Mary Hernandez, and Phillips—who supported Rojas and Edison, but Chong's vote was questionable. It was easy to see how, if trends continued, the next election could sweep a substantial portion of Rojas's coalition out of office in the same way it had removed del Portillo. This election marked the first time that Rojas would face a board that was substantially independent from him.

Coming into the 1999–2001 term, Rojas's coalition had weakened and so had his power to reform the district. In February 1999, the *Ho* case was settled by the court-mandated embrace of race-blind enrollment procedures for all San Francisco schools.[81] While it was not completely killed, the consent decree was fundamentally altered by this decision, weakening Rojas's ability to use its tools

77. SFC, March 19, 1999.
78. SFC, August 6, 1998.
79. SFC, October 30, 1998.
80. SFC, November 5, 1998.
81. SFC, February 16, 1999.

for education reform. In addition, more questions began to arise over Rojas's fiscal management of the district.[82] He had angered teachers, parents, some ethnic constituencies, and even his allies in Sacramento with his tactics and leadership style. A diverse array of constituencies was calling for the superintendent's resignation by early 1999.

In April of that year, he resigned his position to go to the Dallas Independent School District. Kelly, once known to lavish praise on Rojas in the press, remarked that as far as he was concerned, Rojas "can turn in his key tomorrow." Members of the anti-Rojas coalition were angered and disgusted that Rojas had looked for a new job, behind their backs and in violation of his contract. They were glad to see him leave, even as some members of his coalition expressed sadness. Board member Juanita Owens, for example, remarked, "Their gain. Our loss."[83]

There are notable similarities between the types of board opposition faced by Rojas and Alioto. Both had one main opponent—Kopf for Alioto and Wynns for Rojas—who was always suspicious of the superintendent, was in the minority for a long time, and slowly built a coalition against him. Both superintendents became enemies of teachers' unions by their attempts to reform the schools, especially through reconstitution, and for Rojas through the Edison Project as well. And both were ultimately taken down by a defection from their coalition and increasing polarization of the community over their leadership.

Both men were also singularly committed to school reform as envisioned by the consent decree, and—idiosyncrasies aside—both aggressively used reconstitution in the district and fought to expand the scope and reach of the consent decree to redistribute district resources to underprivileged students. Cornejo and Cortines largely ignored the consent decree and, if anything, took steps to dismantle the reforms made by their predecessors.

Arlene Ackerman, 2001–03

In May 2000, more than a year after Rojas's departure, the board of education selected a new superintendent: Arlene Ackerman, then superintendent of public schools for Washington, D.C. Ackerman would become the district's first woman and first African American superintendent. Although a majority of the board was lukewarm on the candidates, Jill Wynns, in the lone quote of a board member in the *Chronicle* article on the selection of Ackerman, praised her as "a highly skilled individual and a rising star."[84] Wynns was and remains one of Ackerman's strongest allies, and because Wynns had solidified her own political coalition in the election of 2000, this alliance translated into protection for Ackerman that extended beyond the usual honeymoon period.

82. SFC, March 19 and April 28, 1999.
83. SFC, April 23, 1999.
84. SFC, May 16, 2000.

The 2000 election came down to a battle between the old Rojas coalition (Steve Phillips, Juanita Owens, and Frank Chong), led by Mary Hernandez, then the board president, and the anti-Rojas, anti-Edison coalition that had put pressure on Rojas to leave (Wynns, Eddie Chin, and Dan Kelly). With Phillips and Owens choosing not to run, Wynns finally got her coalition: she came in first, and the next two spots were filled by newcomers—Eric Mar and Mark Sanchez—who were aligned with Wynns. Hernandez finished fourth, barely beating out another Wynns ally. Wynns became board president in 2001, a position that she would hold for two years.[85] When Hernandez resigned later in 2001, it was widely believed that she had left because she did not like being in the minority faction on the board. Emilio Cruz, who would become another Wynns supporter and succeeded her as president in 2003, was appointed to take Hernandez's place.[86]

During the period of Wynns' presidency (2001 and 2002), relatively little news surfaced about the consent decree or desegregation. The board adopted a strong anti-Edison stance, coming close in 2002 to revoking the 1998 charter for Edison Elementary. New issues divided the board, particularly those surrounding California's recently implemented high-stakes testing programs.[87] Eric Mar and Mark Sanchez became outspoken opponents of Ackerman over her support of these programs, and the 2002 election of another anti-testing member, Sarah Lipson, created a coalition of three that eventually won over a swing vote, that of Emilio Cruz, in exchange for their support of him for board president in January 2003. This did not prevent the board under Wynns from extending Ackerman's contract and increasing her salary to $219,000 (along with a substantial increase in benefits) in December of 2002, a month before the new board was to be seated. Once again, Wynns was at the forefront, telling the press that "Arlene is very much at the bottom of the scale for compensation."[88]

What is perhaps most interesting about Ackerman's leadership is that it is difficult to determine exactly what her position is regarding the consent decree. However, if there is any doubt as to Ackerman's alignment with Wynns on the subject, one story is instructive. In 2003, race issues resurfaced over the district's school assignment plan. The plan used a "diversity index" of six socioeconomic factors (excluding race) to assign its students; the index reflected a compromise reached in the wake of the *Ho* case that attempted to balance the need for race-blind admissions with the stated desegregation goals of the decree. The effects of the index, however, were similar to those of earlier race-based assignment schemes.

85. SFC, November 9, 2000.
86. SFC, October 30, 2001.
87. SFC, November 7, 2002.
88. SFC, December 12, 2002.

Beginning in May of 2003, a string of parent protests against the plan made it a difficult issue to ignore. In October, Eddie Chin proposed doing away with the index and allowing students to attend neighborhood schools.[89] Again, the index already reflected a compromise that had actually succeeded in taking race out of student assignment under the decree. Any further concessions would amount to dismantling the decree entirely. But in November 2003, Ackerman brought a proposal before the board that would do just that, by lessening the importance of the diversity index in favor of assigning students to neighborhood schools. In the end, even Wynns voted against this plan (Chin was its lone supporter). But the atmosphere has changed in San Francisco when the desegregation debate is over whether any index should be used to assign students to schools rather than what the elements of an index should be.

The Limits of Court-Imposed Policy Change

Our examination of the evolution of school board politics in San Francisco reveals that the traditional centers of power in the making of educational policy, especially board factions, can work either to support or to contradict directives issued by federal courts. This is a lesson well worth remembering. As much as rights-based advocacy, such as desegregation litigation, may be necessary to promote policy change to better serve the interests of historically underrepresented communities, it is teachers, administrators, and especially superintendents, as directed by school boards, who ultimately have the responsibility for making policy changes work. Desegregation was pursued in the courts because of the failure of traditional decisionmakers, such as school boards, to respond to the needs and interests of significant segments of the population. Ironically, the support of the same traditional decisionmakers is most critical to the achievement of the courts' goals. Our discussion of the San Francisco case makes this abundantly clear.

This finding directly contradicts the primary policy prescription offered by Sandler and Schoenbrod in their important work *Democracy by Decree: What Happens When Courts Run Governments.*[90] They argue that courts have always been ill equipped to deal with the day-to-day responsibilities of effective policy implementation. Court orders, they continue, serve to seriously limit the capacity of traditional decisionmakers to take responsibility for directing the course of public policy. They state that "[c]onsent decrees transfer power not from politicians to a judge but from one political process to another. The winners are the powerful and the knowledgeable." These winners include "plaintiffs' attorneys,

89. SFC, October 23, 2003.
90. Sandler and Schoenbrod (2003). These authors build on the work of Chayes (1976), Horowitz (1977), Diver (1979), Horowitz (1983), Shuck (1983), DiIulio (1987), McConnell (1987), Rosenberg (1991), Sturm (1993), Posner (1996), and Freeley and Rubin (1998).

various court-appointed functionaries, and lower-echelon officials." In their most forceful recommendation they state, "[t]o the greatest extent practicable, judges should leave policy making to elected policy makers," who are designated to respond to the public's will. These authors have an overwhelming faith in the capacity of traditional decisionmakers to serve as the exclusive means of making effective, responsive public policy.[91]

Contrary to Sandler and Schoenbrod, our examination of school board politics in San Francisco suggests that the power of traditional decisionmakers— school board members—is not necessarily thwarted by a consent decree. They, the elected members of this traditional center of policymaking, can reassert their power and often do in response to the changes in political influence in school district politics. In exercising their most important responsibility, the selection of the school superintendent, they can effectively direct the course of even a highly interventionist consent decree. This can sometimes work to further the original goals of the decree, and sometimes not. When it does not, the traditional operation of politics and policymaking may simply reinforce the disparities and inequalities that the consent decree was intended to remedy.

Our analysis of school board politics in San Francisco as they relate to the implementation of the 1983 consent decree suggests that it is important not to underestimate the great difficulties associated with working to improve educational opportunity for groups that have not usually benefited from the traditional policymaking process.[92] Creative efforts must be made to determine how the interests and power of traditional educational stakeholders, like schools boards, can be included within programs to effect policy change in education.

A return to San Francisco again makes this clear. In 2002–03, in twenty-eight of a total of sixty-nine elementary schools, enrollment of members of one ethnic or racial group exceeded 50 percent. For middle schools, seven of seventeen schools had a majority of students from one ethnic or racial group, and six of nineteen high schools had the same enrollment pattern. This resulted in part from the final resolution of the *Ho* case, which removed the use of race and ethnicity in assigning students to public schools.[93] The achievement gap in San Francisco between African Americans and Hispanics on one hand and Asians and Caucasians on the other also continues.

Of even greater concern, few would argue against the assertion that the current superintendent, Arlene Ackerman, an African American woman, has demonstrated very little support for the most significant aspects of the original consent decree. Everyone, including Ackerman, is for educational reform that

91. Quotes from Sandler and Schoenbrod (2003, pp. 7, 134, 139, 153, 161, 204).

92. See, for example, the excellent discussion of the history of educational reform throughout the twentieth century provided by David Tyack and Larry Cuban in *Tinkering toward Utopia* (2003).

93. *Ho* v. *SFUSD*, 147 F.3d 854 (9th Cir. 1998).

improves the academic performance of all students in San Francisco; however, there has been virtually no attempt to use the special provisions of the consent decree to develop consensus-based, creative policy change that might lead to the realization of that goal. As of 2003, however, Superintendent Ackerman had the unquestioned support of board member Jill Wynns, a majority of the members on the board, and the United Educators of San Francisco.

School boards and supporters of their majority factions remain critical players in setting the course of much educational policy, despite the presence in San Francisco of an activist federal judge and a comprehensive consent decree. As Sandler and Schoenbrod argue, consent decrees are far from a panacea to promote educational reform. Our analysis suggests, however, that relying on traditional educational policymakers, however convincing in theory, is no panacea either. The traditional policies and electoral politics of schools boards can also place many constraints on educational reform.

References

Chayes, Abram. 1976. "The Role of the Judge in Public Law Litigation." *Harvard Law Review* 89 (7): 1281–1316.

DiIulio, John J., Jr. 1987. *Governing Prisons: A Comparative Study of Correctional Management.* New York: Free Press.

Diver, Colin S. 1979. "The Judge as Political Powerbroker: Superintending Structural Change in Public Institutions." *Virginia Law Review* 65 (1): 43–106.

England, Robert E., Kenneth J. Meier, and Luis Ricardo Fraga. 1988. "Barriers to Equal Opportunity: Educational Practices and Minority Students." *Urban Affairs Quarterly* 23 (4): 635–46.

Erlichson, Bari Anhalt, and Luis Ricardo Fraga. 2004. "No Lasting Consensus: The Politics of School Desegregation in San Francisco." Unpublished paper. Rutgers University, Stanford University.

Freely, Malcolm M., and Edward L. Rubin. 1998. *Judicial Policy Making and the Modern State: How the Courts Reformed America's Prisons.* Cambridge University Press.

Heclo, Hugh. 1994. "Ideas, Interests, and Institutions." In *The Dynamics of American Politics,* edited by Lawrence Dodd and Cal Jillson. Boulder, Colo.: Westview Press.

Horowitz, Donald L. 1977. *The Courts and Social Policy.* Brookings.

———. 1983. "Decreeing Organizational Change: Judicial Supervision of Public Institutions." *Duke Law Journal* 1983 (6): 1265–1307.

Kirp, David. 1982. *Just Schools: The Idea of Racial Equality in American Education.* University of California Press.

McConnell, Michael W. 1987. "Why Hold Elections? Using Consent Decrees to Insulate Politics from Political Change." *University of Chicago Legal Forum,* vol. 2: 295–325.

Office of Superintendent Bill Rojas. 1996. "Revised Admissions Process for Lowell High School." San Francisco (January 8).

Orfield, Gary. 1987. *Must We Bus? Segregated Schools and National Policy.* Brookings.

Orfield, Gary, chair. 1992. *Desegregation and Educational Change in San Francisco: Findings and Recommendations on Consent Decree Implementation.* Experts' report, submitted to the court.

Orfield, Gary. 2001. *Schools More Separate: Consequences of a Decade of Resegregation*. Civil Rights Project, Harvard University.

Posner, Richard A. 1996. *The Federal Courts: Challenge and Reform*. Harvard University Press.

Rosenberg, Gerald N. 1991. *The Hollow Hope: Can Courts Bring about Social Change?* University of Chicago Press.

Sandler, Ross, and David Schoenbrod. 2003. *Democracy by Decree: What Happens When Courts Run Government*. Yale University Press.

Shuck, Peter H. 1983. *Suing Government: Citizen Remedies for Official Wrongs*. Yale University Press.

Smith, Rogers. 1996. *Civic Ideals*. Yale University Press.

Sturm, Susan P. 1993. "The Legacy and Future of Corrections Litigation." *University of Pennsylvania Law Review* 142 (May): 639–738.

Tyack, David, and Larry Cuban. 1995. *Tinkering toward Utopia: A Century of Public School Reform*. Harvard University Press.

Articles Cited from the San Francisco Chronicle

May 10, 1983. Charles C. Hardy, "SF School District Moving Slowly on Desegregation Plan."

May 21, 1983. Charles C. Hardy, "San Francisco Desegregation Deal Falling Apart."

June 13, 1984. Castillo, Cathy. "'Mini-School Board' Plan Tabled in S.F."

November 7, 1984. George Williamson, "Miller Wins Seat on S.F. School Board."

January 9, 1985. "Alioto Critic Elected School Board Chief."

July 25, 1985. Diane Curtis, "Alioto Forced Out as S.F. Schools Chief: Pressure from Divided Board."

July 26, 1985. Sarah Dodge, "How Myra Kopf Achieved Power on S.F. School Board."

July 27, 1985. Diane Curtis, "School Politics Threatens Integration, Says NAACP."

July 30, 1985. Diane Curtis, "2 on School Board Ask That Alioto Get His Job Back."

July 31, 1985. Diane Curtis, "Alioto Foe Explains School Board Vote."

August 1, 1985. Joan Marie Shelley, "Alioto Ouster is Long Overdue."

August 9, 1985. Diane Curtis, "School Board President Tells Inside Story of Alioto Ouster."

August 15, 1985. Judy Dellamonica, "Alioto's Dismissal Is Cause for Concern."

August 28, 1985. Diane Curtis, "School Board OKs Reorganization Plan."

November 16, 1985. Diane Curtis and Dave Farrell, "D.A. Urged to Probe Ex, School Chief Alioto."

January 15, 1986. Diane Curtis, "17 Old SF Schools to get Face Lifts."

January 22, 1986. Diane Curtis, "A Necessary Mess in Schools."

March 14, 1986. Diane Curtis, "Acting Schools Chief Wants to Keep Job."

April 6, 1986. Charles C. Hardy, "S.F. Bungled Hunt for Schools Chief, Critics Say."

May 1, 1986. Diane Curtis, "Selection of Schools Chief Upsets S.F. Black Leaders."

May 9, 1986. Diane Curtis, "New Boss Plans to Put S.F. Schools to the Test."

October 8, 1986. Diane Curtis, "Big Money, Power Brokers Spice Up S.F. Schools Race."

November 6, 1986. Diane Curtis, "Kopf Blasts Her Sacramento Opponents."

December 17, 1986. Diane Curtis, "S.F. Parents Protest School Lottery Plan."

June 18, 1987. Diane Curtis, "S.F. Schools Told to Correct Racial Makeup at Lowell High."

July 17, 1987. Angie Cannon, "A Plan to Decrease S.F. School Busing."

August 20, 1987. Edward W. Lempinen, "McAteer High 'Orphans' to Move into Lick School."

August 24, 1987. "School Mess."

August 26, 1987. Leslie Guevarra and Angie Cannon, "Board OKs Plan to Relocate S.F. Schools."

September 2, 1987. Angie Cannon, "Judge Orders School Fixed Up for Lick's Pupils."

October 5, 1987. Angie Cannon, "Lick Students Get New School Today."

April 12, 1988. Charles Burress, "Changes Called for at Balboa High."

May 27, 1989. Nanette Asimov, "S.F. Teachers Switch to New Union."

September 4, 1990. Nanette Asimov, "9 S.F. Schools Try Out 'Restructuring.'"

November 8, 1990. Nanette Asimov, "S.F. Voters Taught a Lesson to School, College Incumbents."

October 7, 1991. Nanette Asimov, "Integration Debate: Many Blacks Unhappy with Busing."

April 13, 1992. Nanette Asimov, "Next Superintendent of S.F. Schools Talks of What He's Facing."

November 4, 1992. Nanette Asimov, "3 Newcomers Win Seats On S.F. School Board."

March 4, 1994. Jean Merl, "Staffs to Be Replaced at 3 San Francisco Schools."

March 23, 1994. Masha Ginsburg, "Burton Parents Irate over Plans to Relocate School; Effort to Create New Alternative Campuses Draws Heavy Fire."

May 11, 1994. Masha Ginsburg, "S.F. School Board Favors Overhaul at 3 Sites."

May 19, 1996. Venise Wagner, "Mayor Gets Involved in Mission High Dispute."

August 21, 1997. Nanette Asimov, "Wilson Sides with S.F. Chinese Americans on Schools Lawsuit to End Court-Supervised Desegregation."

April 29, 1998. Vicki Haddock and Julian Guthrie, "The City Considers Privatizing 2 Schools."

June 22, 1998. Nanette Asimov, "S.F. Schools Plan Drastic Budget Cut."

June 25, 1998. Tanya Schevitz and Nanette Asimov, "Edison School Vote Could Be Invalid."

August 6, 1998. Gregory Lewis and Julian Guthrie, "School Board Appointee Chong Praised as Bridge Builder."

October 18, 1998. Julian Guthrie, "The Fisher King: S.F.'s Edison School, with Additional Funds from the Gap's Don Fisher, Has Been Criticized by Many Groups. Now, Will It Improve?"

October 30, 1998. Julian Guthrie, "Debate over Privatization Dominates Schools Race."

November 5, 1998. Julian Guthrie, "Absentee Voters Decide School Board; Edison Project Major Issue Dividing Leaders on Direction of Local District."

February 16, 1999. Julian Guthrie and Eric Brazil, "S.F. Schools End Race Quotas."

March 19, 1999. Nanette Asimov and Greg Lucas, "Assembly OKs Bailout for S.F. Schools; Irate Lawmakers Slam Rojas' Budget Tactics."

April 23, 1999. Nanette Asimov, "Rojas Set to Bolt S.F. for Dallas School Job."

April 28, 1999. Nanette Asimov, "School Board to Auction Off Empty Building."

May 16, 2000. Julian Guthrie, "S.F.'s Pick for Schools Chief Has Fought, and Won, the Same Battle."

November 9, 2000. Lori Olszewski, "S.F. School Race Still Undecided; Board President Hanging On for Seat."

October 30, 2001. Steve Rubenstein, "Hernandez Quits S.F. School Board—Cruz Appointed."

November 7, 2002. Nanette Asimov, "New S.F. School Board Member not Afraid to Battle over Tests."

December 12, 2002. Ray Delgado, "S.F. School Chief Awarded Raise, More Benefits."

October 23, 2003. Heather Knight, "Leader Calls for Eliminating Diversity Index."

November 13, 2003. Heather Knight, "Schools' Race Plan Endorsed.

6

Local School Boards as Authorizers
of Charter Schools

PAUL TESKE, MARK SCHNEIDER, AND ERIN CASSESE

Since 1983, education reform has occupied a prime spot on the domestic political agenda. School choice has been a focal point of the many programs under consideration, and charter schools have emerged as the central component of choice-based reforms. Given their growing importance, it is not surprising that charter schools have been the subject of considerable research across a wide range of issues. In this chapter, we step back from the theme of much of this work ("Do charter schools improve academic performance?") and instead examine the political process that creates and then oversees these schools.

While "top-down" national pressure has been instrumental to the development of charter schools, the implementation of charter policy is embedded in the American educational system's complex federal structure. In this decentralized system, outcomes are determined by the decisions of many local agencies. All of them have their own incentives and concerns, and sometimes their interests are independent of national interests. Another complicating factor is the well-known penchant in American policy reform to overlay existing systems of government with new ones.

Charter schools can be created by a number of different agencies. The power to authorize charter schools often rests with local school boards, many of which have been in the business of supervising schools for decades. In some instances, states also grant chartering authority to newly created agencies designed specifically for the sole purpose of authorizing and monitoring charter schools. Add to this mix universities, which are now significant players in the chartering game, and a picture emerges of the typically messy institutional structure that characterizes policy reform in the United States. According to the Schools and Staffing Survey of the National Center for Education Statistics, of the 870 charter schools in the country for the 1999–2000 school year, 38 percent were authorized by a local school district, 37 percent by a state board of education, 13 percent by a state chartering authority, 11 percent by a college or university, and 1 percent by some other agency. Many of these schools coexist in the same political jurisdictions and face a range of laws governing their interaction. In short, the practice of creating, overseeing, and renewing or closing charter schools is evolving in a typically complicated American policy environment about which much is speculated and little is really known.

Many education policy analysts have expressed concern that continued reliance on local school boards in granting charters might have adverse effects on the growth and character of charter schools. In particular, charter advocates, who want to see as many well-qualified schools develop as quickly as possible, argue that states allowing bodies other than local school boards, such as state boards and universities, to authorize charters are more likely to have a large and successful charter sector. These advocates fear that local school boards view charter schools as competitors for their students and funds and act both to impede their creation and limit their growth. Chester Finn, with characteristic flair, argues "that placing school boards in charge of charter schools is akin to placing McDonalds in charge of Burger King." In less dramatic language, Finn argues that local school boards do not "want the competition, [have] scant experience in letting some schools be different from others, and [do not] know how to replace command-and-control compliance with results-based accountability."[1]

Indeed, there is ample evidence suggesting that local school boards can create problems for charter schools. For example, Abernathy found that the opposition of some New Jersey school boards to charter school legislation was "quick and intense."[2] According to Abernathy, in 1997 five school boards successfully appealed two of the original charter decisions to the state commissioner of education, and in the following year, thirteen of the first twenty-three charter schools were challenged by local school boards. In addition, many districts sought to block the transfer of funds stipulated in the law.

Such problems are not unique to New Jersey. Fuller describes similar local school board behavior in his discussion of a failed effort to obtain approval for a charter school in Oakland, California. He argues that the school board rejected the application because the board was "caught up in its own bureaucratic aloofness and penned in by the teachers union that feared the emerging threat posed by the new charters."[3]

1. Finn (2003).
2. Abernathy (2004, p. 16).
3. Fuller (2000, p. 2)

Looking at a much larger number of school systems, Bierlein Palmer and Gau contend that local school boards generally do not make good charter authorizers and that they are much more likely to be influenced by political pressure and political considerations than other types of authorizers.[4] In turn, they argue that state policymakers should grant more nonlocal authorizers the power to authorize charters.[5] It is also possible that local boards, even those with good intentions, may have inadequate resources to effectively oversee and monitor the charter schools that they authorize.

Not all studies find such a distinctive and oppositional role for local school boards. Anderson and coauthors found few differences between types of authorizers.[6] For example, initial differences in the resources devoted to overseeing charter schools by state and local authorizers disappeared when they controlled for the numbers of schools that each body was actually supervising.

In this chapter, we contribute to the debate by comparing the chartering activities and outcomes of local school boards with those of other authorizing bodies.

Theoretical Perspectives

The strongest foundation for the belief that local school boards will treat charter schools negatively is the idea that charter schools compete with traditional public schools for students in the market-like environment that choice seeks to stimulate. At least within their own boundaries, school boards have long enjoyed a monopolistic position in providing local public schools, one that they are loath to give up. From this perspective, we would expect school boards to discourage competitors who want to reduce their student "market share" and thereby take funding away from them. Indeed, it should come as no surprise that the number of different authorizers allowed by the chartering law often is used as a critical parameter in rating the strength of state charter laws.[7]

One possible outcome of the no-competition incentive would be for local school boards to authorize fewer charter schools. That is, local boards could simply turn down charter school applicants in large numbers, thereby limiting competition. However, local school boards are driven by a variety of nonmarket considerations that could limit this type of anticompetitive behavior (see chapters 7, 10, and 11 of this volume).

Local school boards operate in an intensely political world that offers them incentives to respond to local political forces and to state institutional rules governing funding and other important issues.[8] Where local and state forces tend to

4. Bierlein Palmer and Gau (2003).
5. See also Hess, Maranto, and Milliman (2001).
6. Anderson and others (2002).
7. Center for Education Reform (2003).
8. See Chubb and Moe (1990).

favor charter schools, local school boards might respond more positively to charter schools, regardless of their own wish to limit competition and retain their
market share of students and funds.

Another strategic response, congruent with this perspective, is that local
school boards will seek to charter "niche schools," especially those serving students who are difficult and potentially expensive to serve. Greene, Forster, and
Winters suggest that the charter approval process in most states encourages the
creation of schools for students considered undesirable by public school districts.[9] The incentive to send these students to charter schools may increase
given the accountability provisions of the federal No Child Left Behind Act.
Indeed, given some political pressure in favor of charter schools, the authorization of niche schools by local boards can serve the dual purpose of diminishing
pressure from charter advocates and at the same time limiting direct competition from broad-based charter schools.

Moreover, in states where less than 100 percent of per-pupil operating funds
follow students to charter schools, local boards may have an additional fiscal
incentive to charter schools that serve more difficult or more expensive students.
In some districts with growing student enrollment, limited facility space, and
some explicit state financial "make-up" support for the loss of charter students,
sloughing off a small percentage of students, particularly some difficult ones, to
charter schools may not seem like a negative prospect, even to local boards that
otherwise would not favor charter schools.[10]

Given the conflicting theoretical perspectives, empirical evidence is required
to sort out the reality of chartering activity. Ideally, researchers could test
whether local school boards have an anticharter bias by employing a range of
indicators central to the process of chartering and supervising new schools—
including initial authorization rates, monitoring and supervision practices,
renewal decisions, and school closures. Unfortunately, as in so many other areas
of education policy, the data necessary to test predictions are scattered across
multiple jurisdictions, many with little or no incentive or administrative capacity to collect, collate, and distribute the data. Therefore our picture of local
school boards in the charter school authorizing process is more of a rough
sketch than a fully completed canvas.

In the next few pages, we review some extant studies and then analyze available national data on patterns of authorization drawn from the most recent
national Schools and Staffing Survey. We supplement the national data with
case studies in Washington, D.C., Pennsylvania, Colorado, and New York.

9. Greene, Forster, and Winters (2003).
10. See Teske and others (2001).

Evidence about Local School Boards as Chartering Bodies

The chartering process involves several steps—application, approval, review, and renewal or closure. The first question of interest concerns the extent to which local school boards are more likely than other authorizing bodies to accept or reject charter school applicants. One would hypothesize that on the basis of self-interest, local school boards would be less likely than other chartering agencies to authorize charter schools, which are their direct competitors.

Unfortunately, there is no national database that includes and tracks all charter applications, and some states do not keep careful records of rejected applications. As Renzulli notes, it is easy to get lists of the charter schools that were approved but difficult to obtain information about applicants that were denied or that withdrew their applications.[11] To address the problem, Renzulli compiled a database of applicants and approvals in twenty-nine states from 1991 to 1998, which covers 85 percent of the states (twenty-nine of thirty-four) that had charter school laws in 1998. She identified 1,147 total charter applications, of which 415 were authorized, for an overall national rate of acceptance of 36 percent. Unfortunately, Renzulli did not focus on the role of the specific authorizing bodies, limiting the utility of the data for our analysis. Nonetheless, the data do provide a rough baseline for overall charter acceptance rates.

Renzulli found a concentration of charter school applications and approvals in large urban districts. Her data highlight an important point—even with the rapid growth of charter schools, most local school boards (97 percent in her data set) had no charter applications. Given the concentration of schools in central cities and the well-known problems with schools there, it is reasonable to expect that there would be more charter applicants in large urban areas. For example, cities such as Washington, D.C., Philadelphia, Chicago, and Boston had received more than twenty applications each by 1998. Local school boards in large cities, which often are already polarized over a range of other educational issues, may act differently in dealing with charter schools than do local school boards in suburban and rural areas. Renzulli used multiple regression analysis to explain the variation in charter application and acceptance rates. She also found that there are both more charter applications and more acceptances in districts with more nonreligious private schools, perhaps because of an existing climate of support for alternatives to traditional public schools.

While our central variable of interest, the role of local school boards, cannot be studied using Renzulli's data, a recent study by Buckley and Kúcsová comes closer to addressing the question.[12] Based on Center for Education Reform

11. Renzulli (2002, p. 15).
12. Buckley and Kúcsová (2003).

(CER) data, they find that states with fewer types of authorizers (states that are more reliant on local school boards to grant charters) had significantly fewer charter schools relative to their school populations, validating the general concern about lower authorization numbers.

Anderson and coauthors found that applications for charters were denied infrequently (fewer than one-quarter of their respondents had ever denied a charter application), but they did find that local school boards were less likely than other authorizing bodies to have turned down an applicant.[13] In part, these results may have to do with the fact that many local school boards have not received charter applications, or they may be a function of who is applying to the local school board, but they do call into question theories of a simple link between competition and high rates of denial.

Once an application has been accepted and a charter school established, the question of oversight and monitoring arises. Again, not much is known here. The recent study by Bierlein Palmer and Gau examines monitoring and finds that many local school boards devote limited resources to monitoring and supervision.[14] This is particularly true of local school boards that have only a single charter school in their jurisdiction. These findings are consistent with those of Anderson and his coauthors, who found that fewer than one-third of authorizers had a separate office or staff dedicated to charter schools. Most often, charter school oversight is a secondary responsibility of a staff member within the authorizing organization.

Anderson and his coauthors did report significant differences in staffing patterns by authorizer type: almost all state-level authorizers (93 percent) had a separate office and staff, while less than half of universities (44 percent) and only about one-quarter of local authorizers (26 percent) did. Anderson and his coauthors also found that local school boards were less likely to be tied into networks that share information or otherwise create support for the process of chartering and monitoring schools.[15] These studies raise the question of whether local school boards are providing the resources or developing the skills necessary to effectively manage the complicated regulatory process surrounding charter schools.

Outcomes of the oversight process feed into charter renewal decisions. Hassel and Batdorff recently studied decisions to renew school charters, looking at all 506 nationwide renewal cases through 2001 and then focusing on fifty randomly selected cases.[16] They found that most charters (84 percent) were renewed but that there was some variation by authorizer: local school boards

13. Anderson and others (2002).
14. Bierlein Palmer and Gau (2003).
15. Anderson and others (2002, p. 24). On the importance of networks for policy implementation, see Heclo (1978), Bardach (1998), Konig and Brauninger (1998), O'Toole (1997), and Schneider and others. (2003).
16. Hassel and Batdorff (2003).

renewed the most (87 percent), while state boards of education renewed 76 percent and university boards renewed 83 percent. From their in-depth case examinations, Hassel and Batdorff argue—as do Bierlein Palmer and Gau—that most local school boards do not have the capacity or the resources to properly monitor charter school performance. These studies present convincing evidence that local school boards are less likely to adequately oversee charter schools than other authorizers.

Examining the final stage of the process, the Center for Education Reform considered charter school closures.[17] The CER found that 154 charter schools had been closed nationwide, about 7 percent of existing charter schools. Of those closures, local school boards closed about two-thirds (ninety-five). Recall that local school boards chartered about 38 percent of schools nationwide in 2000. Thus local boards were far more likely to close schools that they had chartered than were other authorizing agencies. In addition, Hassel and Batdorff indicate that in almost all closings in which "political" considerations seemed to outweigh a school's merit (only about 14 percent of the renewal cases that they examined), local school boards were the agency that shut down schools that were performing adequately.

While filled with considerable gaps, the evidence from these studies suggests that compared with other authorizers, local schools boards authorize fewer schools, monitor them less well, are less careful about renewal decisions, and are more likely to shut schools down. While these results are congruent with anticompetitive behavior, they are not overwhelming proof of it. We return to this point below, but first we turn to our own national data and findings.

Our National Findings

As noted above, there is no single source of data on the number of charter school applications in each state, and states themselves vary widely in the data that they collect and make available to researchers. Therefore we cannot perform a direct national test to determine what percentage of applicants are authorized by different types of chartering agencies. What we can examine is output—that is, how many charter schools have been authorized, who authorized them, and what the characteristics of the schools that resulted from the chartering process were. Here, we employ data from the National Center for Education Statistics's Schools and Staffing Survey (SASS), which includes information on the number of charter schools in each state and on the schools' enrollment, origin (newly created or public-private conversion), characteristics, student demographics, and authorizing agency. Even these data are quite limited: they cover only 870 charter schools for the 1999–2000 period. Thus the

17. Loonie (2002); Braunlich and Loonie (2002).

explosive growth in the number of charter schools that has taken place in the last few years is not reflected in these data.

As noted earlier, SASS data show that less than 40 percent of schools were chartered by local school boards and about the same number by state bodies. Universities chartered another 10 percent, and other agencies chartered the other 6 percent.[18] We divided the schools into three categories based on their authorizer—local school board, state, or university (the twelve "other" schools were dropped)—to see whether schools chartered by local boards differed in systematic ways from schools chartered by other agencies. In estimating our multiple regression models, we controlled for the location of the school (urban, suburban, rural), the state in which the school was located, and the "charter-friendliness" score of the state charter law.[19]

Our analysis centers on eight different school outcome characteristics—the number of tools a school has to encourage parent participation; the number of regulatory waivers granted to the school (such as teacher tenure, variable teacher payment, and the like); total student enrollment; percentage of students with limited English proficiency (LEP); percentage of students with special education requirements or an individual education plan (IEP); magnet school (12 percent of charter schools were magnets); school for at-risk students (6 percent); and conversions of existing schools (27 percent of charters were conversions, and about two-thirds of those were public school conversions).

Our results, presented in table 6-1, show that schools chartered by local school boards shared a profile that differed somewhat from that of schools chartered by universities or state agencies. Most important, in this multiple regression approach controlling for state climate and urban location, local boards were significantly more likely to create "niche" schools. Schools chartered by local school boards had the highest percentage of students with limited English proficiency, had higher percentages of students with learning disabilities (as reflected in IEPs), and were more likely to be schools for at-risk students.

Table 6-1 also shows that schools chartered by local boards had significantly greater numbers of programs designed to encourage parental involvement and had received more administrative waivers. In a related analysis (not reported here), we also found that local school boards chartered relatively fewer elementary schools than did other chartering agencies and relatively more junior and senior high schools. Thus local boards did differ from other authorizers in the types of schools that they chartered. It appears that the most important difference is that they were significantly more likely to charter schools that included

18. In a more recent sample of 2,500 charter schools, Bierlein Palmer and Gau (2003) report a greater percentage chartered by local school boards, 47 percent, with 39 percent chartered by state bodies, 10 percent by universities, and 4 percent by others. Thus since 1999, local school boards may have increased their relative share of charter schools authorized.

19. The charter-friendliness score is from Center for Education Reform (2003).

Table 6-1. *Differences in the Profile of Schools Authorized by Local Chartering Agencies*[a]

School characteristic	Local school district	State	University	Significance level
Number of parental involvement actions	5.5	5.1	4.9	.00
Number of waivers granted	1.8	1.6	1.1	.00
Percent of LEP/NEP students[b]	6.6	4.3	1.9	.01
Percent of students with IEP[b]	12.7	10.9	7.1	.01
Percent converted schools	26	29	16	.04
At risk	9	4	2	.01
Magnet	14	11	7	.16

Source: Authors' calculations.

a. These results were generated using multiple regression techniques, controlling for state charter school "friendliness" and for city, suburb, or rural location. We do not report the coefficients for those variables.

b. LEP: limited English proficiency; NEP: no English proficiency; IEP: individual education plan.

larger numbers of the types of students that might be most difficult or expensive for them to educate—a finding consistent with the "niche" hypothesis.

A More Detailed Look at the Politics of Chartering: Four Case Studies

These results from the SASS data are interesting but limited, since they are based only on the 870 charter schools actually authorized as of the 1999–2000 school year. Recall too that we do not have data on the total number of applicants, so we cannot address the selection bias issues that arise from the possibility that certain types of charter school applicants gravitate to or avoid certain types of authorizers. Thus, given significant state-by-state variation in chartering policies, we undertook a series of case studies to explore these issues further.

We examined four "states": Washington, D.C., Pennsylvania, Colorado, and New York. These jurisdictions include four large cities in which much charter school action takes place—Washington, Philadelphia, Denver, and New York City. In addition, we wanted to avoid states that have already received considerable scholarly attention about their charter schools, such as Arizona, Michigan, and California. While the jurisdictions we study may not be fully representative of all states, they do have charter laws stipulating a variety of ways to authorize charter schools and therefore can help to provide insight into the question we explore in this study.

For the D.C. case study, we had considerable data to compare the authorization outcomes of the local school board to those of the only other authorizing body. In the other case studies, we examined the charter environment more

Table 6-2. *Summary of State Chartering Actions*

Action	Nation	Pennsylvania (local boards with state appeals)	Colorado (local boards, with state appeals)	New York (local boards, SUNY, or Regents)	Washington (board of education or PCSB)
Percent approvals	36[a]	41[b]	50[c]	27[d]	37[e]
Percent successful appeals	. . .	40	30	. . .	. . .
Number of charters authorized	3,000	90	90	44	39
(per year)	(200)	(15)	(8)	(9)	(6)
Charter closures	154	1	2	0	6
(percent of total)	(7)	(1)	(2)	(0)	(13)
Charter consolidations	60	0	1	2	0
Charter schools approved but never opened	84	2	0	0	0

Source: Authors' compilation from various state sources and Loonie (2002).

a. Percent overall (Renzulli 2002).

b. Percent including appeals; 35 percent local school boards only.

c. Percent including appeals; 37 percent local school boards only.

d. Percent overall.

e. Percent overall; 30 percent Public Charter School Board; 50 percent Board of Education.

briefly, focusing on the decisionmaking process and some outcome indicators to better understand how local school boards go about chartering schools. In D.C., two authorities charter schools—the local school board and the Public Charter School Board, which was established specifically for the purpose of authorizing and monitoring charter schools. In New York, there are three authorizing bodies—local school boards, the State University of New York, and the State Board of Regents. In contrast, in both Pennsylvania and Colorado the local school boards are the only chartering agencies, but each state has an appellate board to which many applicants appeal if rejected at the local level.

According to the 2003 Center for Education Reform annual study of the strength of chartering laws, the states in our study are all in the upper third of forty charter law states: D.C. is ranked third, Colorado ninth, New York tenth, and Pennsylvania thirteenth. The weakest laws usually allow only local school boards to authorize charter schools and do not allow for an appeals process. In table 6-2, we illustrate the charter approval rates and other figures associated with each of our state case studies.

Washington D.C.

The charter school movement in D.C. sprang from the perennial problems of low test scores and high dropout rates in the District's public schools, compounded by the city's 1995 fiscal crisis. Congress favored school choice as a response to D.C.'s educational problems, and in the D.C. School Reform Act of 1995 it made provisions for voucher programs, scholarship programs, and charter schools. While voucher programs were dropped after meeting Senate opposition, charter schools were approved, and the D.C. city council then enacted a separate statute defining the terms for establishing charter schools.

For our purposes, the most important element of D.C.'s charter legislation is that it allows two different bodies—the board of education (BOE) of the D.C. public school system and the Public Charter School Board (PCSB)—to authorize charter schools. Each is permitted to authorize a maximum of ten schools every year and is responsible for their oversight. The dual authority structure was designed specifically to address concerns about democratic accountability and conflicts of interest—making D.C. particularly useful for investigating the effects of having multiple authorizers.[20]

Forty-two charter schools now serve about 14 percent of D.C. students, currently the highest density of charter schools in the nation.[21] At present, twenty-five of the District's operational charters were authorized by the PCSB and seventeen were authorized by the BOE. The two agencies differ in composition. The PCSB is composed of eleven members appointed by the mayor from a list provided by the U.S. Department of Education. Following a public referendum, the BOE was reconstituted in 2000 and reduced from eleven elected members to nine members, of whom five were elected (including the board's president) and four appointed by the mayor.

The two agencies are widely perceived to be distinctive in their approach to their charter school responsibilities.[22] The charter-granting behavior of the BOE suggests a vulnerability to local political forces. A recent study by Henig and MacDonald demonstrated that schools chartered by the BOE were concentrated in wards with higher voter turnout and in areas with a large African American population.[23] The PCSB appears to be motivated by more pragmatic concerns centered on school operations. Beyond this, Bierlein Palmer and Gau, in their recent study of charter school authorization, indicate that BOE-authorized charter schools consistently describe their oversight relations with the board as strained and, at times, antagonistic.[24]

In terms of approval rates, the combined rate by both authorizing bodies is 37 percent, essentially the same as the national average generated by Renzulli. Breaking approvals down by authorizer, the PCSB approved twenty-four of the seventy-nine applications it received since 1997, or 30 percent. In contrast, the

20. DC Appleseed Center (2001).

21. Patrick Badgley, "Three Charter School Hopefuls Get OKs," *Washington Times*, August 19, 2003, p. B2.

22. Hill and others (2001).

23. Henig and MacDonald (2002).

24. Bierlein Palmer and Gau (2003); Hill and others (2001).

BOE received a smaller number of applications, forty-two, but approved 50 percent of them, or twenty-one schools.

Six charter schools had been closed in D.C. by 2003, giving the district a closure rate almost twice the national average. The schools were all chartered and closed by the BOE, four for fiscal mismanagement and two for improper reporting and poor learning conditions.[25] The closure rate for the BOE alone, then, is a huge 30 percent. Alternatively, the PCSB has yet to close a school that it chartered.

Some attribute the higher success rate of the PCSB schools to the organization's more rigorous application process, its active participation in school development, and its greater support of its schools through the oversight process.[26] The BOE responded to the 1995 passage of the charter law with the rapid approval of several charter schools, but it did not carefully examine the expertise of applicants, nor did it do much to support its schools following authorization. Such behavior was likely the result of tension caused by a combination of fear of congressional retribution if they did not approve the schools and the BOE's prevailing anticharter sentiment. Following the highly publicized failures of BOE-chartered schools and the 2000 reconstitution of the board so that its members held more favorable attitudes toward charter schools, the BOE has adopted a more careful and professional approach to its schools and applicants that more closely parallels that of the PCSB.

Studies by Henig, Holyoke, Lacireno-Paquet, and Moser in 1999 and 2001 confirm that the two chartering agencies have been perceived differently by stakeholders in D.C.[27] The PCSB is considered to be the more neutral, objective, and professional chartering entity, while the BOE is characterized as hostile, less stringent in its review of applications, and less supportive during the early stages of charter school development. The disparity may prove to be attributable to differences in staffing resources and organizational focus; however, it is important to note that the influence of local politics was borne out in several personal interviews that we ourselves conducted with the staff of pro–charter school interest groups. Interest group staff clearly aligned themselves with the PCSB, suggesting (as did Hill and others) that the BOE authorized only charters with particularly high levels of community political support. Claims of the PCSB's greater neutrality are founded on its distance from the climate of conflicting interests that surrounds the BOE and on its greater likelihood of chartering schools run by private, for-profit firms. Henig and his colleagues suggest, however, that because the PCSB has a vested interest in the success of the charter movement, charter schools may in effect have captured their regulators.

25. Center for Education Reform (2003).
26. Henig and others (1999).
27. Henig and others (1999, 2001).

Table 6-3. *Profile of the Two Washington, D.C., Chartering Agencies*

School characteristic	Board of education	Public Charter School Board	Significance
Number of parental involvement mechanisms	5.3	5.3	.99
Number of waivers granted	3	3.4	.06
Average enrollment	159.2	299.5	.10
Percent of LEP/NEP students[a]	14	9.1	.85
Percent of students with an IEP[a]	7.0	14.7	.19
Percent black students	88.8	89.6	.93
Percent Hispanic students	9.1	10.1	.94
Percent converted schools	25	25	.99
Percent schools focusing on at-risk students	50	0	.01
Percent magnet schools	25	8	.42

Sources: Heath Brown, working with Henig and others, provided much of these data; the rest come from the National Center for Education Statistics, *Schools and Staffing Survey,* 1999–2000 (Washington).

a. LEP: limited English proficiency; NEP: no English proficiency ; IEP: individual education plan.

Despite these differences in the boards, the simple comparative data we present in table 6-3 do not show many differences in the profiles of the schools they have chartered. However, perhaps most important—and mirroring our national data—we do find that the BOE is significantly more likely to charter schools targeting at-risk students. Again, this finding is consistent with the niche hypothesis.

Pennsylvania

Pennsylvania passed its charter law in 1997 as part of a top-down state reform strategy that also emphasized school accountability, driven in part by the efforts of former Republican governor Tom Ridge. Ninety charter schools have been authorized since then, giving Pennsylvania the most rapid rate of expansion among our case studies. The charter schools are geographically clustered—only eighteen of sixty-seven Pennsylvania counties contain charter schools, and in ten of these eighteen counties, charter schools serve a tiny population of students. Not surprisingly, charter school density is highest in the state's urban centers. In Philadelphia, for example, 8 percent of all students are enrolled in charter schools.

Pennsylvania's charter law grants local school boards the sole authority to authorize charter schools, but it provides for an appeals process at the state level. Of the ninety authorized schools, fifteen that were initially rejected by the local school board successfully appealed to the state's Charter Appeals Board (CAB). Twenty-two other schools rejected by local boards also appealed, but they were rejected by the CAB too.

Miron, Nelson, and Risely recently completed a study of Pennsylvania charter schools.[28] While they were not able to pin down precise figures for total charter school applications, they report that the Pennsylvania state government awarded 273 planning grants to potential charter school applicants between 1997 and 2002, which is a rough approximation of the number of serious potential applicants. Through more detailed checks of district and state records, Miron and colleagues believe that there were about 217 actual applications, of which ninety, or 41 percent, were approved—a rate higher than Renzulli's nationwide approval figure of 36 percent. If we exclude the fifteen successful state appeals, the local school boards themselves approved seventy-five of the 217 applications, or 35 percent, essentially the national average figure. Thus the CAB appeals process may have served to boost the state's overall approval rate slightly above the national average. Miron and colleagues show that contrary to the niche hypothesis, the percentage of students with special needs is considerably lower in Pennsylvania charter schools than in their home districts.

The rapid expansion of charter schools seems to be a function of the combination of the credible threat of appeal to the CAB, strong initial support from state politicians (though there is evidence that this is changing), and bottom-up pressure from parents for charter schools. Parental pressure has been strongest in the dramatically failing school system in Philadelphia, where charters have been perceived as a less radical solution than the highly controversial proposal for a complete takeover of the system by the private Edison Schools Corporation. Statewide, the median charter school has a waiting list totaling 28 percent of its current enrollment.[29] Clearly, there exists considerable parental pressure for further expansion.

Perceptions of the competence of Pennsylvania school boards in monitoring charters vary widely. The large urban districts seem to be perceived more positively, perhaps because of the greater resources available to large boards. Miron, Nelson, and Risley argue that the state board has done a good job with its part in monitoring and assisting charter schools, but local boards have played a minimal role in oversight, except when it is time for renewal.[30] As is evident in table 6-2, Pennsylvania boards did not close many charter schools once they were approved.

In short, strong political and parent support for charter schools and the presence of the Charter Appeals Board limit the ability of local school boards to constrain entry into the market for education. Nor do local boards appear to be emphasizing a niche strategy for approvals. These elements could change, however, as the political climate in Pennsylvania continues to shift away from support for charters; in October 2003, Governor Ed Rendell, a Democrat,

28. Miron, Nelson, and Risley (2002).
29. Miron, Nelson, and Risley (2002).
30. Miron, Nelson, and Risley (2002).

appointed a task force to study charter schools that seemed to be stacked with individuals who oppose further charter school expansion.

Colorado

Colorado was one of the earlier states to pass a charter law, in 1993. As in Pennsylvania, state law grants sole charter-granting authority to local school boards, but it also provides for appeal to the state board of education (CBOE). In part, this provision is related to a strong tradition of local school control in the state. The environment for school choice in Colorado is generally positive and offers considerable opportunity for choice both across and within most districts. In 2002, the state passed a voucher law that, if it survives court challenges, will give low-income students in failing schools an opportunity to enroll in private schools. In addition, a state accountability law provides for charter conversion for schools that have "unsatisfactory" test results for three straight years, and at least one traditional public school has applied for conversion.

Charter schools have developed relatively quickly in the state: about 4 percent of Colorado public school children attended the ninety-five charter schools in operation in 2003. Charter schools are somewhat more widely distributed geographically than in Pennsylvania, with at least one school operating in twenty-five of the state's sixty-three counties. In fact, compared with other states, more charter activity is taking place in nonurban areas. "We were known as the white-suburban charter school state for a long time," says Denise Mund, a consultant with the state department of education.

Indeed, unlike in many other states, charter schools do not serve a proportionate share of minorities or low-income families compared with traditional public schools. Overall, minorities represent 34 percent of Colorado's traditional school students, but only 27 percent of those in charter schools. Similarly, students eligible for free or reduced lunches represent 29 percent of Colorado traditional students, but only 17 percent of those in charter schools. And, contrary to the niche hypothesis, the charter schools also serve a smaller aggregate percentage of disabled and at-risk students than are served by the traditional public schools.

Despite the suburban emphasis, higher concentrations of charter schools are found in the biggest city, Denver. Charter schools in Denver serve between 7 and 8 percent of public school children.[31] After initial opposition, the Denver board is now perceived by the League of Charter Schools, a statewide advocacy group, as the most charter-friendly district in the state.

The state does not maintain records of the approval rate for all applications, but according to the League of Charter Schools, there have been about 190 actual applications and ninety-five approvals in Colorado, for an overall acceptance rate

31. Colorado Department of Education (2003).

(including successful appeals) of about 50 percent. This is much higher than Renzulli's national baseline rate of 36 percent and Pennsylvania's 41 percent approval rate after appeals. In addition, ninety-six of the applicants that were initially rejected appealed to the CBOE, and many of these appeals were made prior to 1997, when acceptance rates were below 40 percent. The CBOE returned almost one-quarter of these cases to the local boards, which then approved the applicants. Thus the initial approval rate by local school boards was about seventy-one of 190, or 37 percent, about the overall national average.

Several of the early reversals of local boards involved high-profile charter school applicants. In overturning these rejections, the state board strongly suggested that local school boards view charter applications more positively. The message seems to have been internalized by Colorado's local school boards, given that the approval rate has been about 55 percent since 1997. Early signals from state officials can be understood to have pushed local boards to act more favorably on charter applicants, resulting in approval rates that exceed the national average.

Overall, despite limited resources, the monitoring relationship between local boards and charter schools is better in Colorado than in many other states. Mund notes that, unlike in states such as Arizona that encouraged extremely rapid growth of charter schools, in Colorado "[t]here is more of a personal relationship with the local boards, and they have a better idea of what is going on."[32] This relatively positive relationship between charter schools and many local boards is consistent with Bierlein Palmer and Gau's report, which suggests that some Colorado local boards have been prominent exceptions to the national finding of anticharter attitudes by local boards.[33] Table 6-2 shows two closures of Colorado charter schools, although more recent data show six closed schools. Still, even this higher closure rate does not exceed the national average.

Despite considerable positive interaction, current relationships between local boards and charter schools in Colorado are far from perfect. In 2003, three local school boards voted to impose a moratorium on approving new charter schools. Fights with two local boards in 2003 kept charter school capital bond proposals out of the districts' main bond proposal, putting them on a separate (and losing) ticket instead. A fierce fight over a proposed charter in Steamboat Springs attracted attention from the governor and the state courts. Partly in response to these issues, in 2004 state legislators passed a law establishing a state-level board that can authorize charter schools.

Governor Bill Owens—who, as a legislator, cosponsored the charter bill in 1993—believed that charter schools would fill a badly needed niche for many

32. Quoted in Monte Whaley, "State Education Department Is Charter Friendly," *Denver Post*, October 5, 2003, p. 12A.
33. Bierlein Palmer and Gau (2003).

students that the public system could not provide. Unlike our national findings for local board charters, however, whatever niches may have been filled in Colorado have not been predominantly for special education students or those with limited English proficiency.

Approval rates, monitoring relationships, and closure rates suggest that overall the relatively positive environment for choice has not allowed local school boards to limit the Colorado charter sector. Recent developments, however, suggest that the climate is changing in a way that will influence its further expansion.

New York State

In the five years following passage of New York state's charter school law in 1998, forty-four schools were authorized.[34] The law provides for three authorizing agencies—the State University of New York, the State Board of Regents, and local school boards. Of the forty-four state charter schools authorized since the law's inception, twenty-five were authorized by SUNY (57 percent), twelve by the State Board of Regents (27 percent), and seven by the New York City (NYC) chancellor. The seven approved by the local school board in NYC include five conversions of existing schools and only two new charter schools. No other local school board in New York has yet approved charter schools, although Buffalo and Rochester plan to do so soon. This suggests either a lack of enthusiasm by New York local school boards for charter schools or the availability of alternative authorizing agencies that are perceived by applicants as a better route to approval.

The Charter School Institute (CSI), established by SUNY for the purpose of reviewing applications and providing oversight, has received 160 applications since the charter law's inception. Forty-four schools have been approved, yielding an overall state approval rate of about 27 percent—considerably lower than that of the other case study states and Renzulli's calculated national rate of 36 percent. Despite the presence of active alternative chartering authorities in New York state, authorizing bodies are rejecting a greater percentage of applicants than those in the other states under consideration.

While charter school advocacy groups in New York consider the initial approval process of the CSI to be quite rigorous, charter advocates report that the CSI is a careful and helpful overseer of schools that do get authorized, much like the PCSB in Washington, D.C. A recent independent report on charter school accountability in New York finds that charter authorizers in the state have done a relatively good job of developing and monitoring a range of performance-based fiscal and contractual accountability and oversight mechanisms.[35] No CSI-authorized schools have been closed or consolidated.

---

34. Charter School Institute (2003).
35. Ascher and others (2003).

Generally, local boards in New York have not yet authorized or renewed enough charter schools to determine how well they are monitoring them.

Interestingly, compared with other large cities around the country and in our sample cases, the New York City public school system has not focused on charter schools as a strategy for educational improvement. Instead, in recent years NYC local school board politics has focused on centralization, mayoral control of the school system, funding parity from state sources, the fairness of state tests, and an adequate flow of qualified teachers for the system. Despite substantial shifts in the direction of education policy from different leaders in recent years, in all cases, charter schools have taken a back seat in NYC and serve only a miniscule percentage of the public system's 1.1 million students, in marked contrast to the percentage in many other large cities around the country, including Washington, Philadelphia, and Denver. This may now be changing somewhat, however; in November 2003, the mayor and school chancellor announced a plan to create fifty new charter schools and a newly funded institute to assist schools in reinventing themselves as charters.

Conclusions

There are strong theoretical reasons to believe that local school boards are likely to be more hostile to charter schools than other authorizers, based mainly on anticompetitive incentives. We have found some evidence to support this view. Prior studies demonstrate that in states in which only local boards were authorizers, fewer schools were chartered and local boards were less adequate at oversight, more swayed by political considerations, and more likely to close charter schools.

The national statistical evidence we gather here shows that local boards were more likely to charter niche schools with greater numbers of students that might be difficult or expensive to educate. This validates the idea that local school boards will seek to avoid creating schools that compete directly for most students, while still showing responsiveness to top-down and bottom-up political demands for charter schools. And there are some other differences in the types of schools authorized by local boards. Still, there is substantial variation in local boards across the nation, and some, especially those in large cities where public schools are perceived to be failing dramatically, have proven to be more sympathetic to a wider range of charter schools. Simple demographic data from Pennsylvania and Colorado do not support the niche hypothesis, even though local boards are the only chartering bodies in those states.

While simple authorization rates might seem like the acid test of charter-friendliness, they are problematic. First, good data on applicants simply are not available across the nation. Second, selection issues make it difficult to study the real environment surrounding approval rates. Thus we turned to our case study evidence to get further insight. In particular, a careful look at Colorado and

Pennsylvania, where law grants chartering authority only to local school boards, suggests that local boards do grant charters at a rate comparable to the national average. However, the higher approval rates in the two states may exist only because of the presence of an effective appeals process that provides a credible recourse for overturning inappropriate denials. Similarly, the Washington BOE's concern that Congress was looking closely over its shoulder may have made the board more receptive to charters than it otherwise would have been. In contrast, despite the presence of multiple chartering authorities, New York's acceptance rate is almost 10 percent lower than Renzulli's national average. Ultimately, factors other than the formal composition of the charter-granting authority seem to account for some of the statewide variation in charter acceptance levels.

Anecdotal evidence suggests that local boards do not monitor charter schools well. This may be true because they do not care about the development and health of the schools that they charter or it may be more the result of the weak administrative capacity of local school boards and their placement in a highly charged political environment. Given our inability to fully distinguish between the anticompetition model and the incompetence explanation, it may be best to resort to Hanlon's Razor: "Never attribute to malice that which can be adequately explained by stupidity." In short, many of the problems that charter schools are having with local school boards may prove to be as much a function of the weaknesses of local boards as organizations in a turbulent political and administrative environment as a strategic anticompetitive response.

Finally, we must recognize one further limitation on any desire of a school board to limit competition. Henig and his colleagues have recently examined the extent to which schools run by different types of organizations differ in terms of target population, program focus, size, and marketing behavior, leading them to develop "differentiation" and "convergence" hypotheses.[36] Differentiation suggests that differences in the internal characteristics of the applicant organization (such as institutional origins, norms, mission, and personnel) will be reflected in school characteristics. By contrast, convergence occurs as factors external to the applicant (such as political forces, supply and demand, and regulatory constraints) overwhelm internal differences. Borrowing their convergence perspective, our findings suggest that—despite real differences in the authorization, monitoring, and renewal behavior of local school boards compared with other chartering agencies—external political pressure (from governors, teacher unions, parents, and others) and the general climate surrounding school choice may be as important in distinguishing local boards from other authorizing bodies. Certainly, with changes in political leadership and pressures, the attitudes of some local boards toward charters have become more positive over time, as demonstrated in Washington, D.C., and Colorado and quite recently in New

36. Henig and others (2003).

York City. On the other hand, Pennsylvania may be moving in a more negative direction. To quote Tip O'Neill, a politician with a gift for words, "All politics is local." So it seems with the local school board politics of chartering schools.

References

Abernathy, Scott. 2004. "The Democratic Consequences of School Choice." Ph.D. dissertation, Princeton University, Department of Political Science.

Anderson, Lee, and others. 2002. "A Decade of Public Charter Schools: Evaluation of the Public Charter Schools Program: 2000–2001 Evaluation Report." Palo Alto: SRI International (www.sri.com/policy/cep/choice/yr2.pdf [September 2, 2003]).

Ascher, Carol, and others. 2003. "Charter School Accountability in New York: Findings from a Three-Year Study of Charter School Authorizers." New York University Institute for Education and Social Policy.

Bardach, Eugene. 1998. *Getting Agencies to Work Together: The Practice and Theory of Managerial Craftsmanship.* Brookings.

Bierlein Palmer, Louann, and Rebecca Gau. 2003. "Charter School Authorizing: Are States Making the Grade?" Washington: Thomas Fordham Institute.

Braunlich, Christian, and Melanie Loonie, eds. 2002. "Charter Schools 2002: Results from CER's Annual Survey of American Charter Schools." Washington: Center for Education Reform.

Buckley, Jack, and Simona Kúcsová. 2003. "The Effect of Institutional Variation on Policy Outcomes: the Case of Charter Schools in the States." Occasional Paper Series 79. National Center for the Study of Privatization in Education, Teachers College.

Center for Education Reform. 2003. "Charter School Laws across the States: Ranking Scorecard and Legislative Profiles." Washington.

Charter Schools Institute. 2003. "Charter Schools in New York: A New Choice in Public Education." Staff Report. State University of New York.

Chubb, John, and Terry Moe. 1990. *Politics, Markets, and Schools.* Brookings.

Colorado Department of Education. 2003. "The State of Charter Schools in Colorado 2001–2: The Characteristics, Status, and Performance Record of Colorado Charter Schools." Staff Report. Denver.

DC Appleseed Center. 2001. "Charter Schools in the District of Columbia: Improving Systems for Accountability, Autonomy, and Competition." Washington.

Finn, Chester. 2003. "The War on Charter Schools." *Education Gadfly* 3 (20) (www.edexcellence.net/gadfly/v03/gadfly20.html [September 2, 2003]).

Fuller, Bruce. 2000. "Introduction: Growing Charter Schools, Decentering the State." In *Inside Charter Schools: The Paradox of Radical Decentralization,* edited by Bruce Fuller. Harvard University Press.

Greene, Jay P., Greg Forster, and Marcus A. Winters. 2003. "Apples to Apples: An Evaluation of Charter Schools Serving General Student Populations." Education Working Paper 1. New York: Center for Civil Innovation, Manhattan Institute.

Hassel, Bryan, and Meagan Batdorff. 2003. "High-Stakes: Findings from a National Study of Life-or-Death Decisions by Charter School Authorizers." Draft Report. Chapel Hill, N.C.: Public Impact.

Heclo, Hugh. 1978. "Issue Networks and the Executive Establishment." In *The New American Political System,* edited by A. King, pp. 87–124. Washington: American Enterprise Institute.

Henig, Jeffrey, and Jason MacDonald. 2002. "Locational Decisions of Charter Schools: Probing the Market Metaphor." *Social Science Quarterly* 83 (4): 962–80.

Henig, Jeffrey, and others. 1999. "Making a Choice, Making a Difference? An Evaluation of Charter Schools in the District of Columbia." Center for Washington Area Studies, George Washington University.

———. 2001. "Growing Pains: An Evaluation of Charter Schools in the District of Columbia; 1999–2000." Center for Washington Area Studies, George Washington University.

———. 2003. "The Influence of Founder Type on Charter School Structures and Operations." Paper presented at the annual meeting of the American Political Science Association. Philadelphia, August 28–31.

Hess, Frederick, Robert Maranto, and Scott Milliman. 2001. "Responding to Competition." In *Charters, Vouchers, and Public Education*, edited by Paul Peterson and David Campbell. Brookings.

Hill, Paul, and others. 2001. "A Study of Charter School Accountability." Office of Education Research and Improvement, U.S. Department of Education.

Konig, Thomas, and Thomas Brauninger. 1998. "The Formation of Policy Networks." *Journal of Theoretical Politics* 10: 445–71.

Loonie, Melanie, ed. 2002. "Charter School Closures: The Opportunity for Accountability." Washington: Center for Education Reform.

Miron, Gary, Christopher Nelson, and John Risley. 2002. "Strengthening Pennsylvania's Charter School Reform: Findings from the Statewide Evaluation and Discussion of Relevant Issues." Kalamazoo, Mich.: Evaluation Center, Western Michigan University.

O'Toole, Laurence J., Jr. 1997. "Implementing Public Innovations in Network Settings." *Administration and Society* 29 (2): 115–38.

Renzulli, Linda. 2002. "Charter School Formation: A Test of Density and Cross-Effects on an Emerging Form." Unpublished. University of Georgia, Department of Sociology.

Schneider, Mark, and others. 2003. "Building Consensual Institutions: Networks and the National Estuary Program." *American Journal of Political Science* 47 (1): 143–58.

Teske, Paul, and others. 2001. "Can Charter Schools Change Traditional Public Schools?" In *Charters, Vouchers, and Public Education*, edited by Paul Peterson and David Campbell. Brookings.

7

Democratic Accountability in Public Education

CHRISTOPHER R. BERRY AND WILLIAM G. HOWELL

F ew notions have attracted more attention in education policy over the last few years than *accountability*. From the federal No Child Left Behind Act of 2002 (NCLB) to a host of recently enacted state accountability regimes, policymakers are increasingly concerned with objectively measuring student learning and holding educators responsible for learning progress. This newfound fascination with legislating accountability in education is surprising in a country in which average citizens regularly judge the performance of federal, state, and local government officials by voting them into and out of office. Moreover, there is no comparable movement for legislating accountability in other policy domains—no law to hold the Environmental Protection Agency directly accountable for changes in air and water quality, for instance, or to hold police departments, much less individual officers, directly accountable for changes in crime rates. In these and other policy arenas, the ballot box appeases the public's desire to hold its representatives accountable for policy outcomes. Has democratic accountability failed us when it comes to public education?

As currently used in education circles, *accountability* is a slippery word whose meaning shifts from one legislative enactment to the next. The common core of all accountability systems, however, is regular standardized testing of student achievement. In an approach often labeled *hard accountability*, some state systems, along with NCLB, explicitly tie performance on standardized tests to sanctions and rewards for students, teachers, schools, and even entire districts. Other systems, sometimes called *report card systems*, simply report test results to the public, without attaching explicit consequences for anyone.

If hard accountability systems establish fixed rewards and sanctions, report card systems rely on external forces to generate performance incentives. Report card systems depend on either of two mechanisms to encourage improvements in student test scores: the market or the ballot box. The market works because school quality is capitalized in property values, which in turn influence school budgets. Because land prices reflect the quality of local schools and because school budgets are tied to local property taxes, districts have (admittedly weak) incentives to boost student achievement, especially when test results are widely distributed. The ballot box, on the other hand, establishes a more immediate link between school board members' electoral fortunes and student performance. Voters may reward board members in successful districts with reelection, while they send members in faltering districts packing, or so the theory goes. Although a good deal of empirical evidence confirms that property values do, in fact, fluctuate with school quality, almost nothing is known about whether voters actually hold school board members accountable for student learning. Indeed, we are aware of no existing research that tests the basic proposition that school board members' electoral fortunes are tied to student performance.

This chapter examines whether average voters hold school board members accountable for the performance of their schools. Specifically, it assesses whether voters punish or reward incumbent school board members on the basis of changes in student learning (as measured by test scores) in local and district schools. It also scrutinizes candidate behaviors, assessing the impact of student learning trends on incumbents' decisions to seek reelection and potential challengers' decisions to contest them. The findings from the 2000 elections in South Carolina are striking. From the initial decision to run to the final vote tallies, we observed robust relationships between student learning and incumbents' electoral fortunes. During the 2002 election, however, when turnout dropped by roughly half of that observed in 2000, we found scant evidence that voters held members responsible for changes in test scores. Whether voters hold school board members accountable for recent changes in test scores, we suggest, depends critically on who shows up on election day.

This chapter first reviews the relevant literatures on accountability and voting behavior and identifies forces that contribute to and detract from accountability in school board elections. It then introduces new data from school board elections in South Carolina and tests whether changes in student test scores systematically affected the probability that incumbent school board members would seek reelection and the probability that they would face competitors if they did.

Literature Review

This chapter draws from two bodies of literature, one on accountability systems, which resides within the disciplines of education and economics, and the other on retrospective voting, which is firmly ensconced in political science. We review each in turn.

Accountability

Although performance-based accountability in education remains in its infancy, a significant scholarly literature on the subject is emerging.[1] Considerable attention has been devoted to the optimal design of accountability systems, and questions receiving top billing include how to appropriately measure student achievement, whom to hold accountable, and which rewards and sanctions are most effective.[2] Other authors have provided case studies of a particular state's or district's experience with accountability reforms: for example, Florida (Goldhaber and Hannaway 2004), California (Betts and Dannenberg 2003), and Chicago (Bryk 2003; Jacob 2003). And, of course, a flood of ink has been spilled over the anticipated effects of NCLB (Peterson and West 2003).

Although the empirical evidence on school accountability systems is thin, the initial findings are encouraging. Hanushek and Raymond, for example, found that students in states with either hard accountability or report card systems registered larger gains on the National Assessment of Educational Progress than did students in states lacking accountability systems. It is important to note that although students in hard accountability states outperformed those in report card states, the difference between the two systems was not statistically significant.[3] Thus early results suggest that accountability, of either variety, pushes school test scores in a positive direction.

That hard accountability and report card systems produce comparable results raises questions about whether explicit sanctions and rewards are necessary to produce improvements in student learning. Hanushek and Rivkin found that the mere disclosure of student achievement on the Texas Assessment of Academic Skills generated the competition needed to produce gains in average scores.[4] In his assessments of accountability in California, Florida, and Texas, Martin Carnoy argues that even without the imposition of sanctions, public designation of failing schools led to substantial subsequent improvements, through a mechanism

---

1. For important recent contributions, see Ladd (1996), Evers and Walberg (2002), and Peterson and West (2003).

2. Finn (2002); Izumi and Evers (2002).

3. Hanushek and Raymond (2003). The performance difference between either a report card system or a hard accountability system and no accountability system was statistically significant.

4. Hanushek and Rivkin (2003). In their paper, the authors analyzed the Texas accountability system before direct consequences were linked to performance.

he labels the "scarlet letter effect."[5] On the other hand, Jay Greene contends that in Florida, which provides vouchers to students in schools deemed to be failing, the *threat* of vouchers induces performance gains.[6] That is, schools on the border of being labeled failing generated significant test score gains, suggesting that the mere risk of sanctions induces educational improvements.

Hirschman (1970) observes that where accountability systems rely on information disclosure to produce improvements in quality, two forces may be at work: exit or voice. The first has received considerable scholarly attention. Even prior to the advent of the accountability movement, economists in particular have examined how information about school quality led to increases or decreases in demand for houses in good or bad districts, which was reflected in housing prices, property taxes, and school budgets.[7] Because strong property values generate higher school budgets (through local taxes), the exit option establishes incentives for improving performance even without other explicit rewards or sanctions, a mechanism that Peterson and West (2003) call "self-enforcing accountability." Considerable empirical evidence suggests that housing prices respond as expected to information about district quality and to test scores in particular.[8] Indeed, Weimer and Wolkoff (2001) find that housing prices fluctuate even around the test scores of individual schools.

If the exit option in public education is well understood, voice is not. Relative to the existing theoretical and empirical research on market competition, almost nothing is known about the influence of school quality on voting behavior. As a point of departure, the political science literature on retrospective voting suggests ways to think about the issue; it also provides some clues regarding whether voters can be expected to hold school board members accountable for recent trends in student test scores.

Retrospective Voting

For decades, scholars have examined the ways in which incumbents' electoral fortunes rise and fall with their constituents' material well-being.[9] By placing a minimal informational burden on voters while also recognizing incumbents' attempts to advertise a record of success, retrospective voting posits a simple and powerful voting heuristic: voters support incumbents whose tenures are marked by improvements in the state of the world, and they oppose those who have overseen declines. The electorate thereby assumes the "role [of] an appraiser of past events, past performance, and past actions."[10]

5. Carnoy (2001).
6. Greene (2001).
7. This is a special case of the well-known Tiebout model, which suggests that residential choice leads to efficiency-enhancing competition among local governments.
8. Black (1999); Figlio and Lucas (2000); Weimer and Wolkoff (2001).
9. Monroe (1979); Kiewiet and Rivers (1984); Fiorina (1997); Lewis-Beck and Stegmaier (2000).
10. Key (1966).

Over the past thirty years, scholars have amassed a voluminous body of empirical research on retrospective voting. Considerable evidence supports the naive hypothesis—put simply, that citizens vote strictly in accordance with recent economic fluctuations.[11] Arguments persist, however, over the salience of different economic indicators in voting decisions. Should incumbents worry most about unemployment figures, inflation, earnings, or the gross domestic product? And to the extent that trade-offs among them are unavoidable, should incumbents seek some optimal balance? Lewis-Beck and Stegmaier conclude that "the savvy modeler, given the choice of only one predictor [of elections], would do well to select an economic variable. Which one? The answer varies from country to country. It could be unemployment, inflation, or growth."[12]

Having selected a feature of the domestic economy, it remains unclear whether voters reflect on their own condition or society's more generally when evaluating an incumbent. In a growing economy, will citizens who have become unemployed (or who have had their wages cut or have witnessed their stock portfolio decline in value) nonetheless support the incumbent? Or will citizens who meet personal misfortune instinctively punish the incumbent? To the extent that there is consensus on the matter, most scholars suggest that collective (or sociotropic) considerations dominate pocketbook (or egotropic) concerns.[13] The issue, however, remains far from settled, as other scholars have detected evidence of pocketbook voting.[14]

Finally, arguments endure about whether the electoral fortunes of incumbents in different branches of government facing their constituencies in different elections depend on economic improvements in equal measure. While much of the empirical literature on retrospective voting began by focusing on Congress,[15] supportive evidence appears especially robust in presidential elections, where turnouts are much higher.[16] By extension, scholars have tended to observe more robust relations between economic developments and voting behavior during on-year elections than during off-year elections.[17]

Although the retrospective voting literature offers a sophisticated theoretical apparatus and a set of testable hypotheses, it has yet to examine local elections,

11. Alesina, Londregan, and Rosenthal (1993).

12. Lewis-Beck and Stegmaier (2000, p. 211). A handful of retrospective voting studies examine noneconomic indicators; see, for example, Fiorina, Abrams, and Pope (2003).

13. Kiewiet (1983); Kinder, Adams, and Gronke (1989); Markus (1992); Alvarez and Nagler (1998).

14. Brown and Woods (1991); Romero and Stambough (1996).

15. Tufte (1978); Weatherford (1978); Jacobson and Kernell (1983); Born (1986); Alesina and Rosenthal (1989); Erikson (1990).

16. Fiorina (1981); Kinder and Kiewiet (1981). The 2000 presidential election, for which forecasting models regularly predicted a strong Gore victory, appears exceptional in this regard. See the symposium in the March 2001 issue of the journal *PS*.

17. Fiorina (1978).

much less school board contests. The vista is wide open for scholars to begin exploring the ways in which the number of issue dimensions, egotropic and sociotropic considerations, and turnout affect retrospective voting (and hence democratic accountability) in local elections.

Retrospective Voting in School Board Elections

How do average citizens sort through and then evaluate the confluence of problems for which national office holders are responsible? Does a successful military campaign conducted during an election year offset rising unemployment rates? Or are declining crime rates also needed to tip the scales in an incumbent's favor? Most empirical work on retrospective voting ignores these questions and focuses exclusively on the economy. Given the economy's importance in the minds of voters, the existing literature may justifiably set such issues aside. In the context of school board elections, however, these problems evaporate because officials are responsible for only one issue, education. As Richard Briffault notes in chapter 2 of this volume, "Unlike general purpose local governments (counties and municipalities), school districts have a single function—the provision of public elementary and secondary education." That being the case, a successful tenure on a school board ultimately reduces to a member's ability to demonstrate that student learning has improved.

Of course, board members do many things that do not have a direct impact on the daily lives of students. They negotiate teacher contracts, write budgets, procure new school sites and sell old ones—all vital activities, to be sure, but activities that may be slightly removed from the goings-on in the classroom. Still, many board activities immediately affect the content and quality of student learning. Members may modify the curriculum, establish academic standards, decide whether to accept federal aid for specific educational programs, prescribe textbooks, write disciplinary codes, and hire superintendents. What is more, all board activities presumably contribute to the everyday functioning of schools and hence serve students. To the extent that these activities collectively succeed, student learning should improve.

There is good reason to expect voters to hold school board members accountable for the performance of local schools. Two features about these elections stand out. First, voter discontent with schools can be directed only at board members. The teachers and principals who oversee the daily lives of students and may have a greater impact on their education are shielded from electoral pressures. Hence, even if board members materially affect student learning only at the margins, on Election Day they must face the full brunt of voter discontent when student performance slips, just as they reap all the credit when it improves. Second, because most board elections are nonpartisan, party identification does not rival retrospective evaluation of an incumbent as a basis for voting behavior. Voters, therefore, ought to place disproportionate weight on board members' competency, as measured by the performance of local schools.[18]

Voters also have at their disposal a fair amount of information about student achievement trends. For one thing, they live among the schools that board members oversee. By observing their own children or those of friends and colleagues, voters have ample opportunities to learn about the quality of educational services rendered at local elementary and high schools. With the spread of regular standardized testing nationwide over the last several years, voters have additional sources of information about student achievement. Standardized test scores present several advantages. First, the scores are objective and allow parents to evaluate school quality apart from their assessment of their own child's performance. Second, the scores are benchmarked so that parents can evaluate the performance of their local schools relative to others in the state or region, something they cannot do by observing only their own children's education. Finally, the scores are available to all voters, even those without children in school, who might otherwise have little direct information about local school quality.

It is hardly a forgone conclusion, however, that board members' reelection prospects will rise and fall with average citizens' retrospective judgment of their performance in office. For one thing, citizens may not play much of a role in determining the composition of most boards. If Terry Moe's arguments in this volume about union dominance in school board elections are correct, then vested stakeholders in the public school system (teachers and other district employees) ultimately determine who stays on and who leaves school boards. Members' electoral fortunes therefore may depend only on their ability to improve the compensation and working conditions of public school employees. Indeed, if these elections are defined by low overall turnout, cronyism, and union influence, the reelection of incumbents may have little if anything to do with student learning.

Accountability in school board elections may be limited for other reasons as well. While board members may perceive widespread competition, as a factual matter any competent individual who is willing to serve for little or no compensation may secure a seat. In chapter 10 of this volume, Hess and Leal suggest that at least in small rural districts, competition may appear quite muted.[19]

18. A number of scholars have noted differences in voting behavior and the availability of voting cues in partisan and nonpartisan elections. See, for example, Dubois (1984).

19. Elsewhere, Hess lays out some basic points of fact about school board elections (Hess 2002). More than 90 percent of members run for office in open elections, a majority of which are at large; only 3 to 5 percent of board members are appointed, typically by a mayor (see also Danzberger and others 1987; Danzberger 1994; and Kirst 1994). Candidate spending in these elections typically hovers around $1,000, though costs increase notably in larger, more competitive districts. In large districts, fully 55 percent of school board members claim that elections are "very competitive" or "somewhat competitive." Similarly, roughly half of members claim that they plan on retiring after the end of their current term. Turnout rates, however, are notoriously low, typically

Board turnover may reflect members' disinterest and poor working conditions more than a wrathful electorate banishing incompetents any time student learning declines. Ultimately, willingness to serve may be the only real prerequisite for joining a school board. If true, then there really is no politics to speak of in school board elections. Elections are mere formalities, whereby willing servants declare their candidacy and, more often than not, a grateful electorate ushers them into office.

Finally and perhaps most obviously, student learning (at least that part of student learning captured by test scores) may not be at the forefront of citizens' minds when they enter the voting booth and choose from a slate of school board candidates. Voters instead may be preoccupied with safety issues, the football team's record, the convenience of the busing system, or the attractiveness of the buildings. In principle, the function of schools is to promote and enhance student learning. Voters, however, may not hold school boards strictly to that charge. And if not, then school board elections may be just as complex as the national and state races that have been the focus of the extant retrospective voting literature.

Ultimately, these are empirical questions. If, in fact, board elections are competitive and voters hold members responsible for the academic performance of schools, then changes in student test scores should correlate positively with incumbents' reelection. On the other hand, if unions rig election outcomes, if most races are noncompetitive, or if voters do not pay attention to student learning, then null findings should emerge. We now investigate these possibilities, combining school- and district-level trends on standardized exams with school board election returns in South Carolina.

South Carolina

We analyzed data from South Carolina, which is, to our knowledge, the only state to collect precinct-level election data for local races. Precinct-level data for all local elections are available from the South Carolina Election Commission, while in all other states local election data must be collected from individual counties. Furthermore, South Carolina recently instituted a statewide standardized student achievement test, making school-level data publicly available. This combination of readily available electoral and achievement data make South

---

ranging between 25 and 30 percent when elections are held separately from gubernatorial, congressional, and presidential elections and between 42 and 44 percent when they are held with them. Other scholars have reported turnout rates as low as 5 to 15 percent. See, for example, Wagner (1992); Danzberger (1994); Iannaccone and Lutz (1994); and Hickle (1998). Once elected, most school board members serve four-year terms, and members hold office for a total of 6.7 years on average. Overall, two-thirds of board members are not paid for their service, though again, salaries typically vary by district size and number of hours devoted to service.

Carolina an ideal, and (temporarily) unique, testing ground for theories of democratic accountability in education.

Election and Student Achievement Data

South Carolina is divided into eighty-five school districts. More than 90 percent of school boards have between five and nine members, while the largest board (in Beaufort) has eleven. Of these districts, thirty-nine held school board elections in 2000. We collected precinct-level election returns for all school board races and then computed the vote share, by precinct, for each incumbent running in a competitive election (more on this below). Thus our units of observation are unique incumbent-by-precinct combinations. Because each incumbent runs in more than one precinct, and because each precinct may host more than one school board race, we have multiple observations of most incumbents and precincts.[20] Specifically, in 2000 we had sixty-seven incumbents running in 396 precincts, for a total of 960 observations on incumbents' vote share.

Student achievement data were obtained through the South Carolina Department of Education.[21] Since 1999, South Carolina has administered the Palmetto Achievement Challenge Tests (PACT) to students in grades 3 through 8. These tests, based on the South Carolina Curriculum Standards, are given in English and math. We averaged the English and math scores to arrive at a composite score for each school and then computed district-level and precinct-level average composite scores. The precinct-level percentile scores indicate the performance of the schools nearest the polling place and hence those schools most likely to be attended by a voter's children or those of a neighbor; district-level scores indicate the overall performance of all schools in the district.[22] To test claims about egotropic and sociotropic voting, we estimated models with both precinct-level and district-level scores.

Model Specifications and Results

Our analysis focuses first on the 2000 South Carolina school board elections.[23] In that year, sixty-seven incumbents from thirty-seven school boards ran for reelection in competitive races. Of the sixty-seven incumbents, fifty were reelected, and the median vote share for all incumbents was 58 percent. We estimated simple least squares regressions that posit incumbent vote shares as a function of test score trends and some basic controls, each of which is explained below. Because observations for the same incumbent across precincts and for

20. Below we discuss how we adjust the standard errors in our models to account for this.

21. We gratefully acknowledge Jim Felker at the South Carolina Department of Education for providing 1999 and 2000 achievement data files that were not publicly accessible.

22. Computation of precinct- and district-level test score change is explained in the appendix to this chapter.

23. The PACT was first administered in 1999, so 2000 was the first cycle of school board elections after test scores became available.

Table 7-1. *Incumbent Vote Share in 2000 School Board Elections*[a]

Variable	(1)	(2)
Change in total score, 1999–2000 (precinct)	0.005**	0.004**
	(0.002)	(0.002)
Change in total score, 1999–2000 (district)	–0.007	–0.006
	(0.006)	(0.006)
Incumbent vote share, 1996		0.374**
		(0.090)
Per-pupil expenditures, 2000		0.022
		(0.014)
Percent change in per-pupil expenditures, 1999–2000		–0.136
		(0.150)
Total percentile score, 2000 (district)		–0.000
		(0.001)
Constant	0.580**	0.202
	(0.022)	(0.135)
Summary statistic		
N	960	862
R^2	0.02	0.23

Source: Authors' calculations.

a. Robust standard errors in parentheses, with clustering by school district. Ordinary least squares regressions estimated. * $p < .10$, two-tailed test; ** $p < .05$. Per-pupil expenditures are measured in thousands of dollars.

multiple incumbents in the same school district are not independent, we allowed for clustering of the standard errors by school district.[24]

Table 7-1 presents the results. The first column shows the simplest model, with only precinct-level and district-level test score changes on the right side of the equation and 2000 vote shares on the left. As discussed above, precinct-level test scores represent the performance of voters' nearby schools, while district-level scores reflect the performance of all schools in the district. Only precinct-level test score change is significant in this model, with the expected positive coefficient indicating that incumbents won more votes where test scores showed improvements. That district-level scores were not significant suggests that voters were behaving egotropically—or perhaps more accurately, "egocentrically"—focusing on the performance of their own local schools more than on that of the broader district.[25]

The second column of table 7-1 shows the results from models that control for lagged incumbent vote share (that is, the 2000 incumbent's vote returns in

24. This clustering allows for both types of error dependence, as all observations for a given incumbent are within one school district. For discussion on the topic, see Wooldridge (2002).

25. Strict egotropic voting would consider only the performance of one's own children, which we did not observe.

the same precinct in 1996), test score *levels*, and measures of school expenditures. The lagged vote share should capture unobserved aspects of an incumbent's profile, such as name recognition, experience, endorsements, and fundraising capacity. Not surprisingly, its coefficient is highly significant and positive, indicating that candidates who did well in 1996 also garnered more votes in 2000. Levels of test scores, on the other hand, were nowhere near significant, consistent with the prediction from the retrospective voting literature that rational citizens will base their assessment of incumbents on *changes* during their tenure rather than the absolute *level* of performance. Finally, to account for the possibility that races are more competitive in higher-spending districts and that voters may punish board members for marginal increases in their taxes, we controlled for levels and changes in per-pupil expenditures. Neither of these variables, however, logs significant effects on incumbent vote shares.[26]

Importantly, test score changes are robust to the inclusion of these additional variables. The coefficients reported in column 2, our preferred specification, indicate that a movement from the sample's 25th to 75th percentile of test score change—that is, moving from a loss of 4 percentile points to a gain of 3.8 percentile points between 1999 and 2000—is associated with an increase of 3 percentage points in an incumbent's vote share. Similarly, a movement from the sample's 10th to 90th percentile of test score change is associated with an increase of 4.8 percentage points in an incumbent's vote share. With an average incumbent vote share of 58 percent, these estimates suggest that a major swing in test scores can erode as much as two-thirds of an incumbent's margin of victory in a two-way race.[27]

The results reported in table 7-1 reflect the experience of incumbents running in competitive elections. Many incumbents, however, either did not run for reelection or ran unopposed. Specifically, of the 157 incumbent board members in thirty-nine school districts who were up for election in 2000, 112 sought reelection and forty-five of them did not face a challenger. As a result, the sixty-seven incumbents reflected in the results of table 7-1 represent less than half of the incumbents whose seats were in play in 2000. Because these candidates presumably were not randomly selected into competitive elections, test scores may have influenced electoral outcomes beyond the observed vote shares. Indeed, if board members anticipate citizens' voting behavior, then incumbents in districts with declining test scores should be less likely to seek reelection and more likely to face competition when they do run. If either of these effects is present, then

26. Models that account for test score changes and levels as a function of dollars spent on students generate results virtually identical to those presented below.

27. Virtually identical results for all coefficients are observed when estimating the probability that an incumbent won a majority of the votes in each precinct in a competitive race, rather than the margin by which an incumbent won. In addition, weighting the observations by the number of votes cast in the precinct yields nearly identical results.

Table 7-2. Seeking Reelection and Facing Competition, 2000[a]

Variable	Did incumbent run for reelection? (Logit) (1)	Was race competitive? (Logit) (2)
Change in total score, 1999–2000 (district)	0.178**	–0.186**
	(0.061)	(0.066)
Average percentile score, 2000 (district)	0.001	–0.003
	(0.009)	(0.019)
Incumbent vote share, 1996	–0.031	–1.691
	(0.959)	(1.132)
Per-pupil expenditures, 2000	-0.043	-0.006
	(0.103)	(0.018)
Percent change in per-pupil expenditures, 1999–2000	–5.241**	2.312
	(1.753)	(2.259)
Dummy = 1 if position pays no salary	–1.369**	1.588*
	(0.334)	(0.931)
Total number of registered voters (district)		0.003
		(0.003)
Constant	1.863	1.074
	(1.228)	(1.825)
Summary statistic		
N	152	108
Pseudo R^2	0.09	0.14

Source: Authors' calculations.

a. * $p < .10$, two-tailed test; ** $p < .05$.

the results shown in table 7-1 *underestimate* the effect of test score change on incumbents' electoral prospects.

We therefore ran two logistic regressions, first to estimate the effect of test scores on the incumbents' decision to run and then to estimate the probability that those who did run would face competition. In contrast to the vote share models, we do not have precinct-level observations here because when candidates run, they run in all precincts in the district. Thus our unit of observation is the incumbent, and we have only one observation per incumbent. For this reason, we used only district-level rather than precinct-level test scores and lagged vote share on the right side. Again we allowed for clustering of standard errors within school districts.

Column 1 of table 7-2 presents the results of the first logistic regression model. As in table 7-1, the model controls for test score levels, incumbents' lagged vote share, and measures of per-pupil expenditures. In addition, we included a dummy variable indicating whether board members received remuneration for their service. In our sample, approximately 20 percent of officials received no compensation, while the remainder received a salary, per diem payments, or reimbursement for expenses.[28]

As shown in table 7-2, incumbents were significantly less likely to seek reelection when they were not compensated for their service. In addition, incumbents were less likely to seek reelection in areas where per-pupil expenditures had increased, perhaps because they anticipated a tax revolt at the polls. Neither test score levels nor lagged vote shares were significant, indicating that incumbents in higher-performing districts and incumbents who did especially well in past elections were no more likely to run for office. Most relevant, however, effects of test score changes continue to attain statistical significance and remain in the expected direction: incumbents appear disinclined to seek reelection when their district's test scores drop. This result may indicate that incumbents bow out in anticipation of voter reprisals for poor performance or that serving in a declining district is less rewarding for board members. The point estimates in column 1 indicate that a movement from the 75th to the 25th percentile in the sample's test score change is associated with a drop of 13 percentage points in the probability that the incumbent would seek reelection (from 84 to 71 percent, holding other variables at their median). A movement from the 90th to the 10th percentile is associated with a more than 30 percentage point drop in the probability of seeking reelection (from 90 to 59 percent).[29]

If declining test scores discourage incumbents from seeking reelection, the retrospective voting literature suggests just the opposite in the case of competition: falling test scores should bring out more challengers. Of the 112 incumbents who sought reelection in 2000, forty-five ran unopposed. To test this hypothesis, we ran a logistic regression where the dependent variable is coded 1 if the incumbent faced at least one challenger and zero if he or she ran unopposed. In addition to the three variables introduced in column 1, we added the number of registered voters in the district in the expectation that because larger districts have a bigger pool of potential candidates, they should be more likely to host contested elections.[30]

28. We also estimated models that controlled for whether a race was partisan. All of the main effects presented in table 7-2 hold up when this additional control variable is included. Further, incumbents appeared less likely to run for reelection in partisan races. But as only three districts in our sample (accounting for eleven incumbents) faced partisan elections, we are reluctant to make too much of this result.

29. Assuredly, factors other than those presented here affected incumbents' decisions to run for reelection, for example, the partisan affiliations of the incumbent and the board, whether the incumbent had children in the public schools, and whether the incumbent held a full-time job. It is difficult to think of any, though, that should correlate with changes in test scores, mitigating concerns about omitted variable bias. Much the same logic applies to models estimated in subsequent tables.

30. The number of seats on the school board does not vary proportionately with enrollment, so larger districts have more potential candidates per seat. For instance, school board size ranged from five to eleven seats, while school district enrollment ranged from 600 to 27,000.

Test score changes, once again, are highly significant, and this time they are negatively associated with the probability of competition. The point estimates from column 2 suggest that a movement from the 75th to the 25th percentile in test score change is associated with an 18 percentage point increase in the probability of facing a challenger (from 44 to 62 percent, holding other variables at their median). A movement from the 90th to the 10th percentile in test score change is associated with a whopping 42 percentage point increase in the probability of facing opposition (from 32 to 74 percent). These results suggest that incumbents running in districts where test scores have taken a nose dive are almost certain to face a challenger.[31] All of the control variables, meanwhile, appear insignificant with the exception of whether a position is paid. Curiously, challengers were more willing to take on an incumbent board member when victory did *not* ensure some kind of financial remuneration.

In summary, we identified three major effects of test score change in South Carolina school board elections.[32] First, incumbents were significantly less likely to seek reelection when test scores declined on their watch, because of either anticipated voter retaliation or frustration with serving in a faltering district. Second, those incumbents who did run were significantly more likely to be challenged at the polls if they presided over a test score drop. Third, those incumbents who ran in competitive elections received a significantly lower share of the vote where test scores had fallen. Because test scores influenced the chances that an incumbent ran in a competitive election—essentially deterring the worst performers from running and rewarding the best with an uncontested seat—the results reported in table 7-1 should be considered the *lower bound* estimates of the effects of test scores on incumbents' electoral fortunes.[33]

31. We extended these analyses by examining the possibility that declines in test scores have greater impact than do test score gains. Specifically, we use regression splines on test score change, setting a single knot at zero. Asymmetric effects are apparent in the competitiveness model. While positive improvements in test scores appear unrelated to the probability that an incumbent faces a challenger, test score declines have a substantial impact on the willingness of challengers to enter the race. This finding suggests that the coefficients shown in table 7-2 underestimate the effects of falling test scores on the probability of an incumbent facing competition. The point estimate for negative test scores, in fact, is about three times larger under the spline specification. We did not, however, find evidence of asymmetric effects in models of an incumbent's decision to seek reelection or in models of vote share.

32. In further analyses (not shown) we address the concern that test score change may be a proxy for other conditions that influence voters' assessments of incumbents. If test score change is correlated with broader shifts in the overall health of the local community, then the effects we observed in the preceding analyses may be spurious, merely indicating that all incumbents faced greater electoral pressures in deteriorating communities. To test for this possibility, we modeled the effects of test scores on county council elections. If test scores provide unique information about the performance of the school board, then we expect them to have negligible effects on county council races. Reassuringly, we found no systematic effects of test scores on county council elections.

33. Several considerations dissuaded us from attempting to estimate a Heckman-type selection model in this case. First, we would require at least one identifying variable that strongly affects the chances of observing an incumbent in a competitive election but that is unrelated to incumbent

The 2002 School Board Elections

Here, we replicate the main school board models for the 2002 elections. As previously noted, our theoretical expectations for this midterm election were less clear. Roughly 53 percent of registered voters turned out in 2000; in 2002, meanwhile, just 26 percent did. Unfortunately, available demographic data on the voting population—race, age, and gender—do not provide much of a basis for probing the differences between the two electorates in any depth.[34] It seems fair to assume, however, that voters in 2002 were significantly more educated than their counterparts of two years prior. If Zaller (2004) is correct that retrospective voting occurs principally among low-information voters while high-information voters pay more attention to candidates' policy positions, then test score changes may not impact school board members' electoral prospects during the off-year election.

Consistent with Zaller's argument, the results from 2002 differed markedly from those observed in 2000. As table 7-3 shows, changes in test scores did not affect the probability that an incumbent would seek reelection, the probability that he or she faced competition, or his or her final vote share. These null findings, what is more, do not appear to be a statistical artifact. In models not presented, we added administrative data from teacher, parent, and student ratings of local schools; we experimented with two- and three-year changes in test scores, rather than one-year changes; we looked at changes in the percentage of students who received failing scores on the PACT;[35] and we replicated the spline models for 2002 in an attempt to uncover asymmetric effects. None of these alternative approaches produced any evidence of retrospective voting in the 2002 elections.

Differences between the 2000 and 2002 models also were observed with respect to the control variables. Lagged incumbent vote share, for instance, is only marginally significant in the 2002 vote share model, though it stood out as the most highly significant variable in the 2000 model. This finding, however, is

---

vote share. Given that selection depends on both an incumbent's and a challenger's decision to run, we would require a factor that simultaneously is positively (negatively) correlated with the probability of an incumbent seeking reelection; is positively (negatively) correlated with the probability of a challenger entering the race; and is unrelated to the incumbent's ultimate vote share. We have not been able to uncover such an identifying variable. Second, the two stages of the model (selection and outcome) are observed for different units of analysis. That is, we observe the selection into a competitive race for individual incumbents, whereas we observe vote share at the precinct level, with multiple observations per incumbent. Thus proper estimation of the standard errors for the corresponding selection model would be a challenge. Given these obstacles, the first being paramount, we did not estimate a Heckman-type selection model. Rather, we acknowledge that our estimates of the effects of test score change on vote share and on the probability of facing competition are likely to be lower bounds of the true effects.

34. Nor do they reveal significant differences between the two electorates.

35. These alternative measures of school performance were not available for the 2000 models.

Table 7-3. *2002 School Board Elections*[a]

Variable	Did incumbent run for reelection? (Logit) (1)	Was race competitive? (Logit) (2)	Incumbent vote share, 2002 (least squares) (3)
Change in total score, 2001–02 (district)	0.001	0.004	–0.004
	(0.010)	(0.016)	(0.007)
Change in total score, 2001–02 (precinct)			–0.004
			(0.003)
Total percentile score, 2002 (district)	–0.002	0.003	0.002
	(0.002)	(0.003)	(0.001)
Percent change in per-pupil expenditures, 2001–02	0.959***	–0.264	–0.253
	(0.314)	(0.823)	(0.218)
Per-pupil expenditures, 2002	0.003	0.113*	0.018
	(0.054)	(0.065)	(0.012)
Incumbent vote share, 1998	0.149	–0.030	0.211*
	(0.101)	(0.158)	(0.111)
Dummy = 1 if position pays no salary	0.032	0.119	
	(0.132)	(0.126)	
Total number registered voters		0.006***	
		(0.002)	
Constant	0.588*	–0.274	0.235**
	(0.322)	(0.363)	(0.098)
Summary statistic			
N	184	126	1308
R^2 (pseudo R^2 for logit)	0.03	0.16	0.10
Unit of analysis	Incumbent	Incumbent	Incumbent × Precinct

Source: Authors' calculations.

a. Robust standard errors in parentheses, with clustering by school district. * $p < .10$, two-tailed test; ** $p < .05$. Per-pupil expenditures and registered voters measured in thousands of dollars and voters respectively.

not altogether surprising. Again, because voters in this off-year election were likely more educated, they may have been less influenced by a candidate's name recognition or campaign spending, the kinds of characteristics that lagged vote shares mean to capture.

While high-information voters in off-year local elections may not vote retrospectively, they probably do care about board members' policy positions. Which policy positions? As Moe demonstrates in chapter 11 of this volume, low-turnout school board elections attract a disproportionate share of high-interest stakeholders, such as teachers and administrators. It seems likely that these stakeholders evaluated board members less on the basis of test scores than on their demonstrated commitment to the stakeholders' employment interests. That changes in per-pupil expenditures correlated positively with the probability that incumbents ran for office in 2002 (recall, they registered negative and significant impacts in 2000) certainly is consistent with the claim that vested interests exerted a disproportionate level of influence during this off-year election.

Unfortunately, without individual-level data, we cannot further examine Zaller's and Moe's claims about high- and low-information voters and the composition of school board electorates in on- and off-year elections. We leave it to future research to extend their arguments to different kinds of local elections with variable turnout rates.[36] At a minimum, though, we note that retrospective voting is not a forgone conclusion in all local elections, and, more specifically, that the draw of a presidential election appears to improve the chances that electorates hold board members accountable for the performance of schools.

Still, it is worth recognizing that the 2000 and 2002 races in South Carolina present a tough test for retrospective voting and hence for democratic accountability. First, we are working with aggregate voting data from less than 100 different districts. From a purely statistical standpoint, individual-level data collected from a wider variety of races may produce more pronounced effects. Second, South Carolina's accountability system is relatively new. Over time, as voters grow accustomed to the testing regime and learn more about the performance of their schools, retrospective voting may become more common.[37] And finally, unlike with local elections that revolve around issues of public safety or property taxes, large proportions of the electorate have little reason to be informed about the performance of public schools.

Conclusion

The 2000 findings presented in this chapter suggest that explicit sanctions and rewards associated with hard accountability systems may supplement rather than stand in for accountability systems already built into public education. Those charged with governing public schools currently have strong electoral

36. Individual-level data may permit additional empirical explorations. Evidence of retrospective voting may derive from either a small percentage of high-information voters who vote strictly on the basis of changes in test scores or from a partially informed electorate that pays casual attention to test scores. Similarly, we do not know whether citizens vote on the basis of test scores or changes in student learning more generally. It could be that citizens obtain direct information about how students score on standardized tests and vote accordingly; alternatively, these results might derive from parents observing students and schools—but never test scores—provided that changes in test scores correlate positively with changes in student learning. Plainly, more data are needed to distinguish these various causal pathways.

37. PACT scores in South Carolina have become more widely publicized. The state now sends all parents in the state notification of their school's performance, and districts are required to report school test scores in local newspapers.

incentives to promote policies and develop practices that enhance student learning. When test scores dropped in South Carolina schools, incumbents were less likely to run, they were more likely to face competition, and they won (if they won) by smaller margins. As long as the electorate has the information needed to evaluate student learning—test scores providing one such source—many voters appear willing to punish and reward those who govern public schools according to their performance in office.[38]

An analysis of NCLB, the most important accountability system currently in place, illustrates the specific ways in which formal accountability systems complement—and in some cases conflict with—long-standing forms of democratic accountability. In three ways, NCLB strengthens existing forms of democratic accountability. First, under NCLB, schools and districts are evaluated every single year, while school board elections are held only every two years—and, as the 2002 elections suggest, voters do not always hold board members responsible for changes in student test scores. Second, to avoid penalties under NCLB, public schools must demonstrate annual *improvements* in test scores; it is not enough simply to maintain last year's performance levels. Retrospective voters, meanwhile, appear more likely to rise up and punish their incumbent board members only when test scores decline. Third, NCLB also mandates that schools demonstrate annual improvements for various subgroups: students for whom English is not the primary language, ethnic and racial minorities, and special education students. Without individual-level data, it is extremely difficult to discern whether voters pay attention to the test scores of all students or those within specific subpopulations. If citizens vote primarily on the basis of their own child's test scores or those of their own ethnic group more generally, then minorities cannot hope to affect the composition of a school board. NCLB, however, provides the needed backup, establishing incentives for schools and school boards to improve the test scores of students who come from weak voting blocs in local elections.

In other ways, however, state mandates and democratic accountability systems find themselves in tension with one another. When evaluating schools, NCLB does not make any allowances for temporary setbacks in student learning. For every year that a school fails to make the prescribed gains in test scores, preestablished penalties automatically apply. Retrospective voters, meanwhile, may rightfully see success in constant test scores, especially at schools that confront especially disadvantaged student populations. When NCLB classifies such schools as underperforming and mandates the reallocation of Title I funding, retrospective voters may respond by rallying behind incumbent school board members in defiance of a meddling federal government.

38. We do not know whether voters in South Carolina are responding to test scores per se or whether they are formulating independent evaluations of student achievement for which test score trends are acting as proxies.

Still, as a practical matter, both state mandates and democratic accountability systems may fail to achieve their intended objectives. Test scores may increase because students are learning more, because students have grown accustomed to taking standardized tests, because teachers and students are cheating on tests, or because schools experience an influx of higher-performing students. When dolling out punishments and rewards, NCLB does not distinguish among these possibilities. Unfortunately, the data from South Carolina do not allow us to determine whether retrospective voters attempt to assess the causes of test score changes. Given the difficulties of assessing school quality, however, there is good reason to believe that even the most adept retrospective voters have a hard time doing so. Hence, while state mandates and democratic accountability systems hold schools and school boards accountable, it is not clear that either hold them accountable for their contributions to student learning per se.

It may be years before it is known whether the latest round of accountability reforms have had their intended effects. But it is clear, even now, that accountability is nothing new. NCLB did not introduce accountability into American education, nor did any state's accountability system suddenly make local educators answerable to its citizens. Ironically, even those critics who point to the poor relative performance of American students on international tests as justification for new accountability systems seem oblivious to the fact that American schools are perhaps the most accountable in the world. With nearly 15,000 school districts governed by more than 80,000 popularly elected officials, American public education may be the most democratically accountable institution in this nation or any other. Analysts of the current accountability movement would do well to focus on the specific content of the reform proposals and ignore the rhetoric of accountability. NCLB and other performance-based reforms may bring new standards, new tests, and new incentives to American education. What they will not introduce are systems of accountability. They are already here.

Appendix

Calculation of vote share for multiple-seat elections

School board members are elected at large in thirty-two districts, by "constituent district" (ward) in thirty-eight, and by using a combination of both methods in fifteen districts. Some of the at-large and combination districts allow for "multiple-winner" elections, in which voters are allowed to vote for more than one candidate. For multiple-winner contests, we computed vote share as the number of votes the incumbent received divided by the maximum number of votes he or she could have received. The maximum number of votes that any candidate can receive is equal to the number of voters (a voter cannot vote for the same candidate more than once). For example, consider an election in which 100 voters turn out, each of whom votes for three of five candidates running. If a candidate in this election receives 60 votes, then we compute his or her vote share to be 60 percent, meaning that 60 percent of the voters who could have voted for this candidate actually did so. Put differently, with a total of 300 votes cast by 100 voters, 60 votes is 20 percent of total votes, but 60 percent of possible votes. It is the latter number that we took as our measure of vote share in multiple-seat elections.

Calculation of district- and precinct-level changes in test score

Palmetto Achievement Challenge Tests results are reported both as "scale scores" and as "performance levels." We chose to use the scale scores, which provide more detail to distinguish performance among schools. Scale scores are determined independently for each grade and subject. The South Carolina Department of Education set the average scale score at 100 times the grade level, with a range of 128 scale score points around this average—for example, the initial average score for grade 3 is 300 and the range is 236 to 364.

In developing our performance measure, we began by computing a school-level scale score. Because scores for each grade were on different scales, we first converted them into within-grade statewide percentile rankings. For each school, we then averaged these percentile scores across grades, weighting by enrollment in each grade. These steps were conducted separately for English and math scores, and then the two were averaged to produce a composite score. The result is a school-level percentile score. Based on these school-level scores, we then calculated a score representing the average of nearby schools for each voting precinct. Specifically, for each precinct, we computed the average score of all the schools in the same zip code as the polling place.[39] For zip codes with only one school, that school's performance measures served as the zip code's values. For zip codes in which more than one school was located, we averaged across the schools, weighting by enrollment. For zip codes where no schools were in operation, we imputed the achievement of schools in the nearest zip code with at least one school.[40] The result is a precinct-level percentile score. The district-level test score was based on the same underlying school-level percentile scores,

39. While zip codes are not perfect mappers of "nearness," they are the best possible approximation given our data. Attempts to match schools and precincts based on geocodes did not prove more successful than zip code matching because a large number (nearly half) of the addresses in our database could not be geocoded to a level beneath the zip code.

40. Distance between zip codes was calculated using the "Great Circle" formula, measuring distance between zip code latitude-longitude centroids. The coordinates of the county centroid were used when the zip code could not be located in the Census Bureau's TIGER (Topologically Integrated Geographic Encoding and Referencing system) database (www.census.gov/geo/www/tiger/index.html [December 3, 2004]).

and we simply averaged over all the schools in the district, weighted by enrollment. Test score change for both precincts and districts was computed as the difference between 2000 and 1999 percentile scores. Thus our test score change variable measures the increase or decrease in statewide percentile ranking over the year preceding the election.

References

Alesina, Alberto, and Howard Rosenthal. 1989. "Partisan Cycles in Congressional Elections and the Macroeconomy." *American Political Science Review* 83 (2): 373–98.

Alesina, Alberto, John Londregan, and Howard Rosenthal. 1993. "A Model of the Political Economy of the United States." *American Political Science Review* 87 (1): 12–33.

Alvarez, R. Michael, and Jonathan Nagler. 1998. "Economics, Entitlements, and Social Issues: Voter Choice in the 1996 Presidential Election." *American Journal of Political Science* 42 (4): 1349–63.

Betts, Julian R., and Anne Dannenberg. 2003. "The Effects of Accountability in California." In *No Child Left Behind? The Politics and Practice of School Accountability,* edited by P. E. Peterson and M. West. Brookings.

Black, Sandra. 1999. "Do Better Schools Matter? Parental Valuation of Elementary Education." *Quarterly Journal of Economics* 114 (2): 577–99.

Born, Richard. 1986. "Strategic Politicians and Unresponsive Voters." *American Political Science Review* 80 (2): 599–612.

Brown, Robert, and James Woods. 1991. "Toward a Model of Congressional Elections." *Journal of Politics* 53 (2): 454–73.

Bryk, Anthony S. 2003. "No Child Left Behind, Chicago Style." In *No Child Left Behind? The Politics and Practice of School Accountability,* edited by P. E. Peterson and M. West. Brookings.

Carnoy, Martin. 2001. *School Vouchers: Examining the Evidence.* Washington: Economic Policy Institute.

Danzberger, J. P. 1994. "Governing the Nation's Schools: The Case for Restructuring Local School Boards." *Phi Delta Kappan* 75: 367–73.

Danzberger, J. P., and others. 1987. "School Boards: The Forgotten Players on the Education Team." *Phi Delta Kappan* 69: 53–59.

Dubois, Philip. 1984. "Voting Cues in Nonpartisan Trial Court Elections: A Multivariate Assessment." *Law and Society Review* 18 (3): 395–436.

Erikson, Robert. 1990. "Economic Conditions and the Congressional Vote: A Review of the Macrolevel Evidence." *American Journal of Political Science* 34 (2): 373–99.

Evers, William, and Herbert Walberg, eds. 2002. *School Accountability.* Palo Alto, Calif.: Hoover Institution Press.

Figlio, David N., and Maurice Lucas. 2000. "What's in a Grade? School Report Cards and House Prices." Working Paper 8019. Cambridge, Mass.: National Bureau of Economic Research.

Finn, Chester. 2002. "Real Accountability in K-12 Education: The Marriage of Ted and Alice." In *School Accountability,* edited by William Evers and Herbert Walberg. Palo Alto, Calif.: Hoover Institution Press.

Fiorina, Morris. 1978. "Economic Retrospective Voting in American National Elections: A Micro-Analysis." *American Journal of Political Science* 22 (2): 426–43.

———. 1981. *Retrospective Voting in American National Elections.* Yale University Press.

————. 1997. "Voting Behavior." In *Perspectives on Public Choice: A Handbook,* edited by D. Mueller, pp. 391–415. Cambridge University Press.

Fiorina, Morris, Sam Abrams, and Jeremy Pope. 2003. "Can Retrospective Voting Be Saved?" *British Journal of Political Science* 33 (2): 163–87.

Goldhaber, Dan, and Jane Hannaway. 2004. "Accountability with a Kicker: Observations on the Florida A+ Accountability Plan." *Phi Delta Kappan* 85 (8): 598–605.

Greene, Jay. 2001. *An Evaluation of the Florida A-Plus Accountability and School Choice Program.* New York: Manhattan Institute, Center for Civil Innovation.

Hanushek, Eric, and Mackie Raymond. 2003. "Lessons about the Design of State Accountability Systems." In *No Child Left Behind? The Politics and Practice of School Acccountability,* edited by P. E. Peterson and M. West. Brookings.

Hanushek, Eric, and Steven G. Rivkin. 2003. "Does Public School Competition Affect Teacher Quality?" Unpublished paper. Hoover Institution, Stanford University.

Hess, Frederick. 2002. *School Boards at the Dawn of the Twenty-First Century.* Washington: National School Boards Association.

Hickle, J. 1998. "The Changing Face of School Board Elections." *Updating School Board Policies* 29 (1): 1–5.

Hirschman, Albert O. 1970. *Exit, Voice, and Loyalty: Responses to Decline in Firms, Organizations, and States.* Harvard University Press.

Iannaccone, L., and F. Lutz. 1994. "The Crucible of Democracy: The Local Arena." *Politics of Education Association Yearbook* 9: 39–52.

Izumi, Lance, and William Evers. 2002. "State Accountability Systems." In *School Accountability,* edited by William Evers and Herbert Walberg. Palo Alto, Calif.: Hoover Institution Press.

Jacob, Brian. 2003. "A Closer Look at Achievement Gains under High-Stakes Testing in Chicago." In *No Child Left Behind? The Politics and Practice of School Accountability,* edited by P. E. Peterson and M. West. Brookings.

Jacobson, Gary, and Samuel Kernell. 1983. *Strategy and Choice in Congressional Elections.* Yale University Press.

Key, V. O., Jr. 1966. *The Responsible Electorate.* New York: Vintage.

Kiewiet, D. Roderick. 1983. *Macroeconomics and Micropolitics.* University of Chicago Press.

Kiewiet, D. Roderick., and Douglas Rivers. 1984. "A Retrospective on Retrospective Voting." *Political Behavior* 6 (4): 369–93.

Kinder, Donald, and D. Roderick Kiewiet. 1981. "Sociotropic Politics: The American Case." *British Journal of Political Science* 11 (2): 129–41.

Kinder, Donald, Gordon Adams, and Paul Gronke. 1989. "Economics and Politics in the 1984 American Presidential Election." *American Journal of Political Science* 33 (2): 491–515.

Kirst, Michael. 1994. "A Changing Context Means School Board Reform." *Phi Delta Kappan* 75 (5): 378–81.

Ladd, Helen, ed. 1996. *Holding Schools Accountable: Performance-Based Reform in Education.* Brookings.

Lewis-Beck, Michael, and Mary Stegmaier. 2000. "Economic Determinants of Electoral Outcomes." *Annual Review of Political Science* 3: 183–219.

Markus, Gregory. 1992. "The Impact of Personal and National Economic Conditions on Presidential Voting, 1956–1988." *American Journal of Political Science* 36 (3): 137–54.

Monroe, Kristen. 1979. "Economic Analyses of Electoral Behavior: A Critical Review." *Political Behavior* 1 (2): 137–73.

Peterson, Paul E., and Martin West, eds. 2003. *No Child Left Behind? The Politics and Practice of School Accountability.* Brookings.

Romero, David, and Stephen Stambough. 1996. "Personal Economic Well-Being and the Individual Vote for Congress: A Pooled Analysis, 1980–1990." *Political Research Quarterly* 49 (3): 607–16.

Tufte, Edward. 1978. *Political Control of the Economy.* Princeton University Press.

Wagner, Robert. 1992. "The Case for Local Education Policy Boards." *Phi Delta Kappan* 74 (3): 228–29.

Weatherford, M. Stephen. 1978. "Economic Conditions and Electoral Outcomes: Class Differences in the Political Response to Recession." *American Journal of Political Science* 22 (4): 917–38.

Weimer, David L., and M. Wolkoff. 2001. "School Performance and Housing Values: Using Non-Contiguous District and Incorporation Boundaries to Identify School Effects." *National Tax Journal* 54 (2): 231–53.

Wooldridge, Jeffrey. 2002. *Econometric Analysis of Cross Section and Panel Data.* MIT Press.

Zaller, John. 2004. "Floating Voters in U.S. Presidential Elections, 1948–2000." In *Studies in Public Opinion: Attitudes, Nonattitudes, Measurement Error, and Change,* edited by W. Saris and P. Sniderman. Princeton University Press.

8

Minority Incorporation and Local School Boards

MELISSA J. MARSCHALL

Since passage of the Voting Rights Act in 1965, social scientists have periodi-
cally examined the state of minority representation in U.S. politics.
Although the vast majority of that research has focused on patterns of minority
office holding at the local level, nearly all of it has examined African American
representation in municipal-level offices.[1] To date, considerably less attention
has been paid to black and especially Hispanic representation on local school
boards or in other local elected positions.[2] Numbering approximately 15,000
across the United States, school boards are not only the most prevalent form of
government in this country but also the most common point of entry into public office among those seeking political careers. In addition, schooling is not
simply the most expensive local service provided by state and local governments
but also unquestionably one of the most important public services that government provides. There is much at stake in local school politics, and consequently
minority incorporation in this policy arena warrants greater scholarly attention.

In this chapter, I address the issue of minority incorporation by analyzing
each of its dimensions-descriptive and substantive representation. I begin with
descriptive representation, which refers to the extent of minority representation

1. See, for example, Sass and Pittman (2000), Bullock and MacManus (1987), and Engstrom
and McDonald (1981).
2. But see Meier, Martinez-Ebers, and Leal (2002), Meier and others (2002), Robinson and
England (1981), Robinson, England, and Meier (1985), and Welch and Karnig (1978).

in politics, government, and positions of power, by looking at black and Hispanic school board representation—over time and in the contemporary period—across states. In addition, I review several more recent trends that may be influencing not only the number of blacks and Hispanics on local school boards but also the kinds of candidates who seek and gain access to those positions. From there I look more systematically at the conditions under which minorities are more likely to be represented on local school boards, focusing on selection methods and the demographic composition of local school districts.

I next move beyond descriptive representation to consider the question of how black and Hispanic office holding on local school boards relates to substantive representation—the extent to which minority officials are able to shape policies and outcomes. Though extant research has focused on three primary aspects of minority school board representation—including the minority share of administrative and teaching positions in the district, a set of educational policies and practices commonly referred to as "second-generation school discrimination," and the academic achievement of minority students—I take an alternative approach, investigating whether black and Hispanic representation on local school boards leads to differences in residents' evaluations of their local schools. This is a logical extension of the process of representation described by Meier and Juenke in chapter 9 of this volume. Specifically, if the quality of representation improves because there are blacks and Hispanics on local school boards, there should be higher levels of satisfaction and more positive assessments of local schools among minority parents and residents in districts where minorities are represented on the board.

Though subjective evaluations of the quality of local schools do not directly measure improvements in education and schooling (for example, higher test scores and better teachers), they are nevertheless meaningful. First, residents' assessments of the quality of their schools are a critical indicator of how well a school system is both functioning and meeting the needs of its constituents. Second, as Gilliam points out, the changes in attitude that result from minority empowerment (for example, trust and satisfaction) are significant not only because the level of citizens' trust and confidence in government shapes system stability and the efficacy of representative democracy, but also because attitudes play a key role in determining patterns of political participation.[3]

To investigate both the factors that influence minority representation on local school boards and the extent to which minority representation is associated with more positive evaluations of local schools, I relied on a sample of 190 school districts located in four metropolitan areas (Atlanta, Boston, Detroit, and

---

3. Gilliam (1996, p. 57). On citizens' trust and government stability, see, for example, Dahl (1961). On political orientation and participation, see Converse (1966), Verba and Nie (1972), Shingles (1981), and Zaller (1992).

Los Angeles). Though not a random sample, this group includes not only large, central city school districts, but also a wide array of suburban and county districts. Consequently, the data and analyses employed here have a wider empirical focus than do many earlier studies. My analysis of substantive representation relies on the Multi-City Study of Urban Inequality, a large-scale survey of 9,000 respondents in these same 190 school districts, conducted between 1992 and 1994.[4] I combined these survey data with 1990 census data measuring neighborhood racial and socioeconomic characteristics and data on black and Hispanic school board members to investigate how the racial and ethnic makeup of school boards interacts with the racial and ethnic identity of residents to shape perceptions of local schools. Overall I find that minority representation has a positive effect on minority residents' evaluations of their schools and that these effects are especially strong among blacks.

Descriptive Representation and Local School Boards: An Overview

As with most research on minority representation in municipal-level offices, most research on minority representation on local school boards was conducted in the late 1970s and early 1980s. Since more contemporary patterns of black and Hispanic office holding are less well understood, I begin by reviewing three recent developments that may have implications for the extent and nature of black and Hispanic descriptive representation on local school boards.

Increases in Mexican Immigration and the U.S. Hispanic Population

Data from the Current Population Survey (CPS) indicate that in 2002 the population in the United States included 32.5 million foreign-born residents, constituting 11.5 percent of the total population.[5] With the estimated annual immigration, legal and illegal, of 400,000 Mexicans to the United States in the 1990s, not only are Central Americans the largest immigrant group (11.8 million in 2002), but Hispanics—both native and foreign born—now represent the largest minority group in America.[6] The CPS estimated the number at 30.8 million in 1998, or 11.4 percent of the total U.S. population.[7] Since 1990, there has been a 46 percent increase in the Hispanic population, and today about one in nine Americans is of Hispanic origin. Despite the fact that a sizable share of that population includes illegal immigrants or non-naturalized legal residents, such a significant increase should be reflected in an increase in the number of Hispanics represented on local school boards and in political office more generally.

4. Bobo and others (1998).
5. Schmidley (2003).
6. Mexican immigration is from Hanson (2003).
7. Ramirez (1999).

Although the vast majority of Mexican immigrants continue to concentrate in the Southwest, in the 1990s the South became a new destination for many Mexican and other Hispanic immigrants. As Zuniga and others (2002) note, Mexican migration and settlement in places like Georgia, North Carolina, and Alabama has turned many towns and small cities into border communities, altering the traditional bipolar racial structure of these communities and affecting the dynamics of public and private institutions and the nature of local politics.[8] Given this trend, Hispanics may be increasingly gaining access to public office in states and localities outside the Southwest.

Gains in Black Representation and the Generational Replacement of Black Elected Officials

While Hispanic Americans are making their first significant inroads in political representation, African Americans are experiencing the generational replacement of office holders. Between 1997 and 2000 there were 2,282 newly elected black officials, representing a 25.4 percent turnover. As Bositis (2002) notes, the national population of black elected officials is becoming increasingly younger, and the experiences and views of the new generation differ from those of their predecessors. In particular, the new generation is more educated than the previous generation, its members are less likely to have attended segregated high schools or historically black colleges, and they are less likely to have been active in the civil rights movement or to be members of civil rights organizations.[9] These changes could have implications for schools boards in terms of the number of blacks who seek such positions and the kinds of policies they pursue once in office.

The Shift from Elected to Appointed School Boards

As Wong and Shen point out in chapter 4 of this volume, since the early 1990s a number of large central city school districts have shifted from an elected school board to one in which some or all members are appointed by the mayor, governor, other executive officer, or some combination thereof. Currently, twenty-four states have passed legislation authorizing such changes in local school governance.[10] In some instances, the shift to appointment has been accompanied by a reduction in the size of the school board. For example, in 1999, Detroit moved from an eleven-member elected school board to a seven-member appointed board. Similarly, as one of the earlier reformers, Boston abandoned its thirteen-member elected system in 1991 in favor of a seven-member appointed school committee. In addition to Detroit, Boston, and New York City, which became a mayoral takeover district in 2002 when Mayor

8. See also Henandez-Leon and Zuniga (2002).
9. Bositis (2002, p. 7).
10. Cibulka (1999).

Figure 8-1. *Total Black and Hispanic Elected School Board Members*

Number

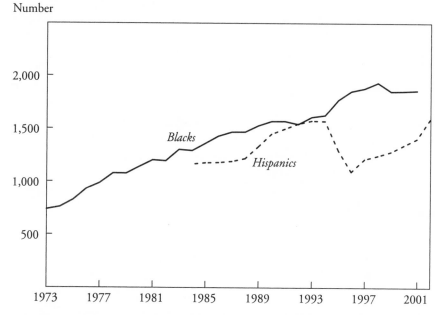

Source: National Association of Latino Elected and Appointed Officials and Joint Center for Political and Economic Studies, various years.

Michael Bloomberg was given control of the public school system, other cities that have at least some appointed school board members include Chicago, Baltimore, Philadelphia, Cleveland, Oakland, and Washington, D.C.[11] The combination of change in the selection method and reduction in the size of some school boards may contribute to a reduction in the number of minority members on the boards.

In light of these developments, how has black and Hispanic representation on local school boards changed over time? To address this question, figure 8-1 reports the total number of blacks and Hispanics elected to local school boards, based on data compiled by the Joint Center for Political and Economic Studies (JCPES) and the National Association of Latino Elected Officials (NALEO).

The overall trend has been toward an increase in the number of both black and Hispanic elected school board officials. Perhaps surprisingly, the number of Hispanic elected officials was roughly on par with the number of black elected officials during the early 1990s. Clearly the substantial increase in Hispanic immigration in the 1980s and 1990s has contributed to the increased Hispanic

11. See Education Commission of the States (2002), Kirst (2002), and Wong and Shen (2003).

presence on local school boards.[12] During the same period blacks saw larger annual increases than they had during the previous decade or so. In fact, the only period in which blacks witnessed any decline in the number of elected school board officials was in more recent years: from 1998 to 2001 the number of black officials dropped from 1,998 to 1,869. Though a relatively small decrease, this drop nevertheless suggests that the generational replacement of black elected officials and perhaps the increasing incidence of mayoral takeovers and reductions in the size of local school boards in predominantly black cities could be having some effect on black representation. Interestingly, the total number of black elected officials (for all levels of government) continued to increase during that period, and no other category of black elected officials (except federal) witnessed a decline.

Although the first elective office won by many individuals seeking a political career is on a local school board, the trend toward appointed school boards may be narrowing this option. In addition, the substantial gains in black representation during the 1970s and 1980s and the concomitant increase in the resources and opportunities available to blacks may also mean that younger blacks with political ambitions could begin to bypass school boards, most of which offer no remuneration, for higher offices.[13] To compare minority representation on school boards with minority representation in politics more generally, figure 8-2 reports black and Hispanic school board officials as a percentage of all black and Hispanic elected officials.

As this figure clearly shows, Hispanic elected officials are much more likely than black elected officials to be school board members. Indeed, for every year that the NALEO has published its roster, the largest number of Hispanic elected officials has been in the category "school boards/education." As Pachon and DeSipio (1992) note, often the first rung on the political ladder for Hispanics is the school board, and it is there that they gain the expertise and experience to run for higher office. In contrast, the largest number of black elected officials has consistently been in the municipal office category. In addition, although there has been a consistent (though gradual) decline over time in black school board members as a percentage of all black officials, that decline has not intensified in recent years. Thus it appears that recent changes in the governing arrangements of big city school systems and the generational replacement of black elected officials has had only marginal effects on the number of blacks elected to school boards.

12. The drop in the number of Hispanic elected officials in 1995 (by about 475 officials) is due to a change in the way NALEO reported data after 1994. Whereas previously the annual rosters included elected officials who had served in office at any time during the year, in 1995 the roster began including only those elected officials who were in office as of January of the year of publication.

13. Hess (2002).

Figure 8-2. *Elected School Board Officials as Percent of All Black and Hispanic Elected Officials*

Percent

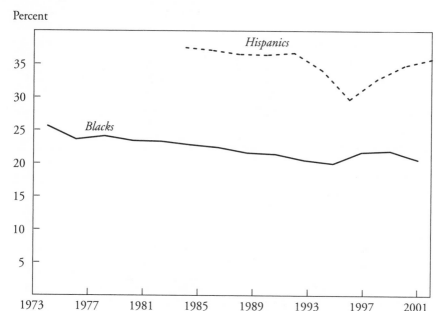

Source: National Association of Latino Elected and Appointed Officials and Joint Center for Political and Economic Studies, various years.

Finally, to illustrate changes in the regional concentrations of black and Hispanic school board members, table 8-1 presents data on minority office holding for 1985 and 2001 by state and region.[14]

As might be expected, there are clear regional patterns. Blacks gained the greatest representation on school boards in the South, while Hispanics were most represented in the West and the South (Texas is included in the South here). In both cases, these are the regions where the percentages of blacks and Hispanics in the total population are largest. Obviously the size of the population matters as well, and the states with the largest (225, Illinois) and fourth-largest (125, New York) numbers of black elected school board members are among the top five when it comes to the size of their black populations. A similar pattern obtains for Hispanics: all but one of the states (New York) with the

14. Given the way the race and ethnicity questions were asked in the 2000 census, it is now much less straightforward to compute these percentages. Percent black here is based on individuals who identified themselves as only black (one race) and is computed from the total number of individuals with only one racial identity. Percent Hispanic includes all individuals identifying themselves as Hispanic (regardless of race or multiple racial or ethnic identities) and is computed from the total number of persons. These categories are not mutually exclusive.

Table 8-1. *Distribution of Black and Hispanic Elected School Board Members by Region and State*

Region	Total school boards	Total popula- tion[a]	Percent black (2000)	Total black elected board members 1985	Total black elected board members 2001	Percent Hispanic (2000)	Total Hispanic elected board members 1985	Total Hispanic elected board members 2001
Northeast	2,954	53.6	6.76	260	260	6.61	80	65
Midwest	5,264	64.4	6.93	224	195	3.94	24	4
South	3,233	99.7	20.1	735	1113	5.79	569	709
West	2,680	63.2	2.72	140	62	14.5	510	632
States with most black elected board members								
Illinois[b]	892	12.4	15.3	70	225	12.3	15	2
Louisiana	67	4.5	32.7	123	161	2.4	1	3
South Carolina	85	4.0	29.8	95	158	2.3	0	0
New York	705	19.0	16.3	135	125	15.1	48	36
Mississippi	149	2.8	36.6	79	123	1.3	0	0
Arkansas	310	2.7	15.9	101	121	3.2	0	0
States with most Hispanic elected board members								
Texas	1,043	20.8	11.7	84	87	32.0	564	701
California	985	33.9	6.9	121	57	32.4	221	354
New Mexico	89	1.8	1.9	1	1	42.1	162	145
Arizona	227	5.1	3.1	3	0	25.2	76	105
New York	705	19.0	16.3	135	125	15.1	48	36
Colorado	178	4.3	3.8	4	1	17.1	45	27

Source: Education Commission of the States, 2002; National Association of Latino Elected Officials, 1985 and 2001; Joint Center for Political and Economic Studies, 1985 and 2001.

a. Population in millions. Regions defined according to census classifications, wherein Northeast includes New England and Mid-Atlantic states (CT, ME, MA, NH, RI, VT, NJ, NY, PA); Midwest includes East North Central and West North Central states (IL, IN, MI, OH, WI, IA, KS, MN, MO, NE, ND, SD); South includes South Atlantic, East South Central, and West South Central states (DE, FL, GA, MD, NC, SC, VA, WVA, AL, KY, MS, TN, AR, LA, OK, TX); and West includes Mountain and Pacific states (AZ, CO, ID, MT, NV, NM, UT, WY, AK, CA, HI, OR, WA).

b. Does not include Local School Councils in Chicago. Total elected school board members (2001): black = 1,855; Hispanic = 1,410. Change in total elected school board members (1985–2001): black = 487; Hispanic = 229.

largest number of Hispanic officials is located in the West or the South. Again, these regions include the states with the largest percentages of Hispanics.

Though not shown in the table, in 2001 there were thirteen states with no black elected school board members and thirty-two states with no Hispanic elected school board members.[15] Clearly, at least by gaining access to school boards in a larger number of states, blacks have made more progress than

15. The mean percent black and Hispanic for all states was 1.5 and 4.25, respectively. Among the states that had elected black and Hispanic school board members in 2001, the mean percent black and Hispanic was 13.0 and 13.97, respectively.

Hispanics. Indeed, while only six states account for 97 percent of all Hispanic elected school board members, the six states with the largest number of black elected school board members account for only 49 percent of the total number of black board members. It appears that although sizable Hispanic communities have recently sprouted across the South, Hispanics have not yet gained representation on school boards in these states.

What Factors Influence Minority Representation on Local School Boards?

As the data presented in table 8-1 suggest, a key factor in determining the extent to which blacks and Hispanics are represented on local school boards is the relative size (or voting strength) of their group in the local population. Indeed, empirical research based on cross-sectional analyses that control for other variables has largely confirmed this pattern; in additon, it has attempted to ascertain the extent to which local elected school boards proportionally represent the racial and ethnic mix of the population. Though early work tended to employ somewhat problematic measures of representation (typically ratios and difference scores), most recent work has relied on the somewhat less problematic proportionality measure adapted by Engstrom and McDonald (1981). Under this approach, the proportion of school board members who are black (Hispanic) is regressed on the proportion of the population that is black (Hispanic). Assuming that the intercept in this regression is statistically indistinguishable from zero, the slope coefficient on the race variable yields a "representation ratio" in which proportional representation is achieved when $b = 1$, whereas overrepresentation occurs when $b > 1$ and underrepresentation exists when $b < 1$.[16]

In fact, what is of primary theoretical and empirical interest in this body of research is the extent to which selection methods structure the nature of minority representation on local school boards. In other words, are blacks and Hispanics generally better (that is, more proportionally) represented under elective or appointive systems? And if they are better represented under elective systems, are there differences across different electoral arrangements, specifically at-large compared with district- or ward-based systems? For the most part empirical research has found that selection methods do indeed matter, particularly when it comes to African American representation. For example, studies examining black school board representation in the mid-1970s found that blacks were

16. See Engstrom and McDonald (1981) for more details. Studies employing this method have relied on samples that contain a minimum threshold for the minority population, since it is assumed that the minority population must be of a minimum size before minorities can have a realistic chance of electing "one of their own"; Engstrom and McDonald (1981, p. 345). There has been, however, no consensus on what this threshold ought to be, with scholars using a minimum population cutoff ranging from 5 to 15 percent.

better than proportionally represented on big city school boards and that appointive systems yielded greater representation than did elective systems.[17] In addition, these studies tended to find that blacks achieved better representation under district- or ward-based electoral systems than in at-large systems.[18]

Findings from several more recent studies of both black and Hispanic school board representation suggest that the relationship between selection methods and minority representation on school boards may depend on the size or type of school district (for example, central city versus rural, predominantly white versus predominantly minority); the nature of the political jurisdiction (for example, unified or independent); or the minority group in question. For example, in their 1987 study of black representation on local school boards in 132 North Carolina school districts, Arrington and Watts (1991) found that overall blacks were underrepresented and that districts with appointive selection methods were associated with the lowest representation ratios while districts with ward-based electoral systems produced more proportional representation than did at-large systems. On the other hand, in a recent study of 1,692 school districts in which blacks constituted less than 50 percent of the population, Eller, Hicklin, and Rocha (2003) found that at-large arrangements were associated with *greater* representation ratios than were district arrangements. However, using a similar sample, Meier and others (2002) and Meier and Juenke (chapter 9 of this book) did not find this to be the case with regard to Hispanic school board representation; instead, ward-based arrangements were associated with more proportional Hispanic representation. Although on balance it appears that the evidence points most strongly to greater proportional representation for both blacks and Hispanics under ward-based arrangements, there are still some inconsistencies in findings.[19]

There are two related issues that might partially explain some of these inconsistencies. First, in a number of cases the assumption regarding the zero intercept (under the proportionality approach) has not been satisfied. This not only makes interpreting the slope coefficient (or the representation ratio) problematic but more generally leads to unreliable results and potentially faulty conclusions. Second, since the number of school districts with no blacks or Hispanics serving on the school board remains large, the distribution of the dependent variable is often severely skewed. Employing a threshold for the minimum percentage of minorities in the population reduces the number of districts without minority elected officials; however, unless a relatively high threshold is used (and thus a

17. Welch and Karnig (1978); Robinson and England (1981).

18. Robinson and England (1981) and Robinson, England, and Meier (1985); but see Welch and Karnig (1978).

19. For positive findings, see Meier and others (2002); Polinard, Wrinkle, and Longoria (1990). For inconsistencies, see Fraga, Meier, and England (1986) and Meier and Juenke's results in chapter 9 of this volume for majority Hispanic districts.

large number of observations are discarded), the skewed distribution typically remains. Moreover, employing a ceiling for the minority population, as nearly all recent studies have done, could also have implications for the results.[20]

Given these problems, an alternative analytic approach may be more appropriate. One method employed by Marschall and Ruhil (2003) focuses on the original measure of representation—the number of minorities serving on the local school board (or city council)—rather than a ratio or proportion of minorities on the board. Using this approach, it is possible to specify a count model that explicitly takes into account the distributional features of the dependent variable. Since in this case the dependent variable is a non-negative count variable, both the maximum-likelihood zero-inflated Poisson and negative binomial estimators are appropriate. In both cases, an equation is first specified to determine whether the observed count is zero (using a probit or logit), then the second equation estimates the Poisson or binomial regression of the dependent variable on the set of independent variables. The benefit of this approach is that it does not make any assumptions about the value of the intercept and also does not require the sample to be censored by employing a threshold or ceiling on the minority population.

Modeling Black and Hispanic Representation on Local School Boards in Four Metropolitan Areas

In the analysis that follows I revisit the question of how selection methods influence minority school board representation by employing count models. My analysis is based on black and Hispanic office holding on local school boards in a sample of 190 school districts. Given the size and nature of the sample, the analysis is not intended to definitively settle the debate on whether and how selection methods are associated with the representation of these two groups on local school boards.[21] On the other hand, because the sample includes a wide array of school districts located in four major metropolitan areas, it provides a wider empirical focus than many earlier studies.

Before reporting results from the multivariate analysis, I begin by presenting descriptive statistics for the sample of school districts as a whole and for each of the four metropolitan areas. As the data in table 8-2 illustrate, there is considerable variation in the size of the school districts across the four metro areas. On

20. Exceptions include Arrington and Watts (1991); Meier and Juenke, chapter 9 in this volume.
21. Because analyzing the relationship between electoral (and other) arrangements and representation requires researchers to compile their own data, often from the political jurisdictions themselves, constructing large, nationally representative samples is no small undertaking. Since I was initially interested in looking at substantive representation, my sample is based on a large-scale survey of residents in four metropolitan areas. Although the number of school districts in which these respondents reside is relatively large (roughly 200), for this analysis the sample cannot be considered a probability sample because school districts were not the primary sampling units. The sample is described in more detail in a later section of the chapter.

Table 8-2. *Summary Statistics for Sample School Districts*[a]

Variables	Full sample	Min-imum	Max-imum	LA metro	Atlanta metro	Boston metro	Detroit metro
Mean schools	53.45	2	659	155.1	68.8	11.8	19.8
	(129.2)			(261.1)	(36.08)	(17.1)	(37.4)
Mean teachers	2,785	61	35,149	8,060	4,217	482	598
	(6,994)			(14,034)	(2,322)	(742)	(1,225)
Mean students	50,820	775	721,346	166,305	65,888	6,263	11,042
	(141,274)			(287,592)	(35,845)	(8,356)	(23,228)
Mean student-teacher ratio	16.91	9.6	25.3	21.38	15.5	13.76	18.37
	(3.40)			(1.01)	(1.02)	(2.56)	(1.83)
Mean school board size	6.56	5	11	5.82	6.8	6.46	7.04
	(1.23)			(.999)	(1.49)	(1.34)	(.658)
Mean percent of district black	12.68	0	87	12.8	29.15	3.82	11.1
	(17.11)			(14.4)	(16.1)	(5.14)	(20.5)
Mean percent of district Hispanic	12.03	0	86.8	40.6	7.4	5.7	2.6
	(17.42)			(18.3)	(3.46)	(10.1)	(2.02)
Mean black school board members	.695	0	11	.71	1.77	.069	.659
	(1.78)			(1.62)	(2.45)	(.317)	(2.03)
Mean Hispanic school board members	.264	0	6	1.29	0	.034	0
	(.893)			(1.64)		(.262)	
Mean percent of school board black	9.80	0	100	12.1	24.5	.90	8.21
	(24.84)			(28.3)	(34.99)	(4.29)	(23.4)
Mean percent of school board Hispanic	4.24	0	100	20.8	0	.493	0
	(14.37)			(26.5)		(3.75)	
Districts with appointed school board	1			0	0	1	0
Districts with at-large system	147			30	4	63	50
Districts with mixed system	1			0	1	0	0
Districts with ward system	48			12	30	6	0
Total districts	197			42	35	70	50

Source: For district demographics: National Center for Education Statistics, School District Demographics (STP2) (http://nces.ed.gov/surveys/sdds/downloadmain.asp [November 1, 2004]).

a. Standard deviations are reported in parentheses.

the other hand, in three of the four metro areas, the at-large system of selecting school board members dominates (Atlanta is the exception). Unfortunately, with only one school district using appointment (Boston) and one relying on a mixed electoral arrangement (Decatur, Georgia), there are too few observations to analyze the effects of these arrangements on minority school board representation.[22] Similarly, since there are no Hispanic school board members in any of the Detroit or Atlanta metro area school districts, the analysis of Hispanics is limited to the Los Angeles and Boston metro areas.

22. Detroit did not adopt its appointed method until 1999; data for this study are based on 1993–94.

Table 8-3. *Black and Hispanic Representation, Zero-Inflated Poisson Models*[a]

Independent variables	Black school board representation		Hispanic school board representation	
	Coefficient	e^bStdχ	Coefficient	e^bStdχ
Percent black in school district	.018**	1.349	−.048**	0.452
	(.006)		(.019)	
Percent Hispanic in school district	.021**	1.480	.014*	1.300
	(.007)		(.008)	
District elections	.683**	1.347	−.655	0.754
	(.221)		(.487)	
Central city	.069	1.015	.665	1.150
	(.320)		(.522)	
Intercept	−2.302**		−1.350**	
	(.355)		(.601)	
Summary statistic				
N	196		196	
Nonzero observations	37		24	
Chi²	23.28**		13.34	
Vuong test	4.06**		2.37	

Source: Author's calculations.

a. Estimates based on Stata 7.0 zip models. e^bStdχ =exp(b*SD of χ) = change in expected count for standard deviation increase in χ (for nonzero observations). * $p < .05$; ** $p < .01$ (one-tailed test). Vuong test of zero-inflated Poisson versus Poisson specification (Z statistic). Standard errors are reported in parentheses.

Table 8-3 reports the results of the zero-inflated Poisson model.[23] Because these are maximum likelihood coefficients and nonlinear models, I also report the change in the expected count for a standard deviation increase in the independent variables for those districts where there is at least one black or Hispanic school board member (that is, nonzero observations). Given the greater flexibility of the count model approach, I also include a control variable for the large central city districts (Atlanta, Boston, Detroit, and Los Angeles) and both percent black and percent Hispanic variables in each of the models. The basic pattern of these results is consistent with the bivariate regression analyses using the conventional proportionality approach.[24]

23. Zero-inflated negative binomial regression models also were estimated; the results are wholly consistent with those of the zero-inflated Poisson.

24. In these models, which excluded school districts with less than 5 percent black or Hispanic populations, the Hispanic results yielded nonzero intercepts whereas black results suggest that proportional representation is more than achieved under at-large arrangements (b = 1.188). On the other hand, blacks failed to achieve proportional representation under district arrangements (b = .837). This finding is contrary to the results reported in most existing research, though again differences in samples and time periods could explain this result.

Looking first at the results for black school board representation, I find that increases in both the percent black and percent Hispanic variables in the school district lead to increases in the number of black board members. Similarly, district elections have a significant positive effect on the number of blacks elected to local boards. In contrast, district elections do not have a significant effect on Hispanic school board representation. At least in this sample of school districts, there does not appear to be a significant difference in the number of Hispanics represented on local school boards under district and at-large arrangements. However, the size of the Hispanic population is positively related to Hispanic office holding, and interestingly, the larger the black population in the district, the fewer the number of Hispanic elected officials.

While the results for black school board representation are consistent with the general pattern of findings in the literature, the nonsignificance of the district electoral arrangements variable in the Hispanic model does not conform to this pattern. For example, Meier and Juenke (chapter 9) find that when Hispanics are a minority they do significantly better in ward-based elections (when they are a majority, electoral arrangements have no effect). On the other hand, Fraga, Meier, and England (1986) found no significant differences in selection mechanisms for Hispanic school board representation. Although in general there has been much less research on Hispanic representation, some of the inconsistencies in findings here could be due to the samples and estimation techniques employed. For example, in the current sample many school districts have relatively small Hispanic populations and school boards with at most only one or two Hispanic members. Clearly more empirical analysis is necessary to better understand how district demographics and selection methods influence Hispanic school board representation. On the other hand, the results presented here do point to important differences in the pattern of black and Hispanic school board representation across the 190 districts included in the four metropolitan areas studied. Moreover, the results suggest that the method of analysis employed can play an important role in what kind of results obtain. In the present case, it appears that key assumptions of the proportionality method do not hold, making this approach less appropriate.

Substantive Representation

Minority incorporation is a two-dimensional concept that encompasses both descriptive and substantive representation. While gaining access to elective office and positions of power is important in its own right, the ability of minority groups to influence policies and outcomes is the ultimate goal. I therefore turn to the question of substantive representation by looking at how Hispanic and black representation on local school boards influences schooling outcomes.

For the most part, this area of inquiry has received only scant empirical scrutiny. Following the approach of scholars investigating substantive representation in urban politics, one approach has been to examine whether minority representation on local school boards leads to an increase in the minority share of district administrative and teaching positions.[25] A second area of inquiry examines the link between minority teachers and a set of policies and practices referred to as second-generation discrimination, which is said to exist when minority students are overrepresented in certain types of classes or outcomes (for example, bilingual, special education, and educable mentally retarded classes; dropping out; and suspensions) and underrepresented in other classes or outcomes (gifted-talented and advanced placement classes; graduation; and college or vocational school attendance).[26] Finally, a third area of empirical research has looked explicitly at minority achievement and the relationship between minority representation in schools and classrooms and the gap between minority and nonminority student achievement.[27]

In fact, these three areas of research tap different aspects of the same general process. This process, summarized in figure 8-3, is essentially one whereby increases in the representation of minorities in various educational positions of authority translate into increases in schools' capacity to address the special educational needs and preferences of minority students and parents. As figure 8-3 illustrates, the process begins with the school board, which not only is responsible for hiring the superintendent—who could be either a minority or a nonminority member who strongly supports minority hiring—but also has the capacity to enact formal policies and exert informal pressure on higher-level school administrators to hire more minorities at lower administrative levels.[28] School administrators, in turn, play an important role in the hiring of teachers and so can influence the extent to which blacks and Hispanics are represented in these positions. Finally, minority teachers not only serve as role models for minority students but also make many day-to-day decisions that affect them.[29] And although teachers are responsible for implementing and enforcing policies and decisions made by school administrators, as "street-level bureaucrats" they also have considerable discretion.

Thus by hiring administrators with certain policy preferences, school boards indirectly influence the hiring of teachers and other lower-level administrators,

25. Fraga, Meier, and England (1986); Polinard, Wrinkle, and Longoria (1990); Stewart, England, and Meier (1989).

26. On second-generation discrimination, see Fraga, Meier, and England (1986); Meier and England (1984); Polinard, Wrinkle, and Longoria (1990).

27. Polinard, Wrinkle, and Meier (1995).

28. Stewart, England, and Meier (1989, pp. 295–96).

29. Fraga, Meier, and England (1986); Thomas and Brown (1982).

Figure 8-3. *Summary of Empirical Research on Minority Incorporation in Educational Politics and Policy*

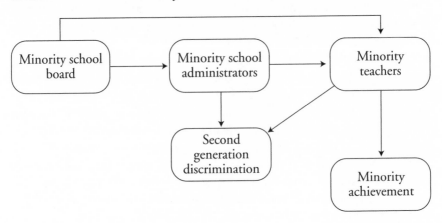

who in turn have a direct influence on shaping minority student outcomes. In this way, gains in descriptive representation within the realm of school politics, administration, and teaching may play an important role in improving the quality, effectiveness, and equality of school outcomes, particularly for black and Hispanic students.

Minority Representation and Residents' Satisfaction with Schools

My analysis of substantive representation builds on the process depicted in figure 8-3. In particular, I focus on policy outcomes as measured by the perceptions of the target audience—the parents and residents served by local school districts. If minority representation on local school boards manifests itself in the ways discussed above, it is reasonable to argue that Hispanic and black parents and residents will feel more positive about their schools. In other words, blacks and Hispanics in districts where members of their own racial or ethnic group are represented on the local school board should rate their schools more favorably and generally be more satisfied with the quality of the education provided in their local school district than those who reside in school districts without minority representation.

In the analysis that follows I examine residents' evaluations of the quality of their neighborhood schools. There are several reasons why such evaluations are reliable indicators of school performance and preferable to other measures of service delivery. First, although survey research suggests that the public is not well informed about the specific arrangements through which their local services are provided, evidence suggests that Americans are remarkably knowledgeable when it comes to evaluating the performance and quality of local services.[30] For instance, using data from two cross-sectional surveys of New Orleans residents, Howell and McLean (2001) found congruence between citizens' perceptions of the general performance of several municipal services and actual changes in performance (for example, reductions in crime). Moreover, DeHoog, Lowery, and Lyons (1990) provide convincing evidence that the level and quality of services positively and significantly influence citizen satisfaction with local public services and that citizens' evaluations of local service quality are valid indicators of actual service quality. Finally, symbolic representation, or the ability of local officials to build constituency trust and broad support, is important in its own right, yet it is often overlooked in the literature on minority representation.[31] Thus the presence of black and Hispanic officials, even on school boards and in other positions that may not be highly visible, can foster increased levels of group pride. Evidence suggests that African Americans derive broad psychic benefits and evince higher levels of political trust, efficacy, and knowledge when their elected representatives are black.[32] The implication of this "symbolic politics" model is that minorities residing in empowered areas ought to feel more positive than those who live in jurisdictions where they have lower levels of representation.

To test the extent to which minority representation on local school boards positively influences residents' evaluations of their schools, I relied on a data set constructed from multiple sources. For individual-level data, I used the Multi-City Study of Urban Inequality (MCSUI), a large-scale survey of residents in the Atlanta, Boston, Detroit, and Los Angeles metropolitan areas conducted between 1992 and 1994.[33] For each metropolitan area, the sample includes a large number of minority and low-income households, allowing for meaningful analysis of both Hispanics and African Americans.[34] The MCSUI data not only tapped respondents' perceptions about the quality of their local schools but also included a variable linking respondents to census block groups, thereby making it possible to match individual-level characteristics and behaviors with data on the economic, racial, and demographic characteristics of neighborhoods. In addition, I recovered the place identifiers for respondents through block group and county information provided in the MCSUI, which allowed me to also match respondents to the school districts in which they resided. Data on school districts were culled from the National Center for Education Statistics and from

30. For the survey research, see Stipak (1977).
31. See Gilliam (1996).
32. On psychic benefits, see Gurin, Hatchett, and Jackson (1989); Tate (1993).
33. Bobo and others (1998).
34. Because the metropolitan areas were quite diverse with regard to their racial and ethnic and income composition, the criteria used to define each stratum were unique to each city. For more details on the sample design of the MCSUI, see Bobo and others (1998, appendix F).

Table 8-4. *Sample Statistics*[a]

	Mean	Standard deviation	Min- imum	Max- imum	Number of observations
Dependent variable (quality of schools)	.51	.50	0	1	8,732
Individual demographics[b]					
Black	.349	.476	0	1	8,899
Hispanic	.200	.400	0	1	8,899
Asian/other	.138	.344	0	1	8,899
School-aged children	.873	1.246	0	1	8,898
Married/partner	.455	.498	0	1	8,899
Years of schooling	12.27	3.377	0	17	8,864
Homeowner	.383	.486	0	1	8,899
Years of residence	8.388	10.782	0	90	8,899
Employed	.533	.499	0	1	8,899
Neighborhood demographics[c]					
Median age of housing	37.378	13.431	0	55	8,886
Median household income ($ thousands)	29.48	17.576	0	150	8,887
School district characteristics[d]					
Student-teacher ratio	17.932	3.912	6.7	25.3	8,884
Number of students (log)	10.97	1.81	6.65	13.5	8,898
Minority school board representation[e]					
Percent of school board black	16.928	31.603	0	100	8,899
Percent of school board Hispanic	12.869	17.474	0	100	8,899
Majority of school board black	.129	.335	0	1	8,899
Majority of school board Hispanic	.029	.168	0	1	8,899
Any black school board representative	.343	.475	0	1	8,899
Any Hispanic school board representative	.420	.493	0	1	8,899

Source: Author's calculations.

a. Sampling weights were not employed in computing these statistics.

b. Bobo and others (1998).

c. 1990 Census of Population and Housing.

d. National Center for Education Statistics, School District Demographics (STP2) (http://nces.ed.gov/surveys/sdds/downloadmain.asp [November 1, 2004]).

e. Joint Center for Political and Economic Studies, 1992–94; National Association of Latino Elected Officials, 1992–94.

the school districts themselves, while information on black and Hispanic elected officials came from the JCPES and NALEO.[35] Table 8-4 reports summary statistics for the sample.

The dependent variable in the analysis is a dichotomous measure of respondents' evaluations of the quality of their local schools (1 = good/excellent; 0 =

35. Minority representation data for the one appointed school board in the sample, Boston, was provided by the Boston School Committee.

fair/poor). To test the effects of black and Hispanic representation on local school boards, I specified three different measures of representation and then interacted these with the race of the respondent to determine whether blacks or Hispanics were more likely to perceive their schools as good or excellent when their local school board included members of their own racial or ethnic group. The basic model can be summarized as follows:

Quality schools = f(individual demographics, neighborhood demographics, school district characteristics, minority school board representation)

Individual demographics refers to a series of respondent-specific control variables. In particular, these include a set of dummy variables (black, Hispanic, Asian/other) corresponding to the respondent's racial or ethnic identity (Anglo is the excluded category), as well as dummy variables for whether the respondent is married or living with a partner (1 = married/partner), is currently employed (1 = employed), is a homeowner (1 = homeowner), or has at least one child under eighteen years of age living at home. Finally, there are variables measuring the respondent's educational attainment (years of schooling) and the length of residence at the current address (in years).

Neighborhood demographics includes two variables that tap the socioeconomic condition of the neighborhood and thus serve as important controls with regard to the quality of the local schools. These include median age of housing structures (measured in years) and median household income (in thousands of dollars). These variables are based on 1990 Census of Population and Housing data measured at the block group level—the lowest level for which the Census Bureau collects data. Although ideally the unit of analysis used to represent the neighborhood would be a spatial subunit that corresponds to the school catchment area, the block group is a reasonable approximation since it ensures not only that respondents live in the same neighborhood and school catchment area but also that their local services and general neighborhood conditions are similar.

School district characteristics includes three measures to control again for factors that are likely to influence the quality of local schools. These include a variable measuring the student-teacher ratio in the school district, the natural log of the total number of students in the district, and a dummy variable indicating whether the respondent lives in one of four primary central city school districts in the metropolitan areas (Atlanta, Boston, Detroit, and Los Angeles).

Minority school board representation corresponds to three different specifications of black and Hispanic office holding on local school boards. The first measures the percentage of blacks and Hispanics, while the second and third include dummy variables indicating whether there is at least one black or Hispanic on the school board (any black/Hispanic school board rep) or whether blacks or Hispanics constitute a majority on the school board (majority black/Hispanic school board).

For each of the three specifications of minority school board representation I estimated two models—a baseline model and a model with the appropriate interaction terms. Because the respondents in the MCSUI were sampled by means of a multistage, stratified, clustered area—probability design, I relied on established routines for regression analysis (Stata's svyprobit routine) that take the clustering of individuals at a specific level into account.[36] In addition, I report the marginal effects, with their corresponding standard errors, to ease interpretation. The results of the three sets of maximum-likelihood probit models are presented in table 8-5.

Beginning with the general pattern of results, I find that independent of the racial or ethnic composition of the school board, blacks' perceptions of their schools did not differ significantly from those of whites, whereas Hispanics were significantly more likely (by roughly 8 percentage points) than whites to rate their schools as good or excellent. In addition, both individual- and neighborhood-level socioeconomic status had the expected effects on residents' evaluations of the quality of their schools: more educated respondents and those living in census blocks with older housing were significantly less likely to perceive their schools as good or excellent, whereas those living in neighborhoods with higher median household incomes were significantly more likely to evaluate their schools positively. And, not surprisingly, the effect of living in a large, central city school district or a district with a high student-teacher ratio translates into a rather substantial decrease in the likelihood of rating a school as high quality. Finally, not considering the race or ethnicity of the respondent, living in a school district where Hispanics held seats on the school board is associated with a lower probability of rating schools positively. The effects are less consistent for districts where blacks were represented on the school board.

Turning to the models that include interaction terms between the race of the respondent and the racial composition of the school board, I find generally positive effects. In Model 1, I find that black respondents who lived in districts with higher percentages of blacks on the school board were significantly more likely to rate their schools as good or excellent than blacks who lived in districts with lower percentages of black board members. For Hispanics the interaction is not significant, indicating that Hispanic evaluations of their schools were not affected by Hispanic school board representation. On the other hand, for both blacks and Hispanics there is a multiplicative effect of having at least one member of their own racial or ethnic group on the school board (Model 2), lending support to the idea that symbolic representation matters. The interaction term is

36. Although the data and hypotheses of this study lend themselves to a full-blown, multilevel analysis, it is not possible to simultaneously specify three levels of sampling weights and additional clusters or levels in the data.

Table 8-5. *Effects of Black and Hispanic School Board Representation on Residents' Evaluations of the Quality of Local Schools*[a]

	Model 1 (Percent black or Hispanic school board members)		Model 2 (Any black or Hispanic school board members)		Model 3 (Majority black or Hispanic school board members)	
Black	−.016	−.080*	−.024	−.089*	−.021	−.056
	(.031)	(.035)	(.031)	(.044)	(.031)	(.032)
Hispanic	.087*	.076	.085*	−.015	.079*	.102**
	(.037)	(.04)	(.037)	(.047)	(.036)	(.032)
Asian/other	.022	.022	.022	.023	.021	.022
	(.041)	(.041)	(.041)	(.042)	(.041)	(.040)
School-aged children	.017	.017	.016	.015	.016	.016
	(.01)	(.010)	(.010)	(.010)	(.010)	(.010)
Married/partner	.005	.005	.008	.009	.005	.003
	(.022)	(.022)	(.023)	(.023)	(.022)	(.022)
Years of schooling	−.008*	−.008*	−.008*	−.007	−.009*	−.009*
	(.004)	(.004)	(.004)	(.004)	(.004)	(.004)
Homeowner	.058*	.057*	.049	.042	.058*	.062*
	(.027)	(.027)	(.028)	(.027)	(.027)	(.027)
Years of residence	.001	.001	.001	.002	.001	.001
	(.001)	(.001)	(.001)	(.001)	(.001)	(.001)
Employed	−.041*	−.042*	−.043*	−.045*	−.040	−.040
	(.021)	(.021)	(.021)	(.021)	(.021)	(.021)
Median age of housing	−.004**	−.004**	−.003**	−.003**	−.004**	−.004**
	(.001)	(.001)	(.001)	(.001)	(.001)	(.001)
Median household income	.003**	.003**	.003**	.003**	.003**	.003**
	(.001)	(.001)	(.001)	(.001)	(.001)	(.001)
Student-teacher ratio	−.014**	−.015**	−.014**	−.013**	−.014**	−.015**
	(.004)	(.004)	(.004)	(.003)	(.004)	(.004)
Number of students (log)	−.003	−.000	.006	.007	−.008	−.007
	(.009)	(.009)	(.010)	(.010)	(.009)	(.009)
Central city	−.173**	−.181**	−.169**	−.173**	−.195**	−.201**
	(.039)	(.039)	(.039)	(.039)	(.040)	(.039)
Black school board representatives	−.001**	−.002**	−.055	−.089*	−.048	−.183**
	(.000)	(.000)	(.031)	(.038)	(.035)	(.053)
Hispanic school board representatives	−.002**	−.002**	−.111**	−.136**	−.126*	−.033
	(.001)	(.001)	(.034)	(.037)	(.054)	(.086)
Black school board representatives*black		.003**		.130**		.217**
		(.001)		(.051)		(.047)
Hispanic school board representatives*Hispanic		.000		−.138**		−.171
		(.001)		(.049)		(.116)
Intercept	1.428	1.410	1.202	1.125	1.559	1.578
	(.363)	(.367)	.398	(.395)	(.353)	(.354)
Summary statistic						
N	8,636	8,636	8,636	8,636	8,636	8,636
Predicted Y	.610	.610	.610	.610	.610	.610
F statistic	16.74**	15.13**	15.90**	14.37**	17.21**	15.89**

Source: Author's calculations.

a. Table entries are marginal effects after Stata survey probit estimation (robust standard errors in parentheses) and correspond to the change in the probability (Y = 1) for a discrete change in χ, when χ is held constant at its mean. Number of Stata = 27; number of primary sampling units = 1,266. * $p < .05$; ** $p < .01$ (one-tailed test).

positive and significant for both blacks and Hispanics, and in both cases substantially attenuates the negative effects of having a minority school board member. Finally, in Model 3, which investigates the effects of having a majority black
or Hispanic school board, I again find significant effects only for blacks.

Taken together, the results from this set of empirical analyses indicate that
Hispanics and especially blacks are more likely to have favorable assessments of
their local schools when their board includes members of their own racial or
ethnic group.[37] Although we cannot rule out the possibility that these attitudinal
effects are strictly symbolic, if the quality of representation improves as a result
of the process of representation described by Meier and Juenke in chapter 9 of
this book, the results presented here suggest that higher levels of satisfaction and
more positive assessments of local schools may also be the result of substantive
changes in the quality of education provided in these districts. To be sure, further research is necessary to examine these relationships more directly; however,
the findings from this study suggest that there may indeed be a link between
minority representation, school policy and outcomes, and residents' perceptions
of how well their local schools are meeting their needs.

Conclusions and Implications

As the data presented in this chapter indicate, both blacks and Hispanics have
made considerable progress in electing members of their own racial and ethnic
groups to local school boards in the past couple of decades. Though Hispanic
representation is still heavily concentrated in school districts in the Southwest,
the total number of Hispanics elected to local school boards has been roughly
equivalent to that of blacks over much of the period between 1984 and 2002.
This is quite a remarkable accomplishment given the substantial percentage of
Hispanics who are not naturalized citizens and who thus are ineligible to vote in
most local school board elections. In addition, the data presented here suggest
that at least at present, concerns about lower rates of office holding among
blacks due to either generational turnover among black elected officials or to the
recent trend toward appointed school boards may be misplaced.

Findings from this study also reveal interesting patterns with regard to the
effect that selection method has on black and Hispanic school board representation. In the case of blacks, my results conform to the predominant findings in
extant research—both district electoral arrangements and the size of the black

37. Though the relationship between minority school board representation and whites' assessments of their neighborhood schools is not the focus of the present analysis, it is worth noting that
the results based on the interaction models (table 5) consistently show that whites are less likely to
rate their schools as good or excellent when Hispanics and especially blacks gain greater representation on the board. For more on how minority representation influences white residents' racial attitudes, policy preferences, and voting behavior, see Hajnal (2001).

population significantly increased the number of blacks represented on local school boards. On the other hand, I find that selection method does not matter for Hispanic school board representation and that while the size of the Hispanic population is positively associated with gains in Hispanic representation, the size of the black population is negatively associated with Hispanic office holding. This is an interesting finding in light of the considerable case study research suggesting that biracial coalitions are playing an increasingly important role in the electoral successes of minority candidates.[38] While the findings presented in this chapter suggest that this may hold true for the electoral prospects of black school board candidates, they suggest otherwise for Hispanics. At least for the sample of school districts examined here, it appears that potential biracial coalitions of blacks and Hispanics were not associated with increased Hispanic school board representation, and that in turn may explain why Hispanics have not made much progress in gaining access to school boards in the districts examined in this study.

Finally, in my investigation of how minority school board representation influences residents' evaluations of their schools, I found that especially among blacks, greater representation translated into more favorable assessments of neighborhood schools. From the simple presence of one black representative on the school board to having a majority of blacks on the school board, blacks were significantly more likely to rate their schools as good or excellent when they lived in school districts where they were represented. These effects were less consistent, though not absent, for Hispanics. Overall, the analysis presented here suggests that minority representation plays an important role in shaping minorities' evaluations of their schools.

As others have demonstrated, even if minority representation is strictly symbolic, it is nevertheless meaningful since it is associated with higher levels of political trust, efficacy, and knowledge.[39] In particular, not only has efficacy been found to be a consistent predictor of political participation, but research also demonstrates that parents who were more satisfied with their local schools were more likely to participate in school-related activities and organizations (for example, parent-teacher associations) and were more likely to trust their child's teacher.[40] The evidence linking parental involvement and a whole array of positive schooling outcomes is well established in research on effective schools.[41] In particular, parental involvement in schools has been consistently associated with

38. See, for example, Browning, Marshall, and Tabb (1986) and other authors in that *PS* symposium.

39. Gilliam (1996); Gurin, Hatchett, and Jackson (1989); Tate (1993).

40. On efficacy as a predictor of political participation, see, for example, Abramson and Aldrich 1982; Berry, Portney, and Thomson (1993); Finkel (1985). On parental involvement in schools, see Schneider, Teske, and Marschall (2000).

41. See Henderson (1987) for a summary of this work.

higher student achievement levels, lower student drop-out rates, and higher graduation rates. In short, the findings presented here suggest that the presence of Hispanics and especially blacks on local school boards can play an important role in improving the quality of schooling outcomes for minority students while at the same time strengthening representative democracy in the United States.

References

Abramson, Paul R., and John H. Aldrich. 1982. "The Decline of Electoral Participation in America." *American Political Science Review* 76 (September): 502–21.

Arrington, Theodore S., and Thomas Gill Watts. 1991. "The Election of Blacks to School Boards in North Carolina." *Western Political Quarterly* 44 (December): 1099–105.

Berry, Jeffrey M., Kent E. Portney, and Ken Thomson. 1993. *The Rebirth of Urban Democracy*. Brookings.

Bobo, Lawrence, and others. 1998. Multi-City Study of Urban Inequality, 1992–94: Atlanta, Boston, Detroit, and Los Angeles (Household Survey Data). 2nd ICPSR version. Distributed by Inter-University Consortium for Political and Social Research (www.icpsr.umich.edu [December 2, 2004]).

Bositis, David A. 2002. "Black Elected Officials: A Statistical Summary, 2000." Washington: Joint Center for Political and Economic Studies.

Browing, Rufus P., Dale R. Marshall, and David H. Tabb. 1986. "Protest Is Not Enough: A Theory of Political Incorporation." *PS: Political Science and Politics* 19 (Summer): 576–81.

Bullock, Charles S., III, and Susan A MacManus. 1987. "Staggered Terms and Black Representation." *Journal of Politics* 49 (May): 543–52.

Cibulka, James. 1999. "Moving toward an Accountable System of K–12 Education: Alternative Approaches and Challenges." In *Handbook of Educational Policy*, edited by Gregory Cizek. San Diego: Academic Press.

Converse, Phillip. 1966. "Mass Belief Systems." In *Ideology and Discontent*, edited by David E. Apter. London: Free Press of Glencoe.

Dahl, Robert. 1961. *Who Governs?* Yale University Press.

DeHoog, Rugh Hoogland, David Lowery, and William E. Lyons. 1990. "Citizen Satisfaction with Local Governance: A Test of Individual, Jurisdictional, and City-Specific Explanations." *Journal of Politics* 53 (August): 807–37.

Education Commission of the States. 2002. "Local School Boards: Types, Elected vs. Appointed, and Number" (www.ecs.org/ecsmain.asp?page=/html/publications/e_newsletters.htm [December 2, 2004]).

Eller, Warren, Alisa Hicklin, and Rene Rocha. 2003. "Political Representation and Ethnic Equality: Assessing the Determinants and Impacts of African American Representation in Education." Paper presented at the annual meeting of the American Political Science Association. Philadelphia, August 28–31.

Engstrom, Richard L., and Michael D. McDonald. 1981. "The Election of Blacks to City Councils: Clarifying the Impact of Electoral Arrangements on the Seats/Population Relationship." *American Political Science Review* 75 (2): 344–54.

Finkel, Steven E. 1985. "Reciprocal Effects of Participation and Political Efficacy: A Panel Analysis." *American Journal of Political Science* 29 (November): 891–913.

Fraga, Luis Ricardo, Kenneth J. Meier, and Robert E. England. 1986. "Hispanic Americans and Educational Policy: Limits to Equal Access." *Journal of Politics* 48 (November): 850–76.

Gilliam, Frank D., Jr. 1996. "Exploring Minority Empowerment: Symbolic Politics, Governing Conditions, and Traces of Political Style in Los Angeles." *American Journal of Political Science* 40 (February): 56–81.

Gurin, Patricia, Shirley Hatchett, and James S. Jackson. 1989. *Hope and Independence: Blacks' Response to Electoral and Party Politics.* New York: Russell Sage Foundation.

Hajnal, Zoltan. 2001. "White Residents, Black Incumbents, and a Declining Racial Divide." *American Political Science Review* 95 (September): 603–17.

Hanson, G. H. 2003. "What Has Happened to Wages in Mexico since NAFTA? Implications for Hemispheric Free Trade." Working Paper 9563. Cambridge, Mass.: National Bureau of Economic Research (March).

Henderson, Anne T. 1987. *The Evidence Continues to Grow: Parent Involvement Improves Student Achievement, an Annotated Bibliography.* Columbia, Md.: National Committee for Citizens in Education.

Hernandez-Leon, Ruben, and Victor Zuniga. 2002. "Mexican Immigrant Communities in the South and Social Capital: The Case of Dalton, Georgia." Working Paper 64. University of California, San Diego (December).

Hess, Frederick M. 2002. "School Boards at the Dawn of the 21st Century: Conditions and Challenges of District Governance." Report prepared for the National School Boards Association, Alexandria, Va.

Howell, Susan E., and William P. McLean. 2001. "Performance and Race in Evaluating Minority Mayors." *Public Opinion Quarterly* 65 (3): 321–43.

Joint Center for Political and Economic Studies. Various years. *Black Elected Officials: A National Roster.* Washington.

Kirst, M. W. 2002. *Mayoral Influence, New Regimes, and Public School Governance.* CPRE Research Report Series RR-049. Consortium for Policy Research in Education, University of Pennsylvania Graduate School of Education.

Marschall, Melissa J., and Anirudh V. S. Ruhil. 2003. "Hues in the House: A Panel Analysis of Black Electoral Gains in City Halls." Paper presented at the annual meeting of the American Political Science Association. Philadelphia, August 28–31.

Meier, Kenneth J., and Robert E. England. 1984. "Black Representation and Education Policy: Are They Related?" *American Political Science Review* 78 (June): 392–403.

Meier, Kenneth J., Valerie Martinez-Ebers, and David Leal. 2002. "The Politics of Latino Education: The Biases of At-Large Elections." Paper presented at the annual meeting of the Western Political Science Association. Long Beach, Calif., March 22–24.

Meier, Kenneth J., and others. 2002. "Political Structure and Representative Effectiveness: The Case of Latino School Board Members." Unpublished paper. Texas A&M University.

National Association of Latino Elected Officials. Various years. *National Directory of Latino Elected Officials.* Los Angeles: NALEO Educational Fund.

Pachon, Harry, and Louis DeSipio. 1992. "Latino Elected Officials in the 1990s." *PS: Political Science and Politics* 25 (2): 212–17.

Polinard, J. L., Robert D. Wrinkle, and Tomas Longoria. 1990. "Education and Governance: Representational Links to Second Generation Discrimination." *Western Political Quarterly* 43 (September): 631–46.

Polinard, J. L., Robert D. Wrinkle, and Kenneth J. Meier. 1995. "The Influence of Educational and Political Resources on Minority Students' Success." *Journal of Negro Education* 64 (Autumn): 463–74.

Ramirez, Roberto R. 1999. "The Hispanic Population in the United States: March 1998." *Current Population Reports.* U.S. Census Bureau (March).

Robinson, Theodore P., and Robert England. 1981. "Black Representation on Central City School Boards Revisited." *Social Science Quarterly* 62 (3): 495–502.

Robinson, Theodore P., Robert E. England, and Kenneth J. Meier. 1985. "Black Resources and Black School Board Representation: Does Political Structure Matter?" *Social Science Quarterly* 66 (December): 976–82.

Sass, Tim R., and Bobby J. Pittman Jr. 2000. "The Changing Impact of Electoral Structure on Black Representation in the South, 1970–1996." *Public Choice* 104 (1–2): 369–88.

Schmidley, Dianne. 2003. "The Foreign Born Population in the United States: March 2002." *Current Population Reports.* U.S. Census Bureau (March).

Schneider, Mark, Paul Teske, and Melissa Marschall. 2000. *Choosing Schools: Consumer Choice and the Quality of American Schools.* Princeton University Press.

Shingles, R. D. 1981. "Black Consciousness and Political Participation: The Missing Link." *American Political Science Review* 75: 76–90.

Stewart, Joseph, Jr., Robert E. England, and Kenneth J. Meier. 1989. "Black Representation in Urban School Districts: From School Board to Office to Classroom." *Western Political Quarterly* 42 (June): 287–305.

Stipak, B. 1977. "Attitudes and Belief Systems Concerning Urban Service Delivery." *Public Opinion Quarterly* 41 (Spring): 41–55.

Tate, Katherine. 1993. *From Protest to Politics: The New Black Voters in American Elections.* Harvard University Press.

Thomas, Gail E., and Frank Brown. 1982. "What Does Educational Research Tell Us about School Desegregation Effects?" *Journal of Black Studies* 13 (2): 155–74.

Verba, Sidney, and Norman H. Nie. 1972. *Participation in America: Political Democracy and Social Equality.* New York: Harper and Row.

Welch, Susan, and Albert K. Karnig. 1978. "Representation of Blacks on Big City School Boards." *Social Science Quarterly* 59 (June): 162–72.

Wong, Kenneth K., and Francis X. Shen. 2003. "When Mayors Lead Urban Schools: Toward Developing a Framework to Assess the Effects of Mayoral Takeover of Urban Districts." Paper prepared for the annual meeting of the American Political Science Association. Philadelphia, August 28–31.

Zaller, John. 1992. *The Nature and Origins of Mass Opinion.* Cambridge University Press.

Zuniga, Victor, and others. 2002. "The New Paths of Mexican Immigrants in the United States: Challenges for Education and the Role of Mexican Universities." In *Education in the New Latino Diaspora: Policy and the Politics of Identity,* edited by W. E. Murillo Jr. and E. Hamann, pp. 99–116. Westport, Conn.: Ablex.

9

Electoral Structure and the Quality of Representation on School Boards

KENNETH J. MEIER AND ERIC GONZALEZ JUENKE

Although an extensive literature exists on how political structure affects representation, particularly representation of political minorities, little is known about how structure affects the quality of representation. A lively debate now exists on designing legislative districts to concentrate minorities and on how such structures affect the policy interests of constituents.[1] Generally ignored in this debate is a parallel literature at the local level that focuses on macrostructural issues—that is, type of election—rather than the issue of how to draw district lines. This chapter looks at the quality of representation produced by school district political structures by focusing on the issue of at-large versus single-member districts.

The analysis proceeds in seven parts. First, we review the literature on structure and representation. Second, we examine the underlying logic of two electoral systems: at-large and ward-based single-member districts. That logic suggests that a group's "minority" status compels it to use electoral structure to its own advantage. Third, we operationalize hypotheses derived from the spatial logic inherent in electoral structures, using a data set for more than 1,000 Texas school districts. Fourth, we examine the influence that structure has on electing

We would like to thank William Howell for his insightful comments on an earlier draft of the manuscript. Thanks also to the two anonymous reviewers, who offered helpful appraisals.

1. On designing districts, see Shotts (2003a, 2003b), and Lublin and Voss (2003), among others.

Hispanic school board members—that is, the impact on descriptive representation. Fifth, we extend the argument beyond descriptive representation to the quality of representation, examining the effectiveness of minority representatives in advancing the interests of the minority community by increasing the number of minority administrators and teachers in the school district. Sixth, we probe whether this array of factors affects the quality of education received by Hispanic students. Seventh, we explore the implications of these school district findings for the study of minority politics, representation, and political structure.

Representation and Structure

Descriptive representation is a term used to characterize representation of constituencies by politicians who share distinctive physical traits with their constituencies.[2] Early studies of minority representation were concerned predominantly with descriptive representation because the initial question of electoral impact centered on the winning candidates' ethnicity. This research questioned whether electoral structures—primarily the change from at-large elections to single-member district (or ward) elections—provided added benefits to minority candidates or whether noninstitutional factors were more important to the process.

Early results held that both socioeconomic and electoral variables were important to African American representation, but contrary findings challenged this conclusion, downplaying the role of structure in the representative process.[3] Later research bolstered the former claim, suggesting that not only were at-large arrangements critical to black losses at the polls but also that those structures were more powerful than socioeconomic characteristics.[4] The most recent studies using data from national samples affirm that structure in general matters for blacks;[5] however, that finding may not hold for other minorities. In Taebel (1978), a study of city council representation, the author found that Hispanics gained only marginal benefits from ward elections, conjecturing that residential segregation was not as prevalent for Hispanics as it was for blacks. Welch (1990), using a national sample of city councils from large U.S. cities, found that Hispanics gained almost nothing from structural variation. Brischetto and others (1994) similarly found that Hispanics achieved little relative to blacks when electoral structures were manipulated; instead, their population size had a

2. Pitkin (1967), but see Mansbridge (1999).
    3. In support, see Karnig (1976) and Robinson and Dye (1978); in opposition, see Cole (1974) and MacManus (1978).
    4. On at-large arrangements, see Davidson and Korbel (1981), Karnig and Welch (1982), Engstrom and McDonald (1981, 1982, 1986), and Welch (1990); for comparison with socioeconomic effects, see Stewart, England, and Meier (1989).
    5. Lublin (1997); Canon (1999).

greater impact on political gains. Polinard and others (1994), however, found strong positive effects on Mexican-American communities in Texas when city councils and school boards changed from at-large to district elections. More recent national findings support these latter findings, suggesting that Hispanics are aided significantly by a change from at-large to district elections.[6]

The debate on the impact of electoral variation (between pure at-large and ward-based single-member district structures) on descriptive representation of blacks appears settled in favor of increased representation in single-member district elections. Many argue, however, that those gains may be offset by losses in substantive representation. We differentiate descriptive and substantive representation as other scholars do: descriptive representation relates to electing minorities to office, and substantive representation involves the policies these elected officials help enact.[7] Swain contends that majority-minority districts (created by subdividing at-large districts into numerous racially concentrated wards) may dilute overall support for black policies because white candidates no longer have to contend with minority constituencies in their own majority districts.[8] She notes that Republicans actually helped create many of the black majority districts in the early 1990s in order to dilute black political power, which tends to vote Democratic overall. Although Swain's argument makes intuitive sense, empirical results appear mixed.

Before comparing the evidence for and against substantive representation trade-offs, it is important to explore why voters might use race as a shortcut in deciding how to vote and in predicting substantive policy gains from election results. The idea of substantive representation rests on the assumption that voters are polarized by race and use it as a cue to select representatives. Eisinger (1980) explains that black voters have good reasons to vote for black candidates. He finds that the presence of a black mayor has a small impact on the percentage of black administrators and professionals in cities. Karnig and Welch (1980) also find that mayoral representation increases social spending on "black" policy issues, although like Eisinger, the authors make no such claims about city council representation. In many circumstances crossover voting by black voters for white candidates makes little sense, and it is not the observed pattern in most elections.[9] All of the studies cited in this chapter make the assumption that voters use race as a primary voting cue, and as we show in a subsequent section, that is important to understanding the formal logic of electoral variation effects.

Two issues arise. First, Swain suggests that a trade-off between descriptive and substantive representation can occur that may keep minority interests from being served. If that is true, then black and Hispanic representatives, even

---

6. Lublin (1997); Leal, Meier, and Martinez-Ebers (2004).
7. Hero and Tolbert (1995, p. 641); Epstein and O'Halloran (1999, p. 385).
8. Swain (1993, pp. 205–06).
9. Bullock (1984).

though full of good intentions and supported by a large (ward) constituency, will fail to deliver on their promises when in office, because their influence in the political arena is diluted. Second, manipulating the electoral system may inadvertently create more racial polarization among voters, in turn creating minority candidates who must behave differently (by supporting majority policy preferences) if they are elected outside of racially gerrymandered wards. We address both issues in this study.

Substantial research examines Swain's argument at the national level, but overall the evidence is inconsistent. Cameron, Epstein, and O'Halloran (1996) used national-level data to look at the effect of the civil rights voting records of black members of the U.S. House of Representatives and found that black political power was reduced by the creation of majority-minority districts. They concluded that the use of this type of electoral solution traded descriptive for substantive gains, leaving blacks at a disadvantage in important policy battles. In a second study Epstein and O'Halloran (1999) got mixed results after examining South Carolina's state senate elections. They found that many majority-minority districts overrepresented minorities and hindered policy gains but that without those districts minorities risked losing descriptive representation. Lublin, using national data, concluded that single-member districts severely hindered black policy gains.[10] He warns (like Swain, Cameron, Epstein, and O'Halloran) that the percentage of blacks in majority-minority districts is too high and should be lowered so that majority-controlled (Republican) seats can be contested in future elections.

The evidence supporting positive electoral effects on substantive representation includes multilevel and multiethnic analyses. Karnig explained why we would expect to see policy losses from minorities elected in at-large districts: "There would likely be a higher incidence of substantively *un*representative Black councilmen in at-large cities, where Black candidates must appeal to the white electorate in order to gain office. If policy attitudes of Black councilmen are basically the same as white councilmen, major changes in policy outcomes are not likely."[11] Stewart, England, and Meier (1989) tested this theory by using a national sample of black school board members and affirmed that single-member district structures created more opportunity for black representation and that this representation translated into more black administrative and teaching positions. Polinard and others (1994) and Leal, Meier, and Martinez-Ebers (2004) found a similar relationship for Hispanic school board members, administrators, and teachers. Canon (1999) examined the U.S. House of Representatives and found that single-member districts increased the quality of black candidates over time. He also contends that the electoral structure positively affects

10. Lublin (1997, p. 119).
11. Karnig (1976, p. 237).

how these members represent their constituents, noting that they "often provide pivotal votes for passing important legislation, they are forceful advocates for Black interests in their speeches and sponsorship of legislation, and the bills they sponsor are more likely to succeed than those with nonblack sponsors."[12]

Political Structure and the Logic of Representation

Thus far we have presented a large amount of at times conflicting findings concerning substantive minority representation. In an effort to clarify a portion of the debate, we contribute empirical evidence regarding Hispanic substantive outcomes in four situations: under at-large and ward systems when Hispanics are a numerical minority, and under at-large and ward systems when Hispanics are a numerical majority. These four environments afford an opportunity to consult the logic of formal theory to provide insight into hypothesis construction. Building on earlier work, we contend that other minority groups use the same electoral mechanisms to their benefit that Hispanic minorities do. Partly because of this, we expect the advantage provided by electoral structure to disappear when Hispanics (or any racial group) make up a majority of the population. This section gives a formal overview pertinent to our analysis and concludes with a specific set of testable hypotheses.

Why might one expect the quality of representation to vary with political structure? That is, why might a black or Hispanic elected in an at-large system be less effective at promoting black or Hispanic interests than one elected from a single-member district? First, let us recap the logic behind the assertion that fewer minorities get elected from at-large systems. We begin by making three assumptions (albeit assumptions with a great deal of empirical support):

—Voters are rational and therefore will vote for candidates who are most likely to represent their interests.

—Candidates are rational and therefore will seek to satisfy their constituency's interests (either because they seek reelection for its own sake or seek reelection to pursue policy goals).

—Ethnicity is an important political issue—that is, individuals' political preferences differ on the basis of their ethnicity.

Figure 9-1 shows this situation for a jurisdiction that is 80 percent white and 20 percent Hispanic (the logic works for other percentages; the illustrations are just more obvious in this case). We have drawn figure 9-1 to show Hispanics with relatively extreme views; however, the logic works as long as the median Hispanic voter M_L is different from the median voter M_V. To illustrate, we take a five-member school board with all members elected at large (see figure 9-1).[13]

12. Canon (1999, p. 245).

13. The presence of many seats and many candidates in our example actually favors the positioning of minority candidates off of the median voter position (Cox 1990; Gerber, Morton, and

Figure 9-1. *At-Large System*

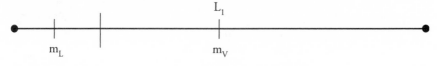

Source: Authors' calculations.

Figure 9-2. *Ward System*

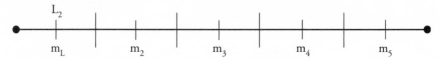

Source: Authors' calculations.

In such a situation, candidates will generally position themselves at the median voter M_V so that no challenger can locate a policy position that will attract a majority of the votes. In a traditional at-large system in which voters get one vote per position, all candidates face the same general electorate. Because the median is well within the white portion of the electorate, whites will capture all five seats and Hispanics will have no representation.

Moving the identical set of circumstances to a ward-based single-member district system changes the calculus. If we assume that electoral districts cannot be created to be an exact microcosm of the entire jurisdiction, then the median voters in each of the five electoral districts are not the same as the median voter in the overall jurisdiction (see figure 9-2).[14] If Hispanics are gerrymandered into a single district, then the median voter in that district (M_L) is the optimal candidate position in that district. In fact, if Hispanics compose a majority of the

---

Rietz 1998). We are not, however, comparing two-candidate at-large elections (where straying from the median voter is *always* a losing strategy) with other multicandidate at-large elections (where this is *generally* the case). Instead, we compare at-large elections with the single-member district structure for two-candidate elections.

14. The assumption that ward boundaries are drawn to reflect racially segregated neighborhoods is extremely reasonable given that they were manipulated in most cases to help segregated minority interests garner policy influence on school boards (specifically in the early 1990s in Texas). Moreover, the assumption does not need to be very strong for the spatial logic to hold. As long as one or more wards contain a substantially higher concentration of minorities than the district as a whole, we can use the rationale to motivate our hypotheses.

electorate in any one of the districts, then the median voter in that district is Hispanic, and a Hispanic is more likely to be elected to the school board.

Thus far, the spatial discussion recapitulates the arguments about the role of structure on the quantity of representation. Our concern, however, is the quality of representation. To understand why the nature of representation is likely to change in different systems, assume that two jurisdictions are identical in all respects except that jurisdiction A (in figure 9-1) elects board members at large and jurisdiction W (figure 9-2) elects them by ward. A Hispanic (L_1) seeking election in jurisdiction A quite rationally positions himself or herself at M_V, the median voter for the entire district. Another Hispanic (L_2), seeking election in jurisdiction W, faces a much different electorate and takes the position at M_L, the median voter in the Hispanic community. L_1, the Hispanic in the at-large system, cannot run at the Hispanic median simply because this leaves a large opening for another candidate to defeat L_1 at the polls by taking a position between L_1 and the median voter. In essence this means that L_1 needs to demonstrate his or her value by taking positions similar to those of M_V while L_2 is free to position at M_L. In less abstract terms, the Hispanic elected in an at-large system must moderate his or her push for Hispanic benefits to avoid alienating the median voter, who is not Hispanic. L_2, the Hispanic elected from a single-member district, faces no such constraint and can push for policies that reflect M_L, the median voter in the Hispanic community.

By defining the match between Hispanic constituents and Hispanic representatives as the quality of representation, the argument suggests the hypothesis that the quality of minority representation will be greater in a ward-based single-member district system than it will in an at-large system. This hypothesis could be tested in a variety of ways, but we will focus initially on the distribution of employment opportunities, thus generating the following testable hypotheses:

—H_1: Minority representatives in a ward-based single-member district system will be more effective in hiring more minority administrators than will minority representatives in an at-large system, all other things being equal.

—H_2: Minority representatives in a ward-based single-member district system will be more effective in hiring more minority teachers than will minority representatives in an at-large system, all other things being equal.

Although one or two Hispanic school board members on a five-member board may not appear to have any policy influence, assuming that they do not ignores the nature of small group dynamics. While the median voter theorem helps motivate our hypotheses about candidate policy preferences (and the construction of tests for the outcomes of these preferences), it is of little use in telling us *how* those preferences are translated into policy in a small legislative body operating in a multidimensional policy space. The question concerns how Hispanic members on a largely white board get their voices heard and their policies adopted. There are a number of possibilities, but the primary ones pertain to the fact that small groups provide greater opportunities for log-rolling, coalitional cooperation, formal and informal bargaining, and the development over time of relationships of trust with other members of the board. Also, Arrow's problem demonstrates the possible "nonrational" outcomes of group decision-making, thus providing bargaining leverage for minority policymakers who have incentives to supply benefits to their minority constituents.[15] We do not directly examine the actual mechanisms used by Hispanic board members to affect policy; instead we assume that there are multiple instruments available to these outnumbered legislators and test for differences in representational quality.

Until now, Hispanic majority districts have been ignored.[16] It is important to reiterate that the formal logic used to generate hypotheses for this study extends to other groups when they are a racial minority, *as long as race is used as a cue for political interests*. Meier and others (forthcoming) demonstrate that both blacks and Hispanics experience very similar descriptive and substantive gains from electoral structural variation; clearly it is not just a benefit for Hispanics. The theory suggests that it is the "minority status" of a group, coupled with the incentive structure, that drives this phenomenon. Thus we expect that the same institutions that operate to the advantage of Hispanics when they are a minority should preclude any (structural) benefits when they constitute a majority of the district population, for two reasons. The first reason is a simple extension of the logic presented thus far and hinges on constituency size and heterogeneity. The second is a little less intuitive and slightly provocative view of the process; perhaps other minority groups use ward structures to thwart Hispanic majority dominance, even to the detriment of substantive Hispanic outcomes.

Understanding how structural impacts on descriptive and substantive outcomes might disappear when Hispanics are no longer a minority is fairly easy. In majority Hispanic school systems, the median district voter is no longer different from the median Hispanic voter.[17] Whether elected at large or by ward, representatives must attend to the policy wishes of the median voter. This means that there should be no difference between the quantity of Hispanic members elected to school boards in majority Hispanic at-large and ward systems *due to structural variance*. Similarly, there should be no difference in the quality of representation based on electoral variation.

Another change occurs, however, in the move from minority to majority

---

15. Downs (1957).

16. We use "majority" rather than "plurality" status because it contributes to a more straightforward theoretical picture. It is plausible, however, that Hispanics who hold a plurality in a district (rather than a majority) will be the ones who begin to experience a decline in structural effects. We test models that use different plurality "break" points (51 percent, 45 percent, 40 percent, and so forth Hispanic), and the results support the use of "majority" status (see footnote 8).

17. In figures 9-1 and 9-2, simply reverse the "Anglo" and "Hispanic" labels to see why this is so.

status. Majority populations are vulnerable to similar strategic behavior by other minority groups (for example, blacks, Asians, whites) when ward structures are in place. This is provocative, because it suggests that not only will electoral variation not benefit Hispanic majority populations in terms of representation and policy, but also that it will actually *hinder* Hispanic policy (relatively speaking)[18] as other groups use wards to achieve quantitative and qualitative representation for their minority constituencies. Black, Asian, and white minority populations should behave similarly under similar incentive structures. On its face, this is not an incendiary perspective, but in the context of race and ethnicity studies it is at the very least counterintuitive. To be clear, this understanding does not discount the cultural, social, and resource differences among these diverse groups. It simply suggests that individuals behave the same when given a set of institutional opportunities, and to the extent that race is used as a voting cue, it allows each of these groups to take similar advantage of ward structures.

The empirical tests in this chapter address the first of these theoretical suggestions. In Hispanic majority school districts, we expect the representation and policy effects due to structure to disappear (to be insignificant). Unfortunately, the data do not allow us to fully examine the second extension of the theory (although the analyses do provide very suggestive evidence). We know from prior research that blacks in minority districts take advantage of structure in a very similar fashion, but we do not know whether it works to the detriment of the majority population's policy preferences.[19] Strict tests of the second type of hypotheses are left to future work, but the evidence below suggests that empirical analysis in this area may provide confirmation. Thus the third and fourth hypotheses tested in this chapter are as follows:

—H_3: In Hispanic *majority* districts, Hispanic school board representation in an at-large system will be no different than Hispanic representation in a ward-based single-member district system, all other things being equal.

—H_4: In Hispanic *majority* districts, Hispanic representatives in an at-large system will be just as effective in hiring minority administrators and teachers as will minority representatives in a ward-based single-member district system, all other things being equal.

18. To think of it differently, we can say that at-large (majoritarian) structures bias electoral results in favor of the majority (whether the majority is Anglo, black, Asian, and so forth), and this should be no different for Hispanics. The alternative to this hypothesis is that individuals from particular groups will act differently given the same set of circumstances, because of their historical experience with the political process and because their policy preferences may not be as concentrated along racial lines as those of other groups. It is the plausibility of the formally derived hypothesis versus the reality of the alternative that forces us to leave this question to more appropriate tests. We lean toward the former, but in this study we expect to find no effect from structure in majority Hispanic districts.

19. Meier and others (forthcoming).

Data

Texas contains one school district that has a nonelected school board and cannot set its own budget, a handful of others with appointed board members, and several that use a cumulative voting system.[20] This study examines all Texas school districts in 1999 that used at-large or ward elections to select their school board. Fewer than 3 percent of the districts (30 of 1,043) were eliminated under this criterion; 875 districts use at-large elections, and the remainder (138) use ward-based single-member district elections. Missing data on other variables, primarily policy variables, left a maximum of 1,012 districts for analysis. These numbers decline in the policy section owing to confidentiality concerns.[21] Data on school board representation were obtained by request from the Texas Association of School Boards (TASB). TASB data had several missing data points, so we contacted 300 of the districts by phone to fill in the gaps. The school board data are for 1999; the census data are population figures for 2000, and all remaining data are from the Texas Education Agency for the year 1999.[22]

Descriptive statistics reveal some telling differences between ward and at-large structures in Hispanic minority and majority districts. The average Hispanic population in districts with at-large structures is 20 percent (with a range from 0 to 99 percent), while in ward districts this number climbs to 36 percent (range 2 percent to 92 percent). Eighty percent of wards (112 of 138) are found in districts where Hispanics are a minority, providing evidence for the representational thrust of this chapter; these structures are present where Hispanics are at a numerical disadvantage to whites. In accordance with this is an underrepresentation of Hispanics in the bureaucracy. In Texas, Hispanics make up 26 percent of the student population in the average district, while they occupy only 9 percent of the teaching, administrative, and legislative positions. The data reveal a representational disconnect between the Hispanic population and elected officials—and between the bureaucracy and its clientele—that motivates questions of structural influence.

Findings

Step one in determining the representational bias of electoral structures is to see whether structure itself has a quantitative impact on representation. To do so, we

20. Engstrom and Barrilleaux (1991); Brischetto and Engstrom (1997).

21. The state of Texas reports data only if five or more students fall into the category. So if a district had fewer than five Hispanic students take AP classes, for example, that case would be reported as missing data.

22. For the census data, districts were apportioned on the basis of the 1990 census. Although initial analyses were run using 1990 census data, the results reported here—using 2000 population measurements that correspond better with the 1999 school district data—are almost identical. The initial (1990 census) results are available from the authors.

Table 9-1. *Impact of Ward Elections and Majority Status on Hispanic Representation on School Boards*[a]

Independent variable	Slope	t score	Slope	t score
Intercept	−1.393	2.09	−.220	.11
Hispanic population	.256	6.46	.269	6.63
Ward elections	−2.232	.85	−1.622	.62
Ward x Hispanic population	.265	2.99	.224	2.51
Hispanic majority	−37.076	6.69	−39.121	7.01
Hispanic majority x				
Hispanic population	.857	10.77	.865	10.84
Ward x Hispanic population	−.337	4.72	−.305	4.26
Hispanic noncitizen percentage	—	—	−.071	2.60
Hispanic education (high school)	—	—	.022	.88
Median family income	—	—	−.013	.35
Summary statistic				
R^2		.64		.65
F statistic		297.48		200.44
Standard Error		11.93		11.90
N		1,012		1,003

Source: Authors' calculations.

a. Dependent variable = percentage of Hispanics on school board.

need to interact political structure with Hispanic population and with a variable indicating whether Hispanics are a majority of the district's population.[23] Two dummy variables are created, one for ward-based elections and one for Hispanics as a population majority (the default case is an at-large election in which Hispanics are a minority). The percentage of Hispanic school board seats is then regressed on Hispanic population, ward elections, whether Hispanics are a majority, the interaction of Hispanic population by ward elections, the interaction of Hispanic population by majority status, and the three-way interaction of majority status, ward elections, and Hispanic population. This equation, a modification of the one popularized by Engstrom and McDonald and used in most analyses of minority representation since then, can be decomposed into separate parts for at-large and ward-based systems in both Hispanic majority and Hispanic minority school districts.[24] The results are in the first two columns of table 9-1.

23. We tested all of the models using different plurality break points (50, 45, 40, 35, 30, 25, and 20 percent Hispanic population) to examine the population percentage at which Hispanics began to see declines in structural effects. The models using "50 percent Hispanic" fit the data best and explained the most variance. This is an interesting finding and should be explored further, but a potential explanation is that school board elections are not well attended, and an absolute population majority (not a simple plurality) is necessary before at-large elections can be successfully contested by Hispanics.

24. Engstrom and McDonald (1981). See also Austin (1998); Meier, Stewart, and England (1989); Meier and Stewart (1991).

When Hispanics are a minority in a district with at-large elections, the last five variables are all reduced to constants (0), producing the following equation:

$$Percent\ seats = -1.39 + .256\ (Hispanic\ population).$$

The intercept is close to zero, so the slope can be treated as a representation ratio. In school districts with at-large elections and a Hispanic minority, a 1 percentage point increase in Hispanic population is associated with a .256 percentage point increase in school board seats held by Hispanics. Continuing the decomposition, when ward elections are used but Hispanics are a minority, the last three coefficients reduce to zero and the remaining coefficients combine to predict Hispanic representation:

$$Percent\ seats = -1.39 + (-2.23) + (.256 + .265)\ Hispanic\ population\ \text{or}$$
$$Percent\ seats = -3.62 + .521\ Hispanic\ population.$$

In table 9-1, the insignificant ward coefficient means that the intercept for ward systems is not different from the intercept for at-large systems. The significant "ward x Hispanic population" coefficient means that the ward *slope* is statistically different from the at-large slope (that is, it is larger). The reduced equation confirms this relationship; in ward systems where Hispanics are a minority, a 1 percentage point increase in Hispanic population is associated with a .521 percentage point increase in Hispanic representation, approximately a 100 percent improvement over the at-large system. These differences can be seen more clearly in figure 9-3.

In Hispanic majority jurisdictions that elect school board members at large, all the ward variables are turned into constants. The representation equation for these districts is as follows:

$$Percent\ seats = -1.39 + (-37.08) + (.256 + .857)\ Hispanic\ population\ \text{or}$$
$$Percent\ seats = -38.47 + 1.113\ Hispanic\ population.$$

The intercept is, of course, well outside the range of the data since population by definition has to equal at least +50 percent Hispanic. In Hispanic majority jurisdictions with at-large elections, a 1 percentage point increase in Hispanic population is associated with a 1.113 percentage point increase in Hispanic representation. This does not mean representational parity, however, since the predicted representation levels range from 20 percent at 50 percent Hispanic population to 72 percent at 100 percent Hispanic population.[25]

25. There are a variety of reasons why Hispanics might not win all the seats in a majoritarian system such as this one. Winning elections is a function of mobilization, and to the extent that Hispanics have lower levels of turnout, as a result of either noncitizenship or other factors, or to the

Figure 9-3. *At-Large versus Ward Structure in Hispanic Minority Districts*

Percent of school board that is Hispanic

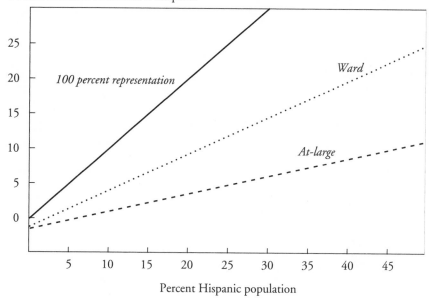

Percent Hispanic population

Source: Authors' calculations.

Determining the representation relationship in Hispanic majority jurisdictions that use ward elections requires using all the coefficients in table 9-1 as follows:

$$Percent\ seats = [-1.39 + (-37.08) + (-2.23)] +$$
$$(.256 + .265 + .857 - .337)\ Hispanic\ population$$
$$Percent\ seats = -40.7 + 1.041\ Hispanic\ population.$$

Note first that the Hispanic representation ratio for ward districts is significantly *less* than that for at-large systems in the case of a Hispanic majority. As shown in figure 9-4, not only do ward structures not help Hispanic representatives (as they do in Hispanic minority districts), they slightly hinder them. In ward systems, a 1 percentage point increase in Hispanic population is associated with a 1.041 percentage point increase in Hispanic school board seats. In actual terms, the predicted levels of representation range from 11 percent at 50 percent of

---

extent that good Hispanic candidates are not running, representation levels will fall. The residual incumbency advantage of sitting Anglo board members might also slow Hispanics' acquisition of seats.

Figure 9-4. *At-Large versus Ward Structure in Hispanic Majority Districts*

Percent of school board that is Hispanic

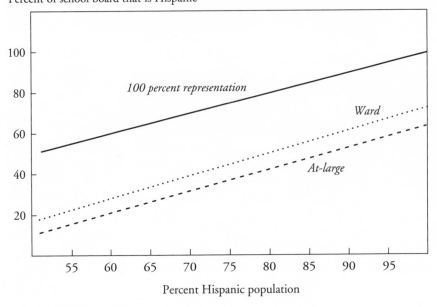

Percent Hispanic population

Source: Authors' calculations.

population to 63 percent at 100 percent of population. These predicted levels have a substantial range, however, and the discontinuity created by using a dummy variable for a population majority means that predictions around 50 percent of population are probably subject to even greater variation. Additional research is needed to determine whether nonlinear curves can be fit to the data that can capture both the minority status effects and the majority status effects.

The findings in the first two columns of table 9-1 hold regardless of whether additional variables are included in the model. As an illustration, the last two columns in table 9-1 control for the percentage of Hispanics who are not citizens, Hispanic median education level, and median family income. Not only do the general findings not change, these additional variables add little explanatory power. Hispanic representation appears determined for the most part by population and electoral structures.

Recapping table 9-1 shows that our hypotheses about electoral structure and minority status are confirmed, while our hypotheses concerning Hispanic majority status are not. When Hispanics are a minority, they do significantly better in electoral systems based on ward elections. When Hispanics are a majority, they receive the same benefits of at-large bias that other majorities do, but we do not know whether that is because other minority groups are using wards to thwart Hispanic policy preferences or because of other unobserved processes. No matter what the system, however, Hispanic representation is never predicted to exceed the Hispanic population percentage.

Influence on the Bureaucracy

Elections are only the first step in determining the policy bias of structure; how the representatives act and their ability to gain policy benefits remain to be studied. The theoretical sections of this chapter argued that at-large elections and minority status would reduce the effectiveness of Hispanic representatives elected in such circumstances. A long literature has linked the election of minorities to governing boards to the subsequent recruitment of minorities to the bureaucracy.[26] Although some condemn such practices as patronage and as detrimental to the performance of school systems, an extensive literature suggests that access to administrative and teaching positions results in policy outcomes that are likely to benefit minority students.[27] We argue that in Hispanic majority systems the median voter structure equalizes the opposition to Hispanic interests compared with a ward system, so that Hispanic representatives elected at large in a Hispanic majority district would be just as effective as their counterparts elected by ward systems (H_4).

To determine the efficacy of representatives elected under various structures, we used the same interaction strategy as in table 9-1. Past research has shown that the major determinants of the number of Hispanic school administrators are the size of the local Hispanic population and Hispanic representation on school boards.[28] At times, labor pool characteristics such as Hispanic education levels or income levels matter statistically, but they rarely make much substantive difference. To keep the presentation as parsimonious as possible, therefore, only representation and population will be used as explanatory factors in combination with how the representatives were selected and the majority or minority status of Hispanics.[29]

26. Mladenka (1989); Kerr and Mladenka (1994); Eisinger (1980); Polinard and others (1994).

27. Meier and Stewart (1991), Meier, Stewart, and England (1989), Polinard and others (1994), Meier, Wrinkle, and Polinard (1999), and Meier and others (2001); for the opposing view, see Rich (1996). This corresponds with "substantive representation" as we have defined it; see also Hero and Tolbert (1995, p. 641) and Epstein and O'Halloran (1999, p. 385). To be clear, it is not possible to directly measure the legislative policies of all 1,012 school boards, but we can capture substantive policy gains—both indirectly, with the outcome measures of Hispanic administrative and teacher recruitment, and directly, because an increase in Hispanic bureaucratic employment is a substantive good in and of itself (for Hispanics).

28. Leal, Meier, and Martinez-Ebers (2004); Meier and Stewart (1991).

29. Adding education and income variables to the model in table 9-2 increases the explained variation by less than one-fifth of 1 percent. Substantively the coefficients are very small, and they do little to change the predicted value of administrative representation.

Table 9-2. *Hispanic Administrators: Effectiveness of Hispanic Representatives Elected under Different Systems*[a]

Independent variable	Slope	t score
Intercept	.137	.24
Hispanic population	.129	3.73
Hispanic board representation	−.028	.45
Hispanic board members x ward system	.319	3.90
Hispanic majority	−62.23	12.37
Hispanic majority x		
Hispanic population	1.34	16.60
Hispanic representation	.143	2.00
Hispanic ward representation	−.440	4.48
Summary statistic		
R^2		.77
F statistic		476.16
Standard error		10.60
N		1,010

Source: Authors' calculations.

a. Dependent variable = percentage of Hispanic administrators.

Table 9-2 presents the results for the determinants of administrative positions. First, the two population coefficients should be compared. When Hispanics are a minority, translation of population numbers into administrative positions is sluggish. A 1 percentage point increase in Hispanic population is associated with only a .129 percentage point increase in Hispanic administrators. In Hispanic majority jurisdictions, this coefficient jumps to 1.47 (1.34 + .129). This difference likely reflects the political pressure that the Hispanic community can put on a school system to hire Hispanic administrators when they constitute a population majority.

Representation on the school board also matters in some cases, and the relative impact is consistent with our hypotheses. In jurisdictions where Hispanics are in the minority, at-large representation has no impact on Hispanic administrative representation at all (β = −.028, ns), but ward representation is significantly related to more Hispanic bureaucratic representation. Figure 9-5 displays the predicted values of each system in minority districts. This figure, in conjunction with figure 9-3, shows that even small descriptive gains can translate into very large substantive returns. In ward systems, a 1 percentage point increase in Hispanic school board representation is associated with a .291 (.319 − .028) percentage point increase in Hispanic administrators. Hispanic representation, in fact, has a larger impact than Hispanic population. In Hispanic majority school districts, however, the school board representation coefficients are .115 (.143 − .028) for at-large elected representatives and −.01 for ward-elected

Figure 9-5. *Substantive Effects, Hispanic Minority Districts*

Percent of Hispanic administrators

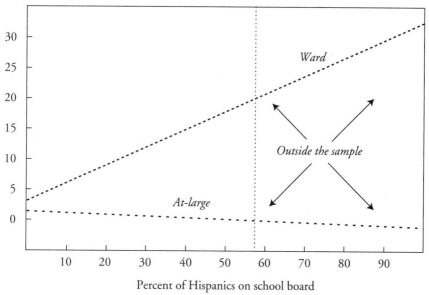

Percent of Hispanics on school board

Source: Authors' calculations.

representatives. These predictions, displayed in figure 9-6, show a very different picture than the one portrayed in the minority context of figure 9-5. Surprisingly, the majority-ward coefficient is much smaller than the minority-ward coefficient (which is negative but practically zero). The primary conclusion is that ward representation (in contrast to at-large representation) actually hurts Hispanic substantive interests when they are a majority (in terms of population numbers, not majority or minority status on the board). At-large representation, in contrast, is effective only in Hispanic majority jurisdictions, and its level of effectiveness is much larger than that of ward representation. This last finding is slightly surprising because it contradicts H_4 in a direction we did not expect given the data. Put simply, Hispanics do much *better* with at-large structures in Hispanic majority districts.[30]

Turning now to the ethnic composition of teachers, we should expect school board influence to be far less, regardless of selection process or majority status. School boards hire the chief administrator directly and are likely to have some

30. We expected no difference due to structure in these majority districts. By "better" we do not refer to the absolute advantages seen in figure 9-6 (due to a larger intercept), we simply note the steeper slope.

Figure 9-6. *Substantive Effects, Hispanic Majority Districts*

Percent of Hispanic administrators

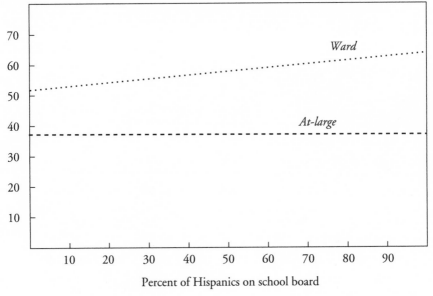

Percent of Hispanics on school board

Source: Authors' calculations.

say in hiring top-level administrators. Teachers, however, are hired by administrators, by the superintendent in small districts, or by a specialized personnel department in larger districts. The influence of school board members is likely to be felt through the policies they advocate—such as affirmative action—rather than through direct hiring. To investigate the question of teacher representation, we use the same equation as in table 9-2, but add the percentage of Hispanic administrators. Our expectation is that the administrator variable will dominate the equation. The influence of the school board is likely to be relatively small if there is any direct influence at all.

Table 9-3 shows that representation on the school board has only a modest impact, but that impact is mostly consistent with our hypotheses. For Hispanic minority districts, at-large representation is significantly related to more teachers, all other things being equal, but the coefficient is small. A 1 percentage point increase in Hispanic representation is associated with a .08 percentage point increase in Hispanic teachers. The coefficient is statistically insignificant for ward systems in Hispanic minority jurisdictions, suggesting that ward representatives are not more effective than at-large representatives in recruiting and hiring Hispanic teachers. In Hispanic majority systems, neither representation coefficient is statistically significant, which means that they are not different

Table 9-3. *Hispanic Teachers: Effectiveness of Hispanic Representatives Elected under Different Systems*[a]

Independent variable	Slope	t score
Intercept	–.018	.07
Population	.151	9.69
Board representation	.080	2.86
Ward representation	.031	.84
Hispanic administrators	.121	5.61
Hispanic population majority x	–44.70	17.76
Hispanic population	.802	17.81
Hispanic representation	–.025	.79
Hispanic ward representation	.047	1.07
Hispanic administrators	.222	7.83
Summary statistic		
R^2		.94
F statistic		1,662.18
Standard error		4.71
N		1,010

Source: Authors' calculations.

a. Dependent variable = percentage of Hispanic teachers.

from the respective Hispanic minority coefficients. In short, there is a fairly consistent but small direct impact of representation on the school board on Hispanic teacher hires, but there is no significant difference between ward and at-large structures.

Although our concern is the influence of political representation, the remainder of table 9-3 provides a wealth of useful information, some of it relevant to political representation. The process in Hispanic minority systems is dramatically different from that in Hispanic majority systems even though the same factors matter. Hispanic population and Hispanic administrators are the major influences on Hispanic teachers in both systems, but the size of influence changes a great deal. For population, a 1 percentage point increase in Hispanic population is associated with a .151 percentage point increase in Hispanic teachers in minority districts; this coefficient increases to .953 (.151 + .802) in Hispanic majority districts. The changes in the administrator coefficients are not quite as large but show a similar pattern. In minority districts, a 1 percentage point increase in Hispanic administrators is associated with a .121 percentage point increase in Hispanic teachers; in Hispanic majority districts, the influence nearly triples, to .343. The size of the regression coefficients also factors into our assessment of the representation question. Because administrators are a major influence in hiring teachers and because the representational structure of school board members matters in terms of hiring administrators, there is also a substantial indirect influence of representation and electoral structure on the composition of the teaching faculty.

Policy Influence

There is more to the question of representational quality than patronage—than who gets jobs. The composition of the teaching faculty is directly related to the educational opportunities afforded students. In a randomized experiment from the Tennessee class size project, Dee (2003) found that minority students performed better in class if the teacher was a member of the same minority. Meier, Wrinkle, and Polinard (1999) and Meier and others (2001) take this argument one step further, contending that both minority students and majority students perform better when taught by diverse teaching faculties. In a study of large urban districts, Hess and Leal (1997) similarly show that minority faculty were associated with more students going on to college regardless of the race of the student.

Although the exact process whereby minority teachers improve the educational circumstances of minority students is in doubt, the literature suggests four different possibilities. First, minority teachers may be more effective at teaching minority students.[31] Second, minority teachers serve as role models for minority students.[32] Third, minority teachers mitigate the negative consequences of grouping, tracking, and discipline either by making individual decisions or by influencing overall policy.[33] Fourth, minority teachers influence the behavior of majority teachers, who in turn adopt teaching methods less likely to put minority students at a disadvantage. Only the first of these methods actually requires a given minority student to come into contact with a specific minority teacher. The others can work indirectly, and they will be missed in studies done at the individual level. The appropriate unit of analysis to investigate such influences is the organizational level. The key independent variable in the analysis is the percentage of Hispanic teachers. The influence of school board members is unlikely to work directly on the fortunes of students but indirectly, through the composition of administrative and teaching personnel.[34]

Dependent Variables. Because schools have multiple goals, this study examines the influence of Hispanic teachers on Hispanic students using ten different policy indicators. Even if one ignores the broader educational objectives of creating democratic citizens and focuses solely on student performance, school

31. Dee (2003); Moore and Johnson (1983, p. 472); Aaron and Powell (1982, p. 55).
32. Cole (1986, p. 332).
33. Meier and Stewart (1991).
34. Including Hispanic board members in the following equations only produces significant direct impacts on the percentage of students taking college boards (but not their scores) and the percentage of students taking AP classes (but not passing the exam).

systems provide numerous programs aimed at a wide variety of goals—ensuring attendance, preventing students from dropping out, teaching students to master basic skills, preparing students for college, and so forth. Even though some goals might be held in higher regard than others, Hispanic politicians and bureaucrats are likely to be concerned with Hispanic student performance relative to all of them. To provide as complete a view as possible, this study uses ten different performance indicators for Hispanic students.

At the low end of the performance scale, students need to attend school and remain in the system until graduation. Two measures are used—the percentage of Hispanic students attending class and the percentage of Hispanic students who drop out of school. Attendance is measured with more accuracy than dropping out. Attendance counts are the basis for state aid, and an elaborate auditing system is used to verify the data. Dropout data in general are problematic: student populations are highly mobile, and schools may not know whether a student has dropped out of school or just moved. Because dropping out reflects negatively on a school system, schools have little incentive to find out whether a missing student has actually dropped out.

Adequate student achievement on tests of basic skills is a moderate-level goal for school districts. At the time of this study, Texas administered the Texas Assessment of Academic Skills (TAAS) to students in grades 3 through 8 and as a high school exit exam. Our performance measure is the percentage of Hispanic students who passed all of the various TAAS tests (math, reading, writing, and so forth) at all grade levels.

Within a school system, the quality of education varies from school to school and classroom to classroom. To tap some of this variation in educational quality, we used three indicators: the percentage of Hispanic students who gained access to advanced classes, the percentage who took advanced placement (AP) classes, and the percentage who passed advanced placement exams. AP classes are designed to be college-level classes; students who take these classes and pass the national exam with a grade of 3 or higher can get college credit.

For top-end indicators, we include four measures of college preparation. These include the percentage of Hispanic students who take either the ACT or SAT exam, the average Hispanic SAT score, the average Hispanic ACT score, and the percentage of Hispanic students who score above 1110 on the SAT or its ACT equivalent. (The 1110 score has been defined by the state of Texas as indicating likely success in college.) Students who do not take either exam are unlikely to attend college. In Texas, large percentages of students take both the SAT and the ACT, so results generally are not affected by the performance of a small number of students.

The ten performance indicators for Hispanic students are clearly distinct from each other. Of the forty-five intercorrelations between the indicators, only twenty-three are statistically significant—that is, different from zero. A factor analysis of the ten indicators revealed three significant factors, with no single factor accounting for more than 30 percent of the variance.[35]

Control Variables. Two distinct types of control variables are included in the analysis. The first represents general school district performance, and the second includes the standard education production function controls.[36] Because Hispanics, especially recent immigrants, face a segmented labor market that discourages them from pursuing many professions, the literature suggests the possibility that the pool of Hispanic teachers could be more talented than the pool of white or black teachers.[37] Other studies argue that nondiscriminatory bureaucracies are more likely to be effective simply because they do not consider nonproductive factors such as race, gender, or ethnicity.[38] Both arguments indicate that a control for non-Hispanic student performance might be appropriate, because Hispanic teachers could be associated with better performance for all students, not just Hispanic students. For each indicator, therefore, we control for white student performance on the same indicator (that is, for Hispanic SAT scores we include white SAT scores in the model). This control requires Hispanic teachers or school board members to have an effect on Hispanic students that exceeds the impact that they might have on white students. The control should also adjust for quality-of-education factors and peer effects, which are outside the control of Hispanic teachers.[39]

Additional controls can be clustered into two groups: resources and constraints. Bureaucracies cannot influence outcomes without resources. Five resource indicators, all commonly used in education production functions, are included in all models: average teacher salary, per-student instructional spending, class size, average years of teacher experience, and percentage of teachers who are not certified.[40] Three measures of constraints include the percentage of African American, Hispanic, and poor students; the last-mentioned is measured by students eligible for free or reduced-price school lunches.

Although the production function literature specifies directional hypotheses for each control variable, the actual direction of relationships in this study is not obvious. Because each equation controls for white student performance, the effect of these control variables on Hispanic performance must exceed their impact on white performance. For teachers' salaries to matter, therefore, better-paid teachers would need to benefit Hispanic students more than they benefit

---

35. The factor scores are not useful for analysis given the list-wise deletion of missing values. The factor analysis as a result is based on less than 20 percent of the total school districts (those with reportable data on every indicator).

36. Hanushek (1996); Hedges and Greenwald (1996).

37. Meier, Wrinkle, and Polinard (1999).

38. Becker (1993).

39. Weiher (2000); Meier and others (2001).

40. See Burtless (1996).

Table 9-4. *Hispanic Teacher Influence on Hispanic Students*[a]

Independent variable	Slope	t score
Hispanic teachers	.114	3.56
White test scores	.771	15.69
Resources		
Teacher salary	.554	2.37
Per-student expenditures	.670	.84
Class size	−.126	.45
Teacher experience	−.066	.32
Noncertified teachers	.029	.36
Constraints		
Percent black Students	−.126	3.67
Percent Hispanic students	−.198	6.79
Percent low-income students	.043	1.31
Summary statistic		
R^2		.30
F statistic		39.44
Standard error		10.08
N		935

Source: Authors' calculations.

a. Dependent variable = Hispanic student test pass rate.

white students. While there is a modest literature on differential impacts, it indicates little consistency in regard to expectations.[41] The controls should be viewed merely as an effort to make sure key factors are not left out of the model rather than to estimate precise impacts for each control variable.[42]

Table 9-4 shows the influence of Hispanic teachers on the TAAS test scores of Hispanic students. While Hispanic teachers are not among the stronger influences on Hispanic test scores (that distinction goes to school quality and the racial composition of the schools), Hispanic teachers are positively associated with higher test scores. Although the size of the coefficient appears small, a 1 percentage point increase in Hispanic teachers is associated with an increase in the Hispanic pass rate by .114 percentage points; in reality the impact is substantial. The equation controls for white test scores, so the appropriate substantive comparison is to the Hispanic-white test score gap, approximately 12.2 percentage points on average. A 1 standard deviation change in Hispanic teachers (about 18.9 percent) is associated with a 2.2 percentage point gain in Hispanic test scores, or approximately 17 percent of the existing gap. A movement of this

41. Jencks and Phillips (1998).

42. Similarly, we are not concerned with collinearity among the control variables.

Table 9-5. *Influence of Hispanic Teachers on Other Policy Indicators*[a]

Indicator	Slope	t score	R^2	Number
Hispanic attendance	.022	6.93	.31	989
Hispanic dropouts	−.005	.82	.11	930
Hispanic advanced classes	.088	3.55	.33	852
Hispanics taking college boards	.388	4.99	.23	490
Hispanic SAT scores	.644	1.83	.46	248
Hispanic ACT scores	−.001	.14	.42	284
Hispanics above 1110 SAT	.084	1.95	.32	360
Hispanics in AP classes	.050	2.50	.44	682
Hispanics passing AP classes	.048	.39	.55	158

Source: Authors' calculations.

a. All equations control for white performance on the same indicator, teacher salary, instructional funds, class size, teacher experience, noncertified teachers, and percent Hispanic, black, and poor students.

size in Hispanic test scores relative to white test scores would be considered a major substantive change.[43]

Although TAAS scores are the most salient educational performance indicator in Texas, a variety of other measures exist. Table 9-5 shows the regression coefficients for nine other measures of Hispanic educational performance. The table reports only the coefficients for the Hispanic teachers variable rather than including those for the control variables. Because our expectation is that Hispanic teachers improve the performance of Hispanic students, we have a directional hypothesis, and a one-tailed test of significance is appropriate. By that standard (t > 1.65), Hispanic teachers are significantly associated with higher levels of Hispanic student attendance, more Hispanics in advanced classes, more Hispanics taking college boards, higher Hispanic SAT scores, more Hispanics scoring above 1110 on the SAT or its ACT equivalent, and more Hispanic students in AP classes. There is no relationship for Hispanic dropouts, ACT scores, and whether or not Hispanics pass AP courses. The findings in tables 9-4 and 9-5 are strong evidence that an increase in Hispanic teachers is associated with an improvement in Hispanic student educational opportunities.

These findings underscore the importance of the findings on political structure and bias. A relatively simple choice—whether to hold school board elections at large or by wards—influences not only the ethnic composition of the school board but also the quality of the Hispanic representation on that board. That representational quality influences the number of Hispanic administrators employed by the school district and, indirectly, the number of Hispanic teachers

43. Whether this estimate for Hispanic teachers is an overestimate or underestimate is an open question. There is some evidence that minority teachers improve the test scores of Anglo students in Texas. If so, then Hispanic scores are likely to rise more than the slope indicates because Anglo scores will rise a corresponding amount.

in the classroom. Hispanic teachers, in turn, affect the quality of education provided to Hispanic students. Biases generated by political structures, therefore, reverberate through the system.

Our examination of policy impacts has followed only a single line of inquiry, that of student performance on various educational outputs. We have not examined a set of other processes that are equally likely to affect the quality of education afforded to Hispanic students. Ability grouping and tracking is a long-standing process of sorting students by perceived ability, and the quality of education varies across sorted groups. Inconsistent applications of disciplinary policy, from minor punishments to expulsions, also can be used to deny students equal access to educational opportunities. Both of these processes show significant differences in how Hispanic and white students are treated, with Hispanic students more likely to be overrepresented in groups and situations with negative connotations and underrepresented in positive circumstances. Both processes have been linked to the representativeness of the teaching faculty.[44] Other processes have not been systematically studied, but the potential for bias clearly exists in the counseling provided to students, teacher interactions with students in classrooms, and access to transportation for extracurricular activities. The total influence of structural bias, therefore, might well be much larger than the evidence reveals.

Conclusion

This study examines the potential double bias of electoral structures. The issue of whether at-large elections are biased in favor of minority candidates, although well studied, is still a matter of controversy. The bias in the *type* of representatives that various electoral systems produce is relatively uncharted territory. In this chapter, at-large and ward election structures are compared in Hispanic minority and majority environments, producing four different demographic and institutional conditions. In Hispanic minority districts, we expected ward structures to provide a significant representational advantage over at-large arrangements. In Hispanic majority districts, however, we expected these structural influences to disappear, although the formal logic strictly suggests a significant reversal of fortune due to structure. For clarity, we treat the minority and majority environments separately below.

Using Texas school districts, this study found that at-large elections were associated with fewer Hispanic school board members in districts where Hispanics make up a minority of the population. The quantity of Hispanic representatives was significantly influenced by the type of election (figure 9-3). Perhaps more important than the descriptive electoral bias, the representatives produced

44. Meier and Stewart (1991).

under at-large systems were less effective at pushing the minority group's agenda in one key area: hiring (figure 9-5). At-large systems were associated with fewer minority administrators being hired and fewer minority teachers in the classroom. An extensive literature shows that Hispanic teachers positively influence the educational experience of minority students. When they are exposed to minority teachers, minority students are less likely to be tracked into low-status classes, more likely to be assigned to advanced and gifted classes, less likely to be disproportionately disciplined, more likely to pass standardized tests, more likely to not drop out and graduate from high school, and more inclined to score highly on college board exams.[45]

In Hispanic majority districts, contrary to our hypotheses (H_3 and H_4), we found that the structure of elections still mattered, but that Hispanics used the at-large system to their advantage. While the formal logic informs us of this outcome, we expected that the differences between racial groups' political experiences (mobilization, residential segregation, and the use of race as a cue), would interact to suppress any purely structural effects in the Hispanic majority environment. That was not the case here. Other minority groups may be using the ward structures in Hispanic majority districts to thwart Hispanic policy. The tests do not explicitly speak to this, but they consistently provide evidence of the effect.

In sum, structure matters; and it matters a great deal more than we expected. In Hispanic minority districts, descriptive and substantive gains are made under ward conditions. In Hispanic majority districts, at-large structures bias outcomes in favor of the majority, and ward structures slightly restrain both the quantity and quality of representation. Finally, using multiple measures, we show that bureaucratic representation was associated with positive educational outcomes. The biases of election structure, therefore, reverberate throughout the entire education system, creating additional biases.

References

Aaron, Robert, and Glen Powell. 1982. "Feedback Practices as a Function of Teacher and Pupil Race during Reading Group Instruction." *Journal of Negro Education* 51 (Winter): 50–59.

Austin, Rory A. 1998. "Testing the Impact of Electoral Structures on Minority Office-Holding and Policy Representation." Ph.D. dissertation, University of Rochester.

Becker, Gary S. 1993. *Human Capital.* University of Chicago Press.

Brischetto, Robert, and Richard Engstrom. 1997. "Cumulative Voting and Latino Representation." *Social Science Quarterly* 78 (December): 978–91.

Brischetto, Robert, and others. 1994. "Texas." In *Quiet Revolution in the South*, edited by Chandler Davidson and Bernard Grofman. Princeton University Press.

45. See Meier and Stewart (1991); Meier, Stewart, and England (1989); Polinard and others (1994); Meier, Wrinkle, and Polinard (1999); Meier and others (2001).

Bullock, Charles S. 1984. "Racial Crossover Voting and the Election of Black Officials." *Journal of Politics* 46 (February): 238–51.

Burtless, Gary. 1996. *Does Money Matter? The Effect of School Resources on Student Achievement and Adult Success.* Brookings.

Cameron, Charles, David Epstein, and Sharyn O'Halloran. 1996. "Do Majority-Minority Districts Maximize Substantive Black Representation in Congress?" *American Political Science Review* 90 (December): 794–812.

Canon, David T. 1999. *Race, Redistricting, and Representation.* University of Chicago Press.

Cole, Leonard A. 1974. *Blacks in Power.* Princeton University Press.

Cole, Beverly P. 1986. "The Black Educator: An Endangered Species." *Journal of Negro Education* 55 (Summer): 326–34.

Cox, Gary. 1990. "Centripetal and Centrifugal Incentives in Electoral Systems." *American Journal of Political Science* 34 (November): 903–35.

———. 1997. *Making Votes Count: Strategic Coordination in the World's Electoral Systems.* Cambridge University Press.

Davidson, Chandler, and George Korbel. 1981. "At-Large Elections and Minority-Group Representation: A Re-examination of Historical and Contemporary Evidence." *Journal of Politics* 43 (November): 982–1005.

Dee, Thomas S. 2003. "Teachers, Race, and Student Achievement in a Randomized Experiment." Unpublished paper. Swarthmore College, Department of Economics.

Downs, Anthony. 1957. *An Economic Theory of Democracy.* New York: Harper-Collins.

Eisinger, Peter K. 1980. *The Politics of Displacement.* New York: Academic Press.

Engstrom, Richard, and Charles Barrilleaux. 1991. "Native Americans and Cumulative Voting: The Sisseton-Wahpeton Sioux." *Social Science Quarterly* 72 (June): 388–93.

Engstrom, Richard, and Michael McDonald. 1981. "The Election of Blacks to City Councils: Clarifying the Impact of Electoral Arrangements on the Seats/Population Relationship." *American Political Science Review* 75 (June): 344–54.

———. 1982. "The Under Representation of Blacks on City Councils." *Journal of Politics* 44 (November): 1088–105.

———. 1986. "The Effect of At-Large versus District Elections on Racial Representation in U.S. Municipalities." In *Electoral Laws and Their Political Consequences,* edited by Bernard Grofman and Arend Lijphart. New York: Agathon Press.

Epstein, David, and Sharyn O'Halloran. 1999. "Measuring the Electoral and Policy Impact of Majority-Minority Voting Districts." *American Journal of Political Science* 43 (April): 367–95.

Gerber, Elisabeth, Rebecca Morton, and Thomas Rietz. 1998. "Minority Representation in Multimember Districts." *American Political Science Review* 92 (March): 127–44.

Hanushek, Eric. 1996. "School Resources and Student Performance." In *Does Money Matter?* edited by Gary Burtless. Brookings.

Hedges, Larry V., and Rob Greenwald 1996. "Have Times Changed? The Relation between School Resources and Student Perfomance." In *Does Money Matter?* edited by Gary Burtless. Brookings.

Hero, Rodney, and Caroline Tolbert. 1995. "Latinos and Substantive Representation in the U.S. House of Representatives: Direct, Indirect, or Nonexistent?" *American Journal of Political Science* 39 (3): 640–52.

Hess, Frederick, and David Leal. 1997. "Minority Teachers, Minority Students, and College Matriculation: A New Look at the Role-Modeling Hypothesis." *Policy Studies Journal* 25 (Summer): 235–48.

Jencks, Christopher, and Meredith Phillips. 1998. *The Black-White Test Score Gap.* Brookings.

Karnig, Albert K. 1976. "Black Representation on City Councils: The Impact of District Elections and Socioeconomic Factors." *Urban Affairs Quarterly* 12 (December): 223–42.

Karnig, Albert K., and Susan Welch. 1980. *Black Representation and Urban Policy*. University of Chicago Press.

_____. 1982. "Electoral Structure and Black Representation on City Councils." *Social Science Quarterly* 63 (March): 99–114.

Kerr, Brinck, and Kenneth R. Mladenka. 1994. "Does Politics Matter? A Time-Series Analysis of Minority Employment Patterns." *American Journal of Political Science* 38 (November): 918–43.

Leal, David, Kenneth J. Meier, and Valerie Martinez–Ebers. 2004. "The Politics of Latino Education: The Biases of At-Large Elections." *Journal of Politics* 66 (November): 1224-44.

Lublin, David. 1997. *The Paradox of Representation: Racial Gerrymandering and Minority Interests in Congress*. Princeton University Press.

Lublin, David, and D. Stephen Voss. 2003. "The Missing Middle: Why Median Voter Theory Can't Save Democrats from Singing the Boll-Weevil Blues." *Journal of Politics* 65 (February): 227–37.

Mansbridge, Jane. 1999. "Should Blacks Represent Blacks and Women Represent Women? A Contingent 'Yes.'" *Journal of Politics* 59 (August): 628–57.

MacManus, Susan. 1978. "City Council Election Procedures and Minority Representation." *Social Science Quarterly* 59 (June): 153–61.

Meier, Kenneth J., and Joseph Stewart Jr. 1991. *The Politics of Hispanic Education*. State University of New York Press.

Meier, Kenneth J., Joseph Stewart Jr., and Robert E. England. 1989. *Race, Class and Education: The Politics of Second Generation Discrimination*. University of Wisconsin Press.

Meier, Kenneth J., Robert D. Wrinkle, and J. L. Polinard. 1999. "Representative Bureaucracy and Distributional Equity: Addressing the Hard Question." *Journal of Politics* 61 (November): 1025–39.

Meier, Kenneth J., and others. 2001. "Zen and the Art of Policy Analysis: A Reply to Nielsen and Wolf." *Journal of Politics* 63 (May): 616–29.

Meier, Kenneth J., and others. Forthcoming. "Electoral Structure and the Post-Election Quality of Representation: The Policy Consequences of School Board Elections." *American Journal of Political Science*.

Mladenka, Kenneth R. 1989. "Blacks and Hispanics in Urban Politics." *American Political Science Review* 83 (March): 165–91.

Moore, Helen A., and David R. Johnson. 1983. "A Reexamination of Elementary School Teachers' Expectations: Evidence of Sex and Ethnic Segmentation." *Social Science Quarterly* 64 (September): 460–75.

Pitkin, Hanna. 1967. *The Concept of Representation*. University of California Press.

Polinard, J. L., and others. 1994. *Electoral Structure and Urban Policy: The Impact on Mexican American Communities*. Armonk, N.Y.: M. E. Sharpe.

Rich, Wilbur C., ed. 1996. *The Politics of Minority Coalitions: Race, Ethnicity, and Shared Uncertainties*. Westport, Conn.: Praeger.

Robinson, Theodore P. and Thomas R. Dye. 1978. "Reformism and Black Representation on City Councils." *Social Science Quarterly* 59 (June): 133–41.

Shotts, Kenneth W. 2003a. "Does Racial Redistricting Cause Conservative Policy Outcomes? Policy Preferences of Southern Representatives in the 1980s and 1990s." *Journal of Politics* 65 (February): 216–26.

_____. 2003b. "Racial Redistricting's Alleged Perverse Effects: Theory, Data and 'Reality.'" *Journal of Politics* 65 (February): 237–44.

Stewart, Joseph, Robert England, and Kenneth Meier. 1989. "Black Representation in Urban School Districts: From School Board to Office to Classroom." *Western Political Quarterly* 42 (June): 287–305.

Swain, Carol M. 1993. *Black Faces and Black Interests: The Representation of African Americans in Congress.* Harvard University Press.

Taebel, Delbert. 1978. "Minority Representation on City Councils." *Social Science Quarterly* 59 (June): 142–52.

Welch, Susan. 1990. "The Impact of At-Large Elections on the Representation of Blacks and Hispanics." *Journal of Politics* 52 (November): 1050–76.

Weiher, Gregory. 2000. "Minority Student Achievement: Passive Representation and Social Context in Schools." *Journal of Politics* 62 (August): 886–95.

10

School House Politics: Expenditures, Interests, and Competition in School Board Elections

FREDERICK M. HESS AND DAVID L. LEAL

For most of the past century, the issue of local school board governance was a subject of on-and-off debate, and the debate continues today. Praised on one hand as pillars of democracy, schools boards have been assailed on the other as an outdated and dysfunctional approach to school governance. In an age of charter schools, national for-profit education providers, and high-profile mayoral and state takeovers of public schools, observers have wondered whether school boards are an anachronism or an important link in the provision of democratic education. Reformers have asserted that boards are no more than gadflies, captives of teacher unions, and breeding grounds for ambitious politicians. (The more than 100,000 board members who serve on the country's approximately 15,000 school boards constitute the largest group of elected officials in the United States.) These various critiques have continued with remarkably little systematic attention to the empirical evidence regarding what boards do, who serves on them, or the realities of board elections.

The contemporary debate has encompassed a variety of reform proposals, each premised on particular critiques of board behavior. For instance, Finn (1992) has called for abolishing the school board as a parochial institution ill-suited to the demands of modern schooling. A similar proposal by Hill (2003)

The authors would like to thank Andrew Kelly and Brett Friedman for their valuable research assistance and the National School Boards Association for its cooperation.

has called for replacing traditional school boards with multiple, competing entities, each of which is free to sponsor "charter districts." A third response, by Glass (2002), has been to call for mayoral control of school boards. This suggestion has occasioned a burst of research, with the findings generally yielding an uncertain verdict as to its desirability.[1]

The Education Commission of the States (1999) offers a fourth response, acknowledging that although boards are a vital element of democratic school governance, some are in need of substantial reform. Meanwhile, a "counterreformation" has emerged, which suggests that boards be made more professional and political and that they be subjected to strengthened electoral accountability.[2]

Although these arguments rest on assertions about the nature of board governance and elections, they have been informed by little systematic evidence on the political pressures that exist in districts. The claims inevitably turn on anecdotal evidence, high-profile cases, ideology, or intuition. This is due in large part to the relative absence in recent decades of systematic analysis of school board elections or electoral processes.

The goal of this chapter is not to endorse any particular set of claims regarding school board efficacy or the desirability of particular reforms. Rather, we seek to provide a firmer empirical basis for considering claims about board elections and electioneering. Reading the popular press, for instance, one might easily think that school board elections have become expensive and heavily professionalized affairs. This is because newspaper coverage tends to focus on those cases, such as the elections in Los Angeles in 2003 or San Diego in 2002, in which heated conflicts and avid campaigns resulted in multimillion dollar contests. How typical are such elections? Our survey will for the first time provide answers to that question.

In addition, critics of teacher unions have suggested that these unions are the predominant political influence in local school districts. However, most of the accounts supporting this analysis have been decidedly union-centric in their mode of inquiry, disregarding the influence of other groups. In chapter 11 of this volume, Moe focuses on teacher unions because "there are good reasons for thinking that teacher unions are ordinarily the most potent political force in school board elections."[3]

It is our goal to study the influence of not only teacher unions but also a number of other potentially influential actors and interests in school board elections. For instance, how active are unions in school board elections, in terms of both fundraising and campaigning? How does their activity compare with that

1. Cibulka (2001); Cuban, Usdan, and Hale (2002); Kirst (2002); and Henig and Rich (2003).
2. Feuerstein (1998); Hess (2003).
3. Although he does note that "their power is constrained in basic ways that can vary across contexts."

of other key interests, particularly religious groups, the business community, and racial and ethnic organizations? How does the monetary or organizational influence of these groups vary with context? In particular, how do community size, wealth, collective bargaining status, and racial composition affect the influence of these actors? How does board professionalization or the manner of election affect their influence?

Using information collected from a stratified random national sample of more than 800 school boards matched with district-level census data, this chapter undertakes a systematic inquiry into the role of money and interest group activism in school board elections. We focus on four sets of questions: How much money do board candidates spend in their campaigns? Which interests supply campaign funding? How active in board elections are the various interests reported to be? And, finally, how competitive are school board campaigns?

In each case, we describe the general landscape and then use multivariate analysis to explore how constituent, institutional, and electoral pressures create differences in group influence and electoral contestation. For instance, do factors such as electoral arrangements, school board professionalism, and the presence of collective bargaining alter the activism of teacher unions? Through our analysis, we hope to provide at least partial answers to some of the questions that have dominated discussions about reform of district governance.

Previous Research

From early in the nineteenth century until the 1970s, political scientists produced many scholarly studies on the nature and politics of school boards.[4] Starting in the late 1970s, political scientists' research on these questions declined precipitously, leaving the field largely to education specialists and journalists. After the publication of *School Politics, Chicago Style* in 1976, it would be more than two decades before a political science volume of any note addressed questions of school district governance, except in the context of choice-based school reform.[5]

A resurgence of interest among political scientists in the politics of education began in the late 1990s, spurred by the growth of a relatively sophisticated literature on choice-based reform and a spate of interest in "civic capacity." Observers have been particularly interested in the influence of teacher/employee unions, long recognized as a powerful interest group at both the national and local levels. The political influence that teacher unions exert on districts has been a subject of debate and occasional empirical inquiry since the 1960s. Most of this work, ranging from the literature on the "new unionism" to ideological

4. See, for example, Dye (1967); Jennings and Zeigler (1971); Meranto (1970); Wirt and Kirst (1972); Zeigler and Jennings (1974).

5. Peterson (1976).

attacks on unions, has offered little by way of balanced or systematic assessment of the extent of the influence of teacher unions or the determinants of that influence.[6] However, Moe is in the midst of extensive and careful research into the influence of unions on school districts, some of which is beginning to establish the parameters of the activity and influence of teacher unions, at least in the union stronghold of California.[7]

Researchers also have been interested in the involvement of other interest groups (Feuerstein 1998), including civic organizations (Portz, Stein, and Jones 1999), the business community (Stone and others 2001), and minority communities and race-based organizations (Henig and others 1999; Orr 1999; Rich 1996). This work coexists with renewed efforts to explain how institutional arrangements constrain school district governance and management.[8] Meanwhile, researchers have noted the influence of Christian Right organizations on state and local politics in various contexts, including school boards.[9] How wide their influence is in district elections is a question of some debate.

Other recent work has focused less on school board elections than on the broader question of how local pressures affect the outcomes of school board policies, whether through elections or other dynamics. Berkman and Plutzer (2001, 2002), for instance, explored how constituent characteristics like age and race influence the outcome of policy decisions on spending and education provision. This work extended a literature that has examined how demographic, fiscal, and institutional forces affect board decisions on policies concerning the provision of classroom technology, sex education programs, school violence prevention policies, the availability of public input to decisionmaking, and bilingual education spending.[10]

The current inquiry, of course, is framed not just by such education research but also by a large and long-standing body of work that examines how interest groups, electoral arrangements, and the professionalism of elected officials influence political outcomes more generally. However, most of this work concerns federal or state government; there is surprisingly little work on how interest groups, campaign finance, electoral arrangements, or institutional factors influence local elections. For instance, perhaps the only issue related to city council and school board elections to have enjoyed sustained empirical attention in recent decades is the question of whether at-large or ward electoral systems promote or impede minority political representation.[11]

6. Brimelow (2003); Lieberman (1997).
7. See chapter 11 in this volume as well as Moe (2003a, b).
8. Hess (1999).
9. Regnerus, Sikkink, and Smith (1999).
10. Hess and Leal (1999, 2001a, 2001b, 2003); Leal and Hess (2000).
11. Davidson and Korbel (1981); Fraga, Meier, and England (1986); Polinard, Wrinkle, and Longoria (1990, 1991); Zax (1990); Meier and Stewart (1991); Bezdek, Billeaux, and Huerta (2000).

Very little of this research, however, involves questions such as interest group activity or the role of money in elections. While the occasional mayoral election may be the focus of attention, there is little systematic research into the factors that determine the election of mayors, city council candidates, or school board members. Given this backdrop, we particularly hope that scholars of both education governance and local government may find our data and analyses useful.

Data

The data for the analysis were obtained from two sources: a 2001 national survey of school boards and the 2000 U.S. census. In 2001, one of the authors conducted an extensive survey of a nationally representative sample of school boards. The eight-page survey, developed in collaboration with the National School Boards Association (NSBA), was sent to a stratified random sample of school districts drawn from the nation's 15,000 districts. The largest districts were oversampled, helping to ensure that large districts would provide enough responses to permit meaningful analysis. Consequently, while 2 percent of the nation's school districts enroll more than 25,000 students, 11.9 percent of the sampled districts do. The survey was mailed by the NSBA, and for each sampled district, one board member was randomly selected from the current school board. Board members who did not respond were contacted up to two more times. Responses were obtained from 827 board members, yielding a response rate of 40.9 percent; response rates were relatively stable across districts of different sizes.[12]

Responses were anonymous, but each survey was identified by an alphanumeric code that permitted the responses to be merged with district-level data. The survey results were merged with data from the 2000 census that were organized by school district. Because of some missing data in the census of school districts, twenty-nine observations were lost. We also added a variable to the merged data set that measured whether the district was in a state that had a collective bargaining law.

Variables

The analysis focuses on four measures of school board political activity. The first examines the amount of money spent in the most recent board election by the respondent. The second examines the percentage of campaign revenue that candidates raised from a variety of local organized interest groups. The third examines the reported activism of those groups in local board elections. The fourth examines several measures of the competitiveness of local board elections.

12. Hess (2002).

The measures are, by necessity and by design, rather broad. They are broad because the dearth of prior systematic examination of school district politics and elections means that it was difficult to determine precisely what questions to ask. This inquiry is intended to be a preliminary effort, and it seeks to sketch some broad contours so that successive efforts are better positioned to adopt a more focused line of inquiry.

Those acquainted with school board members and elections will recognize that such imprecision is largely inevitable, as school board campaigns tend to be amateur affairs marked by imprecise recordkeeping and low levels of candidate interest or expertise in the particulars of fundraising and campaigning. That state of affairs does not pose a major problem for this analysis. While it undoubtedly makes the estimates less precise than we would like them to be, it is not clear how or why the limited level of candidate interest or knowledge would systematically bias the findings in any particular direction.

Dependent variables. Because most of the dependent variables contain four categories, we used ordinal probit regression analysis. The substantive significance of the statistically significant independent variables was analyzed using the program CLARIFY.[13] For each dependent variable, we tested the statistical and substantive significance of fourteen independent variables, which are discussed below.[14] We did so because we were interested not only in the absolute level of organizational activism in school board elections, for example, but also in the determinants of such activism. With regression analysis, we can better understand the independent effects of demographic, institutional, and electoral factors. We wanted to know, for instance, whether poverty, urban location, right-to-work laws, board professionalism, electoral system, or any number of other factors influenced the manner in which organized groups attempted to influence board elections.

Explanatory variables. Consistent with the approach to school district governance sketched out above, this inquiry explores whether and how two kinds of forces affected district politics and local interest group influence. The first set of variables examines the effects of popular and electoral pressures that may influence political practices and outcomes. The second set of variables focuses more on the electoral practices of the district and the relative professionalism of board members and on how these may alter the behavior of candidates or interest groups. Both sets of variables have long been used in the political science

13. Michael Tomz, Jason Wittenberg, and Gary King, CLARIFY: Software for Interpreting and Presenting Statistical Results, version 1.2.1. Harvard University (http://gking.harvard.edu/ [October 29, 2004]).

14. While we could create more narrowly tailored models for each dependent variable, that would require a discussion of each specific regression model. The symmetry of our system is easier to report, and it is unlikely that dropping or adding a few variables here and there would significantly change the relationships reported in the tables.

literature; our innovation is to simultaneously consider the relative effects of this battery of measures in a critical area—local education politics—where they have long been overlooked.

The electoral and demographic variables include the size of the school district, the percentage of the school population that is African American or Hispanic,[15] the percentage of the district population that is more than sixty years of age, the percentage of the district student population that is enrolled in a free or reduced-price lunch program,[16] the percentage of the district adult population that has a college degree, and the percentage of the district deemed urban for census purposes. Each of these variables was measured using the school district data reported in the 2000 census.[17]

The political science literature has investigated some of these variables, particularly measures of education and income, for their relationship with political participation at the individual and aggregate levels. However, it is not entirely clear how such factors might be expected to affect the influence or activity of interest groups. Moreover, there are several variables—such as those measuring district size, urban location, or ethnic composition—whose impact on board politics is decidedly unclear.

The institutional variables include whether board members were elected at large (by the entire school district) or by ward (representing a smaller geographic portion of the district), whether elections were partisan, and whether board elections were conducted concurrently with national elections.[18]

We also tested the impact of features relating to the relative professionalism of the local school board, including whether a salary or stipend is paid to board members, the length of term of office, and the number of hours that board members spend on the job each week.[19] Finally, we also include a dummy variable that takes into account whether the state in question has a collective bargaining law, as that has long been argued to be a significant determinant of the power of employee unions.

15. The variable for Hispanic student percentage is highly correlated with overall Hispanic population percentage (0.96), and the same is the case for African American student and district population (0.93).

16. This variable is highly correlated with median family income ($r = .70$), so the latter is not used.

17. The values of all percentage variables range from 0 to 1.

18. The at-large or ward variable measured the percentage of elected board members elected in each fashion (the number of appointed board members in the sample was negligible, less than 5 percent). The variables for both partisan elections and concurrent elections were dichotomous measures.

19. Because many school boards pay no salary at all and because many others compensate board members primarily with a per-meeting stipend, compensation is measured with a dichotomous variable indicating whether board members received any remuneration or not. In general, political scientists have observed that more partisan and high-profile elections tend to generate higher levels of political competition and participation. Similarly, more professional legislatures have tended to attract higher-quality candidates who campaign more aggressively.

Findings

In the following discussion, we present the results of our analysis for overall expenditures, sources of funding, reported election activity of interest groups, relative activity of teacher unions, and political competition.

Overall Expenditures

How much money do board members spend to get elected? Popular conceptions tend to be colored by politics in high-profile urban districts where heated campaigns draw significant media attention. For instance, in the widely reported 2002 board elections in San Diego, supporters and critics of superintendent Alan Bersin spent more than $1 million for three contested seats on the board—an election that ended with Bersin retaining his 3-2 majority. Similarly, national notice attended the 2003 Los Angeles school board election in which superintendent Roy Romer and his union-backed opponents together spent more than $3 million and Romer's critics succeeded in gaining control of the seven-member board. How typical are such contests?

We were interested first in the average amount of money spent overall in school board campaigns. We asked each board member to report the amount of money he or she spent in the last election. Because respondents might not have been able to remember the precise figure, we provided them with five general categories: $0 to $999, $1,000 to $4,999, $5,000 to $9,999, $10,000 to $24,999, and more than $25,000.

The results in figure 10-1 show the atypical nature of the Los Angeles and San Diego elections. More than 76 percent of respondents indicated that they spent less than $1,000 in their last campaign. Only 10 percent of candidates reported spending more than $5,000, and only 1 percent reported spending as much as $25,000.

The results are heavily influenced by the fact that most board members run in small districts. When we consider only those districts with an enrollment of 50,000 students or more, the races appear moderately more expensive. In such districts, the average candidate reported campaign expenditures just below the $5,000 to $9,999 range. When we examine only those four districts with more than 100,000 students, we find candidates in only two districts reporting expenditures more than $25,000.

These results suggest that, except perhaps in the nation's largest districts, formal campaign contributions appear to play only a small role in elections. In fact, 63 percent of respondents reported that either they or their friends and family supplied more than 50 percent of the funds for their most recent campaign. In total, a reasonable estimation is that fewer than 20 percent of candidates received a majority of their funding from an organized interest of any kind. Outside the largest districts, there is little opportunity for organized interests to

Figure 10-1. *Candidates' Reported Expenditures*

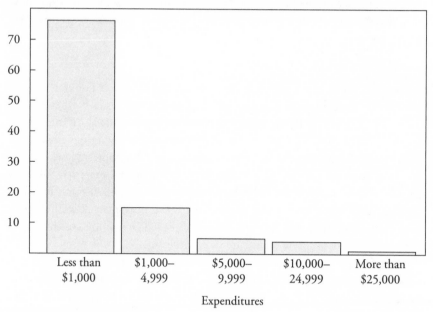

Percent

Source: Authors' data.

influence candidates through traditional campaign contributions of the kind that attract so much attention in the national campaign finance debates. It is important to bear in mind that the respondents were all currently serving on school boards, which means that they were all *winning* candidates in their most recent election. The losers in these elections would most likely have spent even less.

In addition to determining aggregate spending figures, we also were interested in whether and how expenditures vary across school districts. We would expect candidates in larger districts to spend more, but did local wealth, education, or racial composition have an impact on spending? The political science research on legislative elections implies that spending will be higher when the level of legislative professionalism, for instance, is greater. The results of the analysis using the full roster of explanatory variables discussed in the data section are presented in table 10-1 (cut points are not shown in this or subsequent tables because of space constraints).

What do the findings show? As expected, candidates in larger districts tend to have spent more than those in smaller districts, as do candidates in more urban areas and those with more educated constituencies. For reasons that are

Table 10-1. *Factors Determining Overall Expenditures in Most Recent Election*[a]

Independent variable	Expenditures
Percent of board seats elected by ward (0 to 1)	−0.406**
	(0.161)
Length of board term (0 to 6)	0.031
	(0.120)
Partisan election (1 = yes, 0 = no)	0.028
	(0.231)
Board elections concurrent with national elections (1 = yes, 0 = no)	−0.029
	(0.082)
Board member receives some pay (1 = yes, 0 = no)	−0.385***
	(0.146)
District student enrollment	0.027***
	(0.004)
Percent of population over age sixty (0 to 1)	−0.146
	(1.500)
Percent of school population African American (0 to 1)	1.438***
	(0.479)
Percent of school population Hispanic (0 to 1)	0.241
	(0.513)
Percent of students on free or reduced-price lunch (0 to 1)	0.064
	(0.566)
Percent of community classified urban (0 to 1)	0.930***
	(0.326)
Percent of adult population with college degree (0 to 1)	4.481**
	(1.752)
State collective bargaining law (1 = yes, 0 = no)	0.153
	(0.173)
Weekly hours worked by board members	0.005**
	(0.002)
Summary statistic	
N	510
Pseudo R^2	0.26

Source: Authors' data.

a. ** $p < .05$; *** $p < .01$. Standard errors are reported in parentheses.

less clear, candidate spending is positively associated with the percentage of African Americans in the district.

Candidates in districts that elected their board members at large rather than by district tended to spend more, probably because it is more expensive to contest elections in larger districts. Meanwhile, board members who reported working more hours spent more to get elected, perhaps suggesting that board work in their districts is taken more seriously. Surprisingly, the analysis finds that candidates spent less in districts that provided a salary or stipend to board members.

Table 10-2. *Distribution of Responses Regarding Fundraising Sources*[a]

Percentage of support	Teacher unions	Business groups	Religious groups	Personal funds	Family and friends
0	82	76	97	34	49
1–25	12	14	3	16	16
26–50	5	7	0	7	16
More than 50	1	3	0	44	19
Number	425	437	392	608	552

Source: Authors' data.

a. Figures represent the percentage of respondents indicating that the group shown contributed the percentage of total campaign funds shown.

This unexpected finding—that candidates spent more money to win jobs that did not pay—may be an artifact of the way the variable is measured. The compensation variable is a simple yes-no measure in which "salaried" board members frequently earn no more than a few hundred dollars a year. Also, amateur legislative bodies that do not pay sometimes attract candidates who are wealthy and therefore do not need the salary; such candidates might be able to spend more money to secure elections. In the future, we would need a measure of candidate wealth to test this possibility. In addition—and also somewhat surprisingly—there is no evidence that longer terms, partisan elections, or elections that are concurrent with national contests have an impact on candidate expenditures. There is therefore no clear finding that board professionalism is associated with higher expenditures.

Source of Funding

More interesting than the total amount of candidate expenditures may be the source of the contributions. Given popular concerns about the influence on educational affairs of interests such as teacher unions or the business community, just how dependent are candidates on these groups for campaign support?

The survey asked respondents to report the percentage of money they received from teacher unions, business groups, and religiously affiliated organizations, as well as from personal sources and from family and friends. Table 10-2 shows their responses. Expenditures other than direct contributions to a candidate, such as phone banks and get-out-the-vote activities, were not included.

As mentioned, respondents reported that the most popular source of funds was personal resources, followed by donations from friends and family. In fact, 44 percent of respondents reported that they provided more than half of their own campaign funding, and another 19 percent received more than half from their friends or family. Meanwhile, just 6 percent of candidates received more than a quarter of their funding from teacher unions, just 10 percent garnered that much from the business community, and none received that much from religious groups. It is therefore evident that traditional interest groups were playing at best a minor role in the funding of most of these school board campaigns.

While these general patterns are interesting, it is possible that the groups play different roles in different districts. What determines the percentage of funding contributed by particular groups? For instance, are organized interests more active in larger, more urban districts? Do teacher unions contribute significantly more funding in some kinds of communities? Are candidates more likely to contribute to their own campaigns in districts where board service is more professionalized?

The analysis in table 10-3 shows that in larger, more urbanized districts teacher unions tended to provide a larger percentage of candidate funds. In addition, support from the business community tended to be highest in urbanized communities and more affluent districts, results that make intuitive sense.

Surprisingly, business giving constituted a higher percentage of candidate revenue in districts that were located in collective bargaining states and in districts with larger populations of African American students. The collective bargaining result may suggest that business groups attempt to counter the political influence of teacher unions in those districts. The African American student variable is intriguing, and while it could be a statistical artifact, scholars might want to investigate the nature of the business interest in the politics of educating minority children. Otherwise, the analyses generally show that other constituency characteristics, electoral processes, and board professionalism tended to have little impact on the source of candidate funds from business and teacher groups.[20]

Of course, one problem with an analysis of interest group campaign contributions is that the results measure only the money that groups contributed directly to board candidates. Such calculations inevitably exclude expenditures that individual groups might make on their behalf or provide through in-kind contributions like phone banks, literature, advertisements, or yard signs. Moreover, it is likely that some groups, such as teacher unions or religiously affiliated organizations, may find it unnecessary or even counterproductive to make large direct contributions in communities where they exert significant influence through indirect means.

Reported Election Activity of Interest Groups

As noted above, campaign contributions are an imperfect measure of interest group activity in campaigns. Consequently, we also used a second measure—the reported activity of several major potential actors—to see whether the results

20. In the three models, there are some consistent effects. The ward variable is negatively associated with candidate funding from both religiously affiliated organizations and from friends or family. The rural-urban measure also is negatively associated with funding from personal sources and from friends and family.

Table 10-3. *Factors Determining the Percentage of Money Received from Interest Groups and Other Sources*[a]

Independent variable	Teacher unions	Business groups	Religious groups	Personal funds	Family and friends
Percent of board seats	−0.135	−0.079	−1.874*	−0.068	−0.248*
elected by ward (0 to 1)	(0.248)	(0.198)	(0.104)	(0.130)	(0.144)
Length of board term	0.078	−0.109	−0.170	0.158	0.116
(0 to 6)	(0.202)	(0.170)	(0.482)	(0.102)	(0.110)
Partisan election	0.165	0.052	0.601	0.066	0.070
(1 = yes, 0 = no)	(0.337)	(0.298)	(0.683)	(0.202)	(0.212)
Board elections concurrent	0.101	0.047	0.306	−0.071	−0.026
with national elections	(0.123)	(0.108)	(0.321)	(0.071)	(0.076)
(1 = yes, 0 = no)					
Board member receives some	−0.105	−0.163	−0.869	−0.200	−0.189
pay (1 = yes, 0 = no)	(0.211)	(0.188)	(0.573)	(0.128)	(0.136)
District student enrollment	0.017***	0.013***	0.005	0.002	0.003
	(0.004)	(0.004)	(0.010)	(0.003)	(0.003)
Percent of population	0.827	0.762	1.742	−0.837	−1.380
over age sixty (0 to 1)	(1.993)	(1.723)	(5.054)	(1.247)	(1.335)
Percent of school population	0.023	1.781***	2.590	0.053	0.409
African American (0 to 1)	(0.918)	(0.676)	(2.092)	(0.405)	(0.442)
Percent of school population	0.482	0.888	1.161	−0.831*	0.273
Hispanic (0 to 1)	(0.693)	(0.562)	(1.830)	(0.424)	(0.420)
Percent of students on free/	−0.234	−1.111*	1.832	−0.079	0.235
reduced lunch (0 to 1)	(0.827)	(0.651)	(2.301)	(0.464)	(0.498)
Percent of community	2.119***	1.376***	1.456	0.550 ***	1.132***
classified urban (0 to 1)	(0.702)	(0.385)	(1.393)	(0.205)	(0.245)
Percent of adult population	0.121	−1.739	8.982	−2.115	3.858*
with college degree (0 to 1)	(2.637)	(2.232)	(6.960)	(1.587)	(1.675)
State collective bargaining	0.425	−0.138	−0.410	−0.197	−0.217
law (1 = yes, 0 = no)	(0.290)	(0.213)	(0.752)	(0.146)	(0.154)
Weekly hours worked	−0.001	0.002	−0.020	−0.004	0.003
by board members	(0.004)	(0.004)	(0.019)	(0.002)	(0.002)
Summary statistic					
N	296	308	283	420	390
Pseudo R^2	0.26	0.20	0.40	0.03	0.12

Source: Authors' data.

a. * $p < .10$; *** $p < .01$. Standard errors are reported in parentheses.

would reinforce the preceding findings. Because the real world is complex and often difficult to capture in a categorical variable, this measure is problematic, but it offers a useful way to learn whether board officials perceive local interests to be engaging in activities (such as phone banking or erecting signs) that would not be reflected in the question on campaign contributions.

Respondents were asked to gauge how active six interests were in local school

Table 10-4. *Reported Interest Group Activity*[a]

Level of activity	Teacher unions	Parent groups	Business groups	Religious groups	Racial or ethnic groups	School reform groups
Very active	31	19	11	5	5	4
Somewhat active	26	33	22	12	13	9
Occasionally active	20	35	29	28	21	24
Not active	23	13	39	55	61	63
Number of observations	724	730	730	709	696	640

Source: Authors' data.

a. Figures represent the percentage of respondents indicating that the group shown exhibited the level of activity shown.

board elections. Included were teacher organizations, parent groups, the business community, religious organizations, racial and ethnic groups, and school reform organizations. Respondents indicated whether they regarded each of the groups as "very active," "somewhat active," "occasionally active," or "never active."[21] Admittedly, some of these interests, such as parent groups or school reform organizations, are amorphous. In these cases, the reported influence of the organization will not reveal much. In this question, it was appropriate to ask about the influence of religious organizations—including race-based organizations—whereas it did not make sense to ask about formal campaign contributions from these groups in the campaign finance question.

In table 10-4, we see that board members clearly regarded teacher unions as the most active organized interest group in local elections. Teacher unions were regarded as "very active" in 31 percent of districts and as either "very" or "somewhat" active in 57 percent. In comparison, business groups were deemed "very" or "somewhat" active in just 33 percent of districts, less even than the 39 percent in which they were termed "not active." Compared with the results in table 10-2, these findings suggest that the business community's involvement in board elections took place largely through campaign contributions while teacher unions and other employee unions were more likely to engage in electioneering beyond contributions.

In the majority of districts, neither religious nor race-based groups were thought to be active participants; less than 20 percent of respondents labeled either group as "very" or "somewhat" active in local board elections. Parent groups were regarded as "very" or "somewhat" active in the majority of districts, while school reform groups were said to be that active in barely 10 percent of

21. It is worth noting that this question asked about "activity" rather than influence in order to focus respondents on the actual actions undertaken by each group rather than on its reputed influence.

districts. On the other hand, uncertainty about who is included in these latter two categories, what points of view they adopt, and how they choose sides in elections leaves a great deal of ambiguity concerning the substantive significance of this finding.

Note that even the most active groups are reported to be very active in less than one-third of districts, with even the teacher unions deemed "never active" or only "occasionally active" in more than 40 percent of districts. However, it is not clear whether this reflects the relative quietude that tends to pervade many school board races or whether the question inclined respondents to report the levels of activity.

For instance, of concern with the reported activity variable is the possibility that the efforts of some groups may be underestimated because these groups are able to exert influence in ways so subtle that visible activity is not necessary or evident. For instance, if teacher unions are able to win many of their demands regarding wages and working conditions through the collective bargaining process, they may not make a concerted effort to influence routine school board decisions. In such a case, board members might tend to underestimate the "real" influence exerted by teacher unions while overestimating it for a group that is more active in daily board affairs. Such a group may dislike the status quo and want change, but its activism might be only an indicator of its outsider status, not an indictor of its electoral influence.

Is interest group activity consistent across districts, or are various interests more active in certain communities? The regression analyses are presented in table 10-5. In the case of interest group activity, constituency characteristics show strong and consistent effects. Not surprisingly, organized groups of all stripes were reported to be more active in larger districts. A similar result was found in more urban communities, with teacher unions, business groups, and race- or ethnic-based organizations all becoming more active in more urbanized districts. Consistent with the results for campaign spending, board elections in larger, more urban districts were more politicized.

Both a larger African American population and a larger Hispanic population boosted the reported activity of organizations based on race and ethnicity. The percentage of students who were African American was also linked to a reduced rate of teacher union activity, suggesting that the normally large chasm between the efforts of teacher unions and race-based groups may close in heavily minority communities.

As the percentage of the local adult population having a college degree increased, the reported activity of parent groups increased. This is consistent with previous accounts that suggest that more educated communities tend to be more active in school district elections and reform.[22] More educated communi-

---

22. Hess (1999, pp. 139–142); Stone and others (2001).

Table 10-5. *Factors Determining Reported Activity Level of Interest Groups*[a]

Independent variable	Teacher unions	Business groups	Ethnic groups	Religious groups	Parent groups	Reform groups
Percent of board seats elected	−0.039	0.233**	0.040	−0.010	0.005	0.031
by ward (0 to 1)	(0.111)	(0.111)	(0.132)	(0.118)	(0.109)	(0.129)
Length of board term (0 to 6)	0.000	0.069	−0.023	0.042	−0.072	−0.064
	(0.086)	(0.084)	(0.099)	(0.090)	(0.081)	(0.098)
Partisan election (1 = yes, 0 = no)	0.244	0.163	0.160	0.025	0.248	0.100
	(0.179)	(0.170)	(0.187)	(0.182)	(0.165)	(0.195)
Board elections concurrent	−0.007	0.066	0.075	0.085	0.014	−0.026
with national elections	(0.061)	(0.061)	(0.072)	(0.064)	(0.059)	(0.071)
(1 = yes, 0 = no)						
Board member receives	−0.178	0.047	−0.030	0.099	0.084	−0.079
some pay (1 = yes, 0 = no)	(0.114)	(0.112)	(0.130)	(0.120)	(0.110)	(0.128)
District student enrollment	0.021***	0.014***	0.016***	0.013***	0.007**	0.008**
	(0.005)	(0.003)	(0.004)	(0.003)	(0.003)	(0.003)
Percent of population	0.127	0.641	−1.623	−0.795	−2.134 **	−1.572
over age sixty (0 to 1)	(1.109)	(1.080)	(1.289)	(1.126)	(1.043)	(1.285)
Percent of school population	−0.712**	−0.363	2.207***	0.296	−0.163	0.645
African American (0 to 1)	(0.358)	(0.351)	(0.378)	(0.359)	(0.340)	(0.401)
Percent of school population	−0.242	−0.400	0.597*	−0.799 **	−0.141	−0.333
Hispanic (0 to 1)	(0.348)	(0.333)	(0.356)	(0.359)	(0.323)	(0.396)
Percent of students on free or	−0.040	0.236	0.242	0.206	−0.163	−0.529
reduced-price lunch (0 to 1)	(0.362)	(0.359)	(0.403)	(0.375)	(0.345)	(0.413)
Percent of community	0.651***	0.537***	0.532**	0.103	0.163	0.243
classified urban (0 to 1)	(0.178)	(0.174)	(0.222)	(0.186)	(0.166)	(0.213)
Percent of adult population	0.287	−2.452 **	−0.201	−1.306	3.451 ***	−1.115
with college degree (0 to 1)	(1.326)	(1.322)	(0.138)	(1.391)	(1.271)	(1.539)
State collective bargaining	0.759***	−0.265**	−0.201	−0.140	−0.012	0.184
law (1 = yes, 0 = no)	(0.129)	(0.122)	(0.138)	(0.128)	(0.121)	(0.146)
Weekly hours worked	0.004*	0.000	0.002	−0.000	0.002	0.004**
by board members	(0.002)	(0.002)	(0.002)	(0.002)	(0.002)	(0.002)
Summary statistic						
N	520	522	502	511	523	463
Pseudo R^2	0.10	0.05	0.18	0.04	0.04	0.04

Source: Authors' data.

a. * $p < .10$; ** $p < .05$; *** $p < .01$. Standard errors are reported in parentheses.

ties also were the site of less reported activity of business groups and teacher unions. While the cause is not entirely clear, it might be a case in which political activity is diminished when the likelihood of influence is reduced.

In general, teacher union activity appears to decline as the resources available to other constituencies increase. For instance, a greater concentration of African Americans, a more educated adult population, and board members who work longer hours all were associated with lower rates of teacher union activity. Of special note is that teacher unions were reported to be significantly more active in districts located in states with collective bargaining laws. On the one hand that makes perfect sense, because collective bargaining laws strengthen unions, ensuring a larger union membership, a higher profile, and a more central institutional position. On the other hand, the result is slightly surprising in that the ability of unions to exert their influence through collective bargaining might mean that unions in such districts would not engage in as much electoral activity.

Meanwhile, business groups were reported to be less active in districts that operate under collective bargaining laws. One explanation is that business groups are discouraged from making electoral efforts in such states. They may become emboldened where unions are weaker and where their efforts have a greater likelihood of success.[23]

Relative Activity of Teacher Unions

There is reason to consider the relative degree of reported interest group activity as well as the simple level of reported activity. For instance, while an "occasionally active" group may not appear influential, that evaluation takes on more significance if respondents indicate that no other groups are locally active. This question is most salient in the case of the teacher unions, which were viewed by the respondents as the most active interest despite engaging in only a moderate level of election activity.

An examination of the relative activism of teacher unions vis-à-vis the other five interest groups shows that teacher organizations were regarded as more active than any competing group. The larger the differential, the larger the teacher union "activity advantage" was reported to be. Business and parent groups were reported to be nearly as active as unions, though what that means in practice is not clear. Religious, ethnic-racial, and school reform groups, however, lagged significantly in reported electoral activity.[24]

23. It appears that neither legislative professionalism nor electoral arrangements have a consistent effect on interest group activity. Only in a few scattered models are any such variables significant. For instance, a measure of board professionalism (board members' reported number of hours worked per week) is associated with more activity by teacher unions and school reform organizations. This is not entirely surprising, because more professional legislatures attract more professional politicians, who may be more amenable to interest group activities. We also see that business activism is negatively associated with ward electoral schemes. While it makes general sense that interest groups might be more active in ward districts, which are smaller and provide greater odds of electoral success, it is not clear why other groups are not also more active.

24. In addition to the summary statistics in figure 10-2, we also would like to know where the union "activity advantage" is especially high or low (the regression analysis is not presented because of space considerations). Not surprisingly, given the findings from table 10-5, the most consistently significant factor is a collective bargaining law at the state level, which significantly enhances the activity of teacher unions vis-à-vis each of the other five types of groups. Furthermore, the urban variable is significant in four of five cases, being insignificant only in the teacher-business model. Finally, as the percentage of district students who are African American increases, the activity advantage of teacher unions declines in relation to race-based groups, school reform groups, and religious groups. The remaining institutional and constituency variables are only intermittently significant.

Political Competition

Democratic governance rests on the principle that the people hold public officials accountable through the electoral process. Competitive elections are thought to increase the likelihood that officeholders will be attentive to public concerns, while the absence of competition is thought to breed lethargy and irresponsible policymaking. Even the anticipation of elections can promote representation. What Price wrote more than thirty years ago is still true today: "The possibility of opposition . . . remains a powerful factor in attuning the incumbent to the process of representation."[25]

News accounts often depict school districts as stumbling from undisciplined governance to public unrest, to be cleaned up only when sufficient frustration builds up to create a reform slate, which produces a brief surge of healthy electoral competition. Reform advocates have suggested that boards are hobbled by low levels of voter participation and by incoherent elections, suggesting a need for partisan elections, slate-based elections, and holding elections concurrently with national elections.[26] While it is notoriously difficult to predict the consequences of political reform, we can use the data from our survey to ask what effect partisan elections and election timing currently have on the degree of electoral competition.

First, we simply explored how competitive school board elections typically were. How frequently were incumbents defeated? How difficult did board members consider their most recent election to be? Moreover, and particularly relevant to the consideration of reform, how much did electoral arrangements, constituency characteristics, or board professionalism affect board competition? Board competition was measured through several measures, the first of which simply asks respondents to rate the level of electoral competition on a four-point scale. The scale ranged from "not competitive" to "very competitive"; the results are shown in figure 10-2. The respondents depicted board environments that were only occasionally competitive. Fifty-seven percent reported that board elections were never or only occasionally competitive, while just 15 percent described the elections as "very competitive."

Second, board members were asked whether they would describe their last election as "very difficult," "somewhat difficult," "somewhat easy," or "very easy." According to figure 10-3, just 6 percent of respondents termed their election "very difficult," while more than 70 percent said that it was "somewhat" or "very easy" and nearly half reported that it was "very easy." Elections were reported to be somewhat more competitive in larger districts, with 48 percent of respondents in districts of more than 50,000 students terming their election "very difficult" or "somewhat difficult," compared with 25 percent in smaller districts.

25. Price (1973, p. 35).
26. Feuerstein (2002); Hess (2003).

Figure 10-2. *Reported Competitiveness of Local School Board Elections*

Percent of respondents

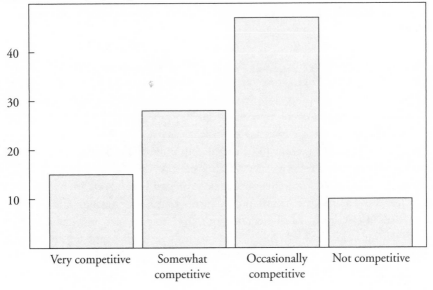

Source: Authors' data.

This indicates that candidates reported their own personal elections to be somewhat less competitive than might be expected given their overall assessment of the district norm. It is not clear whether candidates were overestimating overall competition or overstating the ease of their own elections.

A third question asked how many incumbent school board members seeking reelection were defeated by challengers since January 1, 1997 (the survey was completed in the spring of 2001). The answers ranged from zero to ten, with a mean of 1.01. Because the mean number of elected board members was 6.5 and some percentage of board members do not seek reelection and because probably no more than three-quarters of board members had stood for election between the beginning of 1997 and early 2001, this suggests that 25 percent or more of incumbents had been defeated in that time span.

Although this figure is only a very rough estimate, it may nevertheless surprise political scientists because it is significantly larger than the rate at which incumbents are defeated in elections for the U.S. Congress. According to Ornstein, Mann, and Malbin (1998), the average rate of defeat for House incumbents who sought reelection from 1990 to 1996 was 8.8 percent, while the figure for senators during the same time period was 9.6 percent. In the absolute, the figures indicate that incumbents of any office are highly likely to win reelection, although it is a surprise to see board members in greater electoral jeopardy.

Figure 10-3. *Reported Difficulty of Last Election*

Percent of respondents

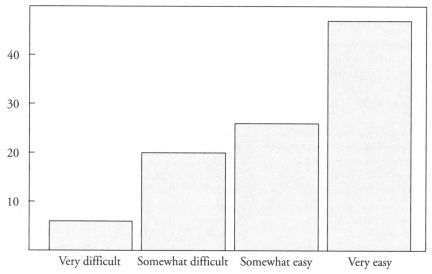

Source: Authors' data.

While city council elections might be a better comparison, there are no equivalent national data on political competition at that level. Scholars do not know the rate at which city council incumbents are defeated, let alone the systematic influence of interest groups in such contests or the source of funds for candidates, nor do they have reliable assessments of the level of competition.

Finally, respondents were asked whether they had run as part of a slate in their most recent election. Given the atomizing tendencies of nonpartisan elections (90 percent of electoral systems in this data set were nonpartisan) and the lack of spending on board member campaigns, how prevalent are efforts to organize and run coherent teams of candidates? Overall, respondents reported running as part of a slate in just 25 percent of the districts. The frequency with which board members had run as part of a slate was not dramatically affected by whether the district used a partisan ballot, with 23 percent of respondents in nonpartisan districts and 36 percent in partisan districts reporting that they had run as part of a slate. Slates were slightly less common in districts with more than 50,000 students than in smaller districts, with 15 percent of candidates in relatively large districts and 25 percent of those in smaller districts reporting themselves to be members of slates.

How was local board competition shaped by constituent, electoral, and institutional characteristics? Table 10-6 shows the results of the regression analyses

Table 10-6. *Factors Determining Reported Measures of Political Competition in Most Recent Election*[a]

Independent variable	Competitive	Easy	Slate	Number defeated
Percent of board seats elected	−0.314*	−0.104	−0.024	0.311***
by ward (0 to 1)	(0.109)	(0.115)	(0.142)	(0.111)
Length of board term (0 to 6)	−0.000	−0.159*	−0.071	−0.115
	(0.082)	(0.089)	(0.107)	(0.085)
Partisan election (1 = yes, 0 = no)	−0.220	0.074	0.445**	0.154
	(0.168)	(0.175)	(0.209)	(0.175)
Board elections concurrent with	0.069	0.043	0.014	0.036
national elections (1 = yes, 0 = no)	(0.060)	(0.063)	(0.078)	(0.062)
Board member receives some	−0.195*	−0.140	0.295**	0.074
pay (1 = yes, 0 = no)	(0.110)	(0.115)	(0.149)	(0.113)
District student enrollment	0.005*	0.007**	−0.001	0.001
	(0.003)	(0.003)	(0.004)	(0.003)
Percent of population over	−1.248	0.249	−1.830	−0.158
age sixty (0 to 1)	(1.048)	(1.115)	(1.424)	(1.082)
Percent of school population	0.521	−0.409	−0.232	0.326
African American (0 to 1)	(0.342)	(0.357)	(0.468)	(0.355)
Percent of school population	−0.510	−0.391	−0.063	0.416
Hispanic (0 to 1)	(0.325)	(0.356)	(0.436)	(0.326)
Percent of students on free or	0.133	0.777**	0.089	−0.438
reduced-price lunch (0 to 1)	(0.350)	(0.376)	(0.463)	(0.350)
Percent of community classified	0.413**	0.080	−0.116	−0.079
urban (0 to 1)	(0.168)	(0.181)	(0.221)	(0.172)
Percent of adult population	−0.825	1.000	−0.861	−4.050***
with college degree (0 to 1)	(1.286)	(1.362)	(1.738)	(1.390)
State collective bargaining	−0.091	0.242*	0.134	0.226*
law (1 = yes, 0 = no)	(0.121)	(0.131)	(0.163)	(0.124)
Weekly hours worked by board	0.005**	0.002	−0.004	0.001
members	(0.002)	(0.002)	(0.003)	(0.002)
Summary statistic				
N	535	512	508	521
Pseudo R^2	0.06	0.03	0.03	0.02

Source: Authors' data.

a. * $p < .10$; ** $p < .05$; *** $p < .01$. Standard errors are reported in parentheses.

conducted for each of the competition measures. As expected, based on our preceding discussion, district size proves to have significant effects on the reported difficulty and competitiveness of board elections. Board members in larger districts rated elections there as both more competitive and more difficult.

Similarly, collective bargaining laws appear to have increased some measures of contestation. Respondents in states with collective bargaining laws deemed their election campaigns to be more difficult; they also reported that incumbent board members were defeated at higher rates in the most recent election. More surprising, and contrary to theoretical expectations, factors such as whether elections were partisan, whether board members were compensated, and the education and poverty levels of the local electorate appear to have had no consistent effect on reported levels of competition.

It is particularly interesting that holding board elections concurrently with national elections does not appear to have had a significant effect on contestation or electoral competition. Previous research found that board elections held in even years had significantly higher levels of turnout than elections held in odd years, but the findings here suggest that such turnout does not necessarily translate into increased competition.[27] The questions of how to reconcile such disparities and whether the survey measures of electoral competition ought to be regarded as reliable on this point require future research.

Conclusion

The findings suggest that several common conceptions regarding school board elections appear to be fundamentally mistaken. Contrary to what is sometimes suggested by popular accounts, for instance, Bushweller (1996), our analysis shows that most school board elections involved minimal campaign spending, few board members received even one-quarter of their campaign funds from teacher unions or the business community, and neither religious organizations nor race-based groups were thought by board members to wield much influence on board decisions or on elections.

More in accord with expectations, the results suggest that teacher unions are generally the leading interest group in local board politics, that union influence is greater in larger, more urbanized districts and in states with collective bargaining laws, and that the influence of race-based groups increases with the size of the local African American and (to a lesser extent) Hispanic population.

An interesting contradiction is that teacher unions were reported to be influential, despite contributing an unexpectedly meager percentage of funds to the campaigns of board members. This suggests that unions, which have many ways of influencing elections and policy besides financial contributions, exert their influence through those other methods. The most notable of these may be their members' votes and the ability to organize, staff phone banks, distribute flyers, and undertake other such labor-intensive activities. Unions also have the ability to constrain district decisions through collective bargaining, a factor that often results in unions supporting district reforms because they are crafted with union concerns in mind.[28] It is entirely possible that unions,

27. Hess (2002); Towney, Sweeney, and Schmieder (1994).
28. See Hess (1999, pp. 77–81).

operating in this relatively stealthy fashion, could exert enormous influence without obviously doing so.

In addition, collective bargaining turns out to significantly boost both the relative influence of teacher unions and the level of contestation in board elections. At the same time, higher concentrations of African American and Hispanic populations boost the activity of race-based groups while moderating the activity of teacher unions. In short, it is a mistake to imagine that teacher unions are unilateral actors in board elections or that their influence is largely unfettered by context.

Teacher unions were clearly the most significant interest in school district elections. However, their advantage in activism was more variable than some have suggested, and their role as a funding source for candidates was generally quite minimal. The diffuse, oftentimes uncompetitive, and amateurish nature of district elections may make it difficult for anyone to consistently dominate outcomes through methods like campaign contributions or electioneering. On the other hand, those very conditions may also make it possible for any given interest group to play a significant role with resources that would seem very modest in a congressional or statewide context. What this implies for the conduct of board elections, electoral outcomes, or the substance of board decisionmaking requires further investigation.

How much does the pressure brought to bear on boards by their constituents ultimately shape policy outcomes after the election? Given their amateur status in comparison with other political institutions (low pay, few staff, and part-time commitment), school boards might be thought to be highly vulnerable to the appeals and exertions of organized interests. However, because school board seats are not very desirable in terms of material gain or prestige, many members may not care all that much about constituent pressure or even about reelection. The present analysis simply cannot tell us much about how the politics and conduct of board elections shape governance. That question must be left to future research.

School board politics in more urbanized districts appear to be significantly more professional, expensive, and competitive and more likely to be influenced by interest groups. This finding, in particular, suggests an empirical basis for crafting two distinct approaches to reforming board governance: one focused on the 100 to 200 largest and most urban districts, which constitute just a tiny percentage of all districts but enroll nearly half of all students, and a second strategy for the 99 percent of boards governing smaller, less urban districts. The results also provide reason to believe that board reforms should be shaped with an eye to local conditions, such as how professional the board is and how elections are conducted.

The bottom line is that efforts to interpret these findings inevitably depend on the point of view of the reader. Two observers can look at the data presented here and reach contradictory conclusions regarding the nature of school district governance and the desirability of prescriptions for reform. The findings we present might seem to suggest that certain interests are active participants in board elections or that they are surprisingly inert. If one sees signs of activity, one can interpret this as an unhealthy sign of interest group domination or alternatively as a reflection of pluralism at work. The objective here is not to advance claims on behalf of one reform agenda or another, but to ensure that all reformers operate with a clear understanding of the realities in the district in question. It is especially important to recognize that the challenges and politics of all districts are not similar. They vary dramatically, and potential remedies ought to be crafted with that variation in mind.

References

Berkman, Michael, and Eric Plutzer. 2001. "Grey Peril or Loyal Support: The Elderly and Expenditures on American Education." Paper presented at the annual meeting of the American Political Science Association. San Francisco, August 30–September 2.

———. 2002. "Paying to Educate 'Other People's Children': Race, Ethnicity, and Public School Finance." Paper presented at the annual meeting of the American Political Science Association. Boston, August 29–September 1.

Bezdek, Robert, David Billeaux, and Juan Carlos Huerta. 2000. "Latinos, At-Large Elections, and Political Change: Evidence from the 'Transition Zone.'" *Social Science Quarterly* 81 (March) : 207–25.

Brimelow, Peter. 2003. *The Worm in the Apple: How the Teacher Unions Are Destroying American Education*. New York: HarperCollins.

Bushweller, Kevin. 1996. "How to Get Elected." *American School Board Journal* 183 (July): 12–16.

Cibulka, James. 2001. "Old Wine, New Bottles." *Education Next* 1 (4): 28–35.

Cuban, Larry, and Michael Usdan. 2003. *Powerful Reforms with Shallow Roots: Improving America's Urban Schools*. New York: Teachers College Press.

Davidson, Chandler, and George Korbel. 1981. "At Large Elections and Minority Group Representation: A Reexamination of Historical and Contemporary Evidence." *Journal of Politics* 43 (4): 982–1005.

Dye, Thomas R. 1967. "Governmental Structure, Urban Environment, and Educational Policy." *Midwest Journal of Political Science* 11 (3): 353–80.

Education Commission of the States. 1999. "Effective School Governance: A Look at Today's Practice and Tomorrow's Promise." Denver.

Feuerstein, Abe. 1998. "Understanding Interest Group Involvement in the Process of Educational Governance." *Planning and Changing* 29 (1): 47–60.

———. 2002. "Elections, Voting, and Democracy in Local School District Governance." *Educational Policy* 16 (1): 15–36.

Finn, Chester E. 1992. "Reinventing Local Control." In *School Boards: Changing Local Control*, edited by Patricia F. First and Herbert J. Walberg, pp. 21–25. Berkeley, Calif.: McCutchan Publishing.

Fraga, Luis R., Kenneth J. Meier, and Robert E. England. 1986. "Hispanic Americans and Educational Policy: Limits to Equal Access." *Journal of Politics* 48 (4) : 850–76.

Glass, Thomas. 2002. "Is It Time for Elected Urban School Boards to Disappear?" Paper presented at Council of Great City Schools Meeting. Fort Lauderdale, Fla., October.

Henig, Jeffrey R., and others. 1999. *The Color of School Reform: Race, Politics, and the Challenge of Urban Education.* Princeton University.

Henig, Jeffrey R., and Wilbur Rich, eds. 2004. *Mayors in the Middle: Politics, Race, and Mayoral Control of Urban Schools.* Princeton University.

Hess, Frederick M. 1999. *Spinning Wheels: The Politics of Urban School Reform.* Brookings.

———. 2002. "School Boards at the Dawn of the Twenty-First Century: Conditions and Challenges of District Governance." Alexandria, Va.: National School Boards Association.

———. 2003. "Voice of the People." *American School Board Journal* 190 (4): 36–39.

Hess, Frederick M., and David L. Leal. 1999. "Politics and Sex-Related Programs in Urban Schooling." *Urban Affairs Review* 35 (1): 24–43.

———. 2001a. "A Shrinking 'Digital Divide'? The Provision of Classroom Computers across Urban School Systems." *Social Science Quarterly* 82 (4): 765–78.

———. 2001b. "The Opportunity to Engage: How Race, Class, and Institutions Structure Access to Educational Deliberation." *Educational Policy* 15 (3): 474–90.

———. 2003. "Technocracies, Bureaucracies, or Responsive Polities? Urban School Systems and the Politics of School Violence Prevention." *Social Science Quarterly* 84 (3): 526–42.

Hill, Paul T. 2003. "School Boards: Focus on School Performance, not Money and Patronage." Policy report. Washington: Progressive Policy Institute (January).

Jennings, M. Kent, and Harmon Zeigler. 1971. "Response Styles and Politics: The Case of School Boards." *Midwest Journal of Political Science* 15 (2): 290–321.

Kirst, Michael W. 2002. *Mayoral Influence, New Regimes, and Public School Governance.* CPRE Research Report Series RR-099. Consortium for Policy Research in Education, University of Pennsylvania, Graduate School of Education.

Leal, David L., and Frederick M. Hess. 2000. "The Politics of Bilingual Education Expenditures in Urban School Districts." *Social Science Quarterly* 81 (4): 1064–72.

Lieberman, Myron. 1997. *The Teacher Unions: How the NEA and AFT Sabotage Reform and Hold Students, Parents, Teachers, and Taxpayers Hostage to Bureaucracy.* New York: Free Press.

Meier, Kenneth J., and Joseph Stewart Jr. 1991. *The Politics of Hispanic Education.* State University of New York Press.

Meranto, Phillip. 1970. *School Politics in the Metropolis.* Columbus, Ohio: Charles E. Merril Publishing.

Moe, Terry M. 2003a. "Teacher Unions and School Board Elections." Paper presented at the conference "School Board Politics." Harvard University, John F. Kennedy School of Government, October 16–17.

———. 2003b. "Politics, Control, and the Future of School Accountability." In *No Child Left Behind? The Politics and Practice of School Accountability*, edited by Paul Peterson and Martin West. Brookings.

Ornstein, Norman, Thomas Mann, and Michael Malbin. 1998. *Vital Statistics on Congress.* Washington: Congressional Quarterly.

Orr, Marion. 1999. *Black Social Capital: The Politics of School Reform in Baltimore, 1986–1998.* University of Kansas.

Peterson, Paul E. 1976. *School Politics, Chicago Style.* University of Chicago.

Polinard, J. L., Robert Wrinkle, and Thomas Longoria. 1990. "Education and Governance: Representational Links to Second Generation Discrimination." *Western Political Quarterly* 43 (September): 631–46.

———. 1991. "The Impact of District Elections on the Mexican American Community: The Electoral Perspective." *Social Science Quarterly* 72 (September): 608–14.

Portz, John, Lana Stein, and Robin R. Jones. 1999. *City Schools and City Politics: Institutions and Leadership in Pittsburgh, Boston, and St. Louis.* University of Kansas.

Price, H. Douglas. 1973. "The Electoral Arena." In *The Congress and America's Future*, 2nd ed., edited by David B. Truman. Englewood Cliffs, N.J.: Prentice-Hall.

Regnerus, Mark D., David Sikkink, and Christian Smith. 1999. "Voting with the Christian Right: Contextual and Individual Patterns of Electoral Influence." *Social Forces* 77 (4): 1375–1401.

Rich, Wilbur C. 1996. *Black Mayors and School Politics: The Failure of Reform in Detroit, Gary, and Newark.* New York: Garland.

Stone, Clarence N., and others. 2001. *Building Civic Capacity: The Politics of Reforming Urban Schools.* University of Kansas.

Towney, Arthur J., Dwight P. Sweeney, and June H. Schmieder. 1994. "School Board Elections: A Study of Citizen Voting Patterns." *Urban Education* 29 (1): 50–62.

Wirt, Frederick M., and Michael W. Kirst. 1972. *The Political Web of American Schools.* New York: Little, Brown.

Zax, Jeffrey. 1990. "Election Methods and Black and Hispanic City Council Membership." *Social Science Quarterly* 71 (June): 340–55.

Zeigler, Harmon L., and M. Kent Jennings. 1974. *Governing American Schools: Political Interaction in Local School Districts.* North Scituate, Mass.: Duxbury Press.

11

Teacher Unions and School Board Elections

TERRY M. MOE

In the folklore of American education, school boards are shining examples of local democracy. But folklore is folklore. During the early years of the twentieth century, school boards were often under the thumb of party machines. And even later, as Progressive reforms weakened the parties, governance of the schools shifted to newly powerful groups—business, middle-class activists, education administrators—with their own special interests to pursue (Peterson 1985; Tyack 1974).

Scholars have rarely studied school board politics, so we may never have a good sense of just how democratic the system was in those days. But one thing is clear. During the 1960s and 1970s, the balance of power within American education underwent yet another dramatic shift, generating a new brand of special interest politics that has been with us ever since—and that poses a serious challenge for democratic governance.

This transformation was brought about by the unionization of teachers. Before the 1960s, states did not have collective bargaining laws for public employees. Few teachers belonged to unions, and teachers had little political power. All that changed during the next two decades, as fierce battles over collective bargaining rights were fought throughout the country. By the early 1980s, virtually all school districts of any size (outside the South) were unionized, and the two major teacher unions—the National Education Association

(NEA) and the American Federation of Teachers (AFT)—had become the de facto political leaders of the education establishment (Moe 2001).

The teacher unions have all the requisites of political power. They are supremely well organized at the local, state, and national levels. They have a guaranteed source of money (member dues) that can be converted into campaign contributions and used for lobbying and political advertising. And most important, they have millions of members spread almost uniformly across the country, along with armies of activists in virtually every political district who participate in electoral campaigns (Lieberman 1997). No other political group in the country can claim such a formidable combination of weapons. Indeed, in an ongoing study of the fifty states, the teacher unions were judged throughout the 1990s to be the single most powerful interest group in the nation, outdistancing trial lawyers, bankers, insurance companies, farm groups, and all others (Thomas and Hrebenar 1999). In the 2002 study they came in second, bested only by general business groups (Thomas and Hrebenar 2004).

From a democratic standpoint, the rise of teacher unions is troubling because it may give one special interest group too much power in the politics of education while other groups, particularly broad-based ones like parents and taxpayers, have too little. But it is also troubling because teachers are not just any social group. They are employees of the education system. And as such they have vested interests—in areas such as job security, higher wages and fringe benefits, costly pensions, restrictive job rules, bigger budgets, higher taxes, lax accountability, limits on parental choice, and many others—that may often conflict with what is good for children, schools, and the public interest.

This "power of the agent" is not unique to education. In all areas of social policy, elected officials make policies on behalf of their constituents and hire agents to carry those policies out. But precisely because the authorities are elected, the agents can take an active part in the electoral process to determine who gets to be an authority in the first place and what their policy preferences are. To the extent that the agents are successful, democratic authority is essentially turned on its head, with the authorities doing the bidding of employees rather than the other way around and government run for the benefit of vested interests rather than society at large. The teacher unions are a notable example of public bureaucrats organizing to gain political power. But they are just the tip of a very big iceberg. Public sector unions are now prominent in virtually every sector of government—not just in the United States, but in every developed democracy—and they are extremely active in politics (Moe 2003a).

We do not know much about public sector unions' actual political clout because they have rarely been studied as political actors. The teacher unions are no exception. In the more popular literature at the fringe of social science, there are a few books and articles that provide insight into what the teacher unions do in politics (Lieberman 1997; Brimelow 2003). But there is little systematic research on the unions and, for that matter, very little on the politics of education as a whole.

One of my purposes here is simply to present some basic facts on the role of teacher unions in school board elections. In a recent paper, I used data on electoral outcomes to show that the teacher unions are quite successful at getting their favored candidates elected to local school boards (Moe 2003a). Here, using a data set derived from interviews with school board candidates, I take a closer look at the political process itself: at what the unions do in elections, what kinds of candidates they support, and what it all means for the composition of school boards.

My second purpose is to offer some theoretical arguments about what we should expect and then to see how those expectations square with the data. The arguments essentially come down to this: there are good reasons for thinking that teacher unions are ordinarily the most potent force in school board elections, but also that their power is constrained in basic ways that can vary across contexts. Thus, while school board politics should often be tilted in the unions' favor—a negative for local democracy—there are built-in limits on what they are able to achieve.

The Survey

This study focuses on school board politics in California, where interviews were conducted with 526 school board candidates from 253 school districts. The interviews were carried out over a period of several years, beginning in 2000 and continuing through 2003, with districts and candidates chosen randomly.

Why California? The obvious alternative is a national cross-section.[1] But because states and localities often do not publish election information for school boards, the information can be gathered only by dealing with each school district individually (and perhaps the county and state election offices). I leave it to other researchers to do that. In California, statewide information on school board elections is readily available through the League of Women Voters.

California is an attractive subject of study anyway. It is the nation's most populous state, enrolling more than 10 percent of the nation's school children. And it is geographically large and demographically diverse, yielding a population of school districts that is enormously varied—urban and rural, big and small, conservative and liberal, white and minority. While the California Teachers Association (CTA) is noted for its political power at the state level, teacher unions in

1. To my knowledge, there is only one national survey on school boards and their elections, which was carried out by Hess (2002) for the National School Boards Association. That survey is the basis for the Hess and Leal analysis in chapter 10 in this volume.

virtually all states are noted for their state-level power too, and there is no reason to think that local politics in California is much different from local politics anywhere else. Indeed, to the extent that California has unique factors that set the state apart, they may well weaken the unions' incentives for local political activity. One of those factors is Proposition 13, adopted in 1978, which drastically limits local property taxes and thus the financial discretion of local school districts. Another is the radical equalization of spending across school districts required by the state supreme court's *Serrano* decisions, which limit local financial discretion still further. If anything, then, school boards may actually be less attractive targets of union influence in California than elsewhere, and the unions less involved in local politics. On the whole, though, I would expect the basic political patterns that turn up in California to be fairly indicative of what happens nationwide.

Now let me provide a few details about the California data. The sample of districts was stratified by enrollment to ensure that roughly equal numbers of small, medium, and large districts would be included in the analysis. While the vast majority of California's school districts are quite small (in terms of enrollment), the vast majority of California's school-age children are enrolled in much larger districts—indeed, 12 percent are enrolled in the Los Angeles unified school district alone. These larger districts needed to be oversampled in order to provide a solid basis for comparison and generalization and for understanding politics in the kinds of districts that matter most.

As this is an analysis of elections, the focus was naturally on districts that actually held elections in recent years. When districts failed to hold elections, it was because there was no competition for seats on their school boards. This absence of competition is unusual in the larger districts but not uncommon in the smaller ones, which sometimes have a hard time finding people who are willing to serve. As a result, the smaller districts that made it into our sample may be somewhat more competitive on average than the entire population of smaller districts statewide.

Once the districts were selected to be part of the sample, an effort was made to contact candidates who had run in these districts' elections. Within any given district, of course, different candidates can be expected to offer somewhat different assessments of district politics, and it is reasonable to worry that the differences could be systematic—for example, that winners may offer perspectives (on union power, say) that differ from those of losers. To try to arrive at more reliable estimates, my assistants and I made an effort to interview at least two candidates from each district and to choose one winner and one loser. Because it proved difficult to get accurate, up-to-date phone numbers on these people and because about a quarter of the elections involved just two candidates vying for one seat, we often (in 43 percent of the cases) had to settle for one interview per district. The sample as a whole is about evenly split between winners and losers, however, ensuring diversity in the aggregate.[2]

Baseline Expectations

The literature on school board politics does not offer a coherent theory to suggest what we should expect or why. But its basic thrust is that politics in this realm is complicated and diverse, with numerous groups competing for power. Indeed, that is the theme of the Hess and Leal analysis in chapter 10 of this volume. Another common claim is that if any group in this pluralist system is predominant, it is the business community (for example, Wirt and Kirst 2001; Wong 1992). In my view, both these arguments are wide of the mark. To explain why, I will set out some simple ideas about school board politics and teacher unions that lead to very different conclusions.

Let's begin with the teacher unions. Their survival and well-being as organizations are rooted in collective bargaining, because this is how they get resources and expand their membership. Their fundamental interests as organizations, then, have to do with gaining collective bargaining rights, and with keeping and increasing their members and resources through successful negotiations with local school boards. These negotiations in turn yield the job security, material benefits, and working conditions that teachers value, and that produce all manner of related policies—bigger budgets and smaller class sizes, for example—that make unions and teachers better off (Moe 2001; Lieberman 1997). Local democracy presents them with attractive opportunities for promoting these fundamental interests. The fact that school boards are elected means that the teacher unions can actually participate in choosing—or even literally choose—the management they will be bargaining with. It goes without saying that they should have strong incentives to take advantage of those opportunities, and thus to seek power in school board elections.

How powerful should we expect them to be? They should often be quite powerful indeed, because the cards are stacked in their favor. Unlike parents, taxpayers, and other broad constituencies, teachers are well organized. With the

---

2. For obvious reasons, this cannot be regarded as a true random sample. But I have no reason to think that the respondents we were able to locate and interview are somehow unrepresentative of the larger population of candidates. It is possible that those who left the area are different in some way from those who did not, but I would be surprised if any differences were relevant to school board issues. Also, it is possible that the union-oriented nature of the survey caused certain people—those especially sympathetic to unions—to refuse to be interviewed and that this biased our sample toward candidates who were less sympathetic. Such a possibility is hard to judge, because we usually did not know why people refused to be interviewed (or even whether they refused at all). But the fact is that, while we did get a few explosive refusals from union partisans, no more than ten people explicitly refused to do the survey. The real problem was locating them, not getting them to participate.

great help (in most states) of favorable labor legislation, they long ago overcame the collective action problems that prevent many groups from participating effectively in politics (Olson 1965). They also have a guaranteed source of money for financing campaigns, paid staff to coordinate political activities, and activist members willing to do the trench-work of campaigning. For these and related reasons, the unions have major advantages over other groups that should translate into electoral power. And this outcome is all the more likely given that school board elections tend to be low-interest, low-turnout affairs in which organized action can be especially consequential (Wirt and Kirst 2001; Moe 2003a).

Any effort to develop a coherent perspective on district-level politics, then, needs to start with the teacher unions. They are the ones to beat. Nonetheless, this is just a baseline. Conditions vary across districts, and there are conditions under which the unions might have a difficult time exercising power. In the following sections, I extend the perspective I have begun to develop here by discussing and then bringing evidence to bear on four basic types of conditions— each of them a potential constraint—that need to be taken into account for a more complete understanding of district politics and union power. They are the size of the union, political pluralism, political culture, and incumbency.

Union Size

The larger unions should typically have more money, more paid staff, and more activists than the smaller unions, and thus a greater organizational capacity for political action. So there is reason to expect, for reasons of size alone, that union activity and power will be at their height in the largest districts and will drop off as districts and unions become smaller.

What do the data have to say? The survey asks candidates whether the unions in their districts engage in certain electoral activities: supporting candidates, giving them money, recruiting people to run, mobilizing members to vote, mobilizing other citizens to vote, making phone calls, campaigning door to door, and providing mailings and publicity. The results, aggregated to the district level, are described in table 11-1.[3]

The relationship between union political activity and the size of the district (and thus the union) is quite dramatic. In districts with enrollments of less than 1,000, teacher unions often seem to play little or no role in school board elections. They regularly support candidates for office in less than 25 percent of

---

3. As there are often multiple candidates per district, we need to move from individual responses to summary scores for each district. One way to do this—a method I rely on throughout this chapter—is to quantify candidate responses, average them within districts, and then categorize districts according to their average scores. In this method, candidate responses for any given dimension of union activity are assigned a 1 for *yes*, a 0 for *no*, and averaged within each district. Districts are then coded as having that type of union activity if their average is greater than .5, and they are categorized as not having it if their average is less than .5. For a relatively small number of districts, the average is exactly .5, and they cannot be placed into one of these categories. They are labeled as "mixed."

Table 11-1. Union Activity and Influence, by District Size[a]

Type of activity	District size					
	Less than 1,000	1,000 to 2,500	2,500 to 5,000	5,000 to 10,000	10,000 to 25,000	More than 25,000
Supporting candidates						
Yes	24	35	45	78	90	92
Mixed	11	6	12	7	5	3
No	66	59	42	15	5	5
Giving money						
Yes	25	23	18	55	72	94
Mixed	0	3	18	7	7	6
No	75	75	64	39	21	0
Recruiting candidates						
Yes	6	23	9	14	27	52
Mixed	15	3	15	14	14	15
No	79	74	76	73	59	33
Mobilizing members						
Yes	29	57	50	76	85	100
Mixed	17	11	24	2	7	0
No	54	31	26	21	8	0
Mobilizing other voters						
Yes	22	46	33	55	73	86
Mixed	17	14	21	12	11	9
No	61	40	45	33	16	6
Making phone calls						
Yes	15	33	16	50	64	97
Mixed	12	3	16	16	12	3
No	73	64	68	34	24	0
Door-to-door campaigning						
Yes	15	21	19	37	38	68
Mixed	9	6	3	15	15	15
No	76	73	78	49	47	18
Mailings and publicity						
Yes	18	26	15	69	75	94
Mixed	0	3	15	5	7	3
No	82	71	70	26	19	3
Union importance in elections						
Important	43	57	57	70	64	82
Mixed	11	11	3	2	13	8
Unimportant	46	31	40	28	23	11
N	36	35	33	43	59	36

Source: Author's data.

a. Figures represent the percentage of districts falling into each category, based on the average scores of its respondents (see footnote 3). District size = number of students enrolled. *N* = number of districts.

these smaller districts, and most of the other political activities are even less common. For example, they make campaign-related phone calls and engage in door-to-door campaigning in just 15 percent of the cases, and they provide mailings and other publicity in only 18 percent.

As districts get larger, however, the unions themselves become larger and more politically capable as organizations. They become much more active along all dimensions, to the point that, in the biggest districts with the biggest unions, every mode of political action (except perhaps recruiting candidates) is common. The unions support candidates for office in 92 percent of these districts. They make phone calls in 97 percent, they campaign door to door in 68 percent, and they provide mailings and publicity in 94 percent.

Given these differences, it is only natural to expect that the teacher unions will be much more powerful in the larger districts than in the smaller ones, and thus more successful at getting sympathetic candidates elected to office. So let's take a first look at (perceived) union influence and see what the data seem to suggest.

As one way of measuring influence, the survey asked candidates a simple question: "In general, how important would you say the teachers union is in your district's school board elections?" Their responses are summarized in the bottom portion of table 11-1. According to the candidates who responded, the teacher unions are often important in elections even in the smaller districts, where they are not very active. In districts with less than 1,000 students, unions are regarded as important in 43 percent of the districts—a rather high level of importance given the unions' starkly low level of activity. Moreover, in districts with 1,000–2,500 students—districts that are still quite tiny, with unions seemingly inactive—the unions are regarded as important in 57 percent of the cases and unimportant in just 31 percent. Something is clearly going on in these districts that is not being picked up by union activity level alone.

Nonetheless, it is also true that assessments of union importance grow with the size of the district. And in the largest districts, the unions are almost always regarded as important (82 percent) and rarely regarded as unimportant (11 percent). Big districts have powerful unions—or so it seems.

Political Pluralism

The other side of the coin, however, is that big districts may also present the teacher unions with certain problems that make it more difficult for them to wield power. If the literature's emphasis on pluralist politics is ever warranted, it would seem to apply best to these larger districts—for they are likely to have a greater number and variety of social groups than smaller districts, and it is reasonable to argue that this social pluralism should tend to generate more competition for the teacher unions and thus limit their power.

As I suggested earlier, we cannot get carried away with this argument. Many broad constituencies are unlikely to achieve effective political organization due to collective action problems. Parents are typically organized only through the local PTA (if then); but the PTA is a parent-teacher organization, not solely a parent organization, and research has shown that it rarely opposes the teacher unions (Haar 2002). Virtually all other groups that manage to get organized—business groups, community groups, ethnic groups, religious groups—do not focus on education. They have broader social and political concerns and allocate their attention and resources accordingly. The unions, meantime, are not just any old group in an apparently pluralist system. Because they have vested interests in public education, they have a strong incentive to be politically active, and they are totally focused on education. In some districts at certain times—times of crisis, scandal, or deep frustration, say—other groups may decide to invest in educational politics. But under most conditions, only the unions are likely to have both the motivation and the resources to do so.

Even so, competition may moderate their power, especially in the larger districts. And this means that district size may be capturing two very different—and countervailing—effects. First, because there is an almost perfect correlation between district and union size, the unions' organizational capacity should grow with district size and so should their power. But second, because political pluralism is also more common in larger districts, the unions should find it more difficult to wield power as districts get bigger. If both effects are indeed operating, that could explain why the small unions in small districts seem to be more politically potent than their miniscule organizational capacity would lead us to expect. They do not have much capacity for political action, but neither do they have much competition.

The survey allows us to explore these issues in a bit more depth. Let's begin by looking at the competitiveness of elections. Candidates were asked to characterize their districts' school board elections in one of two ways: "Usually they are vigorously contested with a lot of campaign activity" or "There is usually little competition or campaign activity." Their responses, displayed in table 11-2, suggest that the electoral context changes radically as the districts increase in size. Elections are seldom vigorously contested in the smaller districts. Of districts with less than 1,000 students, only 13 percent are regarded as having competitive elections. When we turn to districts with between 1,000 and 2,500 students, the corresponding figure is just 14 percent, and for districts with enrollments of 2,500 to 5,000, it is 17 percent. As district size increases, however, the level of competition and campaigning increases dramatically—to the point that, in the largest districts, 61 percent are regarded as having highly competitive elections and just 18 percent are seen as having little competition.[4]

---

4. As mentioned earlier, these figures may tend to overstate the competitiveness of local elections, especially for smaller districts, because our sample is drawn entirely from the population of districts that actually held elections.

Table 11-2. *Electoral Competition and Union Influence, by District Size*[a]

Survey item	Less than 1,000	1,000 to 2,500	2,500 to 5,000	5,000 to 10,000	10,000 to 25,000	More than 25,000
			District size			
How much competition do elections involve?						
Much	13	14	17	24	44	61
Mixed	18	28	43	28	26	21
Little	69	58	40	48	30	18
N	39	36	35	46	61	38
Are unions the most influential group?						
Yes	39	44	38	49	42	50
Mixed	19	9	15	18	19	21
No	42	47	47	33	39	29
N	36	34	34	45	59	38
Are unions the most influential group? (adjusted)						
Yes	59	72	69	70	61	68
Mixed	13	3	6	9	13	13
No	28	25	26	22	26	18
N	39	36	35	46	61	38

Source: Author's data.

a. Figures represent the percentage of districts falling into each category, based on the average scores of its respondents (see footnote 3). District size = number of students enrolled. *N* = number of districts.

We have at least one good indication, then, that the unions in larger districts do indeed face more competition than they do in smaller districts, as we should expect. But does this competition really limit union power very much? And what about the smaller districts—does the lack of competition mean that all groups, including the unions, are without influence? Or does it mean that there are fewer obstacles in the way of union control?

We cannot answer these questions with certainty, of course, but the survey does shed some additional light on them. For instance, it asks candidates whether, compared to all other organized groups in their districts, the teacher unions are the *most* influential. The district-level results, set out in the middle of table 11-2, are interesting on two counts. First, while the unions are regarded as more influential in the larger districts, the differences across contexts are not very impressive or consistent—and the unions again show surprising strength in the smaller districts, where they play little overt role in campaigns. Second, the teacher unions in the larger districts do not come across a consistently dominant political force. They are rated as the single most influential group in 50 percent

Table 11-3. *Influence of Groups Other than Teacher Unions, by District Size*[a]

Other actors	District size	
	Less than 10,000	More than 10,000
Parents	34	13
Party or ideological groups	6	11
Religious groups	4	6
Newspapers	2	17
Other unions	7	26
Prominent individuals	8	12
Community groups	15	13
Ethnic groups	1	4
Business groups	11	22
No groups	36	14
N	131	78

Source: Author's data.

a. Responses are from candidates who, after saying that the teacher union is not the most influential group in the district, were asked to indicate what other groups are more influential. Figures represent the percentage of districts in which the relevant group was mentioned by at least half of the respondents in the district. District size = number of students enrolled. N = number of districts.

of the largest districts and in 42 percent of the next-largest districts. These figures hardly reflect the kind of pluralistic politics that education scholars seem to envision, as any pluralism here is clearly tilted in favor of the teacher unions. But in about half the larger districts, other groups were regarded as either more powerful than the unions or as competing with them on an equal footing.

Table 11-3 provides more detail. Candidates who said that the unions are not the most influential group in district politics were asked to indicate what other organized groups are more influential, and their responses are enlightening. As the table shows, large districts are clearly more pluralistic than small districts (aside from the role of parents), as we would expect, with more groups of different types regarded as influential. But that said, the one group that education scholars would surely expect to rise to the top here—business—is singled out for its influence in just 22 percent of the large districts and 11 percent of the smaller districts. Remember, we are dealing here solely with districts in which the unions are said not to be dominant, so these figures are especially telling about the weak role of business.[5]

With perhaps one exception (parents in small districts), the other types of possible competitors—party and ideological groups, religious groups, newspapers, other unions, prominent individuals, community groups, ethnic groups—

5. In an earlier version of this chapter (Moe 2003b), I also presented data on the occupations of school board members. The findings contradict the conventional wisdom that business interests are prominently represented on school boards (see Wirt and Kirst 2001).

do no better than business and usually do worse. If the teacher unions are being effectively counterbalanced, then it is happening through the action of different types of groups in different districts. In some districts, community groups may be especially influential; in others, prominent individuals; in still others, religious groups. That is quite plausible, and perhaps very important. But still, no group provides a consistent counterweight to union power. In small districts, parents come closest. But they trump the teacher unions in just 34 percent of these districts, which hardly means that they can be counted on. And "parents" may often refer to the PTA, which is typically not a counterbalancing force at all.

A closer look at the numbers in table 11-3 raises additional questions about the potency of pluralism. In the first place, the groups most often singled out in large districts (and sometimes in small districts) as more influential than the teacher unions are *other unions*—meaning, most often, the unions representing classified (nonteaching) employees of the school districts. These unions are allies of the teacher unions. In the second place, many candidates were not able to name *any* group that is more influential than the teacher unions, so there is reason to think that the teacher unions are in fact the most influential organized group in those districts.

If we reclassify the problem districts—the ones in which no other group is mentioned or in which only other unions are mentioned—then things look quite different. As the adjusted figures at the bottom of table 11-2 show, the unions now emerge as the major political force in about two-thirds of all districts—and interestingly, about the same ratio prevails for districts of all sizes.

This reclassification makes some assumptions and may err on the side of attributing too much power to the unions. (The multivariate analysis sheds more light on this issue later on.) I offer it here for the purpose of comparison, knowing that the truth may lie somewhere between the two classifications. Even so, there is good reason to doubt that the diversity of groups often observed in school politics reflects a genuinely pluralistic politics—and good reason for challenging the Hess and Leal analysis in this volume, which sees diversity as evidence for effective pluralism. This is not to claim that the teacher unions always get their way or that other groups do not count. But it does appear that the kind of pluralism operating in local elections is tilted in favor of the teacher unions, and that this is the case for both small and large districts.

Small Districts, Pluralism, and Union Satisfaction

Let's go back and look more closely at the smaller districts. There is clear evidence that the unions are not very active in these districts, yet there is also evidence that they are surprisingly influential. How can they be influential if they are not doing much of anything? Part of the answer may be that they face little competition. So let me elaborate on this theme a bit.

It is reasonable to suggest that when California's teacher unions first came on the scene in the 1960s and early 1970s, they entered a system controlled by other social interests, and they had strong incentives to take control by getting sympathetic people elected to local school boards and keeping them there. Acting on these incentives presumably brought them into conflict with the established interests, a period of upheaval ensued, and a new equilibrium emerged that reflected the newcomers' power.

If this theory is roughly correct, then what we are witnessing today is an outgrowth of political battles that were fought some thirty years ago. In districts where the unions were largely successful, there may be no political battles at all in today's world. The districts are simply in an equilibrium satisfactory to the unions, everyone recognizes the new reality, and politics is peaceful. This could be what has happened in many of the smaller districts, whose environments—because they are relatively homogeneous, stable, and noncompetitive—may help to support such a political equilibrium. In the larger districts, on the other hand, where the political environment is inherently more diverse, competitive, and subject to change, the unions—even if powerful—may be challenged more often by opposing groups, and a high level of union political activity may be required to maintain control. The serenity that prevails in many smaller districts, then, may often hide the fact that teacher unions are satisfied with what they are getting and simply have no need to be more active than they are. In many cases their inactivity may be a sign of power, not of weakness.

Our data suggest as much. Candidates were asked whether, in their own districts, the teacher unions tend to be satisfied with the school boards or would prefer to see members elected who are more pro-union. As table 11-4 shows, the percentage of unions that are regarded as satisfied with their school boards varies with the size of the district. It is in the *small* districts that unions are most likely to be satisfied. In districts with less than 1,000 students, for example, where the teacher unions are almost totally inactive in political campaigns, the unions are satisfied 53 percent of the time. By contrast, they are satisfied in 32 percent of the largest districts, where they are extremely active.

The smaller districts, as we have seen, are contexts in which there is little competition and unions are not very active. So it should come as no surprise that, over the entire population of districts, unions tend to be more satisfied in districts with little competition and where they are not very active. It is worth noting, however, that these same relationships hold up if we look within just the subpopulation of small districts themselves. I will not lay all these numbers out in another table, but suffice it to say that in districts with fewer than 5,000 students, the teacher unions tended to be

—More satisfied in contexts where they are *not* very active: they are satisfied in 50 percent of the small districts with little union political activity, but in 33 percent of the small districts with relatively high levels of union political activity.

Table 11-4. *Union Satisfaction, by District Size*[a]

Survey item	District size					
	Less than 1,000	1,000 to 2,500	2,500 to 5,000	5,000 to 10,000	10,000 to 25,000	More than 25,000
Are unions satisfied with the school board?						
Yes	53	44	42	37	34	32
Mixed	9	27	18	24	14	24
No	38	29	39	39	52	43
N	32	34	33	41	56	37

Source: Author's data.

a. Figures represent the percentage of districts falling into each category, based on the average scores of its respondents (see footnote 3). District size = number of students enrolled. *N* = number of districts.

—More satisfied when they are *not* regarded as important players in electoral politics: they are satisfied in 54 percent of the small districts where they are regarded as unimportant but in 42 percent of the small districts where they are regarded as important.

—More satisfied when there is *little* competition or campaigning on anyone's part: they are satisfied in 55 percent of the small districts that are noncompetitive but in 36 percent of the small districts that are competitive.

Here again, the evidence suggests that the peace and serenity so characteristic of small districts are not indications that the unions are weak, nor that they are not getting what they want. Indeed, there may very well be nothing going on in many of these districts—and no overt union activity—precisely because the unions are happy with the status quo there, a status quo that was essentially determined years ago.

Political Culture

Different districts may have different political cultures, as measured by a variety of social characteristics: party and ideology, ethnicity, income and education, religion, and perhaps others. Group competition aside, if the electoral system is reasonably democratic in responding to the public and reflecting its popular culture—a big "if" that I have left open to question here—these differences in public values should affect the kinds of platforms that attract public support, the kinds of people that get elected, and thus the ability of unions to get what they want. Three implications for union power stand out, which I illustrate with reference to the dimension of political culture on which I have information: party and ideology.

The first implication is that some districts—those that are Democratic and liberal, in this case—will have cultures that are more sympathetic to union demands and more likely to elect union sympathizers to office. Union power should be easier to exercise in culturally friendly environments.

The second is that, in environments that are relatively unfriendly—Republican and conservative ones—the unions do not have to sit by while hostile candidates are elected and their own candidates go down in flames. They can adapt by supporting candidates who are sufficiently representative of the local culture to be electable—sufficiently Republican and conservative, in some sense—but who, on the specific issues that unions care about, are more sympathetic to union positions than the other candidates are. In this way, the unions can gain as much as possible—and become as powerful as possible—under difficult circumstances.

The third is that the content of union power may be very different across these contexts. In friendly contexts, the unions may have high win rates and very sympathetic boards. In unfriendly contexts, their win rates may also be high, due to the compromises they make in endorsing culturally electable candidates; however, their victories may generate school boards that are less sympathetic to their cause. They can be powerful, in the sense of winning elections, yet not highly successful at getting what they want. This is the constraint of political culture.

Now let's take a look at the data. If we categorize districts as Republican, mixed-partisan, or Democratic on the basis of the party registration of the citizens who live there, we find that union endorsements do indeed vary in a systematic way across political cultures (table 11-5).[6] In school districts that are Republican and (presumably) conservative, 55 percent of the candidates endorsed by the teacher union are Republicans and 56 percent are conservatives—figures that would otherwise be something of a shock, given the teacher unions' almost exclusive support of Democrats in state and national politics (Lieberman 1997).[7] As the school district populations get more liberal and Democratic, so do the candidates that the unions endorse—although, interestingly, the unions continue to endorse fair numbers of Republicans (33 percent) and conservatives (38 percent) even in heavily Democratic environments.

These findings are a sign that the usual labels may not mean as much in local politics as they do in state and national politics. In any event, what ultimately counts for the unions is not the labels, but how sympathetic the candidates are

6. The party registration data for each school district were gathered from county election offices. I score districts as Republican if at least 55 percent of the voters who register with one of the two major parties are Republican, Democratic if at least 55 percent are Democratic, and mixed-partisan if the party balance is somewhere in between.

7. A candidate's party identification was measured by asking, "In American politics more generally, do you consider yourself a Democrat, Republican, Independent, or other?" Ideology was measured by asking, "How would you describe your political ideology: Liberal, Moderate, or Conservative?" Moderates were then asked, "Would you say you lean toward being liberal or lean toward being conservative?" Those expressing a leaning were categorized as liberal or conservative in the present analysis.

Table 11-5. *Union-Endorsed Candidates' Party and Ideology, by District Political Culture*[a]

Candidates	Republican district	Mixed district	Democratic district
Party			
Republican	55	46	33
Independent	11	11	13
Democratic	34	44	53
N	47	46	75
Ideology			
Conservative	56	48	38
Moderate	13	20	14
Liberal	31	33	49
N	48	46	74

Source: Author's data.

a. Figures represent the percentage of endorsed candidates with the relevant characteristics. *N* = number of candidates responding.

to union interests. To get at this, the survey asks candidates a number of specific questions about the effects of teacher union influence on various aspects of public education—costs, academic performance, school organization, conflict, teacher professionalism, and teacher quality.[8] As a follow-up, it then asks for a summary evaluation: "In general, what is your attitude toward collective bargaining in public education?" The results (table 11-6) have a lot to say about unions and their political environments:

—The vast majority of school board candidates (66 percent) have positive general attitudes toward collective bargaining. Even among Republicans—indeed, even among Republicans who are not endorsed by the unions—the majority take a positive approach to this most crucial of union concerns. Thus districts that are heavily Republican and conservative may well be unfriendly territory for unions compared with districts that are heavily Democratic and liberal, but they are not necessarily unfriendly in an absolute sense.

—Candidates are more critical of union influence when assessing its specific effects. Almost two-thirds think that union influence leads to higher costs, 42 percent think that it leads to greater conflict, and 40 percent think that it leads to more rigid organizations. But these aspects of schooling are several steps removed from what happens in the classroom, and even supporters of collective bargaining might agree with these criticisms. The more telling finding is that candidates are quite positive on the two items that are most directly related to

8. For these items, the lead-in wording on the survey was "When teachers unions do have influence, what do you consider the most likely effects on public education?" This was followed by various aspects of education (for example, costs) and the possible effects on each (for example, higher costs, lower costs, no effect).

Table 11-6. *Candidate Attitudes toward Effects of Collective Bargaining, by Party and Union Endorsement*[a]

Attitude toward effects of collective bargaining	Republican			Democratic			All
	Not endorsed	Endorsed	Total	Not endorsed	Endorsed	Total	
General effects							
Negative	46	31	40	32	19	25	32
Neutral	3	4	3	2	0	1	2
Positive	51	65	57	67	81	75	66
Effect on cost							
Higher	82	55	70	68	50	59	65
No effect	18	36	26	29	47	38	31
Lower	0	9	4	3	3	3	4
Effect on academic performance							
Lower	42	14	29	17	9	13	22
No effect	32	36	35	41	31	37	35
Higher	26	50	36	41	60	50	42
Effect on organization							
Rigid	53	36	46	42	33	37	40
No effect	18	24	21	35	27	31	25
Flexible	29	40	33	24	39	32	34
Effect on conflict							
More	65	36	52	40	29	34	42
No effect	11	21	16	21	27	25	20
Less	24	43	32	39	44	41	38
Effect on professionalism							
Less	47	19	35	34	18	27	32
No effect	33	32	33	32	35	33	33
More	20	49	32	34	46	40	36
Effect on teaching							
Worse	41	9	27	22	6	14	20
No effect	40	47	43	50	40	46	44
Better	19	45	30	28	54	41	35
Average of specific effects							
Negative	64	34	51	44	25	35	43
Neutral	8	15	12	13	10	12	12
Positive	28	51	38	43	64	53	46
N	76	54	129	60	67	127	256

Source: Author's data.

a. Figures represent the percentage of candidates giving the relevant response. *N* = number of candidates.

how much kids learn—namely, academic performance and teacher quality. Only 22 percent think that union influence has negative consequences for academic performance, and only 20 percent think that it threatens teacher quality.

—Party does make a difference in candidate attitudes. Comparing all Republicans to all Democrats (disregarding endorsements), we see that Republicans are consistently less supportive of collective bargaining than Democrats are. That is true not only for their general evaluations—57 percent positive for Republicans, 75 percent positive for Democrats—but also for each of the more specific items. Just 36 percent of Republicans think that union influence leads to better academic performance, for example, but 50 percent of Democrats did. Similarly, 32 percent of Republicans think that union influence leads to less conflict within the district, but 41 percent of Democrats see it that way. These and other differences are not huge—a reflection of the fact that most candidates for school board are supportive of collective bargaining. But still, party does matter. (If we were to break these results down by ideology instead of party, all of the same patterns would emerge.)

—Most important: the unions *do* appear to use endorsements strategically to promote the candidacies of people who are sympathetic to union interests. Endorsed Republicans are consistently more favorable toward union interests than unendorsed Republicans, and endorsed Democrats are consistently more favorable than unendorsed Democrats. Moreover, the Republicans that the unions endorse tend to be more positive toward union interests than the Democrats they do not endorse. Indeed, the endorsed Republicans are in some ways (on issues of organization, conflict, professionalism) just as positive as the endorsed Democrats. By using endorsements to support candidates who are at once compatible with the local culture (electable) and relatively sympathetic to union interests, then, the unions can take significant steps—especially in districts filled with Republicans and conservatives—toward loosening the constraints of political culture.

If this assessment is basically correct—if the unions are strategically adapting to their constraining environments—then even in relatively unfriendly districts they may well win elections just as often as they do in friendly districts. That, after all, is the reason that they are adapting. The downside, though, is that the content of their victories should tend to be less beneficial. What the constraints ultimately boil down to is not that the unions lose elections, but that in order to win elections they must accept candidates—and school board members—who are less sympathetic than the unions would like.

Evidence on these scores is set out in table 11-7. At the top of the table are figures showing the rates at which endorsed and unendorsed candidates win and how those rates vary across types of districts. We have to remember, in interpreting these figures, that the sample was designed to include roughly equal numbers

Table 11-7. *Election Outcome, Union Influence, and Attitudes toward Effects of Collective Bargaining, by District Political Culture*

Outcome	Republican district	Mixed district	Democratic district	All districts
Win rate (percent of candidates) by type of candidate				
Endorsed				
Win	84	71	74	76
Lose	16	29	26	24
Number of candidates	(49)	(49)	(77)	(175)
Unendorsed				
Win	29	35	28	31
Lose	71	65	72	70
Number of candidates	(49)	(63)	(88)	(200)
How unions are perceived (percent of districts)				
Are unions electorally important?				
Important	85	77	70	76
Mixed	0	8	9	6
Unimportant	15	15	22	18
Number of districts	(47)	(52)	(79)	(178)
Are unions the most influential group?				
Yes	62	35	52	50
Mixed	17	18	18	18
No	21	47	30	33
Number of districts	(47)	(49)	(79)	(175)
Attitude toward effects of collective bargaining (percent of candidates)				
General effects, endorsed winners				
Positive	61	72	83	74
Mixed	3	3	0	2
Negative	35	24	17	25
Number of candidates	(31)	(29)	(46)	(106)
Specific effects (average), endorsed winners				
Positive	45	57	65	57
Mixed	15	10	16	14
Negative	40	33	18	29
Number of candidates	(33)	(30)	(49)	(112)
General effects, all winners				
Positive	58	69	74	68
Mixed	2	2	1	2
Negative	40	29	25	30
Number of candidates	(43)	(49)	(69)	(161)
Specific effects (average), all winners				
Positive	40	45	57	49
Mixed	16	12	14	14
Negative	44	43	30	38
Number of candidates	(45)	(49)	(74)	(168)

Source: Author's data.

of winners and losers; so whatever the true win rate is across all these elections, the probability that a random candidate in our data set turns out to be a winner is about .5 (actually, it is .51). That said, it is clear from the data that the unions' candidates do quite well indeed: 76 percent of endorsed candidates won their elections, while just 31 percent of unendorsed candidates won theirs. Even more important, given our concerns here, the unions do *not* tend to lose more often in districts that are heavily Republican. In our sample, in fact, union candidates do somewhat better in heavily Republican districts (84 percent winners) than in mixed-partisan districts (71 percent) or even in heavily Democratic districts (74 percent). In parallel with these win rates, the unions are more often regarded as electorally important in the Republican districts (85 percent, compared with 77 percent in the mixed-partisan districts and 70 percent in the Democratic districts), and they are more often seen as the single most influential group in school board politics (62 percent, compared with 35 percent for the mixed-partisan districts and 52 percent for the Democratic districts).

In these respects, the unions seem to be adapting with great success. But what is the content of their victories? As the figures at the bottom of table 11-7 reveal, their wins clearly do not gain them as much in the districts where they have had to make trade-offs. Despite their high win rates in Republican districts, their own winning candidates are *less* positive toward union interests than their winning candidates in mixed and Democratic districts. In terms of general attitudes, 61 percent of endorsed winners are positive toward collective bargaining in the Republican districts, compared with 72 percent in the mixed districts and 83 percent in the Democratic districts. Similarly, if we categorize candidates on the basis of the average of their responses to the specific-effects items, the pattern is exactly the same: 45 percent of endorsed winners in Republican districts have positive views on the specific effects of union influence, compared with 57 percent in mixed districts and 65 percent in Democratic districts. Finally, if we look at all winners, endorsed and unendorsed—and thus at all candidates who wind up taking seats on their local school boards—the results are again the same: the unions are faced with less sympathetic school boards the less friendly the local political environment.

So the evidence suggests that the unions *are* constrained by political culture. The teacher unions can loosen these constraints by making their endorsements fit local circumstances, but they cannot avoid making trade-offs in doing so, and in the end they take a substantive hit. All of which is another way of saying that the mechanisms of local democracy do appear to be at least reasonably responsive to ordinary citizens.

Incumbency

Whatever the level of government, incumbents tend to win elections at very high rates (see, for example, Ansolabehere and Snyder 2002). One reason is that

Table 11-8. *Attitudes toward Effects of Collective Bargaining and Election Outcome, by Candidate Incumbency and Endorsement*[a]

Outcome	Type of candidate			
	Endorsed incumbent	Unendorsed incumbent	Endorsed nonincumbent	Unendorsed nonincumbent
Attitude toward effect of collective bargaining				
General effects				
Positive	64	42	84	68
Mixed	3	0	0	3
Negative	33	58	16	29
N	66	53	74	106
Specific effects				
Positive	47	29	70	38
Mixed	19	4	8	12
Negative	34	67	23	50
N	70	55	79	111
Electoral outcome				
Win	92	49	62	22
Lose	8	51	38	78
N	83	63	92	139

Source: Author's data.

a. Figures represent the percentage of candidates giving the relevant response. *N* = number of candidates.

they have name recognition, which, in an electorate poorly informed about politics, counts heavily. Another reason is that, as office holders, they have had a chance to serve their constituencies, build coalitions, and raise money. Yet another is that groups that might otherwise support challengers have to worry that incumbents will win their races anyway—and having won, will wreak vengeance on opponents. So groups that want access in the future may be wise to support incumbents even when they do not like them very much.

For these reasons and more, incumbents have their own sources of electoral power, and the teacher unions may have to make trade-offs in dealing with them. In particular, they may find themselves endorsing incumbents who are not especially sympathetic to collective bargaining or other union concerns. To the extent this is so, the unions may be quite successful at getting their endorsed incumbents into office but less successful at getting what they want from them. The content of their power would suffer, constrained by the power of incumbency.

The data in the top half of table 11-8 suggest that the unions do indeed make these sorts of trade-offs. As we would expect, the incumbents they endorse are more sympathetic to union interests than the incumbents they do not endorse. But it is also true that the incumbents they endorse are considerably *less* sympathetic to union interests than the *non*incumbents they endorse.

Sixty-four percent of endorsed incumbents have positive general attitudes toward collective bargaining—but the comparable figure for endorsed nonincumbents is 84 percent. The results are precisely the same when it comes to candidate attitudes on the specific effects of union influence: 47 percent of the endorsed incumbents are positive, compared with 70 percent of the endorsed nonincumbents. It appears that the unions do not have the free hand in dealing with incumbents that they have in dealing with nonincumbents and that they are constrained to accept candidates less to their liking.

The data on win rates at the bottom of table 11-8 suggest that, despite being constrained, unions are still able to come out ahead. In our sample, which has a baseline win rate of .51, a phenomenal 92 percent of the endorsed incumbents won their races, compared with just 49 percent of the unendorsed incumbents. The latter figure is nothing to sneeze at, because it means that half of these incumbents were able to win even when the unions opposed them. Nonetheless, there is a weeding-out process at work here: incumbents who are especially negative toward union interests are systematically being removed from office, while incumbents who are more sympathetic are being kept. In addition, the losers are often being replaced by union-endorsed nonincumbents, who won 62 percent of their elections and are considerably more positive toward union interests. Nonincumbents who are not endorsed by the unions—and who are less sympathetic toward union interests than those who are endorsed—won at a much lower rate, 22 percent.

The unions may be more successful than these figures indicate. We have data only on the incumbents who chose to run for reelection; and it is quite possible, especially in view of the big effect of union endorsements on win rates, that the incumbents who did not run for reelection were disproportionately those who were unsympathetic to union interests and would not have received union support. Thus the unions may exercise power not only by ensuring that the (endorsed) candidates who win are more pro-union than the (unendorsed) incumbents who lose, but also by scaring the anti-union incumbents out of running for reelection. This is an effect our data cannot measure.

We can, at least, get a sense of what the turnover looks like among the candidates who do run, and table 11-9 helps us do that. Overall, the incumbents who won their elections—a mix of endorsed and unendorsed candidates—are more positive toward union interests than the incumbents who lost. In terms of general attitudes toward collective bargaining, 59 percent of the winners are positive, compared with 42 percent of the losers. And in terms of attitudes about the specific effects of union influence, 44 percent of the winners are positive, compared with 28 percent of the losers. Electoral attrition in the ranks of incumbents clearly favors the unions. Moreover, the new recruits coming onto the school boards are considerably more pro-union than the incumbents who lost. Fully 80 percent of these nonincumbents have positive general attitudes,

Table 11-9. *Attitudes toward Effects of Collective Bargaining,*
by Election Outcome and Incumbency[a]

Attitude toward effects of collective bargaining	Type of candidate			
	Winning incumbent	Losing incumbent	Winning nonincumbent	Losing nonincumbent
General effects				
Positive	59	42	80	68
Mixed	2	0	1	3
Negative	38	58	19	29
N	87	33	74	112
Specific effects				
Positive	44	28	55	47
Mixed	13	8	14	9
Negative	42	64	32	43
N	90	36	78	116

Source: Author's data.

a. Figures represent the percentage of candidates giving the relevant response. N = number of candidates.

and 55 percent have positive attitudes on specific effects. Even if we ignore the incumbents who did not seek reelection, then, the direction of turnover here is very much pro-union.

It seems obvious that we should expect such a result if the teacher unions are genuinely powerful. Yet that cannot be the whole story. For the unions have been powerful for more than two decades, and if they have been racking up incremental gains all this time, then the school boards would long ago have become totally pro-union. We know that this is not the case, so we are faced with a conundrum. Can we explain how the unions might produce pro-union turnovers year after year, yet fail in the end to create totally pro-union school boards?

A plausible answer arises from a fascinating pattern in the data that observant readers may already have noticed. As tables 11-8 and 11-9 show, incumbents in general—whether endorsed or unendorsed, winners or losers—tend to be much less sympathetic to collective bargaining than nonincumbents. This is true even though all incumbents were at one time nonincumbents—which suggests, assuming continuity in these patterns over time, that something happens to nonincumbents after they take office that *changes* their attitudes and makes them less sympathetic to collective bargaining. That such a thing might happen makes perfect sense. When nonincumbents take office—and become incumbents—their new job requires that they represent management and deal with the unions across the bargaining table, experiencing first hand (and probably for the first time) what collective bargaining is all about and how the interests of unions and teachers can come into conflict with the interests of districts and children. If this process of socialization actually occurs—and I suspect that it does—then it would resolve our conundrum: the unions could continually win elections and nonincumbents could continually be more prounion than the incumbents they replaced, yet the process would not lead inexorably to union control.

All this suggests that the unions are doubly constrained by incumbency. First, they find themselves having to endorse certain incumbents who are not as sympathetic as they would like. And second, because there is a sympathy gap between incumbents and nonincumbents, the unions tend to take an even bigger hit when they are constrained to support an incumbent. For both reasons, the impressive frequency of union electoral victories—especially the 92 percent victory rate of endorsed incumbents—overstates the true content of their victories.

Multivariate Analysis

We have now discussed four possible constraints on union power—the size of the union, political pluralism, political culture, and incumbency. In this section, I pull together the various strands of the analysis and carry out some statistical tests. By constructing simple models in which all these factors plus control variables come into play at the same time, we should be able to get a better sense of what effects they have on union power—and indeed, whether they have any effects at all once other things are taken into account.

Various approaches might reasonably be tried, but I estimate two models that seem appropriate in light of our concerns. One puts the potential constraints to use in trying to explain the attitudes of candidates endorsed by the unions. The question is: do these constraints prompt unions to endorse candidates who are less sympathetic to union interests? The second model takes exactly the same approach but focuses on the ultimate electoral outcome, the attitudes of all winning candidates. Here the question is: do the constraints tend to produce school board members who are less pro-union?

The variables are the same in both models.[9] They are

—attitudes toward union interests, a single index that combines the two basic measures we have been using all along: one representing general attitudes, the other representing specific effects.[10]

9. Data on district size come from the California Department of Education. Data on district partisanship come from county election agencies. Data on district education levels and nonurban location come from the National Center for Education Statistics' Common Core of Data; districts are coded as nonurban if they are not in a large city or on the urban fringe of a large city. All other variables are from the candidate survey.

10. The general attitudes variable is measured from 1 (*very negative*) to 5 (*very positive*). The specific attitudes variable is an index of all the items (from cost through teaching) listed in table 11-6, which are combined through factor analysis using the "factor" command within Stata with

—the size of the district, measured as a six-category variable from 1 (*smallest*) to 6 (*largest*), as in the tables.

—electoral competition, an aspect of pluralism, measured as a three-category variable (0, *little competition*; .5, *mixed*; 1, *much competition*), as depicted in table 11-2.

—the perceived power of other groups, another aspect of pluralism, measured as 0-1 dummies for each type of group listed in table 11-3.

—the partisanship of the district, an aspect of political culture, measured as a three-category variable that runs from *Democratic* (0) to *mixed-partisan* (1) to *Republican* (2).[11]

—incumbency, measured as a 0-1 dummy.

—union activism, an index of three variables—union activity in elections, the union's perceived importance in elections, and whether the union is seen as the most influential group.[12]

—percent of district residents who graduated from college, a control variable to capture a relevant feature of the social environment, measured as a fraction between 0 and 1.

—nonurban location, another control variable (measured as a 0-1 dummy), but one that may capture an important aspect of political culture that, for reasons of space and simplicity, we have not considered here. This is a sense of community, as reflected in tight social networks, personal acquaintance with candidates, and norms of civic duty (Putnam 2000). In genuine communities, it could be more difficult for special interests like unions to be overtly active and influential.

The models should be interpreted mainly as tests of the various constraints, not as tests of union power per se. As I noted in our discussion of small unions, there are reasons for thinking that unions may sometimes be powerful—meaning that they ultimately get the kinds of school boards that they want—even when they are quite inactive and unimportant in local politics and not regarded as influential. That is why I have labeled the union variable here as "union activism"—because it indicates how overtly active and apparently influential the unions are in politics, not necessarily how powerful they are (although it may do that).

---

no rotation. The overall index, which combines the general attitudes variable and the specific attitudes index, is created by using factor analysis on just these two variables.

11. As discussed in an earlier footnote, the cut-points separating the three categories are at 55 percent Democratic and 55 percent Republican.

12. The three variables are combined into a single index through factor analysis using the "factor" command within Stata with no rotation. The union activity variable is the sum of all the political activities listed in table 11-1. The other two variables are the ones described in table 11-2 and discussed in the text.

Regression estimates for the first model, focusing on the pro-union attitudes of endorsed candidates, are set out in table 11-10.[13] As a matter of full information, I have presented the initial estimates for all variables. But because there are so many group-influence variables, almost all of them highly insignificant, I have followed a practice here and in table 11-11 of removing those with t scores of less than 1. This simplifies the model and, in reducing collinearity, gives us more precise estimates for the variables that remain.

So let's look at the final estimates, listed in the right-hand portion of table 11-10. They show, first, that both political culture and incumbency have statistically significant effects on the content of union endorsements and operate as we would expect. As districts shift from Democratic to Republican, the unions endorse candidates who are .29 standard deviations less sympathetic to union interests (refer to the table's impact coefficients). And when the unions endorse an incumbent rather than a nonincumbent, the drop in sympathy toward union interests is .49 standard deviations. These are respectable effects, especially the one for incumbency.

Moreover, if we think of the nonurban variable as a proxy for community, we would expect it too to have a constraining effect on union power. And it does. Its impact is a nontrivial .33 standard deviation. If we were to combine the effects of the partisanship and nonurban variables, the total impact of political culture—and thus of local democracy—would be considerable.

The variables that explicitly try to measure pluralism do not perform well. Competition has a statistically significant impact of .36 standard deviations, but it is in the wrong direction: the more competitive the district, the more sympathetic the union's candidates are to union interests. So this aspect of pluralism certainly does not appear to be constraining the unions toward moderation. Nor does the second aspect of pluralism, the other groups that are said to be more powerful than the unions. Of the nine types of groups, only one demonstrates any impact on union endorsements: party and ideological groups, whose involvement in politics is estimated to produce a reduction in union sympathies of .36 standard deviations. Yet these groups are rarely active participants in local elections (see table 11-3), so this impact, if it is real, is usually not a factor.[14]

13. Regression estimation is carried out in Stata using robust estimators of variance with clustering on school districts. Robust estimators and clustering are necessary here because we often have more than one candidate to a district and the individuals within such clusters cannot be regarded as truly independent observations. These methods take that fact into account.

14. Having said this, I want to add that the other-groups test is not entirely fair to the pluralism argument. Because of the way the survey was set up, we have measures of group importance only for districts in which the teacher unions are not regarded as the most influential group, and since these other groups may be active in the remaining districts, our measures do not reflect the true extent to which they may be counterbalancing the unions. Still, these measures do single out the districts where particular groups ought to be the *most* influential in the district—so their influence should show up here. And for the most part, it does not. That is useful information.

Table 11-10. *Estimation: Constraints on the Pro-Union Attitudes of Endorsed Candidates*[a]

Independent variable	Initial model		Final model		
	Coefficient	Robust standard error	Coefficient	Robust standard error	Impact
District size	−.083**	.38	−.079**	.035	−.41
District culture (Republican)	−.095*	.070	−.091*	.060	−.29
Incumbent	−.332***	.094	−.306***	.089	−.49
Competition	.232	.148	.223	.140	.36
Union activism	.157*	.105	.178**	.091	.35
Education (district)	−.496	.536	−.417	.413	−.17
Nonurban	−.222*	.128	−.208*	.123	−.33
Influence					
Parents	.009	.260			
Party groups	−.273	.169	−.223*	.126	−.36
Religious groups	.097	.249			
Newspapers	.184	.195			
Other unions	−.081	.173			
Prominent individuals	−.156	.209			
Community groups	−.025	.160			
Ethnic groups	.033	.352			
Business groups	−.012	.224			
No group	.295*	.159	.314***	.142	.50
Constant	.952***	.219	.825***	.226	
Summary statistic					
N		136		136	
R^2		.24		.23	

Source: Author's data.

a. * $p < .10$, ** $p < .05$, *** $p < .01$. Dependent variable is an index of attitudes toward collective bargaining, as described in text. Analysis was carried out on all endorsed candidates. Significance tests are one-tailed for district culture, incumbent, competition, union activism, and business groups, because we tested for specified directional effects. Tests for all other variables are two-tailed. Regressions were carried out within Stata using robust standard errors with clustering on the school district. For ordinal (including dummy) variables, excluding district size, "impact" measures the effect on the dependent variable, in standard deviation units, of a shift in the independent variable from its lowest value to its highest value. For continuous variables, as well as for district size (which contains six values), the logic is the same except that the independent variable is assumed to undergo a shift of two standard deviations (that is, in effect, from low to high), which simulates what is done with the ordinal variables.

A more interesting result from the other-groups portion of the analysis has nothing to do with the nine groups. Recall that when candidates said the teacher unions are *not* the most influential group in their district, they were asked which groups are more influential. In many cases, however, the candidates were unable to mention any groups at all, and that was especially likely to happen in the small districts. The estimates of table 11-10 now reveal that in districts where no group is mentioned, the unions are likely to endorse candidates who are *more* sympathetic to union interests—and by .50 standard deviations. This is consistent with the argument I made earlier: when no other groups are mentioned, the teacher unions actually *are* likely to be the most influential groups.

This same finding, however, provides support for the pluralist argument. It can be interpreted as saying that when pluralism is at its weakest (with no groups being important), the teacher unions are at their most influential. It also dovetails nicely with the estimation results on district size, which are quite striking. They show that as districts become smaller, the candidates endorsed by unions become *more* sympathetic to union interests. The impact is .41 standard deviations. As discussed earlier, the district size variable may well be capturing the effects of two countervailing variables at once, union size and the pluralism of district context. Union size cannot be responsible for this particular finding, because it should clearly work in the opposite direction, with smaller size (and lower organizational capacity) producing less favorable outcomes. Thus it is reasonable to believe that we are observing a contextual effect: smaller unions benefit because they are in smaller, less pluralistic districts, while larger unions suffer because they are in larger, more pluralistic districts.

The evidence for pluralism as a constraint on union power is therefore mixed. When pluralism is measured explicitly through the competitiveness of elections and the roles of specific groups, there is no evidence of a constraining effect. Nor do business groups, presumably the unions' most potent adversaries, show any strength here. But when we look at other, less direct measures that may serve as proxies for pluralism—district size and the inability of candidates to mention any powerful groups—there is persuasive evidence of constraint. These positive results need to be taken seriously, for the indirect measures could easily be picking up aspects of pluralism that the explicit measures are failing to capture.

Finally, consider the role of union activism. It is important to recognize that while larger unions may well be disadvantaged by their pluralist environments, this is an "all else equal" finding that hardly leaves large unions out in the cold. The fact is, large unions are much more politically active than small unions, and the estimates in table 11-10 show that—holding environmental conditions constant—unions that are more politically active tend to endorse candidates who are more sympathetic to union interests, with an impact of .35 standard deviations. The more active the union, the more successful it is, in this sense. So large unions are being affected both positively and negatively: their success is enhanced by their activism but impeded by their context. The reverse is true for small unions: their lack of activism works against them, but their context works for them.

Now let's turn to the question of how the constraints affect final outcomes, the collective bargaining attitudes of the candidates who win. About half of these candidates are endorsed, so this test is not entirely independent of the one we just carried out. Still, connecting the constraints to final outcomes is essential, plenty of new candidates are tossed into the mix (and old ones deleted), and the sample is broadened to include districts in which no endorsements at all are made—the peace-and-serenity districts that we talked about earlier. So there is much to be learned here. Indeed, this step is the real pay-off. We study endorsements, after all, mainly because they tell us something about the final outcomes.

The estimates are set out in table 11-11. Again, incumbency and political culture show themselves to be effective constraints on union power. Both are statistically quite significant, and both have downward impacts on the pro-union attitudes of winners—impacts of .32 and .39 standard deviations, respectively. The nonurban factor, which may be a proxy for political culture, is also significant and has a downward impact of .35 standard deviations.

Competition, the most direct measure of pluralism, shows no impact at all on final outcomes. The same can be said for eight of the nine groups whose roles have been explored here, including party groups (which raises questions about whether the earlier result about its impact on endorsements is just an anomaly). The exception, interestingly, is business—whose impact is statistically significant (on a one-tailed test, which is appropriate in this case) and which has a downward effect on pro-union attitudes of .36 of a standard deviation. This is the first indication that business may be contributing to a more pluralistic brand of politics. Still, the earlier evidence (table 11-3) suggests that it is usually not a major player, so we cannot exaggerate its role as a counterweight to the unions.

Additional evidence for pluralism, however, is provided by the indirect measures. Once again it is in the smaller districts, not in the larger ones, that unions have the most success at getting sympathetic candidates elected to office, and the impact is a substantial .49 standard deviation. As I argue above, it makes little sense to attribute this effect to union size, and a reasonable interpretation is that smaller unions are more successful than larger ones (all else equal) because they operate in smaller districts that are less pluralistic. A second finding that points in the same direction is that, in districts where candidates are unable to name any groups at all that are especially powerful—as often happens in small districts with small unions—the winning candidates are more likely to be sympathetic toward union interests (by .34 standard deviations).

But while small unions are advantaged by their more benign environments, we also find that unions can gain power by being politically active and important in elections—which small unions usually are not and large unions almost always are. At .52 standard deviations, the impact of union activism is big and significant here. This is especially impressive given that the outcome is not being measured simply in terms of the attitudes of union-endorsed candidates, but in terms of the attitudes of *all winners*, endorsed or not. Other things being equal, unions that are active and important are able to elect more sympathetic school boards.

Table 11-11. *Estimation: Constraints on the Pro-Union Attitudes of All Winning Candidates*[a]

Independent variable	Initial model		Final model		
	Coefficient	Robust standard error	Coefficient	Robust standard error	Impact
District size	−.105***	.39	−.101***	.035	−.49
District culture (Republican)	−.131**	.061	−.130***	.053	−.39
Incumbent	−.204***	.084	−.210***	.081	−.32
Competition	.039	.125	.044	.120	.07
Union activism	.256***	.075	.237***	.078	.52
Education (district)	−.739***	.376	−.571	.357	−.25
Nonurban	−.256***	.102	−.235**	.102	−.35
Influence					
Parents	.150	.144			
Party groups	.001	.172			
Religious groups	.076	.215			
Newspapers	.160	.200			
Other unions	.068	.146			
Prominent individuals	−.180	.281			
Community groups	−.031	.142			
Ethnic groups	−.031	.331			
Business groups	−.201	.182	−.238*	.167	−.36
No group	.266**	.120	.225**	.110	.34
Constant	.983***	.225	.961***	.215	
Summary statistic					
N	203		203		
R^2	.18		.17		

Source: Author's data.

a. * $p < .10$, ** $p < .05$, *** $p < .01$. Dependent variable is an index of attitudes toward collective bargaining, as described in text. Analysis was carried out on all endorsed candidates. Significance tests are one-tailed for district culture, incumbent, competition, union activism, and business groups, because we tested for specified directional effects. Tests for all other variables are two-tailed. Regressions were carried out within Stata using robust standard errors with clustering on the school district. For ordinal (including dummy) variables, excluding district size, "impact" measures the effect on the dependent variable, in standard deviation units, of a shift in the independent variable from its lowest value to its highest value. For continuous variables, as well as for district size (which contains six values), the logic is the same except that the independent variable is assumed to undergo a shift of two standard deviations (that is, in effect, from low to high), which simulates what is done with the ordinal variables.

Conclusion

What passes for a theory of education politics these days is the notion that politics is complex, that many so-called stakeholders have weighty roles to play, and that competition among these groups explains political outcomes. But what is the analytical basis for this view? When we think about which groups have *incentives* to be politically active in school board elections and the *resources* to do it with real power, a balanced system of pluralist politics is unlikely. One group clearly stands out from the others in these respects: the teacher unions. They have vested interests that give them much stronger incentives for political action in this arena than other social groups. And they have resources—money, organization, activists—that usually give them much more formidable means of getting what they want.

In a separate paper, I present an empirical analysis showing that teacher unions do indeed exercise considerable power in school board elections (Moe 2003a). But neither there nor here do I argue that the unions are all-powerful. Despite their advantages in incentives and resources, there are reasons for thinking that certain factors may work to constrain their power, and my aim in this chapter is to put the spotlight on some of the more prominent of these—the size of the union, political pluralism, political culture, and incumbency—and bring evidence to bear on whether they do in fact seem to play such a role.

The evidence comes from a survey of school board candidates in 253 California school districts. California is a good state to study, as it allows for a sample that covers a full range of districts—varying in size, region, political culture, and the like—and provides coherent data on their elections. We have to recognize, of course, that there may be a degree of slippage in generalizing to the nation as a whole. This is especially true for the small set of states, notably those with right-to-work laws, in which collective bargaining is rare or even illegal (Lieberman 1997). More research is required before the bigger picture can be filled in with confidence. But this is always the case in empirical research. We move forward step by step and fill in the picture as we go. Here is what the evidence from this study seems to suggest:

Union size. Large unions in large districts have greater organizational capacity than small unions in small districts, and they are much more active in school board politics. A multivariate analysis shows, moreover, that union activism has a big impact on the kinds of people who get endorsed and who win elections: they are more pro-union. But once electoral activism is factored out, we find that it is in the smaller districts that unions do especially well in securing sympathetic endorsements and winners. This is not because small organization is a plus for them, but because of the beneficence of their local contexts—due most likely to the relative absence of pluralistic politics. The flip side is that large unions, while advantaged by their greater capacity and activism, are disadvantaged—and constrained—by their more pluralistic environments. Given these countervailing factors, it is probably wrong to think that the teacher unions are enormously powerful in the large districts and have little power in the small districts. There may be a power gap, but there is good reason to think they are powerful in both settings.

Political pluralism. Despite the failure of certain measures of pluralism to show effects—the competitiveness of elections, the activity of various social groups—the strength of the positive findings, especially those on district size, suggests that pluralism does constrain union power. To say this, however, is not to embrace the literature's view of pluralism as the norm. For the degree of pluralism can vary considerably across districts, and it is likely to be weak and unconstraining in many (if not most) districts. And even when it is strong and constraining, as is likely in large districts, the evidence suggests—as does the logic of incentives and resources—that the pluralist balance of power tends to tilt in favor of the teacher unions.

Political culture. There is good evidence that union power is moderated by the local political culture. In Republican districts, the teacher unions endorse candidates who are less sympathetic to union interests than the candidates they endorse in Democratic districts. And they wind up with school boards (winning candidates) that are less sympathetic as well. It appears, then, that local democracy is to some degree operating as it is supposed to in reflecting the preferences of ordinary citizens, and that the unions—although still quite powerful—find that they have to adapt strategically to their democratic context (through more moderate endorsements) and accept outcomes whose substantive content is not entirely what they want.

Incumbency. There is also good evidence that union power is moderated by incumbency. Incumbents have their own sources of electoral power, and the unions make trade-offs by endorsing incumbents who are less sympathetic toward union interests than they would like. While they do take steps (successfully) to get rid of incumbents who are especially anti-union and while the incumbents that they endorse are more sympathetic than the ones that they do not, the unions are still settling for people they would not support if they had a free hand. To make matters worse, it appears that the experience of serving on school boards tends to make board members less sympathetic to union interests than they were when they were first elected—which means that the unions cannot count on locking up school boards by getting their supporters elected (because the latter will become less supportive over time) and that the unions have to make even bigger trade-offs in agreeing to endorse incumbents.

It is possible, of course, that the teacher unions are constrained in additional ways as well, and some of the other chapters in this volume point to possibilities. Berry and Howell (chapter 7 of this volume), for instance, argue that citizens hold board members accountable by voting retrospectively on the basis of school performance, rewarding incumbents when the schools are doing well and ousting them when the schools are doing badly. If this argument is true—and the authors provide mixed (but intriguing) evidence on its behalf—then simple democratic responsiveness may be an even more potent factor than my data suggest, with citizens electing performance-oriented board members who are less inclined to do what the unions want. The trouble with this argument, however, is that turnout in school board elections is notoriously low, as is citizen knowledge, and the unions still have huge advantages over all other groups—and certainly over ordinary voters—in promoting favored candidates and shaping electoral outcomes. Moreover, even if voters were aroused enough to throw out the incumbents in light of bad performance, they would have to replace them with nonincumbents—and the union-endorsed nonincumbents would have a big edge.

Another possible constraint on union power is implicit in Meier and Juenke's analysis in chapter 9 of this volume. What they show is that different electoral structures—one in which all board members are elected at large, for example, compared with one in which each member is elected from a separate subdistrict—have important consequences for the representation of minority groups. It is quite possible, however, that different electoral systems would also have different consequences for union power and that some would prove especially constraining. Consider what might happen, for instance, if school board elections were no longer required to be nonpartisan (as they usually are nationwide) and party labels were put on the ballot. Suddenly, citizens would have concrete information on each candidate—and a meaningful voting cue—that they did not have before, and this could affect voting behavior in ways the unions would not want. Their power could well be more constrained.

In view of the constraints suggested by my own data, it would be nice to conclude that democracy is alive and well in the politics of public education. Yet I think it is much more fitting to say that democracy is alive but not well. It is alive because the democratic system does function to put constraints on how the teacher unions can exercise their power, and to ensure that the shared values of local citizens are reflected in their school boards. But democracy still suffers because these constraints serve only to moderate the extent to which local politics is tilted in favor of the teacher unions. The unions still have major advantages over other groups in both incentives and resources, and they appear to use these advantages quite effectively and strategically in getting what they want. If school board democracy can rightly be described as pluralist at all, it is a pluralism that is decidedly unbalanced.

References

Ansolabehere, Stephen, and James M. Snyder. 2002. "The Incumbency Advantage in U.S. Elections: An Analysis of State and Federal Offices, 1942–2000." *Election Law Journal* 1 (3): 315–38.

Brimelow, Peter. 2003. *The Worm in the Apple: How the Teacher Unions are Destroying American Education*. New York: HarperCollins.

Haar, Charlene. 2002. *The Politics of the PTA*. Somerset, N.J.: Transaction.

Hess, Frederick. 2002. *School Boards at the Dawn of the 21st Century: Conditions and Challenges of District Governance.* Alexandria, Va.: National School Boards Association.

Lieberman, Myron. 1997. *The Teacher Unions.* New York: Free Press.

Moe, Terry M. 2001. "Teachers Unions and the Public Schools." In *A Primer on America's Schools,* edited by Terry M. Moe. Stanford, Calif.: Hoover Press.

———. 2003a. "Political Control and the Power of the Agent." Paper presented at the annual meeting of the Midwest Political Science Association. Chicago, April 2–3.

———. 2003b. "Teacher Unions and School Board Elections." Paper presented at the Conference on School Board Politics. Harvard University, October 16–17.

Olson, Mancur, Jr. 1965. *The Logic of Collective Action.* Harvard University Press.

Peterson, Paul E. 1985. *The Politics of School Reform: 1870–1940.* University of Chicago Press.

Putnam, Robert D. 2000. *Bowling Alone.* New York: Simon and Schuster.

Thomas, Clive S., and Ronald J. Hrebenar. 1999. "Interest Groups in the American States." In *Politics in the American States*, 7th ed., edited by Virginia Gray and Herbert Jacobs. Washington: CQ Press.

———. 2004. "Interest Groups in the American States." In *Politics in the American States*, 8th ed., edited by Virginia Gray and Herbert Jacobs. Washington: CQ Press.

Tyack, David B. 1974. *The One Best System: A History of American Urban Education.* Harvard University Press.

Wirt, Frederick M., and Michael W. Kirst. 2001. *The Political Dynamics of American Education.* Berkeley, Calif.: McKutcheon.

Wong, Kenneth K. 1992. "The Politics of Urban Education as a Field of Study: An Interpretive Analysis." In *The Politics of Urban Education in the United States*, edited by James Cibulka, Rodney Reed, and Kenneth K. Wong. Washington: Falmer Press.

12

Contextual Influences on Participation in School Governance

DAVID E. CAMPBELL

Public participation in local politics—including school district politics—reveals something of a paradox. On the one hand, there is some evidence that Americans *in general* show little interest in, awareness of, and engagement in local politics, as demonstrated by the fact that voter turnout rates in local elections are typically abysmally low. But on the other hand, when we look beyond voter turnout and instead turn to specific ways in which participators choose to get involved, engagement in local affairs constitutes a major share of the participatory investment made by Americans. Almost half (44 percent) of Americans report attending at least one meeting on "town or school affairs" in the previous year.[1] And of the issues regularly featured prominently on the local political stage, school politics is often the star of the show. Americans care deeply about their local public schools, enough to put their money where their mouths are. Consider how real estate prices track school quality. Yet the literature on political participation has had little to say about this particular channel for political involvement.

This chapter examines one important means of local engagement in politics:

I would like to express my appreciation to Robert Putnam and Tom Sander for their assistance with the Social Capital Community Benchmark Survey. Also, I am grateful to Christian Poehlmann of the University of Notre Dame's Business Information Center for his help (and considerable patience) in compiling the census data used in this chapter.

1. Data are from the Social Capital Community Benchmark Survey (Saguaro Seminar 2001).

attendance at local meetings, including school board meetings. In particular, this chapter adds to a growing literature on how the characteristics of the communities in which Americans live affect their civic and political participation. Like previous studies, it asks whether where people live affects their degree of political involvement. Unlike prior studies, however, it specifically looks to the school district as the community of interest. The analysis thus uses a unique data set to determine whether the contextual features of school districts affect individuals' levels of participation. In a nutshell, this study is motivated by two interrelated claims. First, place matters. Second, school districts are places with political relevance.

Place matters in the sense that the communities in which we live shape our participation in public affairs. While there has long been a literature exploring what have come to be known as "contextual effects," in recent years this line of research has become a growth stock.[2] Much of the social capital literature, for example, examines the ways that social environments affect our likelihood of engaging in public-spirited behavior.[3] There is also a burgeoning body of research into how the social complexion of local communities shapes participation in civic and political activities, in particular how community heterogeneity affects such engagement. While most of the extant literature focuses on municipalities as political units, I contend that school districts are also politically relevant. Indeed, in regard to local public school policy, we should expect that the school district is the most salient political unit. This is not to claim that the school district is the only geographic unit that matters, even for school-level politics, but only to underscore that the district is understudied as a political jurisdiction.

To date, research on the subject has revealed an intriguing inconsistency about the participatory consequences of heterogeneity. Eric Oliver's recent book, *Democracy in Suburbia*, for example, carefully examines how various features of municipalities—including but not limited to ethnic and racial heterogeneity—impact local political engagement.[4] One of Oliver's more notable findings is that people who live in communities with greater economic diversity have higher levels of engagement in localized political action, for example, by voting in local elections and contacting local elected officials. In contrast, a number of economists have found that economic, racial, and ethnic heterogeneity all lead to a decrease in participation. In a recent essay surveying this literature, Dora Costa and Matthew Kahn note, "Over the past five years, at least 15 different empirical economic papers have studied the consequences of community heterogeneity, and all of these studies have the same punch line: heterogeneity reduces civic engagement."[5]

2. Huckfeldt and Sprague (1993).
3. Putnam (2000).
4. Oliver (2001).
5. Costa and Kahn (2003, p. 104).

At first glance, Oliver's conclusions would seem to be in sharp contrast to those of the economists cited by Costa and Kahn, notably the work of Alberto Alesina and Eliana La Ferrara.[6] While Oliver finds that heterogeneity, or at least economic heterogeneity, ignites local political participation, Alesina and La Ferrara find that three types of heterogeneity—ethnic, racial, and economic—all have a dampening effect on civic activity. A closer look, however, suggests that while their conclusions appear empirically incompatible, they are actually theoretically consistent with one another. It is important to note that these studies examine different forms of participation. Mistakenly, the literature on participation often indiscriminately groups disparate activities together, notwithstanding considerable evidence that various forms of participation are qualitatively different from one another. There are different participatory strokes for different folks. In their classic study of participation, for example, Sidney Verba and Norman Nie draw a distinction between activity that is conflictual and activity that is nonconflictual, contrasting electoral activities like political campaigning with intrinsically cooperative activities like membership in (most) voluntary groups.[7] More recently, Krista Jenkins, Molly Andolina, Scott Keeter, and Cliff Zukin have conducted a massive study of participation in the United States, and upon analyzing an array of different activities, they concluded that there are essentially three participatory dimensions.[8] The dimension of "civic" activity, by which they mean nonpolitical efforts like volunteering in the community, is different from expressing political voice or influencing electoral outcomes. These two studies, based on data collected more than thirty years apart, bear a striking resemblance to one another.

Oliver has examined *political* activism—the sorts of things that people do to express their political preferences. These are activities largely sparked by conflict and competition. Indeed, he explicitly writes that "conflict is essential for fueling civic participation" and that "economic diversity is a primary determinant of local political competition."[9] Alesina and La Ferrara model a very different measure, membership in a voluntary association. Their analysis is grounded in a formal model of group membership based on the assumption that "individuals prefer to interact with others who are similar to themselves in terms of income, race, and ethnicity."[10] Birds of a feather, as it were, flock together.

Once we recognize that there are different types of participation, the empirical results that at first seemed contradictory now appear complementary. Local political engagement is sparked by *conflict*; membership in voluntary associations is facilitated by *commonality*. Therefore, community heterogeneity has a different impact on these different forms of participation. A social context that

---

6. Alesina and La Ferrara (2000).
7. Verba and Nie (1972, p. 53)
8. Jenkins and others (2003).
9. Oliver (2001, p. 86)
10. Alesina and La Ferrara (2000, p. 850).

triggers conflict over differing political preferences will result in higher levels of political activism, while one characterized by people sharing common characteristics—and thus, by implication, preferences—will instead foster collective action motivated by feelings of social solidarity.

This theoretical distinction between conflict and commonality as motivations for participation leads us to an interesting question. Is participation in the governance of a school district more likely to be driven by one or the other? In other words, does heterogeneity—more colloquially, diversity—whether racial or economic in nature, pull people into school district politics or push them out? The answer speaks to how involvement in school board politics is shaped by the design of the political landscape, specifically the geographic lines defining public school districts. While heterogeneity will not be the only contextual factor examined here, given the attention to diversity in the national zeitgeist, it is perhaps of greatest interest to most people.

Data

This analysis relies on the Social Capital Community Benchmark Survey (SCCBS), a rich source of data about myriad forms of civic engagement among Americans, including participation in local and school politics. Unlike most such surveys, the SCCBS does not consist of a single nationally representative sample of a few thousand respondents. Rather, it contains representative samples in forty different communities.[11] As a result, the number of cases included in the SCCBS dwarfs what is found in other, similar sources of data like the National Election Studies and the General Social Survey. More important than the sheer number of cases is the fact that for every survey question asked of an individual, it is possible to construct an aggregate measure for that community—thus permitting the internal construction of contextual measures. While most of the contextual data employed in this analysis are derived from the U.S. census, aggregated to the school district as the relevant geographic context, for a few of the measures that is not possible. Because the Census Bureau does not collect any data that touch on religion or political ideology, measures of both

11. For more information about the SCCBS, including the wording of the survey's items, see www.cfsv.org/communitysurvey/ [October 21, 2004]. The areas included in the study are Rural South Dakota; Bismarck, North Dakota; Newaygo City, Michigan; York, Pennsylvania; Southeastern Michigan; St. Paul, Minnesota; Central Oregon; Rochester, New York; New Hampshire; Kalamazoo, Michigan; Syracuse, New York; Indiana; Chicago, Illinois; Cincinnati, Ohio; Eastern Washington; Maine; Charlotte, North Carolina; "Silicon Valley" (San Mateo and Santa Clara counties, California, and the cities of Fremont, Newark, and Union City); Cleveland, Ohio; Eastern Tennessee; Phoenix, Arizona; Greensboro, North Carolina; Grand Rapids, Michigan; San Francisco, California; Winston-Salem, North Carolina; Atlanta, Georgia; San Diego, California; Delaware; West Virginia (Boone, Kanawha, and Putnam counties); Montana; Houston, Texas; Birmingham, Alabama; Minneapolis, Minnesota; North Minneapolis, Minnesota; Baton Rouge, Louisiana; Los Angeles, California; Seattle, Washington; Denver, Colorado; Boulder, Colorado; Boston, Massachusetts.

religious and ideological context have been constructed from within the SCCBS data set. This is not possible with surveys that simply draw a single random sample nationwide, as there are generally too few respondents in each geographic location to construct a reliable aggregate measure.

For this analysis, I merged data describing the public school district in which each respondent resides. These data were taken from the U.S. Census and then aggregated by school district.[12] Thus for each respondent I have not only individual-level information (for example, whether the respondent is African American), but also information about the respondent's public school district (for example, the percentage of African Americans in the school district).[13]

Unfortunately, the SCCBS's actual measure of attendance at school board meetings is less than ideal. It is worded, "How many times in the past twelve months have you attended any public meeting in which there was discussion of town or school affairs?" obviously lumping various types of meetings together and making it impossible to isolate attendance at school board meetings. While the imprecision of the question does muddy any conclusions drawn using these data, it does not appear to be a fatal flaw. There is evidence from both inside and outside the data to think that much of the participation recorded by this measure is related to the local schools. Outside the data, any observer of American politics should have the intuition that a community's schools attract a lot of attention and generate local political controversy. From inside the data, we observe that one of the largest factors predicting whether people attend a "public meeting on town or school affairs" is having school-age children. However, even with evidence suggesting that this question largely records attendance at meetings on school-related matters, throughout this discussion the reader should keep in mind that the measure of the dependent variable encompasses meetings of various sorts and thus is "fuzzy." One way to assuage this concern is to limit the model to the respondents with the greatest stake and therefore the most immediate interest in the local public schools: parents of school-age children (six to eighteen). In order to maximize the probability that the meetings attended are school related, this analysis thus is limited to parents of school-age children only.

Analysis

The analysis proceeds in three stages. First, I examine the individual-level predictors of meeting attendance, in order to establish a baseline with which to compare the contextual factors that are of primary interest. Second, the model incorporates the contextual measures at both the district and, where necessary,

12. The data themselves were compiled using software produced by a commercial vendor (Geolytics 2001).
13. Data were aggregated over unified school districts—that is, the district covering K–12.

community level. Third, the analysis turns to examining possible interactions between individuals and their context. The dependent variable that is the focus is simply whether an individual reports attending a single meeting in the previous year.

Individual-Level Predictors

Using logistic regression, the first model regresses meeting attendance on an array of individual-level variables, each of which has been long recognized as a predictor of participation in general. The model includes education level and household income, owing to long-standing evidence that participation in America is skewed toward the upper end of the socioeconomic scale.[14] Age is also included in the model, as previous research has found that the greater someone's age, the greater the likelihood of engaging in political activity.

Other variables include a dummy variable for homeownership. Since many Americans purchase a home on the basis of the perceived quality of the local public schools, we should expect homeownership to be a factor contributing to engagement in the governance of the local schools and community. Similarly, the model accounts for how long respondents have lived in their communities. The longer one lives in a place, the deeper one's roots, the thicker one's social networks, and the greater the investment one feels in the community—all of which contribute to political involvement.

The model also controls for gender, coded so that women score a one, men a zero. While women *generally* show a slightly lower level of political participation than men, one area in which they exhibit a greater level of engagement is in regard to education and local schools especially.[15] We should thus expect a positive coefficient for gender. Race and ethnicity is included in the equation, coded into five categories: White, African American, Hispanic,[16] Asian American, and a catch-all "other" category that includes Native Americans, Pacific Islanders, and people who choose not to place themselves in any racial category. Owing to the amalgamation of groups within this category, its coefficient should not be taken as having any theoretically significant meaning. Rather, it is included to keep the interpretation of the other groups' coefficients clear. White is the baseline category, which means that all of the race/ethnicity coefficients are interpreted as a particular group's level of local political involvement relative to that of whites. Note that the categories African American and white include only non-Hispanics and that a Hispanic can be either black or white.

---

14. Verba and Nie (1972); Verba, Schlozman, and Brady (1995).
15. Delli Carpini and Keeter (1996); Burns, Schlozman, and Verba (2001).
16. White, African American, and Hispanic are mutually exclusive categories. The white and African American categories include only people who indicated that they are not Hispanic as well. Hispanic includes people who identify as white Hispanics, black Hispanics, and Hispanics with no further racial classification.

In addition to these demographic variables, the model includes two more measures, one attitudinal and one behavioral. The attitudinal measure is respondents' level of interpersonal trust, specifically whether they trust their neighbors. Interpersonal trust has generally been shown to correlate with greater levels of civic activity.[17] Incorporating trust of one's neighbors into the model will give us the first hint of whether attendance at local public meetings is better characterized as driven by conflict or commonality. If it is conflictual and that conflict is sparked by disagreements among people who live in the same community, we might then expect participants to be less trusting of their neighbors. Conversely, if it is generally based on commonality, the relationship between trust and participation would be positive.

Finally, the model includes a measure of religious involvement, which is a composite index of membership in a church,[18] attendance at religious services, participation in church activities, financial contributions to a religious organization, volunteering for a religious cause, and participation in a religiously affiliated organization.[19] Religious involvement is a strong predictor of community participation, so we should expect it to have a positive coefficient.[20] While denominational affiliation is undoubtedly important in understanding religion's effect on American politics, there is increasing evidence that the most politically salient divide is more likely to be between religiously and secularly oriented people and thus less likely to be between people of different denominations per se.[21] When controls for denominational affiliation are included in the model, the results do not change. To keep these rather cumbersome models as parsimonious as possible, therefore, they have been excluded.

With these introductions out of the way, we can turn to the results of the model. Note that the estimation accounts for the clustered nature of the sample, and so robust standard errors are reported. Also, each variable has been coded on a 0-1 scale, facilitating the comparison of the relative magnitudes of the coefficients. The first column of table 12-1 presents the results. We see that, with only a few exceptions, our expectations are met. More education and higher income are both positive predictors of meeting attendance, each reaching a conventional level of statistical significance. Surprisingly, neither being a homeowner nor the length of time one has lived in a community is a significant factor in meeting attendance, although both are, as expected, positive. Likewise, the coefficient for age is positive, but it misses the standard cut-off for statistical significance. Women are more likely to attend meetings than men, as expected.

17. Burns, Kinder, and Rahn (2003).
18. "Church" is used here in a general sense to include synagogues, mosques, temples, and so forth.
19. By using factor analysis, these have been combined into a single variable. Details available on request.
20. Putnam (2000); Verba, Schlozman, and Brady (1995).
21. Layman (2001).

Table 12-1. *Attendance at Town and School Meetings, Logistic Regression*[a]

	Individual-level factors		Contextual factors		Individual-contextual interactions	
Individual-level factors						
Education	1.281***	(0.134)	1.223***	(0.158)		
College degree					0.192	(0.203)
Household income	0.633***	(0.126)	0.743***	(0.122)	1.295***	(0.411)
Age	0.060	(0.365)	0.149	(0.415)	0.503	(0.374)
Homeowner	0.063	(0.079)	0.031	(0.091)	0.004	(0.097)
Female	0.135**	(0.060)	0.161**	(0.068)	0.174**	(0.073)
Years in community	0.131	(0.130)	0.104	(0.131)	0.091	(0.130)
African American	0.189**	(0.088)	0.127	(0.082)		
Hispanic	−0.163	(0.178)	−0.053	(0.204)		
Asian American	−0.510**	(0.230)	−0.464*	(0.279)		
Other races	0.143	(0.172)	−0.051	(0.193)		
White			0.056	(0.217)		
Religious involvement	1.361***	(0.106)	1.441***	(0.110)	5.950**	(2.327)
Trust in neighbors	0.573***	(0.128)	0.565***	(0.124)	0.555***	(0.123)
Southern state	−0.038	(0.073)	0.034	(0.101)	0.031	(0.111)
Contextual factors						
School district size (area)			20.024*	(11.841)	16.894	(10.387)
School district population			−2.380***	(0.624)	−2.463***	(0.550)
School district population density			1.333	(1.109)	1.187	(1.120)
Percent of college graduates in school district			0.976**	(0.434)	1.223**	(0.549)
Median income in school district			1.395	(5.716)	0.112	(5.706)
Median income squared			−2.511	(5.955)	−1.124	(6.223)
Economic heterogeneity in school district			−0.530	(1.235)	−0.237	(1.363)
Racial heterogeneity in school district			0.005	(0.280)	−0.040	(0.355)
Ideological heterogeneity in community			0.411	(0.979)	0.646	(1.112)
Religious involvement in community			−0.172	(0.204)	−0.121	(0.235)
Religious heterogeneity in community			−0.376*	(0.204)	−0.537**	(0.241)
Individual-contextual interactions						
College degree x percent of college graduates					0.748	(0.647)
Household income x median income in school district					−0.940	(0.993)
White x racial heterogeneity in school district					0.061	(0.389)
Religious involvement x community religious involvement					0.469	(0.401)
Religious involvement x community religious heterogeneity					−4.416*	(2.317)
Relative ideology					−0.305**	(0.150)
Constant	−1.510***	(0.127)	−1.221	(0.904)	−1.599	(1.202)
Summary statistic						
Pseudo R^2	0.10		0.10		0.10	
N	6,368		5,660		5,532	

Source: Saguaro Seminar (2001).

a. Robust standard errors are reported in parentheses. * $p < 0.10$; ** $p < 0.05$; *** $p < 0.01$.

Figure 12-1. *Impact of Individual-Level Factors on Attendance at School and Local Meetings*[a]

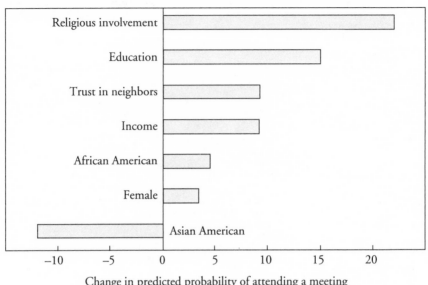

Change in predicted probability of attending a meeting

Source: Author's calculations.

a. Control variables are set to their means. Binary variables vary from 0 to 1, the others from 1 standard deviation below the mean to 1 above (or the categories most closely approximating that range.)

African Americans are more likely than whites to attend meetings on local and school politics, while Asian Americans are less likely. Hispanics, however, attend at the same rate as non-Hispanic whites.

Note that trust in neighbors is positive and highly significant. As suggested above, the fact that a higher degree of trust has a positive impact on meeting attendance suggests, even if only slightly, that this is not a form of participation motivated by localized political conflict. Finally, we see that religious involvement has a substantial, positive impact on whether someone attends a local meeting.

Because these models employ logistic regression, the coefficients are difficult to interpret in substantive terms, and so the coefficients have been translated into a more meaningful metric. Figure 12-1 displays the relative impact of each statistically significant variable on the probability of attending a meeting, holding everything else constant at its mean.[22] For the binary variables, the figure

22. Note that the probabilities are actually reported as percentages, as this is a more intuitive way to think about the results.

shows the impact of having one value versus the other, for example, being either female or male. In order to maintain consistency, the other variables vary between 1 standard deviation above and below the mean or the nominal categories that most closely approximate this range.[23] We see that religious involvement has the single largest impact on attending public meetings (21.6 points). Gender has the smallest impact (3.1) within this population, although the comparison between African Americans and whites is close in terms of magnitude (4.2). Of the factors that achieve statistical significance, being Asian American (as compared with white) is the only one with a negative impact—a substantial 12.3 points. Asian Americans' relatively low rate of meeting attendance suggests that there are significant barriers to the full incorporation of this group into local, particularly school, governance.

Contextual Variables

The model with individual-level factors only is only a warm-up for the headliner, the contextual variables. The individual-level variables, however, do provide a benchmark against which to compare the relative impact of contextual variables. This way, we can be informed as to the substantive as well as statistical significance of the factors included in the model.

While the central focus of our inquiry is the impact of heterogeneity on local and school politics, other contextual factors are of interest as well. They can be divided into three categories: geography, sociodemography, and heterogeneity. Geography includes first the physical size of a school district (the land area it occupies, measured in square miles), as well as the size of its population. This is particularly relevant for a study of school districts, given the wide variation in district size across the United States and, as Berry notes in chapter 3 of this volume, the increasing trend in the United States toward larger districts. Berry finds that larger districts lead to slightly "better" schools—or at least, to graduates who earn slightly more money in the labor force. If we think of school districts as political entities, we are reminded that the ideal size of a polity, both in terms of area and population, has long been a matter of concern to political philosophers, although it has been of only sporadic interest to empirically oriented political scientists. Oliver's work is a notable exception, as he provides evidence that communities of a relatively small geographic size facilitate civic engagement. Like Berry, he concludes that size matters.[24]

We can thus test whether the size of a school district matters in a comparable way. Similarly, we can see whether the second geography variable, the population of a school district, affects the decision to get involved in local and school

23. For example, education changes from high school graduate to a college degree, the two nominal categories that are closest to 1 standard deviation below and 1 standard deviation above the mean.

24. Oliver (2000).

politics. Perhaps a larger population fosters anonymity and a sense of alienation from the workings of local government, thus pulling local participation down. Or it could be that what Madison describes for the nation as a whole in *Federalist 10* applies to school districts as well—a larger population produces more political factionalization, sparking more conflict and stimulating participation.[25] The third geography variable is a measure of population density, which is simply calculated as population divided by area. As with the size of population, the expectation for the impact of population density is not clear. Greater density means a more urban environment, which again might foster anonymity and thus detachment from local politics. However, greater density might also spark conflict and facilitate the work of political mobilizers—face-to-face contact is much easier when large numbers of people are clustered together.

The sociodemographic makeup of a respondent's context is measured with four variables. The first is simply a measure of the percentage of people over age twenty-five with college degrees within the school district. Because an individual's level of education is a potent predictor of participation, we should expect a higher average level of educational attainment within a community to facilitate engagement in local and school politics. The second measure is the district's median income, for which the expected relationship is not so straightforward.[26] Oliver has found that the relationship between the affluence of an area and its residents' participation in local politics is curvilinear—falling in areas with both the lowest and the highest median incomes and rising in between. This pattern can be captured with the third measure, a squared term for median income (which would be negative should this same relationship hold in these data). Fourth, as a complement to the individual-level measure of religious commitment, the equation also incorporates the mean level of religious commitment within the community. Will a high level of religious commitment at the community level facilitate or inhibit individuals' rate of participation in local and school affairs? An important caveat about the contextual measure of religious involvement is in order. While the aforementioned contextual measures are external to the study and thus calculated using the school district as the geographic unit, that is not possible for religiosity. It is measured internally, and so its dispersion is calculated across each of the *communities* in the study, which do not necessarily coincide with school district boundaries. The results for community-level religious involvement, therefore, should not be interpreted as applying to school districts per se but instead to the wider community.

25. Madison (1961).

26. Owing to the aggregate nature of the data, median income is categorical (five categories) and more precisely described as a mean of medians. That is, it has been calculated using the census tract as the basic unit of analysis. Data from the tracts have been aggregated up the public school district boundaries, which means that the district-level measure consists of the average of the tract-level medians.

The model includes a series of variables that measure heterogeneity along four dimensions: economic, racial/ethnic, ideological, and religious. Economic heterogeneity is calculated using the index of qualitative variation (IQV).[27] The ethnoracial composition of each district is measured using a Herfindahl Index, a standard measure of heterogeneity. Intuitively, it is the probability that two randomly chosen people within a community are from different groups.[28] Both variables produce a score where a higher value means greater heterogeneity.

Both economic and racial heterogeneity are measures that have been used in past research, featuring prominently in the work of Oliver as well as Alesina and La Ferrara. In addition to these types of heterogeneity, the SCCBS allows for a measure of the ideological dispersion within a community, which has not been the subject of much research.[29] If, as Oliver suggests, political conflict sparks local political action, then it would follow that communities with greater ideological variance experience higher levels of engagement. Ideological diversity is measured as simply the standard deviation of political ideology within a community. The greater the standard deviation, the more ideologically heterogeneous the community. Because this measure has been constructed from within the SCCBS data, the same caveat that applies to the community-based measure of religious involvement is relevant here: ideological heterogeneity is not calculated across school districts, but communities. Finally, the model includes a measure of religious heterogeneity. It is calculated much like the measure of ideological heterogeneity—the standard deviation of religious commitment. The higher the number, the greater the variation in religious commitment within a community.

Recall that the literature on community heterogeneity leads to divergent expectations about the relationship between an area's social composition and the participation levels of its residents, depending on the type of participation in question. Heterogeneous communities spark disagreement over policy preferences, and thus increase participation motivated by political conflict. Places that are homogeneous, however, facilitate participation that is rooted in commonality rather than conflict—birds of a feather flocking together. The task at hand is to see whether any of these measures of heterogeneity affect attendance at meetings about local and school affairs, and if so whether the impact is positive or negative. If positive, that would suggest that attendance at such meetings is spurred by political conflict. If negative, it would suggest that social solidarity leads people to engage in local or school affairs or both.

27. This is calculated with the following formula: $IQV = k(N2 - Sum\ (f2))/N2\ (k - 1)$, where k = number of income groups (5), N= total number of cases, and $Sum(f2)$ = the sum of the squared frequencies. See Oliver (2001, chapter 3) for more details.

28. This is calculated using the following computational formula: $1 - \sum_r s_{rc}^2$, where r represents each racial group and c each community. Thus s_{rc} is the share of group r in each community c.

29. Although see Rahn and Rudolph (2001).

Column 2 of table 12-1 presents the results of models that parallel those in column 1, the only difference being the addition of the contextual variables. We turn first to the geographic variables: area, population, and density. The effect of a district's area is positive—larger districts have higher meeting attendance— although the coefficient is only marginally significant statistically. The size of a district's population has the opposite impact: the greater the population, the lower the probability of attending a meeting. This latter finding is consistent with Oliver's conclusion for municipal boundaries, that smaller towns and cities foster local participation.

Next, we move to the measures of a district's sociodemographic profile. We see that the percentage of college graduates within a district has a positive effect on attendance at meetings. However, there is no statistically significant impact for either median income or median income squared. This is in sharp contrast to Oliver's conclusion that the affluence of a community is an important factor in explaining the participation of the people who live there. The strength of religious commitment within a community also does not have a significant impact on meeting attendance.

The findings for the heterogeneity variables also diverge from Oliver's findings. Whereas he found that economic diversity leads to greater local political involvement, here it fails to achieve statistical significance. Tellingly, however, its sign is negative, not positive. Racial heterogeneity also comes nowhere near clearing the bar for statistical significance. Ideological heterogeneity (in the community, remember) also has no impact.

Among the heterogeneity variables, only one reaches statistical significance. All other things being equal, people who live in communities characterized by greater religious heterogeneity attend local and school meetings less than those who live in places with less variation in religious commitment. While Oliver does not examine religious heterogeneity per se, this finding is inconsistent with the general tenor of his argument that heterogeneity breeds participation.

Figure 12-2 again presents the substantive magnitude of the contextual variables, calculated as changes in the predicted probability of attending a local meeting as the independent variables shift from one standard deviation below the mean to one standard deviation above (all else being equal). The four variables that achieved statistical significance in the general population are displayed. Of these four, the educational environment has the largest substantive impact, an increase of 6.7 points, while the population of the district has the smallest, a decrease of 2 points. Most notable perhaps is simply the general observation that these variables have a much more muted impact than the individual-level factors.

Taken one by one, these results are a lot to absorb. When taken as a whole, however, some patterns emerge. First, we see that districts that are small in population but high in average education level facilitate attendance at meetings.

Figure 12-2. *Impact of Contextual Factors on Attendance at School and Local Meetings*[a]

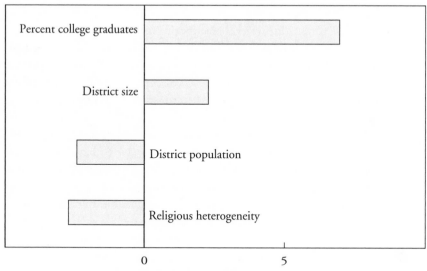

Change in predicted probability of attending a meeting

Source: Author's calculations.

a. Control variables are set to their means. Binary variables vary from 0 to 1, the others from 1 standard deviation below the mean to 1 above (or the categories most closely approximating that range.)

Neither relationship is surprising. School districts with a small population likely foster a sense of local attachment and facilitate the sort of engagement that reinforces social norms. Similarly, a higher average level of education would encourage paying attention to local affairs, especially the schools.

These data also suggest that Oliver's findings for heterogeneity, specifically economic heterogeneity, at the municipal level do not apply to school districts. Far from stimulating participation, living in an economically diverse community has no statistically significant impact on engagement with school governance (in fact, the direction of the relationship is negative, not positive). Neither racial nor ideological heterogeneity affects attendance at meetings either. Of the four heterogeneity variables, only religious heterogeneity has an impact—but in a negative direction. In other words, the more variation in religious commitment within a community, the lower the likelihood its residents will attend meetings related to school affairs. This suggests that it is not conflict but commonality—at least along religious lines—that motivates participation in school (and local) governance.

Interactions

After we have examined the individual and contextual factors that contribute to local political engagement in isolation, the final step is to put them together. Does the impact of individual-level characteristics vary according to social context? For example, even though we found that racial heterogeneity had no impact on involvement in local affairs—which suggests that this form of participation is not stimulated by racially motivated discord—it could be that *whites* become more participatory in a racially heterogeneous environment, which would suggest the presence of conflict after all.

I have tested for possible interactions in five areas: education, race, religion, income, and ideology. Nie, Junn, and Stehlik-Barry (1996) have argued that education has such a potent impact on participation because it is essentially a mechanism by which to sort people by socioeconomic status. According to them, what matters is not your absolute level of education, but your level of education *relative to that of others*. A college degree confers greater social status in a place where it is unusual than in a place where it is the norm. To test this hypothesis, the model includes an interaction between holding a college degree and the percentage of the population over age twenty-five who hold college degrees within one's local school district. If the Nie, Junn, and Stehlik-Barry argument holds up, we should expect this interaction to be negative—holding a college degree has less impact on participation as the average level of education in a school district rises.[30] A similar interaction is tested for income—an individual's own household income has been multiplied against the median in a community. As with education, a negative coefficient would mean that as the median income in a school district increases, the impact of an individual's own income decreases.[31]

For race, the interaction displayed in the model is between being white and the level of racial heterogeneity within a district. A positive coefficient would mean that as racial diversity in a district climbs, so does the likelihood that whites get involved in local politics. Other racial interactions have also been tested but for the sake of space are not presented. As discussed below, this decision seems warranted by the fact that the story is similar across all such interactions.[32]

---

30. Note that this particular application of education's impact as relative, rather than absolute, is an extension of the model developed in Nie, Junn, Stehlik-Barry (1996). They do not incorporate geographic differences into their model, as I do here. Also, in order to keep the interpretation of the coefficients straightforward, the individual-level measure of education is now a dichotomous measure of whether the respondent has graduated from college.

31. Admittedly, it could also mean the opposite, but that seems far less plausible.

32. As with education, here again there has been a slight change in the individual-level race variables included in the model in order to facilitate interpretation of the model. Rather than using "white" as the baseline category, in this case it is the only category included in the model. The substantive effect is, of course, the same either way.

As with race, we might expect that religiosity's impact is relative to the religious character of a community. Given that many anecdotal reports of involvement in school politics center on moral issues—sex education, treatment of homosexuality in the classroom, teaching evolution, and so forth—it could be that religious commitment sparks political conflict if people with strong religious convictions feel that their values are not represented in their public schools.[33] When it comes to religion, therefore, the relevant measure might not be an individual's level of religious involvement or even that of the community as a whole. Rather, what would matter is an individual's level of religious commitment *relative to* the religiosity of the community at large. Being highly religious in a secularly oriented environment—or vice versa—could lead to conflict over the presentation of morally tinged issues in the public schools. On the other hand, if engagement in local affairs is triggered more by social solidarity than political conflict, then we would expect highly religious people to be more likely to attend meetings when surrounded by similar people (and the same might apply to secularly minded people in a secular context). These hypotheses are straightforward enough, but testing them offers two alternatives. One is to think of religious involvement as being analogous to education or income. In this case, we would test for the presence of an interaction effect between individual and community-level religiosity, calculated by multiplying an individual's own level of religious commitment and the mean level in the community. Another, however, is to think of religious involvement as more comparable to race. In this case, the test would be an interaction between an individual's level of religious commitment and the degree of religious heterogeneity within the community. Because existing theory does not speak to this question, the model includes both interaction terms. (The results for each do not change if the other is omitted from the model.)

With either measure, does the religious composition of a community increase the level of participation of people with a high degree of religious commitment—which, as we have seen, is already quite high (that is, the interaction term is positive)? If so, this would support the theory that engagement with school issues is driven by localized conflict. If the interaction term is negative, that would mean that as religious heterogeneity increases, people with a greater level of religious involvement are less likely to attend meetings on school-related matters.[34] In other words, it would suggest that this form of participation is driven by commonality, not conflict.

The final interaction is between personal ideology and ideological context. If

33. Sharp (1999).

34. If we looked at the interaction term alone, it could also mean that people with less religious involvement are more likely to participate as religious heterogeneity increases. When the results are graphed, however, we see that this is not the case, as we would expect given that religious involvement is such a strong positive predictor of attendance (results available on request).

attendance at local meetings is driven by political conflict, then we should expect people who are out of step ideologically with their community to be more likely to get involved. Conversely, if ideological comity has a positive impact on local engagement, that would favor the view that local participation is a product of consensus. The measure of ideological consonance is simply the absolute value of the distance between an individual's own ideology and the mean ideology of the community. The higher the value, the more extreme one's relative ideology. Note that this measure is not dependent on an individual's absolute degree of ideological extremism nor its direction. Thus being a moderate in San Francisco might make you a radical in South Dakota, and a conservative in Boston could be a liberal in Boise. A positive value for the coefficient would mean that ideological extremists are more likely to attend local public meetings, while a negative value would mean that ideological comity brings people out.

Column 3 of table 12-1 displays the results of models that parallel those in columns 1 and 2, only now the interactions have been added to the individual-level and contextual variables. For the education interaction, we do not see evidence in favor of Nie, Junn, and Stehlik-Barry's argument among this population. One's relative education level does not drive local participation. Likewise, the income interaction comes nowhere near statistical significance. There is also no interaction effect for race.[35]

The religious interactions tell an interesting story. The interaction between an individual's religious involvement and the level of religious involvement in the community falls far short of statistical significance. However, the interaction between religious involvement and religious heterogeneity is significant, in a negative direction. In other words, religiously involved people are less, not more, likely to participate in local politics as the mean level of religious heterogeneity in their community rises. The coefficient for relative ideology leads to a similar inference. Recall that relative ideology measures one's distance from the ideological mean of the community. A negative coefficient means that the closer you are to your community's ideological mainstream, the more likely you are to attend a local meeting on town or school affairs.

The substantive impact of the interaction terms can again be determined by calculating predicted probabilities. Without the interaction the simultaneous impact of an increase in an individual's religious involvement and a community's level of religiosity is 21.6 points. Accounting for the interaction drops that slightly, to 17 points. For relative ideology, the range of variation shifts slightly.

---

35. As mentioned above, it is important to note that I have experimented with multiple permutations of racial interactions—different racial groups multiplied against racial heterogeneity. Neither African Americans nor Hispanics are more, or for that matter less, likely to participate in an ethnoracially heterogeneous school district. Nor does the story change when each ethnoracial group is interacted with the share of the population of the same group (for example, African American x percentage African American).

Since the measure is in relation to the mean, the meaningful comparison is to vary the value from the mean to 2 standard deviations above the mean, which decreases the probability of meeting attendance by 3.2 points. (And, obviously, there is no contextual variable to vary.)

From this array of results, we can distill evidence that engagement in local, including school, politics does not increase in environments where political conflict is expected to result because individuals differ from others in their surroundings. On the contrary, the individual-contextual interaction terms for religious involvement and political ideology suggest that people are more likely to make a participatory investment in their communities and schools where they are surrounded by people who share their degree of religious involvement and political ideology.

Conclusion

Imagine that you wanted to design school districts so as to increase their residents' participation in school affairs.[36] What could you learn from this analysis? In answering that question, there are obviously some factors affecting participation that are more amenable to policy manipulation than others. For example, increasing the average education in a district would undoubtedly increase the level of participation, but this would be an extremely tall task for local policymakers.[37] Similarly, it is difficult to see what policymakers could do to affect the level of religious involvement within a community, even if they put aside both its political impracticality and constitutional infeasibility.

Even the one school district characteristic that seems most pliable turns out to be fraught with complexity. As we have seen, size matters. Or at least, size of population matters. Smaller districts have higher levels of participation (although not by much). Therefore, one reform to enhance participation in school affairs might be to create districts with smaller populations. Even this apparently straightforward reform, however, is not as simple as it seems. According to these data, if we wanted to facilitate participation among parents, school districts should simultaneously increase in area and decrease in population!

The findings for heterogeneity are potentially far more explosive, but no less complex. A naïve reading of this analysis might lead to the suggestion that policymakers craft ideologically and religiously homogeneous school districts in order to enhance participation. At the risk of grave understatement, this sort of policy engineering would undoubtedly strike many Americans as morally suspect.

36. It is important to keep in mind that this portion of the discussion focuses on participation in meetings that deal with school affairs, while, as noted, the dependent variable in the forgoing analysis covers a broader range of meetings.

37. Although, as we have seen, there is a diminishing returns process at work. As the average education level increases, the impact of education at the individual level drops off.

At the very least, the lesson to be learned is that America's diversity presents a civic challenge. And the best hope for grappling with that challenge is understanding the nature of local participation. The fact that homogeneous communities, including school districts, have higher levels of localized participation suggests that something other than a Madisonian "clash of interests" generally motivates this type of engagement. To borrow Mansbridge's felicitous terms, attendance at meetings on local and school affairs appears to be better characterized as a form of *unitary* rather than *adversary* democracy.[38] In this respect, these findings for participation in school governance suggest a causal mechanism distinct from that described by Oliver for participation in local politics. This is more than a debate over abstruse social science theories, as it speaks to the reasons that people get involved in local governing institutions. While Oliver paints a picture of local politics (including, presumably, school board politics) driven by conflict, these results suggest that public institutions, or at least school boards, should be designed to foster a sense of solidarity within local communities.

At this point, I am not prepared to offer specific, empirically grounded policy proposals to foster such solidarity and thus enhance participation. However, it is fair to say that far from being a pie-in-the-sky objective, experience has shown that such institutions can be designed at the local level. A compelling study, Berry, Portney, and Thomson (1993), highlights the positive participatory impact when cities create small-scale neighborhood associations with real decisionmaking power. Interestingly, when applied to school districts this would seem to be consistent with the observation that smaller (in terms of population) is better. Nevertheless, with the data at hand it would be premature to propose that school boards adopt any specific institutional features to enhance participation in the governance of the local schools. Before we know what works, two things have to happen. First, school boards must take up the challenge to serve as laboratories of democratic engagement, experimenting with different ways to strengthen the connections between school officials and their constituents. Second, these efforts—many of which are undoubtedly already under way—must be evaluated rigorously, with an eye toward determining the best practices for enhancing participation in the governance of local public schools.

References

Alesina, Alberto, and Eliana La Ferrara. 2000. "Participation in Heterogeneous Communities." *Quarterly Journal of Economics* 115 (August): 847–904.

Berry, Jeffrey M., Kent E. Portney, and Ken Thomson. 1993. *The Rebirth of Urban Democracy*. Brookings.

---

38. Mansbridge (1980).

Burns, Nancy, Donald R. Kinder, and Wendy Rahn. 2003. "Social Trust and Democratic Politics." Paper presented at the annual meeting of the Midwest Political Science Association. Chicago, April 3–6.

Burns, Nancy, Kay Lehman Schlozman, and Sidney Verba. 2001. *The Private Roots of Public Action.* Harvard University Press.

Costa, Dora L., and Matthew E. Kahn. 2003. "Civic Engagement and Community Heterogeneity: An Economist's Perspective." *Perspectives on Politics* 1 (1): 103–11.

Delli Carpini, Michael X., and Scott Keeter. 1996. *What Americans Know about Politics and Why It Matters.* Yale University Press.

Geolytics, Inc. 2001. Neighborhood Change Database 1970–2000. Tract Data (computer file). East Brunswick, N.J.

Huckfeldt, Robert, and John Sprague. 1993. "Citizens, Contexts, and Politics." In *Political Science: The State of the Discipline II*, edited by A. W. Finifter. Washington: American Political Science Association.

Jenkins, Krista, and others. 2003. "Is Civic Behavior Political? Exploring the Multidimensional Nature of Political Participation." Paper presented at the annual meeting of the Midwest Political Science Association. Chicago, April 3–6.

Layman, Geoffrey. 2001. *The Great Divide: Religious and Cultural Conflict in American Party Politics.* Columbia University Press.

Madison, James. 1961. "Federalist 10." In *The Federalist Papers*, edited by C. Rossiter. New York: Mentor (Penguin).

Mansbridge, Jane J. 1980. *Beyond Adversary Democracy.* New York: Basic Books.

Nie, Norman H., Jane Junn, and Kenneth Stehlik-Barry. 1996. *Education and Democratic Citizenship in America.* University of Chicago Press.

Oliver, J. Eric. 2000. "City Size and Civic Involvement in Metropolitan America." *American Political Science Review* 94 (2): 361–73.

———. 2001. *Democracy in Suburbia.* Princeton University Press.

Putnam, Robert D. 2000. *Bowling Alone: The Collapse and Revival of American Community.* New York: Simon and Schuster.

Rahn, Wendy, and Thomas J. Rudolph. 2001. "Spatial Variation in Trust in Local Government: The Roles of Institutions, Culture, and Community Heterogeneity." Paper presented at the Conference on Political Trust. Princeton University, Center for the Study of Democratic Politics, November 30–December 1.

Saguaro Seminar ("Civic Engagement in America"). 2001. Social Capital Community Benchmark Survey 2000. Harvard University, John F. Kennedy School of Government. Distributed by Roper Center for Public Opinion Research, Storrs, Conn.

Sharp, Elaine B., ed. 1999. *Culture Wars and Local Politics.* University of Kansas Press.

Verba, Sidney, and Norman H. Nie. 1972. *Participation in America: Political Democracy and Social Equality.* University of Chicago Press.

Verba, Sidney, Kay Lehman Schlozman, and Henry E. Brady. 1995. *Voice and Equality: Civic Voluntarism in American Politics.* Harvard University Press.

13

The End of Local Politics?

JOSEPH P. VITERITTI

Nearly twenty years have passed since the Institute for Educational Leadership in Washington, D.C., prepared a well-received report on American school boards that might well have served as a primer for "School Board Politics," the symposium that resulted in the publication of this volume.[1] Based on case studies conducted in more than 200 jurisdictions from nine metropolitan areas and three predominantly rural states, the results were both illuminating and discouraging. They revealed that while the American people seemed to support the notion of local control through popularly elected school boards, their support did not extend to the school boards in their own communities. The public did not know very much about the functions and activities of these governing bodies; respondents, nonetheless, shared certain general perceptions that were not particularly flattering. They saw school boards as contentious institutions on which "civically qualified" leaders were reluctant to serve. These negative impressions were mirrored by consistently low voter turnout in school board elections throughout the regions studied. The authors of the report also remarked on the paucity of research that had been conducted on the subject up until that time.

A reading of the preceding chapters suggests that while much has changed in the politics and governance of education since the IEL report was released, the

---

1. Institute for Educational Leadership (1986).

underlying problems persist. Nor has much been written on the topic since then, which the present volume aims to correct. Although the authors of these chapters approach the subject from a variety of perspectives and are not altogether in agreement, certain key themes emerge that point future researchers in productive directions. My assignment, as I take it, is to identify these themes and connect them to a larger body of research.

Since the great majority of American school boards are popularly elected, it stands to reason that they are widely perceived as representative bodies. This, after all, is the way democratic governments are supposed to work. The history of American school boards, however, is somewhat more complicated. In actuality, through the first half of the twentieth century, school board members served as trustees who delegated broad discretion to professionally trained administrators.[2] Boards were commonly dominated by men from business and professional backgrounds who were condescending in their disposition toward the less advantaged children in their charge and the legions of women who staffed the schools.[3] As Robert Salisbury described it, the entire governing scheme was based upon the myth of a unitary community for which school board members could ably speak.[4] When populations grew diverse and issues became divisive in the latter part of the century, competition for vacancies became keen and membership more representative, especially in urban environments.[5] Ethnic rivalries, teacher unions, and the civil rights movement all had a hand in producing the new dynamic. To put it plainly, school boards became political, which is not necessarily a bad thing. The literature of the 1960s and 1970s reflected the growing recognition that policymaking in school districts is a political process responsive to the dictates of interests and power.[6] The rough and tumble portrait that emerged was at least partially due to an increased scholarly focus on cities.

As I read through the preceding chapters, I could not help but to wonder if perhaps we are entering a third stage in the life of American school boards in which politics—conceived as conflict between competing groups and interests—is once again on the decline. That is not necessarily a bad thing either, depending on the causes and effects. The problem is that the causes and effects vary from one place to another. That will take some explaining, which I will get to later in this chapter. First, let me say more about what I think the other chapters, taken as a whole, tell us—and alert the reader that while my observations are based in some part on their contents, I make no assumption that their respective authors or editors are in agreement with me.

2. Tyack and Hansot (1982, pp. 105–201).
3. Counts (1927); Charters (1953).
4. Salisbury (1967).
5. Drachler (1977).
6. Kimbrough (1964); Iannaccone and Lutz (1970); Peterson (1976).

Localism: In Spirit and in Law

Richard Briffault put his finger on one of the great contradictions of school governance in America: while there has always been a strong tradition of localism, the fact is that the weight of legal authority in education policymaking lies at the state level, where the legislature enjoys plenary power. The authority of local school districts and the boards that govern them is even more circumscribed than that of counties and municipalities because school districts are singular in their function and purpose. That being said, one should remember that school boards are not the only depositories of local educational authority. Luis Fraga and his colleagues describe the relationship between the San Francisco school board and a succession of superintendents, observing the differing degrees of latitude that the former allowed the latter. Although school boards have the formal power to appoint and (at times) remove their chief executive, the relationship between them is very often a function of the leadership skills of the superintendent. It is for this reason that by the 1970s and 1980s, scholarly attention turned toward the school superintendent.[7] In at least some instances, depending on the capabilities of the incumbent, it appeared that the big dog of the school board was being wagged by the feisty executive tail. In their monumental study of school boards around the country, Zeigler and Jennings (1974) portrayed the school board as a mere agent for legitimacy that gave the superintendent broad discretion and a wide berth in running the district.

Of course, developments over the 1990s have worked to limit the discretion that remains for local education players to negotiate. States are more apt to exercise their takeover power, big city mayors are seeking direct control, and charter laws are ceding to individual schools powers that once belonged to school boards. Then there is the federal government, which has managed to intrude on local affairs through the aggressive application of judicial power, beginning with the landmark *Brown* v. *Board of Education* ruling and extending through Congress's manipulative spending of federal money. A big question that hung over the "School Board Politics" symposium concerns the impact that President George W. Bush's No Child Left Behind Act (NCLB) will have on the federal-state equation. The most precise answer one can give is "It depends." First of all, it depends on the perspective from which one views the new law. On one hand, it is the boldest assertion of federal power ever made by a president and Congress; on the other hand, it was a big compromise in comparison with other kinds of initiatives discussed in Washington over the previous two decades.[8] In 1989, when President George H. Bush met with the National Governors Association in Charlottesville, Virginia, all the talk was about national education

---

7. See, for example, Cuban (1976), Boyd (1976), McCorry, (1978), Scott (1980), Viteritti (1983).
8. See Ravitch (1995); Ravitch (2000a, pp. 408–52); Viteritti (2004).

goals. The president's plan received a surprisingly warm reception from the state leaders, and it was later incorporated into his America 2000 proposal, which also included voluntary national testing. The program eventually died in Congress. In 1994 President Bill Clinton went so far as to appoint a National Education Goals Panel and a National Education Standards and Improvement Panel, and he too toyed with the idea of national testing. Then the Clinton plan also died in Congress, where Republicans were wary of an expanded federal role and Democrats refused their support without a significant appropriation of new federal money.

President George W. Bush's NCLB legislation has resulted in a 40 percent increase in federal spending and allows the states more flexibility on how to use it. Rather than impose federal standards and tests, it requires the states to develop their own. States must also approve local plans for improving the quality of teaching staff, and parents are to be provided with detailed information on the performance of their children and the schools that they attend. It is undeniable that NCLB will alter the balance of federal-state power, but the more ambiguous question is how it will affect the state-local relationship and, indirectly, the power of school boards. That will depend on the district. Since it will be the responsibility of the states to enforce the new standards, state power will be felt most sharply in districts with a record of low performance—more specifically, districts where large numbers of students do not demonstrate adequate yearly progress, where too few teachers are found to be qualified, and where there are an insufficient number of seats available in good schools for children to exercise the transfer option. These are the same districts that will ultimately face federal sanctions when states come up empty in developing strategies for their improvement. All of this figures to bring a measured loss in local autonomy, but the point is that this effect of NCLB will be felt unevenly across the districts.

School District Size

One recurring theme that appeared throughout the symposium concerns the influence of school district size on other factors. Larger districts tend to be more demographically diverse, but the evidence is mixed as to whether size increases involvement in school board elections or educational matters more generally. Rick Hess and David Leal tell us that money plays a more significant role in determining the outcome of school board elections in larger districts than in smaller ones. According to Terry Moe, teacher unions—generally assumed to be the most powerful force in school politics at all levels of government—are more apt to rely on collective bargaining as a lever for getting what they want in smaller districts, reserving political action in the form of electoral strategies and lobbying for use in larger arenas.

There is some evidence that school board politics (and educational politics in general) is more contentious in larger districts, which might explain in part why teacher unions are inclined to pull out all the stops when doing business in these raucous places. Size can also help determine the level of representation on school boards. When racial minorities are numerical minorities, they tend to do better in elections that are structured around small single-member districts or wards. This finding is consistent with what we know about municipal and congressional elections, although some scholars would argue that concentrating minorities in a few self-contained districts ultimately works to dilute minority influence in the policy realm.[9]

Applying Hannah Pitkin's very useful typology, both the Meier and Juenke and the Marschall research found a correlation between "descriptive representation" on school boards in minority districts and "substantive representation" in the form of school quality.[10] However, they used different criteria for measuring school quality, and neither found compelling evidence for establishing causality. Marschall relied on citizen satisfaction, acknowledging that such satisfaction might also be a response to what Pitkin referred to as "symbolic representation." Meier and Juenke used standardized test scores and further speculated that performance was a function of larger minority representation among teachers and administrators in the better-scoring districts, which also correlated with minority membership on the school board. While the correlations stand, one has to wonder how school board representation might so readily translate into administrative and teaching jobs in an age of civil service examinations. Furthermore, the research evidence supporting the claim that minority children perform better with minority teachers is mixed and inconclusive.[11] I would like to suggest another explanation for what Meier and Juenke found, which admittedly is also speculative. Before taking that up, however, I want to conclude my observations on the size variable.

There also seems to be a connection between size and district performance, at least as it pertains to the process of school district consolidation. As Berry explained, an initial argument for consolidating smaller districts into larger ones was that it would lead to managerial efficiency or economy. He finds, to the contrary, that consolidation has resulted in neither efficiency nor economy nor, more important, effectiveness. Berry hangs his explanation on the fact that larger districts tend to have larger schools, which in turn produce depressed student outcomes. There is a fairly convincing body of research on the connection between school size and student performance, but there is no inherent reason why larger districts brought about through consolidation must engender larger schools, even

9. Swain (1993).
10. Pitkin (1972).
11. See Dee (2004).

though they apparently do.[12] Nonetheless, whether the low performance of these districts is primarily a result of their larger schools is rather speculative. I tend to think that there is more going on here, but before I add my own speculations to the matter, let me make one more observation about the size factor.

While I am persuaded that size is a significant factor that affects a range of other important variables, it is too broad a qualifier to have any meaningful predictive value for social scientists studying school boards and local politics. We need more precise classifications. Suppose we start with the more concise if somewhat untidy classifications of urban, suburban, rural. Notwithstanding the fact that many suburban districts on the edges of major cities have begun to resemble urban districts, the phenomenon of urbanization goes a long way in helping us recognize certain patterns. Urban districts are by definition large, and increasingly they have been associated with low performance. Henceforth, these districts are also more probable candidates for state (and indirectly federal) intervention under NCLB, assuming the law does what it is supposed to do. As Christopher Berry and William Howell found, low performance can also generate retrospective voting and turnover on school boards, thus competition. The politics of urban districts can be especially competitive when new groups are in the process of challenging more established interests. Suburban and rural districts tend to be more homogeneous and less politically volatile than their urban counterparts, though performance patterns in rural areas are more likely to resemble those of the city. Therefore rural districts also face a high probability of state intervention under NCLB, compromising local autonomy.

As we try to sort out some of the patterns that have been observed thus far, we see some inconsistencies that cannot be reconciled with our broad classification. One might have anticipated that as African Americans and Hispanics came to assume a more dominant role in local politics and on school boards, especially in urban areas, school districts would become more responsive to the needs of their children. This is what happened in the Meier and Juenke and the Marschall samples; unfortunately, it is not the general pattern. On the whole, politics has been a disappointing vocation for reform-minded groups in cities. There are some reasonable explanations for this, and they are not entirely speculative because they draw on a body of work that might serve to place the "School Board Politics" symposium in a larger context.

Democracy and Demography

The most elaborate social science investigation of urban educational politics conducted in the past decade is the Civic Capacity and Urban Education Project,

12. Toch (2003).

directed by Clarence Stone and Jeffrey Henig (Stone and others 2001). Generously supported by the National Science Foundation, their research encompassed eleven cities and is associated with six separate books. It involved telephone interviews, field research, and the collection of demographic and financial data. The central purpose of the project was to determine how sustainable coalitions assembled at the local level could be built to promote school reform. Although there are problems with the way the team approaches these subjects, the research offers insights that are relevant to the symposium.[13] First of all, it found that school boards—whether elected or appointed—are not significant centers of policy change.[14] Most board members were preoccupied with constituency service rather than policy innovation. This peripheral role was reinforced by the existence of more visible superintendents and an autonomous bureaucracy.

The most revealing finding to emerge from the effort was the widespread absence of either civic engagement or meaningful reform in the cities studied.[15] Stone and Henig define civic engagement broadly to include cooperative arrangements among diverse public and private institutions that function to establish governing regimes at the local level. Their general realm of concern is not equivalent to the kind of school board politics that is the focus of the present volume, but it is related. Since the governing regimes they observed include parent groups, teacher unions, business leaders, and a variety of other organized interests, they are certainly involved in school board politics. Moreover, the low level of civic involvement registered by local notables in the cities studied is quite consistent with the low level of voter turnout we have seen in school board elections. After all, if local elites do not participate in school politics, it should come as no surprise that average citizens do not either—except, maybe, parents with children in school. Perhaps we need to come to terms with the fact that while citizens register a high level of concern for the condition of American education, very few seem to care enough about educational politics to leap into the fray. Of the eleven cities included in the Civic Capacity project, only San Francisco consistently comes out high on an annual survey conducted by the Council of Great City Schools (2001) on academic performance in fifty-five urban districts. Remarkably, San Francisco scores at the bottom of the civic mobilization scale constructed by the Stone and Henig team; its reform agenda was dictated in a top-down fashion by an aggressive federal court involved in a long dispute over racial desegregation. What does all this tell us about local activity? Does politics really matter?

The Stone and Henig series presents a fascinating analysis of ethnic succession in the urban political environment. If the regime theory to which they subscribe

13. See Viteritti (2003, pp. 242–48).
14. Stone and others (2001, p. 85).
15. Stone and others (2001, pp. 123–40).

represents the next generation of political science research after the reign of the pluralist paradigm, then what regime theorists discovered describes the next generation of political engagement in American cities.[16] Robert Dahl's seminal study of New Haven included an astute historical analysis depicting how white ethnic groups, through their sheer strength in numbers, took control from the older patrician elite.[17] Regime theory—at least as it is presented in the Civic Capacity and Urban Education Project—carries the story to the next chapter, in which African American and Hispanic activists take control from white ethnic groups.

It stands to reason that as African Americans and Hispanics began to gain majority status in urban communities, they inherited the reins of political power—although the transfer did not come without a struggle. This was the goal that black activists in the 1960s and 1970s set for themselves. As the history of New Haven writ large on the broader urban landscape demonstrates, population bulk eventually converts into political muscle. At some point, these same fluctuations in the populations of cities and their surrounding areas also alter the composition of local labor pools, allowing teachers and administrators who work in schools to better reflect the composition of the student body. This suggests that personnel shifts may not be the result of better representation on school boards, but of general population shifts that affect both school boards and the labor pool. The question is, at what point does the latter shift occur? How large a majority of the general population do African Americans and Hispanics need before the shift can significantly affect the profile of those who work in the schools? This is another way to frame the research that was presented in the earlier chapters, but it is even more complex than it may first seem.

The personnel transition in schools is not as automatic as it might be in other public services, such as among sanitation or clerical workers or even fire and police personnel. Because school administrators and teachers are professionals, the transition requires the presence of an educated middle class within the minority population. Baltimore, which has a long history of a black middle class, stands out as an example. Because African Americans were excluded from the private sector, schools were a natural place for them to fulfill their professional aspirations.[18] This again underscores the fact that representation in the staffing of school personnel is as much (and probably more) a function of demography as it is of politics. Let us not forget that the purpose of civil service reforms implemented at the end of the nineteenth century was to ensure that hiring was not determined by politics.[19] Then the target of the reform campaign was the old political machine controlled by white immigrant groups. Since those efforts were largely successful, the civil service system that remains operative

16. Stone (1989); Elkin (1987).
17. Dahl (1961).
18. Orr (1999, pp. 63–80).
19. Hays (1964).

today also works to modify the connection between descriptive representation on school boards and representation among school personnel.

The great disappointment of black and Hispanic political succession in cities is that it did not sensitize school districts to the needs of minority children sufficiently to improve their academic performance. A central assumption of black activists who decades ago rebelled against education bureaucracies dominated by white professionals was that descriptive representation in the power alignment was to result in substantive representation in the output of local services.[20] Part of the explanation for the fact that this did not occurr is also demographic. African American and Hispanic children arrived at school with an accumulation of economic, social, and cultural deficits that made it more difficult to raise academic performance.[21] Another part of the explanation, according to the Stone and Henig team, is political. While minority (African American and Hispanic) political leaders ostensibly support school reform, cities with large black popular and political majorities—most notably Baltimore, Washington, and Detroit— have galvanized into employment regimes.[22] Political leaders with constituents who work in school systems are reluctant to shake things up. Their first instinct is to protect the status quo.

Reading this evidence, I suspect that Terry Moe would again remind us of the power of teacher unions. One cannot overstate the significance of such a finding because it suggests that many black middle-class constituents identify as employees of the school system rather than as parents of students within the school system. This should not be so shocking, however, because many white teachers do the same thing. It all becomes plausible when we recognize that many teachers do not live in the cities where they work, and many of those who do live there send their children to private schools. Here again Baltimore comes to mind. Historically, because of racial segregation and their exclusion from the public schools, many middle-class African Americans in that city developed an allegiance to their own church-based private schools.[23] Thus they may not be a significant part of the client base of the public schools. In most cities, the clientele of the school system is drawn from a less advantaged population—one that lacks the political potency of those who are part of the employment regime.[24] That being the case, one must also concede that when large numbers of teachers live outside the city in which they work, it serves to dilute union influence in school board elections, though only to a point. In large districts with low turnout rates, labor's money, along with its political machinery, goes a long way in determining electoral outcomes.

20. Ravitch (2000b, pp. 251–378); Altshuler (1970).
21. Jencks and Phillips (1998, pp.1–51); Thernstrom and Thernstrom (2003, pp. 83–119).
22. Stone and others (2001, pp. 136–39).
23. Orr (1999, 24–26).
24. Viteritti (1983, pp. 314–22, 335–46).

Before leaving the topic of demography, there is one relevant finding in the Meier and Juenke and the Marschall chapters worthy of reconsideration. That is the connection they found between descriptive representation among school professionals and substantive representation regarding school quality. While there are many good reasons to have more minority teachers in minority classrooms, I am not persuaded that it necessarily improves academic performance. If this were so, then cities like Baltimore, Detroit, and Washington, D.C., which have large numbers of minority teachers, should be among the better-performing urban school districts. So why then does there seem to be such a connection in the sample districts observed above? I do not pretend to have an answer to this puzzle, but I do have a suggestion for future research, one which flows from my earlier comments on demographics. It would be valuable to know whether school professionals and the educated middle-class population of which they are a part send their children to the public schools in the districts where they work. The presence of black or Hispanic middle-class children in the public schools may function to raise overall academic performance—the same way that the presence of white middle-class children usually does. Their presence might also serve to anchor a larger middle-class population in the public schools that is neither black nor Hispanic. Their being there might suggest that there is a critical mass of political constituents—including school professionals—who are more identified with the clientele of their school systems than with the kind of employment regimes that were found in Baltimore, Washington, and Detroit.

Politics versus Civics

One of the more intriguing conversations to emerge from the symposium grew out of David Campbell's distinction between politics and civics. If I understand the difference correctly, politics refers to the kind of competition for influence and favors that political scientists have been discussing since David Truman explained the role that interest groups play in the power game.[25] Civics is what Robert Putnam had in mind when he described the voluntary activity in which citizens partake to improve life in their communities.[26] One is self-interested; the other is public oriented. Each thrives in a different kind of environment. Politics thrives in the tumultuous kind of faction-laden world that James Madison envisioned when he wrote his famous *Federalist No. 10*. Civics thrives in the sort of small pacific precincts that Jefferson imagined, where like-minded neighbors would come together to do the public business, a most important part of which involved education.

25. Truman (1960).
26. Putnam (2000).

The Madisonian model appears most applicable to twenty-first-century school boards in urban settings, which can be diverse, competitive, and factionalized. There, of course, are variations on the urban scene that need to be examined. Let us first, however, consider the other categories in our admittedly broad classification: rural and suburban districts. Writing on school board elections in the early 1970s, Peter Cistone found that demographic homogeneity in suburban and rural districts made elections less contested than was characteristic in their urban counterparts.[27] One has to wonder if such placidity will be shaken by retrospective voting as suburbs become more like cities in demographics and temperament and as NCLB forces rural districts to face the realities of academic failure.

The scene in comfortable suburban districts, however, is the antithesis of urban commotion. Here the population is homogeneous, resources are plentiful, teachers and staff are well-paid, the unions are content, academic performance is high, incumbency is secure, and elections are predictable. When teachers so easily get what they want at the bargaining table, there is no need to be politically aggressive. When students are registering high levels of achievement, there is no reason for retrospective voting. This is hardly politics as we know it in the city. In fact, it is hardly politics. It more resembles the civic activity that Jefferson wrote about in his model of localism. Jefferson sought to divide government into small districts because he believed it would allow citizens to achieve self-government through face-to-face transactions. He assumed that people who lived in small, self-defined communities shared a common perspective and that familiarity among like-minded people would allow decisionmaking to proceed on the basis of consensus.[28] Involvement is an act of civic duty rather than political opportunity. That, for the most part, is what we have today in small homogeneous school districts where parents and citizens are complacent.

But what of educational politics in the city? We actually may be approaching a new era, at least in some jurisdictions. The memory of black militants confronting an educational bureaucracy controlled by white professionals does not square with the picture that was recently presented in Baltimore, Washington, and Detroit. There we find a superficial political quiescence absent the motivational force of racial antagonism, where citizen involvement is low and decisionmaking is controlled by a governing regime that is not focused on change. In reality, demographic homogeneity produces a political apathy that discourages political action. The pattern is reinforced in urban environments, where most residents are educationally, socially, and economically disadvantaged—characteristics that also work to depress voter turnout and political involvement. Of course, this is not the case in all urban districts. Cities like San Francisco, Houston, and Chicago, which have a diversity of racial minority groups that include

27. Cistone (1974).
28. See also Mansbridge (1983, pp. 3–35, 253–89).

Hispanics and Asians, have been the scenes of competitive school board elections, although still with relatively low turnout.[29] All this suggests to future researchers that we should continue to explore the relationship between demographic diversity and competition. Diversity, however, should not be measured solely as an erosion of white dominance. Competition between and among racial minorities is a phenomenon worthy of close examination. Whether such competition will at some point serve to raise participation in school board elections among low-income people remains to be seen.

One of the more interesting developments to have occurred at the local level in cities and elsewhere is the response that parents have had to the availability of choice programs, either in the form of charter schools or vouchers. Unlike electoral participation, participation in choice programs has not been characterized by class or racial bias. Most evidence suggests that poor and minority children are as likely to participate in charter programs as their white middle-class peers.[30] They are even more likely to register for voucher programs, but this skewed effect usually is a result of program design, which in both public and private initiatives has targeted low-income children attending failing public schools. It is noteworthy that so many people who have customarily refrained from political activity have been motivated to join voluntary communities (such as charter or private schools) devoted to the education of their children. Perhaps these parents understand that such engagement is a more productive use of their energy than politics, which tends to be controlled by stakeholders who do not represent their interests. Nonetheless, such activity is a form of civic involvement that helps build social capital at the community level.[31] We need to learn more about this. We need to know how and why the same populations of people who have abstained from political participation have been otherwise engaged. With few exceptions, researchers have focused on school choice as an economic phenomenon, a form of consumer activity. It is also a civic phenomenon.

Perhaps the most important question to be addressed here concerns the kind of activity—political or civic—that will eventually work to improve the overall level of school performance in minority and low-income districts. The learning gap is a chronic condition in American education, and it is most severe in urban, followed by rural, environments. Thus it is becoming common for states to resort to extraordinary institutional mechanisms to address it. As Ken Wong and Francis Shen point out in chapter 4, nearly half the states have passed legislation that would put the control of failing school districts in the hands of either mayors or state officials. These takeovers are designed to circumvent local politics and take authority for day-to-day operations from elected school boards and

29. Stone (1998).
30. Finn and others (2000, p. 157)
31. Schneider and others (1997).

their superintendents. They replace political regimes with management regimes that are supposedly removed from the influence of local politics. Their purpose is to impose accountability through hierarchic top-down management structures that will appropriate resources wisely and improve student outcomes. This is a different picture from the one that was painted earlier in well-heeled suburban districts. In those happy places, civics replaces politics because politics is deemed both irrelevant and unnecessary. In more troubled urban environments, management replaces politics because politics is deemed to be part of the larger problem that results in shabby schooling.

Risks and Trade-Offs

All this may appear discomforting to those who think of school boards as instruments of local democracy. The truth of the matter, however, is that Americans have always been ambivalent about the role of politics in education. They never quite trusted politicians with the care and upbringing of their children. That is why Progressive reformers at the end of the nineteenth century set up a separate governance structure for schools that was a step removed from municipal politics. In retrospect their institutional concoction was a bit naïve; reformers never anticipated how it would eventually serve to produce an insulated politics of its own. The irony of takeover regimes is that they look to municipal and state politicians to rescue schools from the mess of school politics. That mess was very much the product of changes imposed by Progressives in the name of reform. As the conventional wisdom that arose from research thirty years ago found, separate nonpartisan elections kept turnout low, discouraged competition, and protected incumbency.[32] It also provided educational professionals with a level of political protection that made them unaccountable. Writing for the *American Political Science Review* at mid-century, Thomas Eliot perceptively explained that "the school board's primary functions . . . are to hire and support a competent professional as superintendent, defend the schools against public criticism, and persuade the people to open their pocketbooks."[33]

But not all Progressive changes in local governance were for the worse. Their wisdom becomes more apparent when seen in the municipal sphere. Progressive reformers understood that at-large elections would produce a better caliber of candidate than ward politics, and that strong mayors with centralized power would be more visible and therefore more accountable for their actions.[34] The validity of their claims has grown apparent with the passage of time. Jeffersonian

32. Zeigler and Jennings (1974).
33. Eliot (1959, p. 1033).
34. Viteritti (1990, pp. 228–34).

localism had much to say for itself in rural Virginia during the eighteenth century, when familiarity with one's representatives in government was a function of geographical proximity. In the political world of the twenty-first century, there is an inverse relationship between localization and popular participation, and school board elections are no exception. In the modern age of the media, voters are more familiar with the ways and accomplishments of executive officials, and they are more likely to show up at the polls when the latter stand for election. Such visibility creates a level of accountability that is not present in school board elections. Therefore a key argument in support of managerial regimes, whether they are imposed at the behest of city or state executives, is that they potentially are more democratic.

In their review of mayoral takeovers, Wong and Shen found that the more direct involvement of mayors in education matters has contributed to both an increase in spending on schools and an improvement in their performance. In the past, mayors in cities with fiscally dependent school districts have been reluctant to spend money on a service over which they had little or no authority. Responsibility and control provide chief executives with an incentive to invest resources in schools.[35] It remains to be seen whether such responsibility and control can achieve sustained improvement at the school level. If Chicago and New York are any indication of things to come, much will depend on whether the managers empowered by chief executives are better equipped to fix schools than were the educational professionals empowered by the old Progressives. In the most recent generation of reform, the MBA has replaced the Ed.D. as the credential of choice.

And then there is politics. Mayors and governors are not beyond the reach of the same organized interests that have retarded reform on local school boards. The bet here is that chief executives who function in a larger electoral arena where majorities demand school reform can withstand the pressure of such groups better than school boards that operate in a confined arena characterized by low interest and low turnout.[36] Put differently, the hope is that large electoral majorities can serve as a counterbalance to the organized interests that have relied on popular apathy as an ally in preventing schools from changing. This, of course, turns on one final question: whether a new politics of education will inspire informed citizens to participate more energetically in mayoral and gubernatorial elections than they have in school board elections. Let's hope that it does. Such participation would be good for both schools and the democratic process. It probably would not be very good for local school boards.

35. Portz and others (1999).
36. Joseph P. Viteritti, "Abolish the Board of Education," *New York Times*, January 6, 2002, p. A15.

References

Altshuler, Alan. 1970. *Community Control: The Black Demand for Participation in Large Cities.* New York: Pegasus.

Boyd, William L. 1976. "The Public, the Professionals, and Educational Policy Making: Who Governs?" *Teachers College Record* 77 (May): 539–77.

Charters, William W. 1953. "Social Class Analysis and the Control of Public Education." *Harvard Education Review* 23 (Fall): 268–83.

Cistone, Peter J. 1974. "The Ecological Basis of School Board Member Recruitment." *Education and Urban Society* 6: 428–50.

Council of Great City Schools. 2001. *Beating the Odds: A City-by-City Analysis of Student Performance and Achievement Gaps on State Assessment.* Washington.

Counts, George S. 1927. *The Social Composition of Boards of Education.* University of Chicago Press.

Cuban, Larry. 1976. *Urban School Chiefs under Fire.* University of Chicago Press.

Dahl, Robert A. 1961. *Who Governs? Democracy and Power in an American City.* Yale University Press.

Dee, Thomas S. 2004. "The Race Connection: Are Teachers More Effective with Students Who Share Their Identity?" *Education Next* 4: 52–59.

Drachler, Norman. 1977. "Education and Politics in Large Cities." In *The Politics of Education,* edited by Jay D. Scribner. University of Chicago Press.

Eliot, Thomas, H. 1959. "Toward an Understanding of Public School Politics." *American Political Science Review* 52: 1032–51.

Elkin, Steven L. 1987. *City and Regime in the American Republic.* University of Chicago Press.

Finn, Chester, and others. 2000. *Charter Schools in Action: Renewing Public Education.* Princeton University Press.

Hays, Samuel P. 1964. "The Politics of Reform in Municipal Government in the Progressive Era." *Pacific Southwest Quarterly* 55: 137–59.

Iannacconne, Lawrence, and Frank Lutz. 1970. *Politics, Power, and Policy.* Columbus, Ohio: Charles Merrill.

Institute for Educational Leadership. 1986. *School Boards: Strengthening Grass Roots Leadership.* Washington.

Jencks, Christopher, and Meredith Philips, eds. 1998. *The Black-White Test Score Gap.* Brookings.

Kimbrough, Ralph. 1964. *Political Power and Education Decision-Making.* Chicago: Rand-McNally.

Mansbridge, Jane J. 1983. *Beyond Adversary Democracy.* University of Chicago Press.

McCorry, J. J. 1978. *Marcus Foster and the Oakland Public Schools.* University of California Press.

Orr, Marion. 1999. *Black Social Capital: The Politics of School Reform in Baltimore, 1986–1998.* University Press of Kansas.

Peterson, Paul E. 1976. *School Politics Chicago Style.* University of Chicago Press.

Pitkin, Hannah Fenichel. 1972. *The Concept of Representation.* University of California Press.

Portz, John, and others. 1999. *City Schools and City Politics: Institutions and Leadership in Pittsburgh, Boston, and St. Louis.* University Press of Kansas.

Putnam, Robert D. 2000. *Bowling Alone: The Collapse and Revival of American Community.* New York: Simon and Schuster.

Ravitch, Diane. 1995. *National Standards in American Education.* Brookings.

Ravitch, Diane. 2000a. *Left Back: A Century of Failed School Reforms*. New York: Simon and Shuster.

Ravitch, Diane. 2000b. *The Great School Wars: A History of the New York City Public Schools*. Johns Hopkins University Press.

Salisbury, Robert H. 1967. "Schools and Politics in the Big City." *Harvard Education Review* 67 (Summer): 408–24.

Schneider, Mark, and others. 1997. "Institutional Arrangements and the Creation of Social Capital: The Effects of Public School Choice." *American Political Science Review* 91 (1): 82–93.

Scott, Hugh J. 1980. *The Black Superintendent*. Howard University Press.

Stone, Clarence N. 1989. *Regime Politics: Governing Atlanta, 1946–1988*. University Press of Kansas.

———, ed. 1998. *Changing Urban Education*. University Press of Kansas.

Stone, Clarence N., and others. 2001. *Building Civic Capacity: The Politics of Reforming Urban Schools*. University Press of Kansas.

Swain, Carol. M. 1993. *Black Faces and Black Interests: The Representation of African Americans in Congress*. Harvard University Press.

Thernstrom, Abigail, and Stephen Thernstrom. 2003. *No Excuses: Closing the Racial Gap in Learning*. New York: Simon and Schuster.

Toch, Thomas. 2003. *High Schools on a Human Scale*. Boston: Beacon Press.

Truman, David B. 1960. *The Governmental Process: Political Interests and Public Opinion*. New York: Alfred A. Knopf.

Tyack, David, and Elizabeth Hansot. 1982. *Managers of Virtue: Public School Leadership in America. 1820–1980*. New York: Basic Books.

Viteritti, Joseph P. 1983. *Across the River: Politics and Education in the City*. New York: Holmes and Meier.

———. 1990. "The City and the Constitution: A Historical Analysis of Institutional Evolution and Adaptation." *Journal of Urban Affairs* 12: 221–36.

———. 2003. "Schoolyard Revolutions: How Research on Urban School Reform Undermines Reform." *Political Science Quarterly* 118: 233–57.

———. 2004. "From Excellence to Equity: Observations on Politics, History, and Policy." *Peabody Journal of Education* 79: 64–86.

Zeigler, L. Harmon, and M. Kent Jennings. 1974. *Governing American Schools*. North Scituate, Mass.: Duxbury Press.

14

What School Boards Can and Cannot (or Will Not) Accomplish

JENNIFER L. HOCHSCHILD

As intriguing and important as they are, the chapters in this volume pay relatively little attention to what school boards *do*. That is not especially surprising or alarming; most of their authors are political scientists, who typically focus more on processes than on outcomes. Nevertheless, any study of school boards ought at some point to address their actual activities—the functions that boards should perform, the quality of their performance, and the opportunity costs of performing those functions rather than others. In this chapter, I begin to address these issues by drawing out information and arguments from earlier chapters in the hope of opening an additional line of research and evaluation.

The earlier chapters do, of course, indicate a variety of things that school boards do. Among other things, they

—hire and fire superintendents

—oversee budgets and prepare voting taxpayers in their districts for bond issues or increases in school taxes

—negotiate with teachers, often but not always through unions

—explain, legitimate, and speak for the school system in public

—implement, more or less, laws such as the No Child Left Behind Act (NCLB), court orders, and consent decrees

My thanks for financial and institutional support go to the Radcliffe Institute for Advanced Study, the Mellon Foundation, the Guggenheim Foundation, and the Weatherhead Center for International Affairs of Harvard University.

—award contracts for jobs, supplies, and services

—attend to reformers seeking to influence the school system, whether by enacting or repulsing their initiatives

—charter schools in some states and districts

—run for higher political office.

Not many items on this list directly address questions of educational pedagogy and policy, and that seems to reflect reality. We know from other research and commentary that boards spend less than one-tenth of their time developing and overseeing policy; instead, they spend more than half of their time on administration and responding to particular citizens' concerns or problems.[1]

Is this appropriate? Do school boards perform a useful, even essential, function, and do they do it well? More broadly, even if boards do their manifest tasks well, does their existence inhibit the achievement of more important educational goals by some other actor?[2] To answer these questions, I need to abstract from this particular list (or any other) to discuss what roles school boards can be expected to perform and which they cannot.

An Instrument for Local Democracy

School boards were designed to be instruments of local democracy. That is why the United States (unusual among western nations) runs its public school system through a set of relatively small, geographically defined, substantially autonomous school districts, in most of which the school board is elected.

To say that school boards are instruments of local democracy, however, is not to say that school board elections demonstrate very much democracy in action. Voter turnout in board elections is notoriously low, typically well below a quarter of the eligible voters.[3] So one might question citizens' commitment to the actual governance of their schools. Nevertheless, every survey shows fierce attachment to local control of education,[4] and residents of a district almost never choose to give up local control, even for more resources or some other blandishment.[5]

Several factors help to explain the apparent contradiction between citizens' commitment to local democracy and their anemic practice of it. First is the

1. Lynn Olson and Ann Bradley, "Boards of Contention," *Education Week*, April 29, 1992, pp. 2–10; Lee Silver, "My Lesson in School Politics," *New York Times*, September 10, 1997, p. A23.

2. Briffault, in chapter 2 of this volume, provides an excellent overview of the structure of school governance. He shows that if school boards were abolished, under current laws most of their tasks would devolve to the governments of the fifty states.

3. Hochschild and Kolarick (1997); Shen (2003).

4. Hochschild and Scott (1998).

5. Reed (2001); Shelly (2003).

structure of school board elections. Candidates and media alike portray elections as nonpartisan, so voters lack reliable clues about which candidates may share their own views. In addition, school board elections and other elections often are held on different dates; local media can be terrible in reporting the substantive issues at stake; and until recently, more visible leaders such as mayors did everything they could to distance themselves from the public school system.[6] Second, whether correctly or not, most citizens may be sufficiently satisfied with what they see in the schools and therefore not feel impelled to try to overcome these structural barriers. Almost two-thirds of American households have no children under the age of eighteen, and members of these households may lack interest in or knowledge of schooling.[7] And, again whether correctly or not, almost half of parents of public school students give a "grade" of A or B to schools in their community and over two-thirds give the same high grades to their own children's schools.[8] Third, when residents of a school district do get exercised over an issue, participation in school board elections spikes. An election involving, say, a controversial bond issue or a slate of candidates proposing to teach creationism in biology classes can generate turnouts of half or more of the district's voters.[9] Within a few election cycles, turnout drops back down to a quarter or fewer—but the spike shows that citizens can become more involved if they choose to.[10] Similarly, voters appear to have at least a vague idea of whether educators are improving schooling outcomes for students in their district, and they are capable of punishing incumbent school board members if the answer is no (see Berry and Howell, chapter 7 of this volume).

So people may usually skip school board elections because they think that they need not bother to overcome the considerable structural barriers to voting in them. That is not a good commentary on the depth of Americans' commitment to democratic control. And it may be deeply and harmfully misguided if most citizens' quiescence leaves electoral outcomes in the hands of special interests that do not have education as their primary goal (such as business contractors) or that have a self-interested view of how to improve education (such as teacher unions). But that conclusion does permit the claim that most school boards are, for better and for worse, good microcosms of the educational preferences of citizens within their district.

One can have further confidence that school boards are instruments of local democracy by noting that they can in fact respond to long-term changes in

6. Danielson and Hochschild (1998).

7. U.S. Census Bureau, "Children's Living Arrangements and Characteristics: March 2002," table H2 (www.census.gov/population/www/socdemo/hh-fam/cps2002.html [December 26, 2003]).

8. Thirty-Fifth Annual Phi Delta Kappa/Gallup Poll of the Public's Attitudes toward the Public Schools, tables 2 and 3 (www.pdkintl.org/kappan/k0309pol.pdf [December 26, 2003]).

9. Hochschild and Kolarick (1997).

10. Dahl (1961).

populations or in the desires of a community. Studies from the 1980s onward have found that if boards are elected through single-member voting districts rather than at large, they may become reasonably representative of non-white racial or ethnic groups within that school district, even if the majority of voters are European Americans. This descriptive representation can have important substantive results:

> Hispanic representation on school boards [in thirty-five large urban school districts] is . . . a significant determinant of Hispanic employment as teachers. . . . Hispanic teachers have a major impact on the educational environment of the Hispanic student. Districts with larger percentages of Hispanic teachers also have Hispanic students who are more likely to complete school and more likely to attend college.[11]

In this volume, chapter 8 by Melissa Marschall and chapter 9 by Kenneth Meier and Eric Juenke develop this general point in sophisticated detail. Marschall shows that district elections rather than at-large elections significantly increased the number of blacks represented on local school boards, although they appear to have had no impact on Hispanic representation. Meier and Juenke find that the effect of ward structures on Hispanic representation depends on whether Hispanics are a majority of the population in a district, but more generally they too find that school boards can become representative of a district's changing population. Having representation on a school board, in turn, often enables an otherwise disadvantaged group to attain more administrative and teaching jobs for adults and better educational outcomes for children. District residents also become more satisfied with the school system.

Democratic school board elections, then, appear to satisfy most citizens most of the time, and voting can increase the level of political and substantive equality across groups within a school district. Local governance through elected school boards has other virtues as well. Americans have always prided themselves on their attachment to their schools, even though they no longer build them with their own hands on land and with materials donated by community members. Perhaps this local pride in a vital homegrown institution explains why throughout the nineteenth and most of the twentieth century, American children (at least white boys) received more years of schooling, earlier, than did children in comparable European nations. David Campbell (chapter 12 in this volume) shows that at least some citizens attend local school board meetings— which by definition could not happen if there were no local boards—and that attendance rises a little as the population of the district falls: small, homogeneous communities are more participatory. Most important, local governance of schools has enabled our nation—with its vastly disparate cultures, values, goals,

11. Fraga and others (1986, abstract).

and practices—not to tear itself apart over curricula, resource allocation, or educational leadership.

Local Democracy Yields Overall Inequality

However, the virtues of elected boards are largely swamped, in my view, by the fact that elections within geographically defined local districts often work to maintain if not increase political and educational inequality across groups in the larger arena. That is, local democratic governance in the American public school system sustains racial, ethnic, and class hierarchies in the society as a whole.

To say this is not to fault school boards or even voters for being racist, xenophobic, or elitist. When we assume that voters care most about their own children or other children within their district—and when local school board elections are superimposed on a society with a very high (and slowly falling) degree of racial and ethnic residential separation and a high (and rapidly rising) degree of economic residential separation—this outcome is almost inevitable.[12] Intuitively, this is best seen by comparing the effects of gender in schooling with those of race and class. The United States no longer has much gender separation or inequality within public schooling. This outcome may stem from the fact that voters in any district are roughly evenly split between men and women and are parents of both boys and girls. Because of that it is perhaps not surprising that they decided sometime after 1965—when the fact of gender inequality came to be seen as the problem of gender unfairness—that girls deserved roughly the same education (even in extracurricular activities) as boys. These new views were fairly quickly translated into school boards' decisions about superintendents, budgets, and policy guidelines, and the move toward gender equality in treatment and outcomes has proceeded without a lot of controversy. Girls joined boys in shop and calculus class and on the playing fields; boys joined girls in home ec class (typically renamed something along the lines of "skills for living"). These changes may not be complete or well implemented, but that is not the point here. What matters for my purposes is that even though the move toward gender equity happened separately within each bounded district, because districts were essentially the same in their gender ratios, district boundaries did little to retard this transformation.

Contrast this outcome with efforts to mandate racial and ethnic desegregation or funding equalization. Even within districts, school boards have not done as much to promote racial and class equality as gender equality. Schools in wealthier neighborhoods sometimes get more funds than schools in poorer

---

12. By "superimposed," I do not imply any historical periodization or causal argument; this chapter cannot deal with the issue of how the structure of local districts came into being. I use "superimposed" only in an analytic sense.

neighborhoods.[13] Schools within a district frequently remain racially identifiable, and immigrant children are disproportionately located in schools with each other and with native-born African American children.[14] Even in a single school, rigid tracking—or ostensibly more flexible ability grouping—depends partly on achievement (which is itself racially and economically inflected) but also has a very strong direct class bias.[15] Districts vary in the overall proportion of students who pass high-stakes tests, but it is always the case that students who fail are disproportionately poor, belong to a minority group, or both.

School boards could influence budgetary allocations across schools, student assignment to schools, policies such as ability grouping, and preparation of students for high-stakes tests through their choice of superintendent, direct policy mandates, and symbolic statements. But they seldom try and seldom succeed if they do try—largely because of intense opposition from well-off, disproportionately white, parents.[16] Democratic control of locally based school boards works against equal educational opportunities or outcomes even within a single district.

Nevertheless, most racial, ethnic, and class-based separation now occurs *across* rather than within district lines, and by at least some measures it is rising steadily.[17] Almost all large urban districts have very few white students; many suburban districts have few poor students. This is not, of course, a coincidence. People with children and sufficient resources, especially if they are European Americans, typically move out of urban districts and into suburban ones.

Educational separation in accord with district boundaries is particularly problematic because of the strength of peer effects (after all, recognition of the impact of peers in a classroom was one of the motivations for gender equalization and integration). The economic standing of a child's schoolmates and classmates powerfully affects that child's schooling outcomes.[18] Similarly, the racial mix of a child's school and classroom peers has a substantial impact on that child's level of racially integrated activity as an adult.[19] Separation across district lines dramatically affects schooling outcomes for all Americans—some for better and others for worse.

13. Hertert (1995); Rothstein (2000); Iatarola and Stiefel (2003).

14. Van Hook (2002).

15. Hochschild and Scovronick (2003, chapter 6); Jones and others (1995); Dauber and others (1996); Lucas (1999).

16. Shore (1998); Fraga, Rodriguez, and Erlichson, chapter 5 of this volume.

17. On racial separation, see Clotfelter (1999, 2001), Cutler and others (1999), National Center for Education Statistics (2001, 2003), Reardon and Yun (2001), Reardon and others (2000), and Oliver (2001). On ethnic separation, see Rusk (2002) and Orfield and Gordon (2001). On economic separation, see Rusk (2002), Abramson and others (1995), Massey (1996), Madden (2000), Allen and Kirby (2000), Ho (1999), and Orfield (2002).

18. Kahlenberg (2001); Planning and Evaluation Service (1997); Hoxby (2000); Hanushek and others (2003).

19. Braddock and others (1984); Wells (1995); Wells and Crain (1994); Hochschild and Scovronick (2003, chapter 2).

School boards have little ability and even less incentive to address the severe educational consequences of this phenomenon. Voters in well-off (predominantly white) districts usually perceive direct costs and perhaps even a zero-sum game in the prospect of sharing their resources with children in poor (disproportionately non-white) districts. They are willing neither to open their schools to more than a few "outsiders" nor to send much financial assistance or many highly qualified educators into others' districts. Democratically elected school boards reflect and reinforce those views; they have seldom, to put it mildly, taken strong measures to redistribute resources or children across district lines. After all, they owe their position to voters within their own district who do not want to redistribute resources; in political terms they would lose rather than gain by seeking to improve the schools in another district.

In short, the causal chain on which I am focusing runs as follows: high levels of racial and economic separation across geographically based local school districts combine with the fact that school boards are elected by voters within each district; that combination yields school board decisions on superintendents, budgets, student placement, and curricula (among other things) that maintain or exacerbate unequal outcomes of schooling; those outcomes help to create more racial and economic separation across districts.

Other factors intervene, of course, as they always do in complex causal chains. Those factors include the parents' commitment and ability to help the child navigate the complex school environment, the child's commitment and ability to learn in the given context, the serendipity of getting an excellent teacher or having a disability or encountering a bully on the playground. But the causal chain just described overrides most individual-level variations. A predictable mix of values and fears, institutions and procedures, historical trajectories and current incentives—all playing out within boundaries set by states and seldom changed—produce a dynamic in which the greater the amount of local democracy within districts, the less educational equality across states and the nation.

Policy Efforts to Promote Educational Equality

I am far from the first person to note this opposition between local democratic control and schooling equality. Much of the history of the past fifty years of educational reform can be seen as an effort to reduce the tension between the two phenomena, largely by taking power away from school boards and giving it to one or another set of reformers. This effort is epitomized by the decisions of some federal courts and educational agencies between 1954 and 1968 to transfer student (and sometimes teacher) assignment from local elected officials to appointed regulators or judges. School boards were largely irrelevant to school desegregation except for their many efforts to resist or subvert it, although a few did support or even initiate desegregation plans.[20] Other reform efforts have followed the same approach to pursuing equality by working around rather than through school boards. These efforts include the following:

—from the 1940s through the 1960s, state efforts to consolidate thousands of school districts, including the elimination of thousands of school boards, partly in order to increase opportunities for children in small or rural districts (see Berry, chapter 3 of this volume)

—from the 1970s on, judicial decisions to restructure school finance laws, or to require state legislatures to do so, in order to reduce funding disparities between well-off and poor districts[21]

—from the 1980s on, state-level designation of curricular standards and achievement tests designed to raise the floor for students in the lower tracks or in especially weak schools[22]

—from the 1990s on, mayoral or state takeover of failing schools or districts (Wong and Shen, chapter 4 of this volume), laws permitting universities and other entities to charter schools, and public funding of vouchers to permit low-income students to attend private and parochial schools—all in order to change the opportunity structure for students in unsatisfactory systems, schools, or classrooms.

Reformers have met with varying degrees of success. District consolidation was sustained, although reformers now seek to offset some of its effects in high schools by promoting smaller schools that target specific student populations or create a stronger sense of community among all participants in the school. School desegregation has stalled and has even been partly reversed. So far, the movement for public provision of vouchers has mostly failed (although recent Supreme Court activism may override popular preferences, as earlier Court activism did for a while with regard to desegregation). Charter schools and new funding formulas are in place but have had less impact than supporters hoped. It is too early to judge the success of NCLB.[23] As a result of this mélange of reform success and failure, schooling outcomes are arguably more equal across race, gender, class, population density, immigration status, and disability status than they were half a century ago. But not by much, and seldom because of school boards.

20. See Smith and others (2004) for a case in which local democratic control of school boards has recently led several boards to promote rather than oppose school desegregation plans. They remain, of course, limited to activity within their own district.

21. Hochschild and Scovronick (2003, chapter 3).

22. Dee (2003).

23. Reed (2003), Hess and Finn (2004), and Meier and Wood (2004) present varying views on the effects of NCLB.

Policy Efforts to Promote Local Democracy

While one set of reformers evades school boards in order to make schooling more equal, another set focuses on whether local boards are effective in their core mission of promoting democratic participation in educational decision-making. Some are dismayed by what they have found. After all, if fewer than a quarter of citizens vote in board elections, it is easy for boards to be captured by special interests such as teacher unions (see Moe, chapter 11, but also Hess and Leal, chapter 10, in this volume), contractors or other business interests,[24] or by an activist minority such as prosperous whites or proponents of Afrocentrism or creationism.[25] Alternatively, even duly elected school boards may be too weak, disorganized, or distracted by other incentives to effectively promote the desires of any set of residents or interests within a given district.

So a different group of reforms has sought to strengthen democracy in local schools or districts, sometimes directly through school boards and sometimes in spite of them. These reforms include

—school-based management[26]
—efforts to develop shared civic capacity in the community[27]
—efforts to develop social capital in the community[28]
—promotion of reform within teacher unions in order to facilitate school reforms.[29]

They too have had mixed results, and arguably even less success than the equality-minded reformers.[30]

Policy Efforts That Might Harm or Help Both Democracy and Equality

Some analysts and activists argue that the real problem is not a trade-off between local democracy, which entails strengthening school boards and districts, and greater equality, which entails working around local boards and districts. They fear instead that one or another particular reform effort will weaken *both* values. Thus critics worry that NCLB will remove accountability from local

24. Stone (1998a, part 3).
25. Hochschild and Scovronick (2003, chapter 6); Binder (2002).
26. Anderson (1999); Keith (1999); Malen (1999).
27. Stone (1998b); Henig and others (1999).
28. Putnam and others (2003); Warren (2001).
29. Kate Zernike, "A Tough Union Backs Change; Schools Benefit," *New York Times*, July 31, 2001, p. A1; Chase (1997–98).
30. Yet a different set of reformers seeks to move schooling even further from the realm of local school boards. Libertarian supporters of vouchers for all students, proponents of public funding for parochial schools, supporters of home schooling, and supporters of contracting with private corporations to run public schools are examples. I do not consider these efforts in this paper, since they seldom seek to contribute either to local democracy or to educational equalization.

school boards *and* deny diplomas to weak (or merely badly taught) students through no fault of their own. Some see school finance reform in the same light—it denies local districts the right to determine their own financial picture *and* pours money into dysfunctional districts that cannot or will not improve students' outcomes. Others see publicly funded voucher programs as doubly harmful—a broad voucher system would turn decisionmaking about public functions over to the private sector *and* would make it even easier for wealthy suburbanites to keep their children away from "undesirables."

A few reformers claim that their preferred policy can both strengthen local democracy and promote equal schooling outcomes. Afrocentrists, for example, argue that hiring black faculty and administrators and teaching an Afrocentric curriculum instead of the current Eurocentric one will both be more responsive to the community's desires and motivate students to learn more. Supporters of bilingual education programs that promote maintenance of cultural identity make a similar argument for predominantly Hispanic immigrant communities. I know of no evidence that systematically supports (or refutes) either claim.[31] Even if students in particular schools or whole districts benefit from ethnically or racially specific programs, no one has figured out how to enable these students to make a successful transition into mainstream society. In my judgment, therefore, unless our nation's sharp geographic divisions by race, ethnicity, and class are significantly reduced, promoting local democracy while equalizing schooling outcomes for a large number of students seems to be beyond realistic conception.

Should School Boards Be Abolished?

Given that local school boards are unable or unwilling to promote much equality in student opportunities and outcomes, and given that they may not promote democracy very well even within their own districts, should they nevertheless remain in existence? That question yields three others: What tasks can we expect school boards to do well? How well do they do those tasks? Is the accomplishment of those tasks sufficiently important to justify maintaining boards even though they do poorly at promoting democracy and equality?

These questions frame a fairly substantial research agenda, and I shall not attempt to answer them fully here. Let me instead suggest, or rather revive, a theoretical framework that can help us to develop a set of answers.[32] Paul Peterson's *City Limits* argues that each level of government—local, state, and federal—has distinctive virtues and defects that shape what policies it should

31. For a discussion of both types of programs, see Hochschild and Scovronick (2003, chapter 7).

32. My thanks to Luis Fraga for pointing out the usefulness of Peterson's framework for the issues in this paper.

promulgate in a well-ordered polity.[33] We can apply a variant of that theory to the single policy arena of public schooling. Thus the local level—the mayor and school board—are best suited to allocating resources such as contracts and jobs and to overseeing development, that is, promoting the health or growth of a given school system. The national level, through laws and budgetary allocations, is best suited to the redistribution of resources across district and state lines. State governments should presumably function more like the national than local governments since they hold most of the statutory authority for public school-ing (see Briffault, chapter 2 of this volume) and since their scope is broad enough for them to ensure considerable redistribution of resources even within their borders.[34] The theory is silent on the appropriate role for courts; one would have to decide whether they should be understood to be a potentially countermajoritarian institution (in which case they can redistribute, like the federal or state governments) or more like a local system with limited autonomy and considerable responsiveness to voters' desires. A full development of the logic of *City Limits* might also want to consider appropriate roles for nongovern-ment actors such as reformers, experts, parents, and students themselves.

According to this theory, the school board chores listed at the beginning of this chapter may be about right. Many of those tasks have to do with allocating and managing jobs and contracts and with promoting support for and develop-ment of the school system among district residents. Thus one cannot fairly call for the abolition of boards on the grounds that their tasks are too mundane or trivial; someone has to do them. That leads to the second question—how well do school boards accomplish their appropriate tasks? That question will lead us to consider everything from corruption, efficiency, and administrative weakness to broader issues of accountability and capacity for institutional learning and change.[35] If a school board can allocate resources and develop the system well, *and* if it can bind the residents of the district to the public educational system through descriptive and substantive representation, responsiveness to powerful concerns, and flexibility in the face of change, then it passes the second test and does not (yet) warrant abolition.

Thinking more systematically about what school boards should do—and learning more about what they in fact do and how well they do it—are sub-stantial research agendas in themselves. But the most important issue lies in

33. Peterson (1981).

34. According to some researchers, at least a third of the variation in students' achievement is related to the state in which they live, although causation is hard to tease out in such a claim (Mur-ray and others 1998; National Center for Education Statistics 2000). Even so, that leaves a lot of scope for action within any state.

35. See, for a good start, chapter 6 in this volume, by Paul Teske and colleagues. They show that "many of the problems that charter schools are having with local school boards may prove to be as much a function of the weaknesses of local boards as organizations in a turbulent political and administrative environment as a strategic anticompetitive response."

response to the third question—whether school boards provide services that are so essential that they should be maintained even if they cannot promote robust democracy or greater equality of outcomes among students. Some reformers have argued, for example, that most budgetary and hiring decisions should be devolved downward to individual schools and the rest passed upward to regional associations with more professional management and more clout in purchasing supplies than local boards can muster. In such a fashion, boards could be eliminated and their functions better served. Systematic research on the combination of downward and upward reallocation of tasks—perhaps in other policy arenas such as health care—would be useful. It might help us to decide whether boards could safely and usefully be eliminated in order to widen the arena for the pursuit of equality without losing democratic accountability. Comparisons across states would also be useful—Hawaii has one statewide school district, while New Jersey has about 600, some with school boards but no schools or students. Do states with many small districts and therefore many boards do a better or worse job of development and resource allocation than states with a few large ones? To my knowledge, we have no systematic research on the point.

One would also need to look at educational policy and practice—which is, after all, the point of public schooling. Do school boards mainly inhibit achievement by squelching innovative charter schools, caving in to rigid and self-serving teacher unions, or kowtowing to equally rigid and self-serving business elites? Or do they mainly encourage achievement by translating national and state mandates into workable policies and by hiring effective and committed superintendents? Does their apparently excessive attention to individual cases divert them from urgent systemwide priorities, or does it create an essential safety valve so that the drive toward bureaucratic conformity is not permitted to run roughshod over idiosyncratic needs and circumstances? Here too, careful systematic research could help us judge how much Americans need local school boards in order to educate their children well.

In the end, however, school boards should not be released completely from the largest concerns about democracy and educational equality. The federalist logic of *City Limits* has been answered by research that suggests more maneuvering room for local governments than Peterson saw. Clarence Stone, for example, argues that leaders of a city can choose to govern either by responding to the most dominant and self-interested powers (as some chapters in this volume argue that school boards do) or by responding to the needs and desires of local neighborhoods, small businesses, and non-elites.[36] The latter choice is electorally and substantively difficult, and it may fail. But the existence of this option implies that a school board can do more than most currently do to fight against

---

36. Stone (1989).

resource and teaching inequities within its own district and to promote genuine democratic deliberation among all of the district's residents.

Reformers, in short, are usually correct when they seek to work around or hollow out school boards in order to promote more equality or more democracy. But that judgment does not mean that boards cannot allocate resources or develop support for schools well, nor does it let them off the hook with regard to some redistribution of resources. As with everything else, the question is "School boards compared with what?"—and the chapters in this book help us begin to find an answer.

References

Abramson, Alan, and others. 1995. "The Changing Geography of Metropolitan Opportunity." *Housing Policy Debate* 6 (1): 45–72.

Allen, Katherine, and Maria Kirby. 2000. *Unfinished Business: Why Cities Matter to Welfare Reform*. Brookings.

Anderson, Gary. 1999. "The Politics of Participatory Reforms in Education." *Theory into Practice* 38 (4): 191–95.

Binder, Amy. 2002. *Contentious Curricula: Afrocentrism and Creationism in American Public Schools*. Princeton University Press.

Braddock, Jomills II., and others. 1984. "A Long-Term View of School Desegregation: Some Recent Studies of Graduates as Adults." *Phi Delta Kappan* 66 (4): 259-64.

Chase, Bob. 1997–98. "The New NEA: Reinventing Teacher Unions for a New Era." *American Educator* (Winter): 12–15.

Clotfelter, Charles. 1999. "Public School Segregation in Metropolitan Areas." *Land Economics* 75 (4): 487–504.

———. 2001. "Are Whites Still Fleeing? Racial Patterns and Enrollment Shifts in Urban Public Schools, 1987–1996." *Journal of Policy Analysis and Management* 20 (2): 199–221.

Cutler, David, and others. 1999. "The Rise and Decline of the American Ghetto." *Journal of Political Economy* 107 (3): 455–506.

Dahl, Robert. 1961. *Who Governs?* Yale University Press.

Danielson, Michael, and Jennifer Hochschild. 1998. "Changing Urban Education: Lessons, Cautions, Prospects." In *Changing Urban Education*, edited by Clarence Stone, pp. 277–95. University Press of Kansas.

Dauber, Susan, and others. 1996. "Tracking and Transitions through the Middle Grades: Channeling Educational Trajectories." *Sociology of Education* 69 (4): 290–307.

Dee, Thomas. 2003. "The "First Wave" of Accountability." In *No Child Left Behind: The Politics and Practice of School Accountability*, edited by Paul Peterson and Martin West, pp. 215–41. Brookings.

Fraga, Luis, and others. 1986. "Hispanic Americans and Educational Policy: Limits to Equal Access." *Journal of Politics* 48 (4): 850–76.

Hanushek, Eric, and others. 2003. "Does Peer Ability Affect Student Achievement?" *Journal of Applied Econometrics* 18 (5): 527–44.

Henig, Jeffrey, and others. 1999. *The Color of School Reform: Race, Politics, and the Challenge of Urban Education*. Princeton University Press.

Hertert, Linda. 1995. "Does Equal Funding for Districts Mean Equal Funding for Classroom Students? Evidence from California." In *Where Does the Money Go? Resource Allocations in*

Elementary and Secondary Schools, edited by Laurence Picus and James Wattenbarger, pp. 71–84. Thousand Oaks, Calif.: Corwin.

Hess, Frederick, and Chester Finn, eds. 2004. *Leaving No Child Behind? Options for Kids in Failing Schools.* New York: Palgrave Macmillan.

Ho, Alfred. 1999. "Did School Finance Reforms Achieve Better Equity?" Iowa State University, Department of Political Science.

Hochschild, Jennifer, and Deidre Kolarick. 1997. "'Do as I Say, Not as I Do . . .': Americans' Involvement with Public Education." Washington: National Academy of Sciences Committee on Educational Finance.

Hochschild, Jennifer, and Bridget Scott. 1998. "Poll Trends: Governance and Reform of Public Education in the United States." *Public Opinion Quarterly* 62 (1): 79–120.

Hochschild, Jennifer, and Nathan Scovronick. 2003. *The American Dream and the Public Schools.* Oxford University Press.

Hoxby, Caroline. 2000. "Peer Effects in the Classroom: Learning from Gender and Race Variation." Working Paper W7867. Cambridge, Mass.: National Bureau of Economic Research.

Iatarola, Patrice, and Leanna Stiefel. 2003. "Intradistrict Equity of Public Education Resources and Performance." *Economics of Education Review* 22 (1): 69–78.

Jones, James, and others. 1995. "Individual and Organizational Predictors of High School Track Placement." *Sociology of Education* 68 (4): 287–300.

Kahlenberg, Richard. 2001. *All Together Now: Creating Middle Class Schools through Public School Choice.* Brookings.

Keith, Novella. 1999. "Whose Community Schools? New Discourses, New Patterns." *Theory into Practice* 38 (4): 225–34.

Lucas, Samuel. 1999. *Tracking Inequality: Stratification and Mobility in American High Schools.* New York: Teachers College Press.

Madden, Janice. 2000. *Changes in Income Inequality within U.S. Metropolitan Areas.* Kalamazoo, Mich.: Upjohn Institute for Employment Research.

Malen, Betty. 1999. "The Promises and Perils of Participation on Site-Based Councils." *Theory into Practice* 38 (4): 209–16.

Massey, Douglas. 1996. "The Age of Extremes: Concentrated Affluence and Poverty in the Twenty-first Century." *Demography* 33 (4): 395–412.

Meier, Deborah, and George Wood, eds. 2004. *Many Children Left Behind: How the No Child Left Behind Act Is Damaging Our Children and Our Schools.* Boston: Beacon Press.

Murray, Sheila, and others. 1998. "Education Finance Reform and the Distribution of Education Resources." *American Economic Review* 88 (4): 789–812.

National Center for Education Statistics. 2000. *School-Level Correlates of Academic Achievement.* NCES 2000-203. U.S. Department of Education.

———. 2001. *Characteristics of the 100 Largest Public Elementary and Secondary School Districts in the United States: 1999–2000.* NCES 2001-346. U.S. Department of Education.

———. 2003. *Characteristics of the 100 Largest Public Elementary and Secondary School Districts in the United States: 2001–02.* NCES 2003-353. U.S. Department of Education.

Oliver, Eric. 2001. *Democracy in Suburbia.* Princeton University Press.

Orfield, Gary, and Nora Gordon. 2001. *Schools More Separate: Consequences of a Decade of Resegregation.* Harvard University, Civil Rights Project.

Orfield, Myron. 2002. *American Metropolitics: The New Suburban Reality.* Brookings.

Peterson, Paul. 1981. *City Limits.* University of Chicago Press.

Planning and Evaluation Service. 1997. *Prospects: Final Report on Student Outcomes.* U.S. Department of Education.

Putnam, Robert, and others. 2003. *Better Together: Restoring the American Community.* New York: Simon and Schuster.

Reardon, Sean, and John Yun. 2001. "Suburban Racial Change and Suburban School Segregation, 1987–1995." *Sociology of Education* 74 (2): 79–101.

Reardon, Sean, and others. 2000. "The Changing Structure of School Segregation: Measurement and Evidence of Multiracial Metropolitan-Area School Segregation, 1989–1995." *Demography* 37 (3): 351–64.

Reed, Douglas. 2001. *On Equal Terms: The Constitutional Politics of Educational Opportunity.* Princeton University Press.

———. 2003. "Whither Localism?: No Child Left Behind and the Local Politics of Federal Evaluation Reform." Paper presented at the conference "School Board Politics." Harvard University, October 16–17 (www.ksg.harvard.edu/pepg/pdf/SBConfPDF/papers/PEPG_03-04Reed.pdf [December 3, 2004]).

Rothstein, Richard. 2000. "Equalizing Education Resources on Behalf of Disadvantaged Children." In *A Notion at Risk: Preserving Public Education as an Engine for Social Mobility*, edited by Richard Kahlenberg, pp. 31–92. New York: Century Foundation Press.

Rusk, David. 2002. "Trends in School Segregation." In *Divided We Fail: Coming Together through Public School Choice*, edited by Richard Kahlenberg, pp. 61–85. New York: Century Foundation Press.

Shelly, Bryan. 2003. "Funding Centralization and School Board Discretionary Authority: A Preliminary Analysis." Paper presented at the annual meeting of the American Political Science Association. Philadelphia, August 28–September 1.

Shen, Francis. 2003. "Who Elects the Gorgeous Company? Estimating a National Average of Voter Turnout for U.S. School Board Elections." Harvard University, Department of Government.

Shore, Alexa. 1998. "Detracking: The Politics of Creating Heterogeneous Ability Classrooms." Princeton University, Woodrow Wilson School of Public and International Affairs.

Smith, Stephen, and others. 2004. "Electoral Structures, Venue Selection, and the (New?) Politics of School Desegregation." *Perspectives on Politics* 2 (4): 795–801.

Stone, Clarence. 1989. *Regime Politics: Governing Atlanta, 1948–1988*. University Press of Kansas.

———. 1998a. *Changing Urban Education*. University Press of Kansas.

———. 1998b. "Civic Capacity and Urban School Reform." In *Changing Urban Education*, edited by Clarence Stone, pp. 250–73. University Press of Kansas.

Van Hook, Jennifer. 2002. "Immigration and African American Educational Opportunity: The Transformation of Minority Schools." *Sociology of Education* 75 (2): 169–89.

Warren, Mark. 2001. *Dry Bones Rattling: Community Building to Revitalize American Democracy*. Princeton University Press.

Wells, Amy. 1995. "Reexamining Social Science Research on School Desegregation: Long- versus Short-Term Effects." *Teachers College Record* 96 (4): 691–706.

Wells, Amy, and Robert Crain. 1994. "Perpetuation Theory and the Long-Term Effects of School Desegregation." *Review of Educational Research* 64 (4): 531–55.

Contributors

William G. Howell
Harvard University

Christopher R. Berry
University of Chicago

Richard Briffault
Columbia University

David E. Campbell
University of Notre Dame

Erin Cassese
*State University of New York
   at Stony Brook*

Bari Anhalt Erlichson
Rutgers University

Luis Ricardo Fraga
Stanford University

Frederick M. Hess
American Enterprise Institute

Jennifer L. Hochschild
Harvard University

Eric Gonzalez Juenke
Texas A & M University

David L. Leal
University of Texas at Austin

Melissa J. Marschall
Rice University

Kenneth J. Meier
Texas A & M University

Terry M. Moe
Stanford University

Nick Rodriguez
Stanford University

Mark Schneider
*State University of New York
   at Stony Brook*

Francis X. Shen
Harvard University

Paul Teske
University of Colorado at Denver

Joseph P. Viteritti
Hunter College, University of New York

Kenneth K. Wong
Vanderbilt University

Index

Abernathy, Scott, 130

Accountability: definition and meaning, 150; design of accountability systems, 152–53; hard accountability, 150, 152, 166; literature review of, 152–53; market forces, 151, 153; mayoral takeover of school boards, 84, 319–20; NCLB and, 6–7, 18, 132, 150–51, 167, 332–33; in public education, 18; of public officials, 245; reforms and, 4, 6; report card systems, 151, 152; sanctions and rewards, 152–53, 166; school boards and, 7, 17–18, 21, 45, 77, 151, 155–57, 167, 229, 285–86; student achievement and, 151, 152, 153, 155, 156, 167–68; testing and, 150–51, 156, 157–58, 160–61, 162–63, 164, 167–68; voters and voting, 45, 150, 151, 153–68

Ackerman, Arlene, 107, 122–24, 125–26. *See also* San Francisco

ACT Test, 219

ADA. *See* Average daily attendance

Administrators and administration: historical role of, 309; implementation of public policy and, 102–03; public education

and schools, 16, 76–77, 187–88; racial and minority issues, 187–88, 202, 207, 213–18, 222–24, 315, 327; school boards and, 215–16, 217–18, 325

Advanced placement (AP), 219, 222

African Americans: *Brown* v. *Board of Education of Topeka, KS* and, 102; elections and, 236–37, 239; gains in representation and elected officials, 176, 178, 186, 189, 201; mayoral takeover of school boards, 91; political engagement and participation, 296, 297; political issues, 178, 202; public policies and, 201–02; representation and structure, 200–201; satisfaction with schools, 188–94, 195; school boards and, 18, 177, 178, 179–82, 186, 194–95, 327; school size and, 65. *See also* Racial and minority issues

AFT. *See* American Federation of Teachers

Alabama, 65, 176

Alesina, Alberto, 64, 290, 299

Alioto, Joseph, 105

Alioto, Robert, 105, 107, 108–12, 113, 114, 116, 121, 122